Discovering Modern C++

 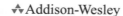

Discovering Modern C++

An Intensive Course for Scientists, Engineers, and Programmers

Peter Gottschling

♦ Addison-Wesley

Boston • Columbus • Indianapolis • New York • San Francisco • Amsterdam • Cape Town
Dubai • London • Madrid • Milan • Munich • Paris • Montreal • Toronto • Delhi • Mexico City
Sao Paulo • Sidney • Hong Kong • Seoul • Singapore • Taipei • Tokyo

For information about buying this title in bulk quantities, or for special sales opportunities (which may include electronic versions; custom cover designs; and content particular to your business, training goals, marketing focus, or branding interests), please contact our corporate sales department at corpsales@pearsoned.com or (800) 382-3419.

For government sales inquiries, please contact governmentsales@pearsoned.com.

For questions about sales outside the U.S., please contact international@pearsoned.com.

Visit us on the Web: informit.com/aw

Library of Congress Control Number: 2015955339

ISBN-13: 978-0-13-438358-3
ISBN-10: 0-13-438358-3
Text printed in the United States on recycled paper at Edwards Brothers Malloy in Ann Arbor, Michigan.
First printing, December 2015

To my parents, Helga and Hans-Werner

Contents

Preface

"The world is built on C++ (and its C subset)."

—Herb Sutter

The infrastructures of Google, Amazon, and Facebook are built to a large extent in C++. In addition, a considerable fraction of the underlying technology is implemented in C++. In telecommunications, almost all landline and cellular phone connections are driven by C++ software. Most importantly, all the major transmission nodes in Germany are handled with C++, which means that peace in the author's family unconditionally relies on C++ software.

Even software written in other programming languages depends on C++ since the most popular compilers are realized in C++: Visual Studio, clang, and newer parts of Gnu and the Intel compiler. This is even more true for software running on Windows which is also implemented in C++ (as well as the Office package). The language is omnipresent; even your cell phone and your car certainly contain components driven by C++. Its inventor, Bjarne Stroustrup, set up a web page with applications where most examples here come from.

In science and engineering, many high-quality software packages are implemented in C++. The strength of the language is manifested in particular when projects exceed a certain size and data structures are rather complex. No wonder that many—if not most—simulation software programs in science and engineering are realized today in C++: the leaders Abaqus, deal.II, FEniCS, OpenFOAM, to name only a few; likewise the leading CAD software CATIA. Even embedded systems are increasingly realized in C++ thanks to more powerful processors and improved compilers (in which not all modern language features and libraries can always be used). Finally, we do not know how many projects would be realized in C++ instead of C if they had been started later. For instance, the author's good friend Matt Knepley, who is coauthor of the very successful scientific library PETSc, admitted that he would program the library today in C++ if rewriting was affordable.

Reasons to Learn C++

Like no other language, C++ masters the full spectrum from programming sufficiently close to the hardware on one end to abstract high-level programming on the other. The lower-level programming—like user-definable memory management—empowers you as a programmer to understand what really happens during execution, which in turn helps you to understand the behavior of programs in other languages. In C++ you can write extremely efficient programs that can only be slightly out-performed by code written in machine language with ridiculous effort. However, you should wait a little with the hardcore performance tuning and focus first on clear and expressive software.

This is where the high-level features of C++ come into play. The language supports a wide variety of programming paradigms directly: object-oriented programming (Chapter 6), generic programming (Chapter 3), meta-programming (Chapter 5), concurrent programming (§4.6), and procedural programming (§1.5), among others.

Several programming techniques—like RAII (§2.4.2.1) and expression templates (§5.3)—were invented in and for C++. As the language is so expressive, it was often possible to establish these new techniques without changing the language. And who knows, maybe one day you will invent a new technique.

Reasons to Read This Book

The material of the book has been tested on real humans. The author taught his class "C++ for Scientists" over three years (i.e., three times two semesters). The students, mostly from the mathematics department, plus some from the physics and engineering departments, often did not know C++ before the class and were able to implement advanced techniques like expression templates (§5.3) by the end of the course. You can read this book at your own pace: straight to the point by following the main path or more thoroughly by reading additional examples and background information in Appendix A.

The Beauty and the Beast

C++ programs can be written in so many ways. In this book, we will lead you smoothly to the more sophisticated styles. This requires the use of advanced features that might be intimidating at first but will become less so once you get used to them. Actually high-level programming is not only applicable in a wider range but is usually equally or more efficient and readable.

We will give you a first impression with a simple example: gradient descent with constant step size. The principle is extremely simple: we compute the steepest descent of $f(x)$ with its gradient, say $g(x)$, and follow this direction with fixed-size steps to the next local minimum. Even the algorithmic pseudo-code is as simple as this description:

Algorithm 1: Gradient descent algorithm

Input: Start value x, step size s, termination criterion ε, function f, gradient g
Output: Local minimum x

1 **do**
2 $\quad\big|\quad x = x - s \cdot g(x)$
3 **while** $|\Delta f(x)| \geqslant \varepsilon$;

For this simple algorithm, we wrote two quite different implementations. Please have a look and let it sink in without trying to understand the technical details.

```
void gradient_descent(double* x,          template <typename Value, typename P1,
    double* y, double s, double eps,                   typename P2, typename F,
    double(*f)(double, double),                        typename G>
    double(*gx)(double, double),          Value gradient_descent(Value x, P1 s,
    double(*gy)(double, double))              P2 eps, F f, G g)
{                                         {
    double val= f(*x, *y), delta;             auto val= f(x), delta= val;
    do {                                      do {
        *x-= s * gx(*x, *y);                      x-= s * g(x);
        *y-= s * gy(*x, *y);                      auto new_val= f(x);
        double new_val= f(*x, *y);                delta= abs(new_val - val);
        delta= abs(new_val - val);                val= new_val;
        val= new_val;                         } while (delta > eps);
    } while (delta > eps);                    return x;
}                                         }
```

At first glance, they look pretty similar, and we will tell you which one we like more. The first version is in principle pure C, i.e., compilable with a C compiler too. The benefit is that what is optimized is directly visible: a 2D function with `double` values (indicated by the **highlighted** function parameters). We prefer the second version as it is more widely usable: to functions of arbitrary dimension with arbitrary value types (visible by the **marked** type and function parameters). Surprisingly the versatile implementation is not less efficient. To the contrary, the functions given for F and G may be inlined (see §1.5.3) so that the function call overhead is saved, whereas the explicit use of (ugly) function pointers in the left version makes this optimization difficult.

A longer example comparing old and new style is found in Appendix A (§A.1) for the really patient reader. There the benefit of modern programming is much more evident than in the toy example here. But we do not want to hold you back too long with preliminary skirmishing.

Languages in Science and Engineering

"It would be nice if every kind of numeric software could be written in C++ without loss of efficiency, but unless something can be found that achieves this without compromising the C++-type system it may be preferable to rely on Fortran, assembler or architecture-specific extensions."

—Bjarne Stroustrup

Scientific and engineering software is written in different languages, and which one is the most appropriate depends on the goals and available resources—as everywhere:

- Math tools like MATLAB, Mathematica, or R are excellent when we can use their existing algorithms. When we implement our own algorithms with fine-grained (e.g., scalar) operations, we will experience a significant decrease in performance. This might not be an issue—the problems are small or the user is infinitely patient; otherwise we should consider alternative languages.

- Python is excellent for rapid software development and already contains scientific libraries like "scipy" and "numpy," and applications based on these libraries (often implemented in C and C++) are reasonably efficient. Again, user-defined algorithms from fine-grained operations pay a performance penalty. Python is an excellent way to implement small and medium-size tasks efficiently. When projects grow sufficiently large, it becomes increasingly important that the compiler is stricter (e.g., assignments are rejected when the arguments do not match).

- Fortran is also great when we can rely on existing, well-tuned operations like dense matrix operations. It is well suited to accomplish old professors' homework (because they only ask for what is easy in Fortran). Introducing new data structures is in the author's experience quite cumbersome, and writing a large simulation program in Fortran is quite a challenge—today only done voluntarily by a shrinking minority.

- C allows for good performance, and a large amount of software is written in C. The core language is relatively small and easy to learn. The challenge is to write large and bug-free software with the simple and dangerous language features, especially pointers (§1.8.2) and macros (§1.9.2.1).

- Languages like Java, C#, and PHP are probably good choices when the main component of the application is a web or graphic interface and not too many calculations are performed.

- C++ shines particularly when we develop large, high-quality software with good performance. Nonetheless, the development process does not need to be slow and painful. With the right abstractions at hand, we can write C++ programs quite rapidly. We are optimistic that in future C++ standards, more scientific libraries will be included.

Evidently, the more languages we know, the more choice we have. Moreover, the better we know those languages, the more educated our choice will be. In addition, large projects often contain components in different languages, whereas in most cases at least the performance-critical kernels are realized in C or C++. All this said, learning C++ is an intriguing journey, and having a deep understanding of it will make you a great programmer in any case.

Typographical Conventions

New terms are set in *clear blue and italic*. C++ sources are printed blue and `monospace`. Important details are marked in **boldface**. Classes, functions, variables, and constants are lowercase, optionally containing underscores. An exception is matrices, which are usually named with a single capital letter. Template parameters and concepts start with a capital letter and may contain further capitals (CamelCase). Program output and commands are `light blue in typewriter font`.

Programs requiring C++3, C++11, or C++14 features are marked with corresponding margin boxes. Several programs making light use of a C++11 feature that is easily substituted by a C++03 expression are not explicitly marked.

$\Rightarrow$ `directory/source_code.cpp`

Except for very short code illustrations, all programming examples in this book were tested on at least one compiler. Indicated by an arrow, the paths of the complete programs are given at the beginning of the paragraph or section in which the contained code snippets are discussed.

All programs are available on GitHub in the public repository **https://github.com/ petergottschling/discovering_modern_cpp** and can thus be cloned by:

```
git clone https://github.com/petergottschling/discovering_modern_cpp.git
```

On Windows, it is more convenient to use TortoiseGit; see **tortoisegit.org**.

Acknowledgments

Starting chronologically, the author would like to thank Karl Meerbergen and his colleagues for the initial 80-page text used as a block lecture at KU Leuven taught by Karl and me in 2008. Over time, most passages have been rewritten, but the original document provided the initial momentum that was essential for the entire writing process. I truly owe Mario Mulanasky a great debt for contributing to Section 7.1, Implementation of ODE Solvers.

I am tremendously grateful to Jan Christiaan van Winkel and Fabio Fracassi, who back-checked every tiny detail of the manuscript and gave many suggestions toward standard compliance and comprehensibility.

I would especially like to thank Bjarne Stroustrup for giving strategic tips to shape the book, establishing contact with Addison-Wesley, generously allowing me to reuse his well-prepared material, and (not to forget) for creating C++. All these proofreaders pushed me hard to update the old lecture material with C++11 and C++14 features as far as possible.

In addition, I thank Karsten Ahnert for his recommendations and Markus Abel for helping me to get rid of the Preface's verbosity.

When I was looking for an interesting random number application for Section 4.2.2.6, Jan Rudl suggested the share price evolution he used in his class [60].

I am obliged to Technische Universität, Dresden, which let me teach C++ in the mathematics department over 3 years, and I appreciate the constructive feedback from the students from this course. Likewise, I am grateful to the attendees of my C++ training.

I am deeply in debt to my editor, Greg Doench, for accepting my half-serious, half-casual style in this book, for enduring long-lasting discussions about strategic decisions until we were both satisfied, and for providing professional support, without which the book would never have reached publication.

Elizabeth Ryan deserves credit for managing the entire production process while having patience for all my special requests.

Last but not least, I wholeheartedly thank my family—my wife, Yasmine, and my children Yanis, Anissa, Vincent, and Daniely—for sacrificing so much of our time together so I could work on the book instead.

About the Author

Peter Gottschling's professional passion is writing leading-edge scientific software, and he hopes to infect many readers with this virus. This vocation resulted in writing the Matrix Template Library 4 and coauthoring other libraries including the Boost Graph Library. These programming experiences were shared in several C++ courses at universities and in professional training sessions—finally leading to this book.

He is a member of the ISO C++ standards committee, vice-chair of Germany's programming language standards committee, and founder of the C++ User Group in Dresden. In his young and wild years at TU Dresden, he studied computer science and mathematics in parallel up to a bachelor-like level and finished the former with a PhD. After an odyssey through academic institutions, he founded his own company, SimuNova, and returned to his beloved hometown of Leipzig, just in time for its 1000th anniversary. He is married and has four children.

Chapter 1

C++ Basics

In this first chapter, we will guide you through the fundamental features of C++. As for the entire book, we will look at it from different angles but we will not try to expose every possible detail—which is not feasible anyway. For more detailed questions on specific features, we recommend the online manuals `http://www.cplusplus.com/` and `http://en.cppreference.com`.

1.1 Our First Program

As an introduction to the C++ language, let us look at the following example:

```cpp
#include <iostream>

int main ()
{
    std::cout << "The answer to the Ultimate Question of Life,\n"
              << "the Universe, and Everything is:"
              << std::endl << 6 * 7 << std::endl;
    return 0;
}
```

which yields

```
The answer to the Ultimate Question of Life,
the Universe, and Everything is:
42
```

according to Douglas Adams [2]. This short example already illustrates several features of C++:

- Input and output are not part of the core language but are provided by the library. They must be included explicitly; otherwise we cannot read or write.

- The standard I/O has a stream model and is therefore named `<iostream>`. To enable its functionality, we `include` `<iostream>` in the first line.

1

- Every C++ program starts by calling the function `main`. It does `return` an integer value where 0 represents a successful termination.

- Braces {} denote a block/group of code (also called a compound statement).

- `std::cout` and `std::endl` are defined in `<iostream>`. The former is an output stream that prints text on the screen. `std::endl` terminates a line. We can also go to a new line with the special character `\n`.

- The operator $\ll$ can be used to pass objects to an output stream such as `std::cout` for performing an output operation.

- `std::` denotes that the type or function is used from the standard *Namespace*. Namespaces help us to organize our names and to deal with naming conflicts; see §3.2.1.

- String constants (more precisely literals) are enclosed in double quotes.

- The expression `6 * 7` is evaluated and passed as an integer to `std::cout`. In C++, every expression has a type. Sometimes, we as programmers have to declare the type explicitly and other times the compiler can deduce it for us. 6 and 7 are literal constants of type `int` and accordingly their product is `int` as well.

Before you continue reading, we strongly recommend that you compile and run this little program on your computer. Once it compiles and runs, you can play a little bit with it, for example, adding more operations and output (and looking at some error messages). Finally, the only way to really learn a language is to use it. If you already know how to use a compiler or even a C++ IDE, you can skip the remainder of this section.

Linux: Every distribution provides at least the GNU C++ compiler—usually already installed (see the short intro in Section B.1). Say we call our program `hello42.cpp`; it is easily compiled with the command

```
g++ hello42.cpp
```

Following a last-century tradition, the resulting binary is called `a.out` by default. One day we might have more than one program, and then we can use more meaningful names with the output flag:

```
g++ hello42.cpp -o hello42
```

We can also use the build tool `make` (overview in §7.2.2.1) that provides (in recent versions) default rules for building binaries. Thus, we could call

```
make hello42
```

and `make` will look in the current directory for a similarly named program source. It will find `hello42.cpp`, and as `.cpp` is a standard file suffix for C++ sources, it will call the system's default C++ compiler. Once we have compiled our program, we can call it on the command line as

```
./hello42
```

Our binary can be executed without needing any other software, and we can copy it to another compatible Linux system[1] and run it there.

Windows: If you are running MinGW, you can compile in the same manner as under Linux. If you use Visual Studio, you will need to create a project first. To begin, the easiest way is to use the project template for a console application, as described, for instance, at `http://www.cplusplus.com/doc/tutorial/introduction/visualstudio`. When you run the program, you have a few milliseconds to read the output before the console closes. To extend the reading phase to a second, simply insert the non-portable command `Sleep(1000);` and include `<windows.h>`. With C++11 or higher, the waiting phase can be implemented portably:

```
std::this_thread::sleep_for(std::chrono::seconds(1));
```

after including `<chrono>` and `<thread>`. Microsoft offers free versions of Visual Studio called "Express" which provide the support for the standard language like their professional counterparts. The difference is that the professional editions come with more developer libraries. Since those are not used in this book, you can use the "Express" version to try our examples.

IDE: Short programs like the examples in this book can be easily handled with an ordinary editor. In larger projects it is advisable to use an *Integrated Development Environment* to see where a function is defined or used, to show the in-code documentation, to search or replace names project-wide, et cetera. KDevelop is a free IDE from the KDE community written in C++. It is probably the most efficient IDE on Linux and integrates well with `git` and `CMake`. Eclipse is developed in Java and perceivably slower. However, a lot of effort was recently put into it for improving the C++ support, and many developers are quite productive with it. Visual Studio is a very solid IDE that comes with some unique features such as a miniaturized colored page view as scroll bar.

To find the most productive environment takes some time and experimentation and is of course subject to personal and collaborative taste. As such, it will also evolve over time.

1.2 Variables

C++ is a strongly typed language (in contrast to many scripting languages). This means that every variable has a type and this type never changes. A variable is declared by a statement beginning with a type followed by a variable name with optional initialization—or a list thereof:

```
int     i1= 2;              // Alignment for readability only
int     i2, i3= 5;
```

---

1. Often the standard library is linked dynamically (cf. §7.2.1.4) and then its presence in the same version on the other system is part of the compatibility requirements.

```
float   pi= 3.14159;
double  x= -1.5e6;              // -1500000
double  y= -1.5e-6;            // -0.0000015
char    c1= 'a', c2= 35;
bool    cmp= i1 < pi,          // -> true
        happy= true;
```

The two slashes **//** here start a single-line comment; i.e., everything from the double slashes to the end of the line is ignored. In principle, this is all that really matters about comments. So as not to leave you with the feeling that something important on the topic is still missing, we will discuss it a little more in Section 1.9.1.

Back to the variables! Their basic types—also called *Intrinsic Types*—are given in Table 1–1.

The first five types are integer numbers of non-decreasing length. For instance, int is at least as long as short; i.e., it is usually but not necessarily longer. The exact length of each type is implementation-dependent; e.g., int could be 16, 32, or 64 bits. All these types can be qualified as signed or unsigned. The former has no effect on integer numbers (except char) since they are signed by default.

When we declare an integer type as unsigned, we will have no negative values but twice as many positive ones (plus one when we consider zero as neither positive nor negative). signed and unsigned can be considered adjectives for the nouns short, int, et cetera with int as the default noun when the adjective only is declared.

The type char can be used in two ways: for letters and rather short numbers. Except for really exotic architectures, it almost always has a length of 8 bits. Thus, we can either represent values from -128 to 127 (signed) in or from 0 to 255 (unsigned) and perform all numeric operations on them that are available for integers. When neither signed nor unsigned is declared, it depends on the implementation of the compiler which one is used. We can also represent any letter whose code fits into 8 bits. It can be even mixed; e.g., 'a' + 7 usually leads to 'h' depending on the underlying coding of the letters. We strongly recommend not playing with this since the potential confusion will likely lead to a perceivable waste of time.

Table 1–1: Intrinsic Types

Name	Semantics
char	letter and very short integer number
short	rather short integer number
int	regular integer number
long	long integer number
long long	very long integer number
unsigned	unsigned versions of all the former
signed	signed versions of all the former
float	single-precision floating-point number
double	double-precision floating-point number
long double;	long floating-point number
bool	boolean

Using char or unsigned char for small numbers, however, can be useful when there are large containers of them.

Logic values are best represented as bool. A boolean variable can store true and false.

The non-decreasing length property applies in the same manner to floating-point numbers: float is shorter than or equally as long as double, which in turn is shorter than or equally as long as long double. Typical sizes are 32 bits for float, 64 bits for double, and 80 bits for long double.

In the following section, we show operations that are often applied to integer and float types. In contrast to other languages like Python, where ' and " are used for both characters and strings, C++ distinguishes between the two of them. The C++ compiler considers 'a' as the character "a" (it has type char) and "a" is the string containing "a" and a binary 0 as termination (i.e., its type is char[2]). If you are used to Python, please pay attention to this.

Advice

Declare variables as late as possible, usually right before using them the first time and whenever possible not before you can initialize them.

This makes programs more readable when they grow long. It also allows the compiler to use the memory more efficiently with nested scopes.

C++11 can deduce the type of a variable for us, e.g.:

C++11

```
auto i4= i3 + 7;
```

The type of i4 is the same as that of i3 + 7, which is int. Although the type is automatically determined, it remains the same, and whatever is assigned to i4 afterward will be converted to int. We will see later how useful auto is in advanced programming. For simple variable declarations like those in this section it is usually better to declare the type explicitly. auto will be discussed thoroughly in Section 3.4.

1.2.1 Constants

Syntactically, constants are like special variables in C++ with the additional attribute of constancy.

```
const int    ci1= 2;
const int    ci3;              // Error: no value
const float  pi= 3.14159;
const char   cc 'a';
const bool   cmp= ci1 < pi;
```

As they cannot be changed, it is mandatory to set their values in the declaration. The second constant declaration violates this rule, and the compiler will not tolerate such misbehavior.

Constants can be used wherever variables are allowed—as long as they are not modified, of course. On the other hand, constants like those above are already known during compilation. This enables many kinds of optimizations, and the constants can even be used as arguments of types (we will come back to this later in §5.1.4).

1.2.2 Literals

Literals like 2 or 3.14 are typed as well. Simply put, integral numbers are treated as int, long, or unsigned long depending on the number of digits. Every number with a dot or an exponent (e.g., 3e12 $\equiv 3 \cdot 10^{12}$) is considered a double.

Literals of other types can be written by adding a suffix from the following table:

Literal	Type
2	int
2u	unsigned
2l	long
2ul	unsigned long
2.0	double
2.0f	float
2.0l	long double

In most cases, it is not necessary to declare the type of literals explicitly since the implicit conversion (a.k.a. *Coercion*) between built-in numeric types usually sets the values at the programmer's expectation.

There are, however, three major reasons why we should pay attention to the types of literals:

Availability: The standard library provides a type for complex numbers where the type for the real and imaginary parts can be parameterized by the user:

```
std::complex<float> z(1.3, 2.4), z2;
```

Unfortunately, operations are only provided between the type itself and the underlying real type (and arguments are not converted here).[2] As a consequence, we cannot multiply z with an int or double but with float:

```
z2= 2 * z;        // Error: no int * complex<float>
z2= 2.0 * z;      // Error: no double * complex<float>
z2= 2.0f * z;     // Okay:  float * complex<float>
```

Ambiguity: When a function is overloaded for different argument types (§1.5.4), an argument like 0 might be ambiguous whereas a unique match may exist for a qualified argument like 0u.

Accuracy: The accuracy issue comes up when we work with long double. Since the non-qualified literal is a double, we might lose digits before we assign it to a long double variable:

```
long double third1= 0.3333333333333333333;   // may lose digits
long double third2= 0.3333333333333333333l;  // accurate
```

If the previous three paragraphs were too brief for your taste, there is a more detailed version in Section A.2.1.

---

2. Mixed arithmetic is implementable, however, as demonstrated at [18].

Non-decimal Numbers: Integer literals starting with a zero are interpreted as octal numbers, e.g.:

```
int o1= 042;          // int o1= 34;
int o2= 084;          // Error! No 8 or 9 in octals!
```

Hexadecimal literals can be written by prefixing them with 0x or 0X:

```
int h1= 0x42;         // int h1= 66;
int h2= 0xfa;         // int h2= 250;
```

C++14 introduces binary literals which are prefixed by 0b or 0B:

```
int b1= 0b11111010;   // int b1= 250;
```

`C++14`

To improve readability of long literals, C++14 allows us to separate the digits with apostrophes:

`C++14`

```
long             d=   6'546'687'616'861'129l;
unsigned long    ulx= 0x139'ae3b'2ab0'94f3;
int              b=   0b101'1001'0011'1010'1101'1010'0001;
const long double pi= 3.141'592'653'589'793'238'462l;
```

String literals are typed as arrays of char:

```
char s1[]= "Old C style"; // better not
```

However, these arrays are everything but convenient and we are better off with the true string type from the library <string>. It can be created directly from a string literal:

```
#include <string>

std::string s2= "In C++ better like this";
```

Very long text can be split into multiple sub-strings:

```
std::string s3= "This is a very long and clumsy text "
                "that is too long for one line.";
```

For more details on literals, see for instance [43, §6.2].

1.2.3 Non-narrowing Initialization

`C++11`

Say we initialize a long variable with a long number:

```
long l2= 1234567890123;
```

This compiles just fine and works correctly—when long takes 64 bits as on most 64-bit platforms. When long is only 32 bits long (we can emulate this by compiling with flags like -m32), the value above is too long. However, the program will still compile (maybe with a warning) and runs with another value, e.g., where the leading bits are cut off.

C++11 introduces an initialization that ascertains that no data is lost or in other words that the values are not *Narrowed*. This is achieved with the *Uniform Initialization* or *Braced*

Initialization that we only touch upon here and expand in Section 2.3.4. Values in braces cannot be narrowed:

```
long l= {1234567890123};
```

Now, the compiler will check if the variable l can hold the value on the target architecture.

The compiler's narrowing protection allows us to verify that values do not lose precision in initializations. Whereas an ordinary initialization of an int by a floating-point number is allowed due to implicit conversion:

```
int i1= 3.14;          // compiles despite narrowing (our risk)
int i1n= {3.14};       // Narrowing ERROR: fractional part lost
```

The new initialization form in the second line forbids this because it cuts off the fractional part of the floating-point number. Likewise, assigning negative values to unsigned variables or constants is tolerated with traditional initialization but denounced in the new form:

```
unsigned u2= -3;       // Compiles despite narrowing (our risk)
unsigned u2n= {-3};    // Narrowing ERROR: no negative values
```

In the previous examples, we used literal values in the initializations and the compiler checks whether a specific value is representable with that type:

```
float f1= {3.14};      // okay
```

Well, the value 3.14 cannot be represented with absolute accuracy in any binary floating-point format, but the compiler can set f1 to the value closest to 3.14. When a float is initialized from a double variable or constant (not a literal), we have to consider all possible double values and whether they are all convertible to float in a loss-free manner.

```
double d;
...
float f2= {d};         // narrowing ERROR
```

Note that the narrowing can be mutual between two types:

```
unsigned u3= {3};
int      i2= {2};

unsigned u4= {i2};     // narrowing ERROR: no negative values
int      i3= {u3};     // narrowing ERROR: not all large values
```

The types signed int and unsigned int have the same size, but not all values of each type are representable in the other.

1.2.4 Scopes

Scopes determine the lifetime and visibility of (non-static) variables and constants and contribute to establishing a structure in our programs.

1.2.4.1 Global Definition

Every variable that we intend to use in a program must have been declared with its type specifier at an earlier point in the code. A variable can be located in either the global or local scope. A global variable is declared outside all functions. After their declaration, global variables can be referred to from anywhere in the code, even inside functions. This sounds very handy at first because it makes the variables easily available, but when your software grows, it becomes more difficult and painful to keep track of the global variables' modifications. At some point, every code change bears the potential of triggering an avalanche of errors.

Advice

Do not use global variables.

If you do use them, sooner or later you will regret it. Believe us. Global constants like

```
const double pi= 3.14159265358979323846264338327950288419716939;
```

are fine because they cannot cause side effects.

1.2.4.2 Local Definition

A local variable is declared within the body of a function. Its visibility/availability is limited to the { }-enclosed block of its declaration. More precisely, the scope of a variable starts with its declaration and ends with the closing brace of the declaration block.

If we define π in the function `main`:

```
int main ()
{
    const double pi= 3.14159265358979323846264338327950288419716939;
    std::cout << "pi is " << pi << ".\n";
}
```

the variable π only exists in the `main` function. We can define blocks within functions and within other blocks:

```
int main ()
{
    {
        const double pi= 3.14159265358979323846264338327950288419716939;
    }
    std::cout << "pi is " << pi << ".\n"; // ERROR: pi is out of scope
}
```

In this example, the definition of π is limited to the block within the function, and an output in the remainder of the function is therefore an error:

```
»pi« is not defined in this scope.
```

because π is *Out of Scope*.

1.2.4.3 Hiding

When a variable with the same name exists in nested scopes, then only one variable is visible. The variable in the inner scope hides the homonymous variables in the outer scopes. For instance:

```
int main ()
{
    int a= 5;               // define a#1
    {
        a= 3;               // assign a#1, a#2 is not defined yet
        int a;              // define a#2
        a= 8;               // assign a#2, a#1 is hidden
        {
            a= 7;           // assign a#2
        }
    }                       // end of a#2's scope
    a= 11;                  // assign to a#1 (a#2 out of scope)

    return 0;
}
```

Due to hiding, we must distinguish the lifetime and the visibility of variables. For instance, a#1 lives from its declaration until the end of the main function. However, it is only visible from its declaration until the declaration of a#2 and again after closing the block containing a#2. In fact, the visibility is the lifetime minus the time when it is hidden.

Defining the same variable name twice in one scope is an error.

The advantage of scopes is that we do not need to worry about whether a variable is already defined somewhere outside the scope. It is just hidden but does not create a conflict.[3] Unfortunately, the hiding makes the homonymous variables in the outer scope inaccessible. We can cope with this to some extent with clever renaming. A better solution, however, to manage nesting and accessibility is namespaces; see Section 3.2.1.

static variables are the exception that confirms the rule: they live till the end of the execution but are only visible in the scope. We are afraid that their detailed introduction is more distracting than helpful at this stage and have postponed the discussion to Section A.2.2.

1.3 Operators

C++ is rich in built-in operators. There are different kinds of operators:

- Computational:

    - Arithmetic: ++, +, *, %, ...

---

3. As opposed to macros, an obsolete and reckless legacy feature from C that should be avoided at any price because it undermines all structure and reliability of the language.

- Boolean:
  - ∗ Comparison: <=, !=, ...
  - ∗ Logic: && and ||
- Bitwise: $\sim$, $\ll$ and $\gg$, &, ^, and |

- Assignment: =, +=, ...

- Program flow: function call, ?:, and ,

- Memory handling: new and delete

- Access: ., ->, [ ], *, ...

- Type handling: dynamic_cast, typeid, sizeof, alignof ...

- Error handling: throw

This section will give an overview of the operators. Some operators are better described elsewhere in the context of the appropriate language feature; e.g., scope resolution is best explained together with namespaces. Most operators can be overloaded for user types; i.e., we can decide which calculations are performed when one or multiple arguments in an expression are our types.

At the end of this section (Table 1–8), you will find a concise table of operator precedence. It might be a good idea to print or copy this page and pin it next to your monitor; many people do so and almost nobody knows the entire priority list by heart. Neither should you hesitate to put parentheses around sub-expressions if you are uncertain about the priorities or if you believe it will be more understandable for other programmers working with your sources. If you ask your compiler to be pedantic, it often takes this job too seriously and prompts you to add surplus parentheses assuming you are overwhelmed by the precedence rules. In Section C.2, we will give you a complete list of all operators with brief descriptions and references.

1.3.1 Arithmetic Operators

Table 1–2 lists the arithmetic operators available in C++. We have sorted them by their priorities, but let us look at them one by one.

The first kinds of operations are increment and decrement. These operations can be used to increase or decrease a number by 1. As they change the value of the number, they only make sense for variables and not for temporary results, for instance:

```
int i= 3;
i++;                // i is now 4
const int j= 5;
j++;                // error, j is constant
(3 + 5)++;          // error, 3 + 5 is only a temporary
```

In short, the increment and decrement operations need something that is modifiable and addressable. The technical term for an addressable data item is *Lvalue* (see Definition C–1

Table 1–2: Arithmetic Operators

Operation	Expression
Post-increment	x++
Post-decrement	x--
Pre-increment	++x
Pre-decrement	--x
Unary plus	+x
Unary minus	-x
Multiplication	x * y
Division	x / y
Modulo	x \% y
Addition	x + y
Subtraction	x - y

in Appendix C). In our code snippet above, this is true for i only. In contrast to it, j is constant and 3 + 5 is not addressable.

Both notations—prefix and postfix—have the effect on a variable that they add or subtract 1 from it. The value of an increment and decrement expression is different for prefix and postfix operators: the prefix operators return the modified value and postfix the old one, e.g.:

```
int i= 3, j= 3;
int k= ++i + 4;    // i is 4, k is 8
int l= j++ + 4;    // j is 4, l is 7
```

At the end, both i and j are 4. However in the calculation of l, the old value of j was used while the first addition used the already incremented value of i.

In general, it is better to refrain from using increment and decrement in mathematical expressions and to replace it with j+1 and the like or to perform the in/decrement separately. It is easier for human readers to understand and for the compiler to optimize when mathematical expressions have no *Side Effects*. We will see quite soon why (§1.3.12).

The unary minus negates the value of a number:

```
int i= 3;
int j= -i;         // j is -3
```

The unary plus has no arithmetic effect on standard types. For user types, we can define the behavior of both unary plus and minus. As shown in Table 1–2, these unary operators have the same priority as pre-increment and pre-decrement.

The operations * and / are naturally multiplication and division, and both are defined on all numeric types. When both arguments in a division are integers, then the fractional part of the result is truncated (rounding toward zero). The operator % yields the remainder of the integer division. Thus, both arguments should have an integral type.

Last but not least, the operators + and - between two variables or expressions symbolize addition and subtraction.

The semantic details of the operations—how results are rounded or how overflow is handled—are not specified in the language. For performance reasons, C++ leaves this typically to the underlying hardware.

In general, unary operators have higher priority than binary. On the rare occasions that both postfix and prefix unary notations have been applied, prefix notations are prioritized over postfix notations.

Among the binary operators, we have the same behavior that we know from math: multiplication and division precede addition and subtraction and the operations are left associative, i.e.:

```
x - y + z
```

is always interpreted as

```
(x - y) + z
```

Something really important to remember: the order of evaluation of the arguments is not defined. For instance:

```
int i= 3, j= 7, k;
k= f(++i) + g(++i) + j;
```

In this example, associativity guarantees that the first addition is performed before the second. But whether the expression f(++i) or g(++i) is computed first depends on the compiler implementation. Thus, k might be either f(4) + g(5) + 7 or f(5) + g(4) + 7. Furthermore, we cannot assume that the result is the same on a different platform. In general, it is dangerous to modify values within expressions. It works under some conditions, but we always have to test it and pay enormous attention to it. Altogether, our time is better spent by typing some extra letters and doing the modifications separately. More about this topic in Section 1.3.12.

$\Rightarrow$ c++03/num_1.cpp

With these operators, we can write our first (complete) numeric program:

```
#include <iostream>

int main ()
{
    const float r1= 3.5, r2 = 7.3, pi = 3.14159;

    float area1 = pi * r1*r1;
    std::cout << "A circle of radius " << r1 << " has area "
            << area1 << "." << std::endl;

    std::cout << "The average of " << r1 << " and " << r2 << " is "
            << (r1 + r2) / 2 << "." << std::endl;
}
```

When the arguments of a binary operation have different types, one or both arguments are automatically converted (coerced) to a common type according to the rules in Section C.3.

The conversion may lead to a loss of precision. Floating-point numbers are preferred over integer numbers, and evidently the conversion of a 64-bit long to a 32-bit float yields an accuracy loss; even a 32-bit int cannot always be represented correctly as a 32-bit float since some bits are needed for the exponent. There are also cases where the target variable could hold the correct result but the accuracy was already lost in the intermediate calculations. To illustrate this conversion behavior, let us look at the following example:

```
long l= 1234567890123;
long l2= l + 1.0f - 1.0;    // imprecise
long l3= l + (1.0f - 1.0); // correct
```

This leads on the author's platform to

```
l2 = 1234567954431
l3 = 1234567890123
```

In the case of l2 we lose accuracy due to the intermediate conversions, whereas l3 was computed correctly. This is admittedly an artificial example, but you should be aware of the risk of imprecise intermediate results.

The issue of inaccuracy will fortunately not bother us in the next section.

1.3.2 Boolean Operators

Boolean operators are logical and relational operators. Both return bool values as the name suggests. These operators and their meaning are listed in Table 1–3, grouped by precedence.

Binary relational and logical operators are preceded by all arithmetic operators. This means that an expression like 4 >= 1 + 7 is evaluated as if it were written 4 >= (1 + 7). Conversely, the unary operator ! for logic negation is prioritized over all binary operators.

In old (or old-fashioned) code, you might see logical operations performed on int values. Please refrain from this: it is less readable and subject to unexpected behavior.

Advice

Always use bool for logical expressions.

Table 1–3: Boolean Operators

Operation	Expression
Not	!b
Greater than	x > y
Greater than or equal to	x >= y
Less than	x < y
Less than or equal to	x < y
Equal to	x == y
Not equal to	x != y
Logical AND	b && c
Logical OR	b || c

Please note that comparisons cannot be chained like this:

```
bool in_bound= min <= x <= y <= max;      // Error
```

Instead we need the more verbose logical reduction:

```
bool in_bound= min <= x && x <= y && y <= max;
```

In the following section, we will see quite similar operators.

1.3.3 Bitwise Operators

These operators allow us to test or manipulate single bits of integral types. They are important for system programming but less so for modern application development. Table 1–4 lists all operators by precedence.

The operation $x \ll y$ shifts the bits of x to the left by y positions. Conversely, $x \gg y$ moves x's bits y times to the right. In most cases, 0s are moved in except for negative signed values in a right shift where it is implementation-defined. The bitwise AND can be used to test a specific bit of a value. Bitwise inclusive OR can set a bit and exclusive OR flip it. These operations are more important in system programming than scientific applications. As algorithmic entertainment, we will use them in §3.6.1.

1.3.4 Assignment

The value of an object (modifiable lvalue) can be set by an assignment:

```
object= expr;
```

When the types do not match, expr is converted to the type of object if possible. The assignment is right-associative so that a value can be successively assigned to multiple objects in one expression:

```
o3= o2= o1= expr;
```

Speaking of assignments, the author will now explain why he left-justifies the symbol. Most binary operators are symmetric in the sense that both arguments are values. In contrast, assignments have a modifiable variable on the left-hand side. While other languages use asymmetric symbols (e.g., := in Pascal), the author uses an asymmetric spacing in C++.

Table 1–4: Bitwise Operators

Operation	Expression
One's complement	$\sim x$
Left shift	$x \ll y$
Right shift	$x \gg y$
Bitwise AND	x & y
Bitwise exclusive OR	x ^ y
Bitwise inclusive OR	x | y

   The compound assignment operators apply an arithmetic or bitwise operation to the object on the left side with the argument on the right side; for instance, the following two operations are equivalent:

```
a+= b;              // corresponds to
a= a + b;
```

All assignment operators have a lower precedence than every arithmetic or bitwise operation so the right-hand side expression is always evaluated before the compound assignment:

```
a*= b + c;          // corresponds to
a= a * (b + c);
```

The assignment operators are listed in Table 1–5. They are all right-associative and of the same priority.

1.3.5 Program Flow

There are three operators to control the program flow. First, a function call in C++ is handled like an operator. For a detailed description of functions and their calls, see Section 1.5.

   The conditional operator c ? x : y evaluates the condition c, and when it is true the expression has the value of x, otherwise y. It can be used as an alternative to branches with if, especially in places where only an expression is allowed and not a statement; see Section 1.4.3.1.

   A very special operator in C++ is the *Comma Operator* that provides a sequential evaluation. The meaning is simply evaluating first the sub-expression to the left of the comma and then that to the right of it. The value of the whole expression is that of the right sub-expression:

```
3 + 4, 7 * 9.3
```

The result of the expression is 65.1 and the computation of the first sub-expression is entirely irrelevant. The sub-expressions can contain the comma operator as well so that arbitrarily long sequences can be defined. With the help of the comma operator, one can

Table 1–5: Assignment Operators

Operation	Expression
Simple assignment	x= y
Multiply and assign	x*= y
Divide and assign	x/= y
Modulo and assign	x%= y
Add and assign	x+= y
Subtract and assign	x-= y
Shift left and assign	x≪= y
Shift right and assign	x≫= y
AND and assign	x&= y
Inclusive OR and assign	x|= y
Exclusive OR and assign	x^= y

evaluate multiple expressions in program locations where only one expression is allowed. A typical example is the increment of multiple indices in a for-loop (§1.4.4.2):

```
++i, ++j
```

When used as a function argument, the comma expression needs surrounding parentheses; otherwise the comma is interpreted as separation of function arguments.

1.3.6   Memory Handling

The operators new and delete allocate and deallocate memory respectively; see Section 1.8.2.

1.3.7   Access Operators

C++ provides several operators for accessing sub-structures, for referring—i.e., taking the address of a variable—and dereferencing—i.e., accessing the memory referred to by an address. Discussing these operators before talking about pointers and classes makes no sense. We thus postpone their description to the sections given in Table 1–6.

1.3.8   Type Handling

The operators for dealing with types will be presented in Chapter 5 when we will write compile-time programs that work on types. The available operators are listed in Table 1–7.

Table 1–6: Access Operators

Operation	Expression	Reference
Member selection	x.m	§2.2.3
Dereferred member selection	p->m	§2.2.3
Subscripting	x[i]	§1.8.1
Dereference	*x	§1.8.2
Member dereference	x.*q	§2.2.3
Dereferred member dereference	p->*q	§2.2.3

Table 1–7: Type-Handling Operators

Operation	Expression
Run-time type identification	typeid(x)
Identification of a type	typeid(t)
Size of object	sizeof(x) or sizeof x
Size of type	sizeof(t)
Number of arguments	sizeof...(p)
Number of type arguments	sizeof...(P)
Alignment	alignof(x)
Alignment of type	alignof(t)

Note that the `sizeof` operator when used on an expression is the only one that is applicable without parentheses. `alignof` is introduced in C++11; all others exist since 98 (at least).

1.3.9   Error Handling

The `throw` operator is used to indicate an exception in the execution (e.g., insufficient memory); see Section 1.6.2.

1.3.10   Overloading

A very powerful aspect of C++ is that the programmer can define operators for new types. This will be explained in Section 2.7. Operators of built-in types cannot be changed. However, we can define how built-in types interact with new types; i.e., we can overload mixed operations like double times matrix.

Most operators can be overloaded. Exceptions are:

`::`	Scope resolution;
`.`	Member selection (may be added in C++17);
`.*`	Member selection through pointer;
`?:`	Conditional;
`sizeof`	Size of a type or object;
`sizeof...`	Number of arguments;
`alignof`	Memory alignment of a type or object; and
`typeid`	Type identifier.

The operator overloading in C++ gives us a lot of freedom and we have to use this freedom wisely. We come back to this topic in the next chapter when we actually overload operators (wait till Section 2.7).

1.3.11   Operator Precedence

Table 1–8 gives a concise overview of the operator priorities. For compactness, we combined notations for types and expressions (e.g., `typeid`) and fused the different notations for `new` and `delete`. The symbol `@=` represents all computational assignments like `+=`, `-=`, and so on. A more detailed summary of operators with semantics is given in Appendix C, Table C–1.

1.3.12   Avoid Side Effects!

"Insanity: doing the same thing over and over again and expecting different results."

—Unknown[4]

In applications with side effects it is not insane to expect a different result for the same input. To the contrary, it is very difficult to predict the behavior of a program whose components

---

4. Misattributed to Albert Einstein, Benjamin Franklin, and Mark Twain. It is cited in *Sudden Death* by Rita Mae Brown but the original source seems to be unknown. Maybe the quote itself is beset with some insanity.

Table 1–8: Operator Precedence

Operator Precedence			
$class::member$	$nspace::member$	$::name$	$::qualified\text{-}name$
$object.member$	$pointer\text{-}>member$	$expr[\,expr\,]$	$expr(expr\_list)$
$type(expr\_list)$	$lvalue$++	$lvalue$--	typeid($type/expr$)
*_cast<$type$>($expr$)			
sizeof $expr$	sizeof($type$)	sizeof...($pack$)	alignof($type/expr$)
++$lvalue$	--$lvalue$	$\sim expr$	! $expr$
- $expr$	+ $expr$	&$lvalue$	* $expr$
new ... $type$...	delete $[]_{opt}$ $pointer$	($type$) $expr$	
$object.*member\_ptr$	$pointer\text{-}>*member\_ptr$		
$expr$ * $expr$	$expr$ / $expr$	$expr$ % $expr$	
$expr$ + $expr$	$expr$ - $expr$		
$expr \ll expr$	$expr \gg expr$		
$expr$ < $expr$	$expr$ <= $expr$	$expr$ > $expr$	$expr$ >= $expr$
$expr$ == $expr$	$expr$!= $expr$		
$expr$ & $expr$			
$expr$ ^ $expr$			
$expr$ | $expr$			
$expr$ && $expr$			
$expr$ || $expr$			
$expr$? $expr$: $expr$			
$lvalue$ = $expr$	$lvalue$ @= $expr$		
throw $expr$			
$expr$, $expr$			

interfere massively. Moreover, it is probably better to have a deterministic program with the wrong result than one that occasionally yields the right result since the latter is usually much harder to fix.

In the C standard library, there is a function to copy a string (strcpy). The function takes pointers to the first char of the source and the target and copies the subsequent letters until it finds a zero. This can be implemented with one single loop that even has an empty body and performs the copy and the increments as side effects of the continuation test:

```
while (*tgt++= *src++) ;
```

Looks scary? Well, it is somehow. However, this is absolutely legal C++ code, although some compilers might grumble in pedantic mode. It is a good mental exercise to spend some time thinking about operator priorities, types of sub-expressions, and evaluation order.

Let us think about something simpler: we assign the value i to the i-th entry of an array and increment the value i for the next iteration:

```
v[i]= i++;
```

Looks like no problem. But it is: the behavior of this expression is undefined. Why? The post-increment of i guarantees that we assign the old value of i and increment i afterward.

However, this increment can still be performed before the expression v[i] is evaluated so that we possibly assign i to v[i+1].

The last example should give you an impression that side effects are not always evident at first glance. Some quite tricky stuff might work but much simpler things might not. Even worse, something might work for a while until somebody compiles it on a different compiler or the new release of your compiler changes some implementation details.

The first snippet is an example of excellent programming skills and evidence that the operator precedence makes sense—no parentheses were needed. Nonetheless, such programming style is not appropriate for modern C++. The eagerness to shorten code as much as possible dates back to the times of early C when typing was more demanding, with typewriters that were more mechanical than electrical, and card punchers, all without a monitor. With today's technology, it should not be an issue for the digital natives to type some extra letters.

Another unfavorable aspect of the terse copy implementation is the mingling of different concerns: testing, modification, and traversal. An important concept in software design is *Separation of Concerns*. It contributes to increasing flexibility and decreasing complexity. In this case, we want to decrease the complexity of the mental processes needed to understand the implementation. Applying the principle to the infamous copy one-liner could yield

```
for (; *src; tgt++, src++)
    *tgt= *src;
*tgt= *src; // copy the final 0
```

Now, we can clearly distinguish the three concerns:

- Testing: *src

- Modification: *tgt= *src;

- Traversal: tgt++, src++

It is also more apparent that the incrementing is performed on the pointers and the testing and assignment on their referred content. The implementation is not as compact as before, but it is much easier to check the correctness. It is also advisable to make the non-zero test more obvious (*src != 0).

There is a class of programming languages that are called *Functional Languages*. Values in these languages cannot be changed once they are set. C++ is obviously not that way. But we do ourselves a big favor when we program as much as is reasonable in a functional style. For instance, when we write an assignment, the only thing that should change is the variable to the left of the assignment symbol. To this end, we have to replace mutating with a constant expression: for instance, ++i with i+1. A right-hand side expression without side effects helps us to understand the program behavior and makes it easier for the compiler to optimize the code. As a rule of thumb: more comprehensible programs have a better potential for optimization.

1.4   Expressions and Statements

C++ distinguishes between expressions and statements. Very casually, we could say that every expression becomes a statement if a semicolon is appended. However, we would like to discuss this topic a bit more.

1.4.1   Expressions

Let us build this recursively from the bottom up. Any variable name (x, y, z, . . .), constant, or literal is an expression. One or more expressions combined by an operator constitute an expression, e.g., x + y or x * y + z. In several languages, such as Pascal, the assignment is a statement. In C++, it is an expression, e.g., x= y + z. As a consequence, it can be used within another assignment: x2= x= y + z. Assignments are evaluated from right to left. Input and output operations such as

```
std::cout ≪ "x is " ≪ x ≪ "\n"
```

are also expressions.

A function call with expressions as arguments is an expression, e.g., abs(x) or abs(x * y + z). Therefore, function calls can be nested: pow(abs(x), y). Note that nesting would not be possible if function calls were statements.

Since assignment is an expression, it can be used as an argument of a function: abs(x= y). Or I/O operations such as those above, e.g.:

```
print(std::cout ≪ "x is " ≪ x ≪ "\n", "I am such a nerd!");
```

Needless to say this is not particularly readable and it would cause more confusion than doing something useful. An expression surrounded by parentheses is an expression as well, e.g., (x + y). As this grouping by parentheses precedes all operators, we can change the order of evaluation to suit our needs: x * (y + z) computes the addition first.

1.4.2   Statements

Any of the expressions above followed by a semicolon is a statement, e.g.:

```
x= y + z;
y= f(x + z) * 3.5;
```

A statement like

```
y + z;
```

is allowed despite being useless (most likely). During program execution, the sum of y and z is computed and then thrown away. Recent compilers optimize out such useless computations. However, it is not guaranteed that this statement can always be omitted. If y or z is an object of a user type, then the addition is also user-defined and might change y or z or something else. This is obviously bad programming style (hidden side effect) but legitimate in C++.

A single semicolon is an empty statement, and we can thus put as many semicolons after an expression as we want. Some statements do not end with a semicolon, e.g., function definitions. If a semicolon is appended to such a statement it is not an error but just an extra empty statement. Nonetheless some compilers print a warning in pedantic mode. Any sequence of statements surrounded by curly braces is a statement—called a *Compound Statement*.

The variable and constant declarations we have seen before are also statements. As the initial value of a variable or constant, we can use any expression (except another assignment or comma operator). Other statements—to be discussed later—are function and class definitions, as well as control statements that we will introduce in the next section.

With the exception of the conditional operator, program flow is controlled by statements. Here we will distinguish between branches and loops.

1.4.3   Branching

In this section, we will present the different features that allow us to select a branch in the program execution.

1.4.3.1   if-Statement

This is the simplest form of control and its meaning is intuitively clear, for instance in

```
if (weight > 100.0)
    cout ≪ "This is quite heavy.\n";
else
    cout ≪ "I can carry this.\n";
```

Often, the else branch is not needed and can be omitted. Say we have some value in variable x and compute something on its magnitude:

```
if (x < 0.0)
    x= -x;
// Now we know that x >= 0.0 (post-condition)
```

The branches of the if-statement are scopes, rendering the following statements erroneous:

```
if (x < 0.0)
    int absx= -x;
else
    int absx= x;
cout ≪ "|x| is " ≪ absx ≪ "\n"; // absx already out of scope
```

Above, we introduced two new variables, both named absx. They are not in conflict because they reside in different scopes. Neither of them exists after the if-statement, and accessing absx in the last line is an error. In fact, variables declared in a branch can only be used within this branch.

Each branch of if consists of one single statement. To perform multiple operations, we can use braces as in Cardano's method:

```
double D= q*q/4.0 + p*p*p/27.0;
if (D > 0.0) {
    double z1= ...;
```

```
      complex<double> z2= ..., z3= ...;
      ...
} else if (D == 0.0) {
      double z1= ..., z2= ..., z3= ...;
      ...
} else {                        // D < 0.0
      complex<double> z1= ..., z2= ..., z3= ...;
      ...
}
```

In the beginning, it is helpful to always write the braces. Many style guides also enforce curly braces on single statements whereas the author prefers them without braces. Irrespective of this, it is highly advisable to indent the branches for better readability.

if-statements can be nested whereas each else is associated with the last open if. If you are interested in examples, have a look at Section A.2.3. Finally, we give you the following:

Advice

Although spaces do not affect the compilation in C++, the indentation should reflect the structure of the program. Editors that understand C++ (like Visual Studio's IDE or emacs in C++ mode) and indent automatically are a great help with structured programming. Whenever a line is not indented as expected, something is most likely not nested as intended.

1.4.3.2   Conditional Expression

Although this section describes statements, we like to talk about the conditional expression here because of its proximity to the if-statement. The result of

```
condition ? result_for_true : result_for_false
```

is the second sub-expression (i.e., result_for_true) when condition evaluates to true and result_for_false otherwise. For instance,

```
min= x <= y ? x : y;
```

corresponds to the following if-statement:

```
if (x <= y)
    min= x;
else
    min= y;
```

For a beginner, the second version might be more readable while experienced programmers often prefer the first form for its brevity.

?: is an expression and can therefore be used to initialize variables:

```
int x= f(a),
    y= x < 0 ? -x : 2 * x;
```

Calling functions with several selected arguments is easy with the operator:

```
f(a, (x < 0 ? b : c), (y < 0 ? d : e));
```

but quite clumsy with an `if`-statement. If you do not believe us, try it.

In most cases it is not important whether an `if` or a conditional expression is used. So use what feels most convenient to you.

Anecdote: An example where the choice between `if` and `?:` makes a difference is the `replace_copy` operation in the Standard Template Library (STL), §4.1. It used to be implemented with the conditional operator whereas `if` would be more general. This "bug" remained undiscovered for approximately 10 years and was only detected by an automatic analysis in Jeremy Siek's Ph.D. thesis [38].

1.4.3.3 `switch` **Statement**

A `switch` is like a special kind of `if`. It provides a concise notation when different computations for different cases of an integral value are performed:

```
switch(op_code) {
  case 0: z= x + y; break;
  case 1: z= x - y; cout ≪ "compute diff\n"; break;
  case 2:
  case 3: z= x * y; break;
  default: z= x / y;
}
```

A somewhat surprising behavior is that the code of the following cases is also performed unless we terminate it with `break`. Thus, the same operations are performed in our example for cases 2 and 3. An advanced use of `switch` is found in Appendix A.2.4.

1.4.4 **Loops**

1.4.4.1 `while`- **and** `do-while`-**Loops**

As the name suggests, a `while`-loop is repeated as long as a certain condition holds. Let us implement as an example the Collatz series that is defined by

$$\textbf{Algorithm 1–1: Collatz series}$$

Input: x_0

1 **while** $x_i \neq 1$ **do**

2 $\quad x_i = \begin{cases} 3\,x_{i-1} + 1 & \text{if } x_{i-1} \text{ is odd} \\ x_{i-1}/2 & \text{if } x_{i-1} \text{ is even} \end{cases}$

As long as we do not worry about overflow, this is easily implemented with a `while`-loop:

```
int x= 19;
while (x != 1) {
    cout ≪ x ≪ '\n';
```

```
    if (x % 2 == 1)      // odd
        x= 3 * x + 1;
    else                 // even
        x= x / 2;
}
```

Like the if-statement, the loop can be written without braces when there is only one statement.

C++ also offers a do-while-loop. In this case, the condition for continuation is tested at the end:

```
double eps= 0.001;
do {
    cout << "eps= " << eps << '\n';
    eps /= 2.0;
} while (eps > 0.0001);
```

The loop is performed at least one time—even with an extremely small value for eps in our example.

1.4.4.2 for-Loop

The most common loop in C++ is the for-loop. As a simple example, we add two vectors[5] and print the result afterward:

```
double v[3], w[]= {2., 4., 6.}, x[]= {6., 5., 4};
for (int i= 0; i < 3; ++i)
    v[i]= w[i] + x[i];

for (int i= 0; i < 3; ++i)
    cout << "v[" << i << "]= " << v[i] << '\n';
```

The loop head consists of three components:

- The initialization;

- A *Continuation* criterion; and

- A step operation.

The example above is a typical for-loop. In the initialization, we typically declare a new variable and initialize it with 0—this is the start index of most indexed data structures. The condition usually tests whether the loop index is smaller than a certain size and the last operation typically increments the loop index. In the example, we pre-incremented the loop variable i. For intrinsic types like int, it does not matter whether we write ++i or i++. However, it does for user types where the post-increment causes an unnecessary copy; cf. §3.3.2.5. To be consistent in this book, we always use a pre-increment for loop indices.

It is a very popular beginners' mistake to write conditions like i <= size(..). Since indices are zero-based in C++, the index i == size(..) is already out of range. People with

---

5. Later we will introduce true vector classes. For the moment we take simple arrays.

experience in Fortran or MATLAB need some time to get used to zero-based indexing. One-based indexing seems more natural to many and is also used in mathematical literature. However, calculations on indices and addresses are almost always simpler with zero-based indexing.

As another example, we like to compute the Taylor series of the exponential function:

$$e^x = \sum_{i=0}^{\infty} \frac{x^n}{n!}$$

up to the tenth term:

```
double x= 2.0, xn= 1.0, exp_x= 1.0;
unsigned long fac= 1;
for (unsigned long i= 1; i <= 10; ++i) {
    xn*= x;
    fac*= i;
    exp_x+= xn / fac;
    cout << "e^x is " << exp_x << '\n';
}
```

Here it was simpler to compute term 0 separately and start the loop with term 1. We also used less-equal to assure that the term $x^{10}/10!$ is considered.

The for-loop in C++ is very flexible. The initialization part can be any expression, a variable declaration, or empty. It is possible to introduce multiple new variables of the same type. This can be used to avoid repeating the same operation in the condition, e.g.:

```
for (int i= xyz.begin(), end= xyz.end(); i < end; ++i) ...
```

Variables declared in the initialization are only visible within the loop and hide variables of the same names from outside the loop.

The condition can be any expression that is convertible to a bool. An empty condition is always true and the loop is repeated infinitely. It can still be terminated inside the body as we will discuss in the next section. We already mentioned that a loop index is typically incremented in the third sub-expression of for. In principle, we can modify it within the loop body as well. However, programs are much clearer if it is done in the loop head. On the other hand, there is no limitation that only one variable is increased by 1. We can modify as many variables as wanted using the comma operator (§1.3.5) and by any modification desired such as

```
for (int i= 0, j= 0, p= 1; ...; ++i, j+= 4, p*= 2) ...
```

This is of course more complex than having just one loop index but still more readable than declaring/modifying indices before the loop or inside the loop body.

C++11 **1.4.4.3 Range-Based for-Loop**

A very compact notation is provided by the new feature called *Range-Based* for-*Loop*. We will tell you more about its background once we come to the iterator concept (§4.1.2).

For now, we will consider it as a concise form to iterate over all entries of an array or other containers:

```
int primes[]= {2, 3, 5, 7, 11, 13, 17, 19};
for (int i : primes)
    std::cout << i << " ";
```

This will print out the primes from the array separated by spaces.

1.4.4.4 Loop Control

There are two statements to deviate from the regular loop evaluation:

- break and

- continue.

A break terminates the loop entirely, and continue ends only the current iteration and continues the loop with the next iteration, for instance:

```
for (...; ...; ...) {
    ...
    if (dx == 0.0) continue;
        x+= dx;
    ...
    if (r < eps) break;
    ...
}
```

In the example above we assumed that the remainder of the iteration is not needed when dx == 0.0. In some iterative computations it might be clear in the middle of an iteration (here when r < eps) that work is already done.

1.4.5 goto

All branches and loops are internally realized by jumps. C++ provides explicit jumps called goto. However:

Advice

Do not use goto! Never! Ever!

The applicability of goto is more restrictive in C++ than in C (e.g., we cannot jump over initializations); it still has the power to ruin the structure of our program.

Writing software without goto is called *Structured Programming*. However, the term is rarely used nowadays as it is taken for granted in high-quality software.

1.5 Functions

Functions are important building blocks of C++ programs. The first example we have seen is the main function in the hello-world program. We will say a little more about main in Section 1.5.5.

The general form of a C++ function is

```
[inline] return_type function_name (argument_list)
{
    body of the function
}
```

In this section, we discuss these components in more detail.

1.5.1 Arguments

C++ distinguishes two forms of passing arguments: by value and by reference.

1.5.1.1 Call by Value

When we pass an argument to a function, it creates a copy by default. For instance, the following function increments x but not visibly to the outside world:

```
void increment(int x)
{
    x++;
}

int main()
{
    int i= 4;
    increment(i);        // Does not increment i
    cout << "i is " << i << '\n';
}
```

The output is 4. The operation x++ within the increment function only increments a local copy of i but not i itself. This kind of argument transfer is referred to as *Call-by-Value* or *Pass-by-Value*.

1.5.1.2 Call by Reference

To modify function parameters, we have to *Pass* the argument *by Reference*:

```
void increment(int& x)
{
    x++;
}
```

Now, the variable itself is incremented and the output will be 5 as expected. We will discuss references in more detail in §1.8.4.

Temporary variables—like the result of an operation—cannot be passed by reference:

```
increment(i + 9); // Error: temporary not referable
```

since we could not compute (i + 9)++ anyway. In order to call such a function with some temporary value, we need to store it first in a variable and pass this variable to the function.

Larger data structures like vectors and matrices are almost always passed by reference to avoid expensive copy operations:

```
double two_norm(vector& v) { ... }
```

An operation like a norm should not change its argument. But passing the vector by reference bears the risk of accidentally overwriting it. To make sure that our vector is not changed (and not copied either), we pass it as a constant reference:

```
double two_norm(const vector& v) { ... }
```

If we tried to change v in this function the compiler would emit an error.

Both call-by-value and constant references ascertain that the argument is not altered but by different means:

- Arguments that are passed by value can be changed in the function since the function works with a copy.[6]

- With const references we work directly on the passed argument, but all operations that might change the argument are forbidden. In particular, const-reference arguments cannot appear on the left-hand side (LHS) of an assignment or be passed as non-const references to other functions (in fact, the LHS of an assignment is also a non-const reference).

In contrast to mutable[7] references, constant ones allow for passing temporaries:

```
alpha= two_norm(v + w);
```

This is admittedly not entirely consequential on the language design side, but it makes the life of programmers much easier.

1.5.1.3 Defaults

If an argument usually has the same value, we can declare it with a default value. Say we implement a function that computes the n-th root and mostly the square root, then we can write

```
double root(double x, int degree= 2) { ... }
```

---

6. Assuming the argument is properly copied. User types with broken copy implementations can undermine the integrity of the passed-in data.

7. Note that we use the word *mutable* for linguistic reasons as a synonym for non-const in this book. In C++, we also have the keyword mutable (§2.6.3) which we do not use very often.

This function can be called with one or two arguments:

```
x= root(3.5, 3);
y= root(7.0);        // like root(7.0, 2)
```

We can declare multiple defaults but only at the end of the argument list. In other words, after an argument with a default value we cannot have one without.

Default values are also helpful when extra parameters are added. Let us assume that we have a function that draws circles:

```
draw_circle(int x, int y, float radius);
```

These circles are all black. Later, we add a color:

```
draw_circle(int x, int y, float radius, color c= black);
```

Thanks to the default argument, we do not need to refactor our application since the calls of draw_circle with three arguments still work.

1.5.2   Returning Results

In the examples before, we only returned double or int. These are well-behaved return types. Now we will look at the extremes: large or no data.

1.5.2.1   Returning Large Amounts of Data

Functions that compute new values of large data structures are more difficult. For the details, we will put you off till later and only mention the options here. The good news is that compilers are smart enough to elide the copy of the return value in many cases; see Section 2.3.5.3. In addition, the move semantics (Section 2.3.5) where data of temporaries is stolen avoids copies when the before-mentioned elision does not apply. Advanced libraries avoid returning large data structures altogether with a technique called expression templates and delay the computation until it is known where to store the result (Section 5.3.2). In any case, we must not return references to local function variables (Section 1.8.6).

1.5.2.2   Returning Nothing

Syntactically, each function must return something even if there is nothing to return. This dilemma is solved by the void type named void. For instance, a function that just prints x does not need to return something:

```
void print_x(int x)
{
    std::cout << "The value x is " << x << '\n';
}
```

void is not a real type but more of a placeholder that enables us to omit returning a value. We cannot define void objects:

```
void nothing;      // Error: no void objects
```

A void function can be terminated earlier:

```
void heavy_compute(const vector& x, double eps, vector& y)
{
    for (...) {
        ...
        if (two_norm(y) < eps)
            return;
    }
}
```

with a no-argument return.

1.5.3 Inlining

Calling a function is relatively expensive: registers must be stored, arguments copied on the stack, and so on. To avoid this overhead, the compiler can inline function calls. In this case, the function call is substituted with the operations contained in the function. The programmer can ask the compiler to do so with the appropriate keyword:

```
inline double square(double x) { return x*x; }
```

However, the compiler is not obliged to inline. Conversely, it can inline functions without the keyword if this seems promising for performance. The inline declaration still has its use: for including a function in multiple compile units, which we will discuss in Section 7.2.3.2.

1.5.4 Overloading

In C++, functions can share the same name as long as their parameter declarations are sufficiently different. This is called *Function Overloading*. Let us first look at an example:

```
#include <iostream>
#include <cmath>

int divide(int a, int b) {
    return a / b ;
}

float divide(float a, float b) {
    return std::floor( a / b ) ;
}

int main() {
    int   x= 5, y= 2;
    float n= 5.0, m= 2.0;
    std::cout << divide(x, y) << std::endl;
    std::cout << divide(n, m) << std::endl;
    std::cout << divide(x, m) << std::endl; // Error: ambiguous
}
```

Here we defined the function `divide` twice: with `int` and `double` parameters. When we call `divide`, the compiler performs an *Overload Resolution*:

1. Is there an overload that matches the argument type(s) exactly? Take it; otherwise:

2. Are there overloads that match after conversion? How many?

    - 0: Error: No matching function found.
    - 1: Take it.
    - > 1: Error: ambiguous call.

How does this apply to our example? The calls `divide(x, y)` and `divide(n, m)` are exact matches. For `divide(x, m)`, no overload matches exactly and both by *Implicit Conversion* so that it's ambiguous.

The term "implicit conversion" requires some explanation. We have already seen that the numeric types can be converted one to another. These are implicit conversions as demonstrated in the example. When we later define our own types, we can implement a conversion from another type to it or conversely from our new type to an existing one. These conversions can be declared `explicit` and are then only applied when a conversion is explicitly requested but not for matching function arguments.

$\Rightarrow$ `c++11/overload_testing.cpp`

More formally phrased, function overloads must differ in their *Signature*. The signature consists in C++ of

- The function name;

- The number of arguments, called *Arity*, and

- The types of the arguments (in their respective order).

In contrast, overloads varying only in the `return` type or the argument names have the same signature and are considered as (forbidden) redefinitions:

```
void f(int x) {}
void f(int y) {} // Redefinition: only argument name different
long f(int x) {} // Redefinition: only return type different
```

That functions with different names or arity are distinct goes without saying. The presence of a reference symbol turns the argument type into another argument type (thus, `f(int)` and `f(int&)` can coexist). The following three overloads have different signatures:

```
void f(int x) {}
void f(int& x) {}
void f(const int& x) {}
```

This code snippet compiles. Problems will arise, however, when we call f:

```
int         i= 3;
const int ci= 4;

f(3);
f(i);
f(ci);
```

All three function calls are ambiguous because the best matches are in every case the first overload with the value argument and one of the reference-argument overloads respectively. Mixing overloads of reference and value arguments almost always fails. Thus, when one overload has a reference-qualified argument, then the corresponding argument of the other overloads should be reference-qualified as well. We can achieve this in our toy example by omitting the value-argument overload. Then f(3) and f(ci) will resolve to the overload with the constant reference and f(i) to that with the mutable one.

1.5.5 main Function

The main function is not fundamentally different from any other function. There are two signatures allowed in the standard:

```
int main()
```

or

```
int main(int argc, char* argv[])
```

The latter is equivalent to

```
int main(int argc, char** argv)
```

The parameter argv contains the list of arguments and argc its length. The first argument (argc[0]) is on most systems the name of the called executable (which may be different from the source code name). To play with the arguments, we can write a short program called argc_argv_test:

```
int main (int argc, char* argv[])
{
    for (int i= 0; i < argc; ++i)
        cout ≪ argv[i] ≪ '\n';
    return 0;
}
```

Calling this program with the following options

```
argc_argv_test first second third fourth
```

yields:

```
argc_argv_test
first
second
third
fourth
```

As you can see, each space in the command splits the arguments. The `main` function returns an integer as exit code which states whether the program finished correctly or not. Returning 0 (or the macro `EXIT_SUCCESS` from `<cstdlib>`) represents success and every other value a failure. It is standard-compliant to omit the `return` statement in the `main` function. In this case, `return 0;` is automatically inserted. Some extra details are found in Section A.2.5.

1.6   Error Handling

> *"An error doesn't become a mistake until you refuse to correct it."*
>
> —John F. Kennedy

The two principal ways to deal with unexpected behavior in C++ are assertions and exceptions. The former is intended for detecting programming errors and the latter for exceptional situations that prevent proper continuation of the program. To be honest, the distinction is not always obvious.

1.6.1   Assertions

The macro `assert` from header `<cassert>` is inherited from C but still useful. It evaluates an expression, and when the result is `false` then the program is terminated immediately. It should be used to detect programming errors. Say we implement a cool algorithm computing a square root of a non-negative real number. Then we know from mathematics that the result is non-negative. Otherwise something is wrong in our calculation:

```
#include <cassert>

double square_root(double x)
{
    check_somehow(x >= 0);
    ...
    assert(result >= 0.0);
    return result;
}
```

How to implement the initial check is left open for the moment. When our result is negative, the program execution will print an error like

```
assert_test: assert_test.cpp:10: double square_root(double):
Assertion 'result >= 0.0' failed.
```

The fact is when our result is less than zero, our implementation contains a bug and we must fix it before we use this function for serious applications.

After we fixed the bug we might be tempted to remove the assertion(s). We should not do so. Maybe one day we will change the implementation; then we still have all our sanity tests working. Actually, assertions on post-conditions are somehow like mini-unit tests.

A great advantage of assert is that we can let it disappear entirely by a simple macro declaration. Before including <cassert> we can define NDEBUG:

```
#define NDEBUG
#include <cassert>
```

and all assertions are disabled; i.e., they do not cause any operation in the executable. Instead of changing our program sources each time we switch between debug and release mode, it is better and cleaner to declare NDEBUG in the compiler flags (usually -D on Linux and /D on Windows):

```
g++ my_app.cpp -o my_app -O3 -DNDEBUG
```

Software with assertions in critical kernels can be slowed down by a factor of two or more when the assertions are not disabled in the release mode. Good build systems like CMake include -DNDEBUG automatically in the release mode's compile flags.

Since assertions can be disabled so easily, we should follow this advice:

Defensive Programming

Test as many properties as you can.

Even if you are sure that a property obviously holds for your implementation, write an assertion. Sometimes the system does not behave precisely as we assumed, or the compiler might be buggy (extremely rare but possible), or we did something slightly different from what we intended originally. No matter how much we reason and how carefully we implement, sooner or later one assertion may be raised. In the case that there are so many properties that the actual functionality gets cluttered by the tests, one can outsource the tests into another function.

Responsible programmers implement large sets of tests. Nonetheless, this is no guarantee that the program works under all circumstances. An application can run for years like a charm and one day it crashes. In this situation, we can run the application in debug mode with all the assertions enabled, and in most cases they will be a great help to find the reason for the crash. However, this requires that the crashing situation is reproducible and that the program in slower debug mode reaches the critical section in reasonable time.

1.6.2 Exceptions

In the preceding section, we looked at how assertions help us to detect programming errors. However, there are many critical situations that we cannot prevent even with the smartest programming, like files that we need to read but which are deleted. Or our program needs more memory than is available on the actual machine. Other problems are preventable in theory but the practical effort is disproportionally high, e.g., to check whether a matrix is regular is feasible but might be as much or more work than the actual task. In such cases, it is usually more efficient to try to accomplish the task and check for *Exceptions* along the way.

1.6.2.1   Motivation

Before illustrating the old-style error handling, we introduce our anti-hero Herbert[8] who is an ingenious mathematician and considers programming a necessary evil for demonstrating how magnificently his algorithms work. He learned to program like a real man and is immune to the newfangled nonsense of modern programming.

His favorite approach to deal with computational problems is to return an error code (like the main function does). Say we want to read a matrix from a file and check whether the file is really there. If not, we return an error code of 1:

```
int read_matrix_file(const char* fname, ...)
{
    fstream f(fname);
    if (!f.is_open())
        return 1;
        ...
    return 0;
}
```

So, we checked for everything that can go wrong and informed the caller with the appropriate error code. This is fine when the caller evaluated the error and reacted appropriately. But what happens when the caller simply ignores our return code? Nothing! The program keeps going and might crash later on absurd data or even worse produce nonsensical results that careless people might use to build cars or planes. Of course, car and plane builders are not that careless, but in more realistic software even careful people cannot have an eye on each tiny detail.

Nonetheless, bringing this point across to programming dinosaurs like Herbert might not convince them: "Not only are you dumb enough to pass in a non-existing file to my perfectly implemented function, then you do not even check the return code. You do everything wrong, not me."

Another disadvantage of the error codes is that we cannot return our computational results and have to pass them as reference arguments. This prevents us from building expressions with the result. The other way around is to return the result and pass the error code as a (referred) function argument which is not much less cumbersome.

1.6.2.2   Throwing

The better approach is to throw an exception:

```
matrix read_matrix_file(const char* fname, ...)
{
    fstream f(fname);
```

---

8. To all readers named Herbert: Please accept our honest apology for having picked your name.

```
        if (!f.is_open())
            throw "Cannot open file.";
        ...
    }
```

In this version, we throw an exception. The calling application is now obliged to react on it—otherwise the program crashes.

The advantage of exception handling over error codes is that we only need to bother with a problem where we can handle it. For instance, in the function that called read_matrix_file it might not be possible to deal with a non-existing file. In this case, the code is implemented as there is no exception thrown. So, we do not need to obfuscate our program with returning error codes. In the case of an exception, it is passed up to the appropriate exception handling. In our scenario, this handling might be contained in the GUI where a new file is requested from the user. Thus, exceptions lead at the same time to more readable sources and more reliable error handling.

C++ allows us to throw everything as an exception: strings, numbers, user types, et cetera. However, to deal with the exceptions properly it is better to define exception types or to use those from the standard library:

```
    struct cannot_open_file {};

    void read_matrix_file(const char* fname, ...)
    {
        fstream f(fname);
        if (!f.is_open())
            throw cannot_open_file{};
        ...
    }
```

Here, we introduced our own exception type. In Chapter 2, we will explain in detail how classes can be defined. In the example above, we defined an empty class that only requires opening and closing brackets followed by a semicolon. Larger projects usually establish an entire hierarchy of exception types that are often derived (Chapter 6) from std::exception.

1.6.2.3   Catching

To react to an exception, we have to catch it. This is done in a try-catch-block:

```
    try {
        ...
    } catch (e1_type& e1)
    { ...
    } catch (e2_type& e2) { ... }
```

Wherever we expect a problem that we can solve (or at least do something about), we open a try-block. After the closing braces, we can catch exceptions and start a rescue depending on the type of the exception and possibly on its value. It is recommended to catch exceptions by reference [45, Topic 73], especially when polymorphic types (Definition 6–1 in §6.1.3) are involved. When an exception is thrown, the first catch-block with a matching type is executed. Further catch-blocks of the same type (or sub-types; §6.1.1) are ignored. A catch-block with an ellipsis, i.e., three dots literally, catches all exceptions:

```
try {    ...
} catch (e1_type& e1) { ... }
  catch (e2_type& e2) { ... }
  catch (...) { // deal with all other exceptions
}
```

Obviously, the catch-all handler should be the last one.

If nothing else, we can catch the exception to provide an informative error message before terminating the program:

```
try {
    A= read_matrix_file("does_not_exist.dat");
} catch (cannot_open_file& e) {
    cerr << "Hey guys, your file does not exist! I'm out.\n";
    exit(EXIT_FAILURE);
}
```

Once the exception is caught, the problem is considered to be solved and the execution continues after the catch-block(s). To terminate the execution, we used exit from the header <cstdlib>. The function exit ends the execution even when we are not in the main function. It should only be used when further execution is too dangerous and there is no hope that the calling functions have any cure for the exception either.

Alternatively we can continue after the complaint or a partial rescue action by rethrowing the exception which might be dealt with later:

```
try {
    A= read_matrix_file("does_not_exist.dat");
} catch (cannot_open_file& e) {
    cerr << "O my gosh, the file is not there! Please caller help me.\n";
    throw e;
}
```

In our case, we are already in the main function and there is nothing else on the call stack to catch our exception. For rethrowing the current one, there exists a shorter notation:

```
} catch (cannot_open_file&) {
    ...
    throw;
}
```

This shortcut is preferred since it is less error-prone and shows more clearly that we rethrow the original exception. Ignoring an exception is easily implemented by an empty block:

```
} catch (cannot_open_file&) {} // File is rubbish, keep going
```

So far, our exception handling did not really solve our problem of missing a file. If the file name is provided by a user, we can pester him/her until we get one that makes us happy:

```
bool keep_trying= true;
do {
```

```
        char fname[80]; // std::string is better
        cout ≪ "Please enter the file name: ";
        cin ≫ fname;
        try {
            A= read_matrix_file(fname);
            ...
            keep_trying= false;
        } catch (cannot_open_file& e) {
            cout ≪ "Could not open the file. Try another one!\n";
        } catch (...)
            cout ≪ "Something is fishy here. Try another file!\n";
        }
    } while (keep_trying);
```

When we reach the end of the try-block, we know that no exception was thrown and we can call it a day. Otherwise, we land in one of the catch-blocks and keep_trying remains true.

A great advantage of exceptions is that issues that cannot be handled in the context where they are detected can be postponed for later. An example from the author's practice concerned an LU factorization. It cannot be computed for a singular matrix. There is nothing we can do about it. However, in the case that the factorization was part of an iterative computation, we were able to continue the iteration somehow without that factorization. Although this would be possible with traditional error handling as well, exceptions allow us to implement it much more readably and elegantly. We can program the factorization for the regular case and when we detect the singularity, we throw an exception. Then it is up to the caller how to deal with the singularity in the respective context—if possible.

1.6.2.4 Who Throws?

C++11

Already C++03 allowed specifying which types of exceptions can be thrown from a function. Without going into details, these specifications turned out to be not very useful and are deprecated now.

C++11 added a new qualification for specifying that no exceptions must be thrown out of the function, e.g.:

```
double square_root(double x) noexcept { ... }
```

The benefit of this qualification is that the calling code never needs to check for thrown exceptions after square_root. If an exception is thrown despite the qualification, the program is terminated.

In templated functions, it can depend on the argument type(s) whether an exception is thrown. To handle this properly, noexcept can depend on a compile-time condition; see Section 5.2.2.

Whether an assertion or an exception is preferable is not an easy question and we have no short answer to it. The question will probably not bother you now. We therefore postpone the discussion to Section A.2.6 and leave it to you when you read it.

C++11 ### 1.6.3 Static Assertions

Program errors that can already be detected during compilation can raise a static_assert. In this case, an error message is emitted and the compilation stopped. An example would not make sense at this point and we postpone it till Section 5.2.5.

1.7 I/O

C++ uses a convenient abstraction called streams to perform I/O operations in sequential media such as screens or keyboards. A stream is an object where a program can either insert characters or extract them. The standard C++ library contains the header <iostream> where the standard input and output stream objects are declared.

1.7.1 Standard Output

By default, the standard output of a program is written to the screen, and we can access it with the C++ stream named cout. It is used with the insertion operator which is denoted by ≪ (like left shift). We have already seen that it may be used more than once within a single statement. This is especially useful when we want to print a combination of text, variables, and constants, e.g.:

```
cout ≪ "The square root of " ≪ x ≪ " is " ≪ sqrt(x) ≪ endl;
```

with an output like

```
The square root of 5 is 2.23607
```

endl produces a newline character. An alternative representation of endl is the character \n. For the sake of efficiency, the output may be buffered. In this regard, endl and \n differ: the former flushes the buffer while the latter does not. Flushing can help us when we are debugging (without a debugger) to find out between which outputs the program crashes. In contrast, when a large amount of text is written to files, flushing after every line slows down I/O considerably.

Fortunately, the insertion operator has a relatively low priority so that arithmetic operations can be written directly:

```
std::cout ≪ "11 * 19 = " ≪ 11 * 19 ≪ std::endl;
```

All comparisons and logical and bitwise operations must be grouped by surrounding parentheses. Likewise the conditional operator:

```
std::cout ≪ (age > 65 ? "I'm a wise guy\n" : "I am still half-baked.\n");
```

When we forget the parentheses, the compiler will remind us (offering us an enigmatic message to decipher).

1.7.2 Standard Input

The standard input device is usually the keyboard. Handling the standard input in C++ is done by applying the overloaded operator of extraction $\gg$ on the cin stream:

```
int age;
std::cin ≫ age;
```

std::cin reads characters from the input device and interprets them as a value of the variable type (here int) it is stored to (here age). The input from the keyboard is processed once the RETURN key has been pressed.

We can also use cin to request more than one data input from the user:

```
std::cin ≫ width ≫ length;
```

which is equivalent to

```
std::cin ≫ width;
std::cin ≫ length;
```

In both cases the user must provide two values: one for width and another for length. They can be separated by any valid blank separator: a space, a tab character, or a newline.

1.7.3 Input/Output with Files

C++ provides the following classes to perform input and output of characters from/to files:

ofstream	write to files
ifstream	read from files
fstream	both read and write from/to files

We can use file streams in the same fashion as cin and cout, with the only difference that we have to associate these streams with physical files. Here is an example:

```
#include <fstream>

int main ()
{
    std::ofstream myfile;
    square_file.open("squares.txt");
    for (int i= 0; i < 10; ++i)
        square_file ≪ i ≪ "^2 = " i*i ≪ std::endl;
    square_file.close();
}
```

This code creates a file named squares.txt (or overwrites it if it already exists) and writes a sentence to it—like we write to cout. C++ establishes a general stream concept that is satisfied by an output file and by std::cout. This means we can write everything to a file that we can write to std::cout and vice versa. When we define operator≪ for a new type, we do this once for ostream (Section 2.7.3) and it will work with the console, with files, and with any other output stream.

Alternatively, we can pass the file name as an argument to the constructor of the stream to open the file implicitly. The file is also implicitly closed when square_file goes out of scope,[9] in this case at the end of the main function. The short version of the previous program is

```cpp
#include <fstream>

int main ()
{
    std::ofstream square_file("squares.txt");
    for (int i= 0; i < 10; ++i)
        square_file << i << "^2 = " << i*i << std::endl;
}
```

We prefer the short form (as usual). The explicit form is only necessary when the file is first declared and opened later for some reason. Likewise, the explicit close is only needed when the file should be closed before it goes out of scope.

1.7.4 Generic Stream Concept

Streams are not limited to screens, keyboards, and files; every class can be used as a stream when it is derived[10] from istream, ostream, or iostream and provides implementations for the functions of those classes. For instance, Boost.Asio offers streams for TCP/IP and Boost.IOStream as alternatives to the I/O above. The standard library contains a stringstream that can be used to create a string from any kind of printable type. stringstream's method str() returns the stream's internal string.

We can write output functions that accept every kind of output stream by using a mutable reference to ostream as an argument:

```cpp
#include <iostream>
#include <fstream>
#include <sstream>

void write_something(std::ostream& os)
{
    os << "Hi stream, did you know that 3 * 3 = " << 3 * 3 << std::endl;
}

int main (int argc, char* argv[])
{
    std::ofstream myfile("example.txt");
    std::stringstream mysstream;

    write_something(std::cout);
    write_something(myfile);
```

---

9. Thanks to the powerful technique named RAII, which we will discuss in Section 2.4.2.1.

10. How classes are derived is shown in Chapter 6. Let us here just take notice that being an output stream is technically realized by deriving it from std::ostream.

```
    write_something(mysstream);

    std::cout << "mysstream is: " << mysstream.str(); // newline contained
}
```

Likewise, generic input can be implemented with istream and read/write I/O with iostream.

1.7.5 Formatting

⇒ c++03/formatting.cpp

I/O streams are formatted by so-called I/O manipulators which are found in the header file <iomanip>. By default, C++ only prints a few digits of floating-point numbers. Thus, we increase the precision:

```
double pi= M_PI;
cout << "pi is " << pi << '\n';
cout << "pi is " << setprecision(16) << pi << '\n';
```

and yield a more accurate number:

```
pi is 3.14159
pi is 3.141592653589793
```

In Section 4.3.1, we will show how the precision can be adjusted to the type's representable number of digits.

When we write a table, vector, or matrix, we need to align values for readability. Therefore, we next set the width of the output:

```
cout << "pi is " << setw(30) << pi << '\n';
```

This results in

```
pi is              3.141592653589793
```

setw changes only the next output while setprecision affects all following (numerical) outputs, like the other manipulators. The provided width is understood as a minimum, and if the printed value needs more space, our tables will get ugly.

We can further request that the values be left aligned, and the empty space be filled with a character of our choice, say, -:

```
cout << "pi is " << setfill('-') << left
     << setw(30) << pi << '\n';
```

yielding

```
pi is 3.141592653589793------------
```

Another way of formatting is setting the flags directly. Some less frequently used format options can only be set this way, e.g., whether the sign is shown for positive values as well. Furthermore, we force the "scientific" notation in the normalized exponential representation:

```
cout.setf(ios_base::showpos);
cout << "pi is " << scientific << pi << '\n';
```

resulting in

```
pi is +3.1415926535897931e+00
```

Integer numbers can be represented in octal and hexadecimal base by

```
cout ≪ "63 octal is " ≪ oct ≪ 63 ≪ ".\n";
cout ≪ "63 hexadecimal is " ≪ hex ≪ 63 ≪ ".\n";
cout ≪ "63 decimal is " ≪ dec ≪ 63 ≪ ".\n";
```

with the expected output:

```
63 octal is 77.
63 hexadecimal is 3f.
63 decimal is 63.
```

Boolean values are by default printed as integers 0 and 1. On demand, we can present them as true and false:

```
cout ≪ "pi < 3 is " ≪ (pi < 3) ≪ '\n';
cout ≪ "pi < 3 is " ≪ boolalpha ≪ (pi < 3) ≪ '\n';
```

Finally, we can reset all the format options that we changed:

```
int old_precision= cout.precision();
cout ≪ setprecision(16)
...
cout.unsetf(ios_base::adjustfield | ios_base::basefield
        | ios_base::floatfield | ios_base::showpos | ios_base::boolalpha);
cout.precision(old_precision);
```

Each option is represented by a bit in a status variable. To enable multiple options, we can combine their bit patterns with a binary OR.

1.7.6   Dealing with I/O Errors

To make one thing clear from the beginning: I/O in C++ is not fail-safe (let alone idiot-proof). Errors can be reported in different ways and our error handling must comply to them. Let us try the following example program:

```
int main ()
{
    std::ifstream infile("some_missing_file.xyz");

    int i;
    double d;
    infile ≫ i ≫ d;

    std::cout ≪ "i is " ≪ i ≪ ", d is " ≪ d ≪ '\n';
    infile.close();
}
```

Although the file does not exist, the opening operation does not fail. We can even read from the non-existing file and the program goes on. Needless to say that the values in i and d are nonsense:

```
i is 1, d is 2.3452e-310
```

By default, the streams do not throw exceptions. The reason is historical: they are older than the exceptions and later the behavior was kept to not break software written in the meantime.

To be sure that everything went well, we have to check error flags, in principle, after each I/O operation. The following program asks the user for new file names until a file can be opened. After reading its content, we check again for success:

```cpp
int main ()
{
    std::ifstream infile;
    std::string filename{"some_missing_file.xyz"};
    bool opened= false;
    while (!opened) {
        infile.open(filename);
        if (infile.good()) {
            opened= true;
        } else {
            std::cout << "The file '" << filename
                      << "' doesn't exist, give a new file name: ";
            std::cin >> filename;
        }
    }
    int i;
    double d;
    infile >> i >> d;

    if (infile.good())
        std::cout << "i is " << i << ", d is " << d << '\n';
    else
        std::cout << "Could not correctly read the content.\n";
    infile.close();
}
```

You can see from this simple example that writing robust applications with file I/O can create some work.

If we want to use exceptions, we have to enable them during run time for each stream:

```cpp
cin.exceptions(ios_base::badbit | ios_base::failbit);
cout.exceptions(ios_base::badbit | ios_base::failbit);

std::ifstream infile("f.txt");
infile.exceptions(ios_base::badbit | ios_base::failbit);
```

The streams throw an exception every time an operation fails or when they are in a "bad" state. Exceptions could be thrown at (unexpected) file end as well. However, the end of file is more conveniently handled by testing (e.g., while (!f.eof())).

In the example above, the exceptions for infile are only enabled after opening the file (or the attempt thereof). For checking the opening operation, we have to create the stream first, then turn on the exceptions and finally open the file explicitly. Enabling the exceptions gives us at least the guarantee that all I/O operations went well when the program terminates properly. We can make our program more robust by catching exceptions that might be thrown.

The exceptions in file I/O only protect us partially from making errors. For instance, the following small program is obviously wrong (types don't match and numbers aren't separated):

```
void with_io_exceptions(ios& io)
{   io.exceptions(ios_base::badbit | ios_base::failbit); }

int main ()
{
    std::ofstream outfile;
    with_io_exceptions(outfile);
    outfile.open("f.txt");

    double o1= 5.2, o2= 6.2;
    outfile ≪ o1 ≪ o2 ≪ std::endl;   // no separation
    outfile.close();

    std::ifstream infile;
    with_io_exceptions(infile);
    infile.open("f.txt");

    int  i1, i2;
    char c;
    infile ≫ i1 ≫ c ≫ i2;              // mismatching types
    std::cout ≪ "i1 = " ≪ i1 ≪ ", i2 = " ≪ i2 ≪ "\n";
}
```

Nonetheless, it does not throw exceptions and fabricates the following output:

```
i1 = 5, i2 = 26
```

As we all know, testing does not prove the correctness of a program. This is even more obvious when I/O is involved. Stream input reads the incoming characters and passes them as values of the appropriate variable type, e.g., int when setting i1. It stops at the first character that cannot be part of the value, first at the . for the int value i1. If we read another int afterward, it would fail because an empty string cannot be interpreted as an int value. But we do not; instead we read a char next to which the dot is assigned. When parsing the input for i2 we find first the fractional part from o1 and then the integer part from o1 before we get a character that cannot belong to an int value.

Unfortunately, not every violation of the grammatical rules causes an exception in practice: .3 parsed as an int yields zero (while the next input probably fails); -5 parsed as an unsigned results in 4294967291 (when unsigned is 32 bits long). The narrowing principle apparently has not found its way into I/O streams yet (if it ever will for backward compatibility's sake).

At any rate, the I/O part of an application needs utter attention. Numbers must be separated properly (e.g., by spaces) and read with the same type as they were written. When the output contains branches such that the file format can vary, the input code is considerably more complicated and might even be ambiguous.

There are two other forms of I/O we want to mention: binary and C-style I/O. The interested reader will find them in Sections A.2.7 and A.2.8, respectively. You can also read this later when you need it.

1.8 Arrays, Pointers, and References

1.8.1 Arrays

The intrinsic array support of C++ has certain limitations and some strange behaviors. Nonetheless, we feel that every C++ programmer should know it and be aware of its problems.

An array is declared as follows:

```
int x[10];
```

The variable x is an array with 10 int entries. In standard C++, the size of the array must be constant and known at compile time. Some compilers (e.g., gcc) support run-time sizes.

Arrays are accessed by square brackets: x[i] is a reference to the i-th element of x. The first element is x[0]; the last one is x[9]. Arrays can be initialized at the definition:

```
float v[]= {1.0, 2.0, 3.0}, w[]= {7.0, 8.0, 9.0};
```

In this case, the array size is deduced.

The list initialization in C++11 cannot be narrowed any further. This will rarely make a difference in practice. For instance, the following:

C++11

```
int v[]= {1.0, 2.0, 3.0};    // Error in C++11: narrowing
```

was legal in C++03 but not in C++11 since the conversion from a floating-point literal to int potentially loses precision. However, we would not write such ugly code anyway.

Operations on arrays are typically performed in loops; e.g., to compute $x = v - 3w$ as a vector operation is realized by

```
float x[3];
for (int i= 0; i < 3; ++i)
    x[i]= v[i] - 3.0 * w[i];
```

We can also define arrays of higher dimensions:

```
float A[7][9];       // a 7 by 9 matrix
int   q[3][2][3];    // a 3 by 2 by 3 array
```

The language does not provide linear algebra operations upon the arrays. Implementations based on arrays are inelegant and error-prone. For instance, a function for a vector addition would look like this:

```
void vector_add(unsigned size, const double v1[], const double v2[],
                double s[])
{
    for (unsigned i= 0; i < size; ++i)
        s[i]= v1[i] + v2[i];
}
```

Note that we passed the size of the arrays as first function parameter whereas array parameters don't contain size information.[11] In this case, the function's caller is responsible for passing the correct size of the arrays:

```
int main ()
{
    double x[]= {2, 3, 4}, y[]= {4, 2, 0}, sum[3];
    vector_add(3, x, y, sum);
    ...
}
```

Since the array size is known during compilation, we can compute it by dividing the byte size of the array by that of a single entry:

```
vector_add(sizeof x / sizeof x[0], x, y, sum);
```

With this old-fashioned interface, we are also unable to test whether our arrays match in size. Sadly enough, C and Fortran libraries with such interfaces where size information is passed as function arguments are still realized today. They crash at the slightest user mistake, and it can take enormous efforts to trace back the reasons for crashing. For that reason, we will show in this book how we can realize our own math software that is easier to use and less prone to errors. Hopefully, future C++ standards will come with more higher mathematics, especially a linear-algebra library.

Arrays have the following two disadvantages:

- Indices are not checked before accessing an array, and we can find ourselves outside the array and the program crashes with segmentation fault/violation. This is not even the worst case; at least we see that something goes wrong. The false access can also mess up our data; the program keeps running and produces entirely wrong results with whatever consequence you can imagine. We could even overwrite the program code. Then our data is interpreted as machine operations leading to any possible nonsense.

- The size of the array must be known at compile time.[12] For instance, we have an array stored to a file and need to read it back into memory:

```
ifstream ifs("some_array.dat");
ifs >> size;
float v[size];   // Error: size not known at compile time
```

This does not work because the size needs to be known during compilation.

The first problem can only be solved with new array types and the second one with dynamic allocation. This leads us to pointers.

---

11. When passing arrays of higher dimensions, only the first dimension can be open while the others must be known during compilation. However, such programs get easily nasty and we have better techniques for it in C++.

12. Some compilers support run-time values as array sizes. Since this is not guaranteed with other compilers one should avoid this in portable software. This feature was considered for C++14 but its inclusion postponed as not all subtleties were entirely clarified.

1.8.2   Pointers

A pointer is a variable that contains a memory address. This address can be that of another variable that we can get with the address operator (e.g., &x) or dynamically allocated memory. Let's start with the latter as we were looking for arrays of dynamic size.

```
int* y= new int[10];
```

This allocates an array of 10 int. The size can now be chosen at run time. We can also implement the vector reading example from the previous section:

```
ifstream ifs("some_array.dat");
int size;
ifs >> size;
float* v= new float[size];
for (int i= 0; i < size; ++i)
    ifs >> v[i];
```

Pointers bear the same danger as arrays: accessing data out of range which can cause program crashes or silent data invalidation. When dealing with dynamically allocated arrays, it is the programmer's responsibility to store the array size.

Furthermore, the programmer is responsible for releasing the memory when not needed anymore. This is done by

```
delete[] v;
```

Since arrays as function parameters are treated internally as pointers, the vector_add function from page 47 works with pointers as well:

```
int main (int argc, char* argv[])
{
    double *x= new double[3], *y= new double[3], *sum= new double[3];
    for (unsigned i= 0; i < 3; ++i)
        x[i]= i+2, y[i]= 4-2*i;
    vector_add(3, x, y, sum);
    ...
}
```

With pointers, we cannot use the sizeof trick; it would only give us the byte size of the pointer itself which is of course independent of the number of entries. Other than that, pointers and arrays are interchangeable in most situations: a pointer can be passed as an array argument (as in the previous listing) and an array as a pointer argument. The only place where they are really different is the definition: whereas defining an array of size n reserves space for n entries, defining a pointer only reserves the space to hold an address.

Since we started with arrays, we took the second step before the first one regarding pointer usage. The simple use of pointers is allocating one single data item:

```
int* ip= new int;
```

Releasing this memory is performed by

```
delete ip;
```

Note the duality of allocation and release: the single-object allocation requires a single-object release and the array allocation demands an array release. Otherwise the run-time system will handle the deallocation incorrectly and most likely crash at this point. Pointers can also refer to other variables:

```
int   i= 3;
int* ip2= &i;
```

The operator & takes an object and returns its address. The opposite operator is * which takes an address and returns an object:

```
int   j= *ip2;
```

This is called *Dereferencing*. Given the operator priorities and the grammar rules, the meaning of the symbol * as dereference or multiplication cannot be confused—at least not by the compiler.

Pointers that are not initialized contain a random value (whatever bits are set in the corresponding memory). Using uninitialized pointers can cause any kind of error. To say explicitly that a pointer is not pointing to something, we should set it to

C++11

```
int* ip3= nullptr;    // >= C++11
int* ip4{};           // ditto
```

or in old compilers:

```
int* ip3= 0;          // better not in C++11 and later
int* ip4= NULL;       // ditto
```

C++11   The address 0 is guaranteed never to be used for applications, so it is safe to indicate this way that the pointer is empty (not referring to something). Nonetheless the literal 0 does not clearly convey its intention and can cause ambiguities in function overloading. The macro NULL is not better: it just evaluates to 0. C++11 introduces nullptr as a keyword for a pointer literal. It can be assigned to or compared with all pointer types. As it cannot be confused with other types and is self-explanatory, it is preferred over the other notations. The initialization with an empty braced list also sets a nullptr.

The biggest danger of pointers is *Memory Leaks*. For instance, our array y became too small and we want to assign a new array:

```
int* y= new int[15];
```

We can now use more space in y. Nice. But what happened to the memory that we allocated before? It is still there but we have no access to it anymore. We cannot even release it because this requires the address too. This memory is lost for the rest of our program execution. Only when the program is finished will the operating system be able to free it. In our example, we only lost 40 bytes out of several gigabytes that we might have. But if this happens in an iterative process, the unused memory grows continuously until at some point the whole (virtual) memory is exhausted.

Even if the wasted memory is not critical for the application at hand, when we write high-quality scientific software, memory leaks are unacceptable. When many people are using our software, sooner or later somebody will criticize us for it and eventually discourage other people from using our software. Fortunately, there are tools to help you to find memory leaks, as demonstrated in Section B.3.

The demonstrated issues with pointers are not intended as fun killers. And we do not discourage the use of pointers. Many things can only be achieved with pointers: lists, queues, trees, graphs, et cetera. But pointers must be used with utter care to avoid all the really severe problems mentioned above.

There are three strategies to minimize pointer-related errors:

Use standard containers: from the standard library or other validated libraries. `std::vector` from the standard library provides us all the functionality of dynamic arrays, including resizing and range check, and the memory is released automatically.

Encapsulate: dynamic memory management in classes. Then we have to deal with it only once per class.[13] When all memory allocated by an object is released when the object is destroyed, then it does not matter how often we allocate memory. If we have 738 objects with dynamic memory, then it will be released 738 times. The memory should be allocated in the object construction and deallocated in its destruction. This principle is called *Resource Allocation Is Initialization* (RAII). In contrast, if we called `new` 738 times, partly in loops and branches, can we be sure that we have called `delete` exactly 738 times? We know that there are tools for this but these are errors that are better to prevent than to fix.[14] Of course, the encapsulation idea is not idiot-proof but it is much less work to get it right than sprinkling (raw) pointers all over our program. We will discuss RAII in more detail in Section 2.4.2.1.

Use smart pointers: which we will introduce in the next section (§1.8.3).

Pointers serve two purposes:

- Referring to objects; and

- Managing dynamic memory.

The problem with so-called *Raw Pointers* is that we have no notion whether a pointer is only referring to data or also in charge of releasing the memory when it is not needed any longer. To make this distinction explicit at the type level, we can use *Smart Pointers*.

1.8.3   Smart Pointers

C++11

Three new smart-pointer types are introduced in C++11: `unique_ptr`, `shared_ptr`, and `weak_ptr`. The already existing smart pointer from C++03 named `auto_ptr` is generally considered as a failed attempt on the way to `unique_ptr` since the language was not ready at the time. It should not be used anymore. All smart pointers are defined in the header `<memory>`. If you cannot use C++11 features on your platform (e.g., in embedded programming), the smart pointers in Boost are a decent replacement.

---

13. It is safe to assume that there are many more objects than classes; otherwise there is something wrong with the entire program design.

14. In addition, the tool only shows that the current run had no errors but this might be different with other input.

C++11   **1.8.3.1   Unique Pointer**

This pointer's name indicates *Unique Ownership* of the referred data. It can be used essentially like an ordinary pointer:

```
#include <memory>

int main ()
{
    unique_ptr<double> dp{new double};
    *dp= 7;
    ...
}
```

The main difference from a raw pointer is that the memory is automatically released when the pointer expires. Therefore, it is a bug to assign addresses that are not allocated dynamically:

```
double d;
unique_ptr<double> dd{&d}; // Error: causes illegal deletion
```

The destructor of pointer dd will try to delete d.

Unique pointers cannot be assigned to other pointer types or implicitly converted. For referring to the pointer's data in a raw pointer, we can use the member function get:

```
double* raw_dp= dp.get();
```

It cannot even be assigned to another unique pointer:

```
unique_ptr<double> dp2{dp}; // Error: no copy allowed
dp2= dp;                    // ditto
```

It can only be moved:

```
unique_ptr<double> dp2{move(dp)}, dp3;
dp3= move(dp2);
```

We will discuss move semantics in Section 2.3.5. Right now let us just say this much: whereas a copy duplicates the data, a *Move* transfers the data from the source to the target. In our example, the ownership of the referred memory is first passed from dp to dp2 and then to dp3. dp and dp2 are nullptr afterward, and the destructor of dp3 will release the memory. In the same manner, the memory's ownership is passed when a unique_ptr is returned from a function. In the following example, dp3 takes over the memory allocated in f():

```
std::unique_ptr<double> f()
{    return std::unique_ptr<double>{new double}; }

int main ()
{
    unique_ptr<double> dp3;
    dp3= f();
}
```

In this case, move() is not needed since the function result is a temporary that will be moved (again, details in §2.3.5).

   Unique pointer has a special implementation[15] for arrays. This is necessary for properly
releasing the memory (with delete[]). In addition, the specialization provides array-like
access to the elements:

```
unique_ptr<double[]> da{new double[3]};
for (unsigned i= 0; i < 3; ++i)
    da[i]= i+2;
```

In return, the operator* is not available for arrays.

   An important benefit of unique_ptr is that it has absolutely no overhead over raw pointers:
neither in time nor in memory.

Further reading: An advanced feature of unique pointers is to provide our own *Deleter*;
for details see [26, §5.2.5f], [43, §34.3.1], or an online reference (e.g., **cppreference.com**).

1.8.3.2   Shared Pointer   C++11

As its name indicates, a shared_ptr manages memory that is used in common by multiple
parties (each holding a pointer to it). The memory is automatically released as soon as
no shared_ptr is referring the data any longer. This can simplify a program considerably,
especially with complicated data structures. An extremely important application area is
concurrency: the memory is automatically freed when all threads have terminated their
access to it.

   In contrast to a unique_ptr, a shared_ptr can be copied as often as desired, e.g.:

```
shared_ptr<double> f()
{
    shared_ptr<double> p1{new double};
    shared_ptr<double> p2{new double}, p3= p2;
    cout << "p3.use_count() = " << p3.use_count() << endl;
    return p3;
}

int main ()
{
    shared_ptr<double> p= f();
    cout << "p.use_count() = " << p.use_count() << endl;
}
```

In the example, we allocated memory for two double values: in p1 and in p2. The pointer p2
is copied into p3 so that both point to the same memory as illustrated in Figure 1–1.

   We can see this from the output of use_count:

```
p3.use_count() = 2
p.use_count() = 1
```

When the function returns, the pointers are destroyed and the memory referred to by p1 is
released (without ever being used). The second allocated memory block still exists since p
from the main function is still referring to it.

---

15. Specialization will be discussed in §3.6.1 and §3.6.3.

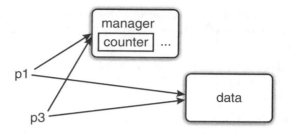

Figure 1–1: Shared pointer in memory

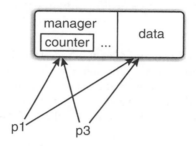

Figure 1–2: Shared pointer in memory after `make_shared`

If possible, a `shared_ptr` should be created with `make_shared`:

```
shared_ptr<double> p1= make_shared<double>();
```

Then the management and business data are stored together in memory—as shown in Figure 1–2—and the memory caching is more efficient. Since `make_shared` returns a shared pointer, we can use automatic type detection (§3.4.1) for simplicity:

```
auto p1= make_shared<double>();
```

We have to admit that a `shared_ptr` has some overhead in memory and run time. On the other hand, the simplification of our programs thanks to `shared_ptr` is in most cases worth some small overhead.

Further reading: For deleters and other details of `shared_ptr` see the library reference [26, §5.2], [43, §34.3.2], or an online reference.

C++11   **1.8.3.3   Weak Pointer**

A problem that can occur with shared pointers is *Cyclic References* that impede the memory to be released. Such cycles can be broken by `weak_ptrs`. They do not claim ownership of the memory, not even a shared one. At this point, we only mention them for completeness and suggest that you read appropriate references when their need is established: [26, §5.2.2], [43, §34.3.3], or `cppreference.com`.

For managing memory dynamically, there is no alternative to pointers. To only refer to other objects, we can use another language feature called *Reference* (surprise, surprise), which we introduce in the next section.

1.8.4 References

The following code introduces a reference:

```
int i= 5;
int& j= i;
j= 4;
std::cout << "j = " << j << '\n';
```

The variable j is referring to i. Changing j will also alter i and vice versa, as in the example. i and j will always have the same value. One can think of a reference as an alias: it introduces a new name for an existing object or sub-object. Whenever we define a reference, we must directly declare what it is referring to (other than pointers). It is not possible to refer to another variable later.

So far, that does not sound extremely useful. References are extremely useful for function arguments (§1.5), for referring to parts of other objects (e.g., the seventh entry of a vector), and for building views (e.g., §5.2.3).

As a compromise between pointers and references, the new standard offers a `reference_wrapper` class which behaves similarly to references but avoids some of their limitations. For instance, it can be used within containers; see §4.4.2.

C++11

1.8.5 Comparison between Pointers and References

The main advantage of pointers over references is the ability of dynamic memory management and address calculation. On the other hand, references are forced to refer to existing locations.[16] Thus, they do not leave memory leaks (unless you play really evil tricks), and they have the same notation in usage as the referred object. Unfortunately, it is almost impossible to construct containers of references.

In short, references are not fail-safe but are much less error-prone than pointers. Pointers should be only used when dealing with dynamic memory, for instance when we create data structures like lists or trees dynamically. Even then we should do this via well-tested types or encapsulate the pointer(s) within a class whenever possible. Smart pointers take care of memory allocation and should be preferred over raw pointers, even within classes. The pointer-reference comparison is summarized in Table 1-9.

1.8.6 Do Not Refer to Outdated Data!

Function-local variables are only valid within the function's scope, for instance:

```
double& square_ref(double d) // DO NOT!
{
    double s= d * d;
    return s;
}
```

---

16. References can also refer to arbitrary addresses but you must work harder to achieve this. For your own safety, we will not show you how to make references behave as badly as pointers.

Table 1–9: Comparison between Pointers and References

Feature	Pointers	References
Referring to defined location		✓
Mandatory initialization		✓
Avoidance of memory leaks		✓
Object-like notation		✓
Memory management	✓	
Address calculation	✓	
Build containers thereof	✓	

Here, our function result refers the local variable s which does not exist anymore. The memory where it was stored is still there and we might be lucky (mistakenly) that it is not overwritten yet. But this is nothing we can count on. Actually, such hidden errors are even worse than the obvious ones because they can ruin our program only under certain conditions and then they are very hard to find.

Such references are called *Stale References*. Good compilers will warn us when we are referring to a local variable. Sadly enough, we have seen such examples in web tutorials.

The same applies to pointers:

```
double* square_ptr(double d) // DO NOT!
{
    double s= d * d;
    return &s;
}
```

This pointer holds a local address that has gone out of scope. This is called a *Dangling Pointer*.

Returning references or pointers can be correct in member functions when member data is referred to; see Section 2.6.

Advice

Only return pointers and references to dynamically allocated data, data that existed before the function was called, or static data.

1.8.7 Containers for Arrays

As alternatives to the traditional C arrays, we want to introduce two container types that can be used in similar ways.

1.8.7.1 Standard Vector

Arrays and pointers are part of the C++ core language. In contrast, std::vector belongs to the standard library and is implemented as a class template. Nonetheless, it can be used very similarly to arrays. For instance, the example from Section 1.8.1 of setting up two arrays v and w looks for vectors as follows:

```cpp
#include <vector>

int main ()
{
    std::vector<float> v(3), w(3);
    v[0]= 1; v[1]= 2; v[2]= 3;
    w[0]= 7; w[1]= 8; w[2]= 9;
}
```

The size of the vector does not need to be known at compile time. Vectors can even be resized during their lifetime, as will be shown in Section 4.1.3.1.

The element-wise setting is not particularly compact. C++11 allows the initialization with initializer lists:

C++11

```cpp
std::vector<float> v= {1, 2, 3}, w= {7, 8, 9};
```

In this case, the size of the vector is implied by the length of the list. The vector addition shown before can be implemented more reliably:

```cpp
void vector_add(const vector<float>& v1, const vector<float>& v2,
                vector<float>& s)
{
    assert(v1.size() == v2.size());
    assert(v1.size() == s.size());
    for (unsigned i= 0; i < v1.size(); ++i)
        s[i]= v1[i] + v2[i];
}
```

In contrast to C arrays and pointers, the vector arguments know their sizes and we can now check whether they match. Note: The array size can be deduced with templates, which we leave as an exercise for later (see §3.11.9).

Vectors are copyable and can be returned by functions. This allows us to use a more natural notation:

```cpp
vector<float> add(const vector<float>& v1, const vector<float>& v2)
{
    assert(v1.size() == v2.size());
    vector<float> s(v1.size());
    for (unsigned i= 0; i < v1.size(); ++i)
        s[i]= v1[i] + v2[i];
    return s;
}

int main ()
{
    std::vector<float> v= {1, 2, 3}, w= {7, 8, 9}, s= add(v, w);
}
```

This implementation is potentially more expensive than the previous one where the target vector is passed in as a reference. We will later discuss the possibilities of optimization: both on the compiler and on the user side. In our experience, it is more important to start with a productive interface and deal with performance later. It is easier to make a correct program fast than to make a fast program correct. Thus, aim first for a good program design. In almost all cases, the favorable interface can be realized with sufficient performance.

The container `std::vector` is not a vector in the mathematical sense. There are no arithmetic operations. Nonetheless, the container proved very useful in scientific applications to handle non-scalar intermediate results.

1.8.7.2   `valarray`

A `valarray` is a one-dimensional array with element-wise operations; even the multiplication is performed element-wise. Operations with a scalar value are performed respectively with each element of the `valarray`. Thus, the `valarray` of a floating-point number is a vector space.

The following example demonstrates some operations:

```cpp
#include <iostream>
#include <valarray>

int main ()
{
    std::valarray<float> v= {1, 2, 3}, w= {7, 8, 9}, s= v + 2.0f * w;
    v= sin(s);
    for (float x : v)
        std::cout << x << ' ';
    std::cout << '\n';
}
```

Note that a `valarray<float>` can only operate with itself or `float`. For instance, `2 * w` would fail since it is an unsupported multiplication of `int` with `valarray<float>`.

A strength of `valarray` is the ability to access slices of it. This allows us to *Emulate* matrices and higher-order tensors including their respective operations. Nonetheless, due to the lack of direct support of most linear-algebra operations, `valarray` is not widely used in the numeric community. We also recommend using established C++ libraries for linear algebra. Hopefully, future standards will contain one.

In Section A.2.9, we make some comments on *Garbage Collection* which is essentially saying that we can live well enough without it.

1.9   Structuring Software Projects

A big problem of large projects is name conflicts. For this reason, we will discuss how macros aggravate this problem. On the other hand, we will show later in Section 3.2.1 how namespaces help us to master name conflicts.

In order to understand how the files in a C++ software project interact, it is necessary to understand the build process, i.e., how an executable is generated from the sources. This will be the subject of our first sub-section. In this light, we will present the macro mechanism and other language features.

First of all, we want to discuss briefly a feature that contributes to structuring a program: comments.

1.9.1   Comments

The primary purpose of a comment is evidently to describe in plain language what is not obvious to everybody in the program sources, like this:

```
// Transmogrification of the anti-binoxe in O(n log n)
while (cryptographic(trans_thingy) < end_of(whatever)) {
    ....
```

Often, the comment is a clarifying pseudo-code of an obfuscated implementation:

```
// A= B * C
for ( ... ) {
    int x78zy97= yo6954fq, y89haf= q6843, ...
    for ( ... ) {
        y89haf+= ab6899(fa69f) + omygosh(fdab); ...
        for ( ... ) {
            A(dyoa929, oa9978)+= ...
```

In such a case, we should ask ourselves whether we can restructure our software such that such obscure implementations are realized once in a dark corner of a library and everywhere else we write clear and simple statements such as

```
A= B * C;
```

as program and not as pseudo-code. This is one of the main goals of this book: to show you how to write the expression you want while the implementation under the hood squeezes out the maximal performance.

Another frequent usage of comments is to let code fractions disappear temporarily to experiment with alternative implementations, e.g.:

```
for ( ... ) {
    // int x78zy97= yo6954fq, y89haf= q6843, ...
    int x78zy98= yo6953fq, y89haf= q6842, ...
    for ( ... ) {
        ...
```

Like C, C++ provides a form of block comments, surrounded by /* and */. They can be used to render an arbitrary part of a code line or multiple lines into a comment. Unfortunately, they cannot be nested: no matter how many levels of comments are opened with /*, the first */ ends all block comments. Almost all programmers run into this trap: they want to comment out a longer fraction of code that already contains a block comment so that the comment ends earlier than intended, for instance:

```
for ( ... ) {
    /* int x78zy97= yo6954fq;        // start new comment
    int x78zy98= yo6953fq;
```

```
/* int x78zy99= yo6952fq;         // start old comment
int x78zy9a= yo6951fq;      */   // end old comment
int x78zy9b= yo6950fq;      */   // end new comment (presumably)
int x78zy9c= yo6949fq;
for ( ... ) {
```

Here, the line for setting x78zy9b should have been disabled but the preceeding */ terminated the comment prematurely.

Nested comments can be realized (correctly) with the preprocessor directive #if as we will illustrate in Section 1.9.2.4. Another possibility to deactivate multiple lines conveniently is by using the appropriate function of IDEs and language-aware editors.

1.9.2   Preprocessor Directives

In this section, we will present the commands (directives) that can be used in preprocessing. As they are mostly language-independent, we recommend limiting their usage to an absolute minimum, especially macros.

1.9.2.1   Macros

> *"Almost every macro demonstrates a flaw in the programming language, in the program, or the programmer."*
>
> —Bjarne Stroustrup

This is an old technique of code reuse by expanding macro names to their text definition, potentially with arguments. The use of macros gives a lot of possibilities to empower your program but much more for ruining it. Macros are resistant against namespaces, scopes, or any other language feature because they are reckless text substitution without any notion of types. Unfortunately, some libraries define macros with common names like major. We uncompromisingly undefine such macros, e.g., #undef major, without mercy for people who might want use those macros. Visual Studio defines—even today!!!—min and max as macros, and we strongly advise you to disable this by compiling with /DNO_MIN_MAX. Almost all macros can be replaced by other techniques (constants, templates, inline functions). But if you really do not find another way of implementing something:

Macro Names

Use LONG_AND_UGLY_NAMES_IN_CAPITALS for macros!

Macros can create weird problems in almost every thinkable and unthinkable way. To give you a general idea, we look at few examples in Appendix A.2.10 with some tips for how to deal with them. Feel free to postpone the reading until you run into some issue.

As you will see throughout this book, C++ provides better alternatives like constants, inline functions, and constexpr.

1.9.2.2 Inclusion

To keep the language C simple, many features such as I/O were excluded from the core language and realized by the library instead. C++ follows this design and realizes new features whenever possible by the standard library, and yet nobody would call C++ a simple language.

As a consequence, almost every program needs to include one or more headers. The most frequent one is that for I/O as seen before:

```
#include <iostream>
```

The preprocessor searches that file in standard include directories like /usr/include, /usr/local/include, and so on. We can add more directories to this search path with a compiler flag—usually -I in the Unix/Linux/Mac OS world and /I in Windows.

When we write the file name within double quotes, e.g.:

```
#include "herberts_math_functions.hpp"
```

the compiler usually searches first in the current directory and then in the standard paths.[17] This is equivalent to quoting with angle brackets and adding the current directory to the search path. Some people argue that angle brackets should only be used for system headers and user headers should use double quotes.

To avoid name clashes, often the include's parent directory is added to the search path and a relative path is used in the directive:

```
#include "herberts_includes/math_functions.hpp"
#include <another_project/more_functions.h>
```

The slashes are portable and also work under Windows despite the fact that sub-directories are denoted by backslashes there.

Include guards: Frequently used header files may be included multiple times in one translation unit due to indirect inclusion. To avoid forbidden repetitions and to limit the text expansion, so-called *Include Guards* ensure that only the first inclusion is performed. These guards are ordinary macros that state the inclusion of a certain file. A typical include file looks like this:

```
// Author: me
// License: Pay me $100 every time you read this

#ifndef HERBERTS_MATH_FUNCTIONS_INCLUDE
#define HERBERTS_MATH_FUNCTIONS_INCLUDE

#include <cmath>

double sine(double x);
...

#endif // HERBERTS_MATH_FUNCTIONS_INCLUDE
```

---

17. However, which directories are searched with double-quoted file names is implementation-dependent and not stipulated by the standard.

Thus, the content of the file is only included when the guard is not yet defined. Within the content, we define the guard to suppress further inclusions.

As with all macros, we have to pay utter attention that the name is unique, not only in our project but also within all other headers that we include directly or indirectly. Ideally the name should represent the project and file name. It can also contain project-relative paths or namespaces (§3.2.1). It is common practice to terminate it with _INCLUDE or _HEADER. Accidentally reusing a guard can produce a multitude of different error messages. In our experience it can take an unpleasantly long time to discover the root of that evil. Advanced developers generate them automatically from the before-mentioned information or using random generators.

A convenient alternative is #pragma once. The preceding example simplifies to

```
// Author: me
// License: Pay me $100 every time you read this

#pragma once

#include <cmath>

double sine(double x);
...
```

This pragma is not part of the standard but all major compilers support it today. By using the pragma, it becomes the compiler's responsibility to avoid double inclusions.

1.9.2.3 Conditional Compilation

An important and necessary usage of preprocessor directives is the control of conditional compilation. The preprocessor provides the directives #if, #else, #elif, and #endif for branching. Conditions can be comparisons, checking for definitions, or logical expressions thereof. The directives #ifdef and #ifndef are shortcuts for, respectively:

```
#if defined(MACRO_NAME)
```

```
#if !defined(MACRO_NAME)
```

The long form must be used when the definition check is combined with other conditions. Likewise, #elif is a shortcut for #else and #if.

In a perfect world, we would only write portable standard-compliant C++ programs. In reality, we sometimes have to use non-portable libraries. Say we have a library only available on Windows, more precisely only with Visual Studio. For all other relevant compilers, we have an alternative library. The simplest way for the platform-dependent implementation is to provide alternative code fragments for different compilers:

```
#ifdef _MSC_VER
    ... Windows code
#else
    ... Linux/Unix code
#endif
```

Similarly, we need conditional compilation when we want to use a new language feature that is not available on all target platforms, say, move semantics (§2.3.5):

```
#ifdef MY_LIBRARY_WITH_MOVE_SEMANTICS
    ... make something efficient with move
#else
    ... make something less efficient but portable
#endif
```

Here we can use the feature when available and still keep the portability to compilers without this feature. Of course, we need reliable tools that define the macro only when the feature is really available. Conditional compilation is quite powerful but it has its price: the maintenance of the sources and the testing are more laborious and error-prone. These disadvantages can be lessened by well-designed encapsulation so that the different implementations are used over a common interfaces.

1.9.2.4 Nestable Comments

The directive #if can be used to comment out code blocks:

```
#if 0
    ... Here we wrote pretty evil code! One day we fix it. Seriously.
#enif
```

The advantage over /* ... */ is that it can be nested:

```
#if 0
    ... Here the nonsense begins.
#if 0
    ... Here we have nonsense within nonsense.
#enif
    ... The finale of our nonsense. (Fortunately ignored.)
#enif
```

Nonetheless, this technique should be used with moderation: if three-quarters of the program are comments, we should consider a serious revision.

Recapitulating this chapter, we illustrate the fundamental features of C++ in Appendix A.3. We haven't included it in the main reading track to keep the high pace for the impatient audience. For those not in such a rush we recommend taking the time to read it and to see how non-trivial software evolves.

1.10 Exercises

1.10.1 Age

Write a program that asks input from the keyboard and prints the result on the screen and writes it to a file. The question is: "What is your age?"

1.10.2   Arrays and Pointers

1. Write the following declarations: pointer to a character, array of 10 integers, pointer to an array of 10 integers, pointer to an array of character strings, pointer to pointer to a character, integer constant, pointer to an integer constant, constant pointer to an integer. Initialize all these objects.

2. Make a small program that creates arrays on the stack (fixed-size arrays) and arrays on the heap (using allocation). Use `valgrind` to check what happens when you do not `delete` them correctly.

1.10.3   Read the Header of a Matrix Market File

The Matrix Market data format is used to store dense and sparse matrices in ASCII format. The header contains some information about the type and the size of the matrix. For a sparse matrix, the data is stored in three columns. The first column is the row number, the second column the column number, and the third column the numerical value. When the value type of the matrix is complex, a fourth column is added for the imaginary part.

An example of a Matrix Market file is

```
%%MatrixMarket matrix coordinate real general
%
% ATHENS course matrix
%
          2025              2025              100015
             1                 1      .9273558001498543E-01
             1                 2      .3545880644900583E-01
.................
```

The first line that does not start with % contains the number of rows, the number of columns, and the number of non-zero elements on the sparse matrix.

Use `fstream` to read the header of a Matrix Market file and print the number of rows and columns, and the number of non-zeroes on the screen.

Chapter 2

Classes

"Computer science is no more about computers than astronomy is about telescopes."

—Edsger W. Dijkstra

Accordingly, computer science is more than drilling on programming language details. That said, this chapter will not only provide information on declaring classes but also give an idea of how we can make the best use of them, how they best serve our needs. Or even better: how a class can be used conveniently and efficiently in a broad spectrum of situations. We see classes primarily as instruments to establish new abstractions in our software.

2.1 Program for Universal Meaning Not for Technical Details

Writing leading-edge engineering or scientific software with a mere focus on performance details is very painful and likely to fail. The most important tasks in scientific and engineering programming are

- Identifying the mathematical abstractions that are important in the domain, and

- Representing these abstractions comprehensively and efficiently in software.

Focusing on finding the right representation for domain-specific software is so important that this approach evolved into a programming paradigm: *Domain-Driven Design* (DDD). The core idea is that software developers regularly talk with the domain experts about how software components should be named and behave so that the resulting software is as intuitive as possible (not only for the programmer but for the user as well). The paradigm is not thoroughly discussed in this book and we rather refer to other literature like [50].

Common abstractions that appear in almost every scientific application are vector spaces and linear operators. The latter project from one vector space into another.

First, we should decide how to represent these abstractions in a program. Let v be an element of a vector space and L a linear operator. Then C++ allows us to express the application of L on v as

```
L(v)
```

or

```
L * v
```

Which one is better suited in general is not so easy to say. However, it is obvious that both notations are much better than

```
apply_symm_blk2x2_rowmajor_dnsvec_multhr_athlon(L.data_addr, L.nrows,
    L.ncols, L.ldim, L.blksch, v.data_addr, v.size);
```

which exposes lots of technical details and distracts from the principal tasks.

Developing software in that style is far from being fun. It wastes so much energy of the programmer. Even getting the function calls right is much more work than with a simple and clear interface. Slight modifications of the program—like using another data structure for some object—can cause a cascade of modifications that must be meticulously made. Remember that the person who implements the linear projection wants to do science, actually.

The cardinal error of scientific software providing such interfaces (we have seen even worse than our example) is to commit to too many technical details in the user interface. The reason lies partly in the usage of simpler programming languages such as C and Fortran 77 or in the effort to interoperate with software written in one those languages.

Advice

If you ever are forced to write software that interoperates with C or Fortran, write your software first with a concise and intuitive interface in C++ for yourself and other C++ programmers and encapsulate the interface to the C and Fortran libraries so that it is not exposed to the developers.

It is admittedly easier to call a C or Fortran function from a C++ application than the other way around. Nonetheless, developing large projects in those languages is so much more inefficient that the extra effort for calling C++ functions from C or Fortran is absolutely justified. Stefanus Du Toit demonstrated in his *Hourglass API* an example of how to interface programs in C++ and other languages through a thin C API [12].

The elegant way of writing scientific software is to provide the best abstraction. A good implementation reduces the user interface to the essential behavior and omits all unnecessary commitments to technical details. Applications with a concise and intuitive interface can be as efficient as their ugly and detail-obsessed counterparts.

Our abstractions here are linear operators and vector spaces. What is important for the developer is how these abstractions are used, in our case, how a linear operator is applied on a vector. Let's say the application is denoted by the symbol * as in L * v or A * x. Evidently, we expect that the result of this operation yields an object of a vector type (thus, the statement w= L * v; should compile) and that the mathematical properties of linearity hold. That is all that developers need to know for using a linear operator.

How the linear operator is stored internally is irrelevant for the correctness of the program—as long as the operation meets all mathematical requirements and the implementation has no accidental side effect like overwriting other objects' memory. Therefore, two different implementations that provide the necessary interface and semantic behavior are interchangeable; i.e., the program still compiles and yields the same results. The different implementations can of course vary dramatically in their performance. For that reason, it is important that choosing the best implementation for a target platform or a specific application can be achieved with little (or no) program modifications.

This is why the most important benefit of classes in C++ for us is not the inheritance mechanisms (Chapter 6) but the ability to establish new abstractions and to provide alternative realizations for them. This chapter will lay the foundations for it, and we will elaborate on this programming style in the subsequent chapters with more advanced techniques.

2.2 Members

After the long plea for classes, it is high time to define one. A class defines a new data type which can contain

- Data: referred to as *Member Variables* or for short as *Members*; the standard also calls it *Data Member*;

- Functions: referred to as *Methods* or *Member Functions*;

- Type definitions; and

- Contained classes.

Data members and methods are discussed in this section.

2.2.1 Member Variables

A concise class example is a type for representing complex numbers. Of course, there already exists such a class in C++ but for illustration purposes we write our own:

```
class complex
{
  public:
    double r, i;
};
```

The class contains variables to store the real and the imaginary parts of a complex number. A common mental picture for the role of a class definition is a blueprint. That is, we have not yet defined any single complex number. We only said that complex numbers contain two variables of type `double` which are named `r` and `i`.

Now we are going to create *Objects* of our type:

```
complex z, c;
z.r= 3.5; z.i= 2;
c.r= 2; c.i= -3.5;
std::cout << "z is (" << z.r << ", " << z.i << ")\n";
```

This snippet defines the objects z and c with variable declarations. Such declarations do not differ from intrinsic types: a type name followed by a variable name or a list thereof. The members of an object can be accessed with the dot operator . as illustrated above. As we can see, member variables can be read and written like ordinary variables—when they are accessible.

2.2.2 Accessibility

Each member of a class has a specified *Accessibility*. C++ provides three of them:

- public: accessible from everywhere;

- protected: accessible in the class itself and its derived classes.

- private: accessible only within the class; and

This gives the class designer good control of how the class users can work with each member. Defining more public members gives more freedom in usage but less control. On the other hand, more private members establish a more restrictive user interface.

The accessibility of class members is controlled by *Access Modifiers*. Say we want to implement a class rational with public methods and private data:

```
class rational
{
  public:
    ...
    rational operator+(...) {...}
    rational operator-(...) {...}
  private:
    int p;
    int q;
};
```

An access modifier applies to all following members until another modifier appears. We can put as many modifiers as we want. Please note our linguistic distinction between a specifier that declares a property of a single item and a modifier that characterizes multiple items: all methods and data members preceding the next modifier. It is better to have many access modifiers than a confusing order of class members. Class members before the first modifier are all private.

2.2.2.1 Hiding Details

Purists of object-oriented programming declare all data members private. Then it is possible to guarantee properties for all objects, for instance, when we want to establish in the before-mentioned class rational the invariant that the denominator is always positive. Then we declare our numerator and denominator private (as we did) and implement all methods such that they keep this invariant. If the data members were public, we could not guarantee this invariant because users can violate it in their modifications.

private members also increase our freedom regarding code modifications. When we change the interface of **private** methods or the type of a **private** variable, all applications of this class will continue working after recompilation. Modifying the interfaces of **public** methods can (and usually will) break user code. Differently phrased: the public variables and the interfaces of public methods build the interface of a class. As long as we do not change this interface, we can modify a class and all applications will still compile (and work when we did not introduce bugs). And when the public methods keep their behavior, all applications will. How we design our private members is completely up to us (as long as we do not waste all memory or compute power). By solely defining the behavior of a class in its external interface but not how it is implemented, we establish an *Abstract Data Type* (ADT).

On the other hand, for small helper classes it can be unnecessarily cumbersome to access their data only through getter and setter functions:

```
z.set_real(z.get_real()*2);
```

instead of

```
z.real*= 2;
```

Where to draw the line between simple classes with `public` members and full-blown classes with `private` data is a rather subjective question (thus offering great potential for arguing in developer teams). Herb Sutter and Andrei Alexandrescu phrased the distinction nicely: when you establish a new abstraction, make all internal details `private`; and when you merely aggregate existing abstractions, the data member can be `public` [45, Item 11]. We like to add a more provocative phrasing: when all member variables of your abstract data type have trivial getters and setters, the type is not abstract at all and you can turn your variables `public` without losing anything except the clumsy interface.

`protected` members only make sense for types with derived classes. Section 6.3.2.2 will give an example for a good use case of `protected`.

C++ also contains the `struct` keyword from C. It declares a class as well, with all features available for classes. The only difference is that all members are by default `public`. Thus,

```
struct xyz
{
    ...
};
```

is the same as

```
class xyz
{
  public:
    ...
};
```

As a rule of thumb:

Advice

Prefer `class` and use `struct` only for helper types with limited functionality and without invariants.

2.2.2.2 Friends

Although we do not provide our internal data to everybody, we might make an exception for a good `friend`. Within our class, we can grant free functions and classes the special allowance to access `private` and `protected` members, for instance:

```
class complex
{
    ...
    friend std::ostream& operator≪(std::ostream&, const complex&);
    friend class complex_algebra;
};
```

We permitted in this example the output operator and a class named complex_algebra access to internal data and functionality. A friend declaration can be located in the public, private, or protected part of the class. Of course, we should use the friend declaration as rarely as possible because we must be certain that every friend preserves the integrity of our internal data.

2.2.3 Access Operators

There are four such operators. The first one we have already seen: the member selection with a dot, x.m. All other operators deal with pointers in one way or another.

First, we consider a pointer to the class complex and how to access member variables through this pointer:

```
complex  c;
complex* p= &c;

*p.r= 3.5;              // Error: means *(p.r)
(*p).r= 3.5;            // okay
```

Accessing members through pointers is not particularly elegant since the selection operator . has a higher priority than the dereference *. Just for the sake of self-torturing, imagine the member itself is a pointer to another class whose member we want to access. Then we would need another parenthesis to precede the second selection:

```
(*(*p).pm).m2= 11;   // oh boy
```

A more convenient member access through pointers is provided by ->:

```
p->r= 3.5;             // looks so much better ;-)
```

Even the before-mentioned indirect access is no problem any longer:

```
p->pm->m2= 11;         // even more so
```

In C++, we can define *Pointers to Members* which are probably not relevant to all readers (the author has not used them outside this book till today). If you can think of a use case, please read Appendix A.4.1.

2.2.4 The Static Declarator for Classes

Member variables that are declared static exist only once per class. This allows us to share a resource between the objects of a class. Another use case is for creating a *Singleton*: a design pattern ensuring that only one instance of a certain class exists [14, pages 127–136].

Thus, a data member that is both static and const exists only once and cannot be changed. As a consequence, it is available at compile time. We will use this for meta-programming in Chapter 5.

Methods can also be declared static. This means that they can only access static data and call static functions. This might enable extra optimizations when a method does not need to access object data.

Our examples use static data members only in their constant form and no static methods. However, the latter appears in the standard libraries in Chapter 4.

2.2.5 Member Functions

Functions in classes are called *Member Functions* or *Methods*. Typical member functions in object-oriented software are getters and setters:

Listing 2–1: Class with getters and setters

```
class complex
{
  public:
    double get_r() { return r; }          // Causes clumsy
    void set_r(double newr) { r = newr; }  //    code
    double get_i() { return i; }
    void set_i(double newi) { i = newi; }
  private:
    double r, i;
};
```

Methods are like every member by default private; i.e., they can only be called by functions within the class. Evidently, this would not be particularly useful for our getters and setters. Therefore, we give them public accessibility. Now, we can write c.get_r() but not c.r. The class above can be used in the following way:

Listing 2–2: Using getters and setters

```
int main()
{
  complex c1, c2;
  // set c1
  c1.set_r(3.0);                          // Clumsy init
  c1.set_i(2.0);

  // copy c1 to c2
  c2.set_r(c1.get_r());                   // Clumsy copy
  c2.set_i(c1.get_i());
  return 0;
}
```

At the beginning of our main function, we create two objects of type complex. Then we set one of the objects and copy it to the other one. This works but it is a bit clumsy, isn't it?

Our member variables can only be accessed via functions. This gives the class designer the maximal control over the behavior. For instance, we could limit the range of values that are accepted by the setters. We could count for each complex number how often it is read or written during the execution. The functions could have additional printouts for debugging (a debugger is usually a better alternative than putting printouts into programs). We could even allow reading only at certain times of the day or writing only when the program runs on a computer with a certain IP. We will most likely not do the latter, at least not for complex numbers, but we could. If the variables are public and accessed directly, such behavior would not be possible. Nevertheless, handling the real and imaginary parts of a complex number in this fashion is cumbersome and we will discuss better alternatives.

Most C++ programmers would not implement it this way. What would a C++ programmer then do first? Write constructors.

2.3   Setting Values: Constructors and Assignments

Construction and assignment are two mechanisms to set the value of an object, either at its creation or later. Therefore, these two mechanisms have much in common and are introduced here together.

2.3.1   Constructors

Constructors are methods that initialize objects of classes and create a working environment for member functions. Sometimes such an environment includes resources like files, memory, or locks that have to be freed after their use. We come back to this later.

Our first constructor will set the real and imaginary values of our complex:

```
class complex
{
  public:
    complex(double rnew, double inew)
    {
        r= rnew; i= inew;
    }
  // ...
};
```

A constructor is a member function with the same name as the class itself. It can possess an arbitrary number of arguments. This constructor allows us to set the values of c1 directly in the definition:

```
complex c1(2.0, 3.0);
```

There is a special syntax for setting member variables and constants in constructors called *Member Initialization List* or for short *Initialization List*:

```
class complex
{
  public:
    complex(double rnew, double inew) : r(rnew), i(inew) {}
  // ...
};
```

An initialization list starts with a colon after the constructor's function head. It is in principle a non-empty list of constructor calls for the member variables (and base classes) or a subset thereof (whereby compilers emit warnings when the order of initialization doesn't match the definition order). The compiler wants to ascertain that all member variables are initialized. Therefore, it generates a call to the constructor with no arguments for all those members that we do not initialize ourselves. This argumentless constructor is called *Default Constructor* (we will discuss it more in §2.3.1.1). Thus, our first constructor example is (somehow) equivalent to

```cpp
class complex
{
  public:
    complex(double rnew, double inew)
      : r(), i() // generated by the compiler
    {
        r= rnew; i= inew;
    }
};
```

For simple arithmetic types like int and double, it is not important whether we set their values in the initialization list or the constructor body. Data members of intrinsic types that do not appear in the initialization list remain uninitialized. A member data item of a class type is implicitly default-constructed when it is not contained in the initialization list.

How members are initialized becomes more important when the members themselves are classes. Imagine we have written a class that solves linear systems with a given matrix which we store in our class:

```cpp
class solver
{
  public:
    solver(int nrows, int ncols)
    // : A()    #1  Error: calls non-existing default constructor
    {
        A(nrows, ncols); // #2 Error: not a ctor call here
    }
  // ...
  private:
    matrix_type A;
};
```

Suppose our matrix class has a constructor setting the two dimensions. This constructor cannot be called in the function body of the constructor (#2). The expression in #2 is not interpreted as a constructor but as a function call: A.operator()(nrows, ncols); see §3.8.

As all member variables are constructed before the constructor body is reached, our matrix A will be default-constructed at #1. Unfortunately, matrix is not *Default-Constructible* causing the following error message:

```
Operator »matrix_type::matrix_type()« not found.
```

Thus, we need to write:

```
class solver
{
  public:
    solver(int nrows, int ncols) : A(nrows, ncols) {}
  // ...
};
```

to call the right constructor of the matrix.

In the preceding examples, the matrix was part of the solver. A more likely scenario is that the matrix already exists. Then we would not want to waste all the memory for a copy but refer to the matrix. Now our class contains a reference as a member and we are again obliged to set the reference in the initialization list (since references are not default-constructible either):

```
class solver
{
  public:
    solver(const matrix_type& A) : A(A) {}
  // ...
  private:
    const matrix_type& A;
};
```

The code also demonstrates that we can give the constructor argument(s) the same name(s) as the member variable(s). This raises the question of to which objects the names are referring, in our case which A is meant in the different occurrences? The rule is that names in the initialization list outside the parentheses always refer to members. Inside the parentheses, the names follow the scoping rules of a member function. Names local to the member function—including argument names—hide names from the class. The same applies to the body of the constructor: names of arguments and of local variables hide the names in the class. This is confusing at the beginning but you will get used to it quicker than you think.

Let us return to our complex example. So far, we have a constructor allowing us to set the real and the imaginary parts. Often only the real part is set and the imaginary is defaulted to 0.

```
class complex
{
  public:
    complex(double r, double i) : r(r), i(i) {}
    complex(double r) : r(r), i(0) {}
  // ...
};
```

We can also say that the number is $0 + 0i$ when no value is given, i.e., if the complex number is default-constructed:

```
    complex() : r(0), i(0) {}
```

We will focus more on the default constructor in the next section.

The three different constructors above can be combined into a single one by using default arguments:

```
class complex
{
  public:
    complex(double r= 0, double i= 0) : r(r), i(i) {}
 // ...
};
```

This constructor now allows various forms of initialization:

```
complex z1,        // default-constructed
        z2(),      // default-constructed ????????
        z3(4),     // short for z3(4.0, 0.0)
        z4= 4;,    // short for z4(4.0, 0.0)
        z5(0, 1);
```

The definition of z2 is a mean trap. It looks absolutely like a call for the default constructor but it is not. Instead it is interpreted as the declaration of the function named z2 that takes no argument and returns a complex. Scott Meyers called this interpretation the *Most Vexing Parse*. Construction with a single argument can be written with an assignment-like notation using = as for z4. In old books you might read sometimes that this causes an overhead because a temporary is first built and then copied. This is not true; it might have been in the very early days of C++ but today no compiler will do that.

C++ knows three special constructors:

- The before-mentioned default constructor,

- The *Copy Constructor*, and

- The *Move Constructor* (in C++11 and higher; §2.3.5.1).

In the following sections, we will look more closely at them.

2.3.1.1 Default Constructor

A *Default Constructor* is nothing more than a constructor without arguments or one that has default values for every argument. It is not mandatory that a class contains a default constructor.

At first glance, many classes do not need a default constructor. However, in real life it is much easier having one. For the complex class, it seems that we could live without a default constructor since we can delay its declaration until we know the object's value. The absence of a default constructor creates (at least) two problems:

- Variables that are initialized in an inner scope but live for algorithmic reasons in an outer scope must be already constructed without a meaningful value. In this case, it is more appropriate to declare the variable with a default constructor.

- The most important reason is that it is quite cumbersome (however possible) to implement containers—like lists, trees, vectors, matrices—of types without default constructors.

In short, one can live without a default constructor but sooner or later it becomes a hard life.

Advice
Define a default constructor whenever possible.

For some classes, however, it is very difficult to define a default constructor, e.g., when some of the members are references or contain them. In those cases, it can be preferable to accept the before-mentioned drawbacks instead of building badly designed default constructors.

2.3.1.2 Copy Constructor

In the main function of our introductory getter-setter example (Listing 2–2), we defined two objects, one being a copy of the other. The copy operation was realized by reading and writing every member variable in the application. Better for copying objects is using a copy constructor:

```
class complex
{
  public:
    complex(const complex& c) : i(c.i), r(c.r) {}
    // ...
};

int main()
{
    complex z1(3.0, 2.0),
            z2(z1);        // copy
            z3{z1};        // C++11: non-narrowing
}
```

If the user does not write a copy constructor, the compiler will generate one in the standard way: calling the copy constructors of all members (and base classes) in the order of their definition, just as we did in our example.

In cases like this where copying all members is precisely what we want for our copy constructor we should use the default for the following reasons:

- It is less verbose;

- It is less error-prone;

- Other people directly know what our copy constructor does without reading our code; and

- Compilers might find more optimizations.

In general, it is not advisable to use a mutable reference as an argument:

```
complex(complex& c) : i(c.i), r(c.r) {}
```

Then one can copy only mutable objects. However, there may be situations where we need this.

The arguments of the copy constructor must not be passed by value:

```
complex(complex c) // Error!
```

Please think about why for few minutes. We will tell you at the end of this section.

$\Rightarrow$ c++03/vector_test.cpp

There are cases where the default copy constructor does not work, especially when the class contains pointers. Say we have a simple vector class with a copy constructor:

```
class vector
{
  public:
    vector(const vector& v)
      : my_size(v.my_size), data(new double[my_size])
    {
        for (unsigned i= 0; i < my_size; ++i)
            data[i]= v.data[i];
    }
    // Destructor, anticipated from §2.4.2
    ~vector() { delete[] data; }
  // ...
  private:
    unsigned my_size;
    double   *data;
};
```

If we omitted this copy constructor, the compiler would not complain and voluntarily build one for us. We are glad that our program is shorter and sexier, but sooner or later we find that it behaves bizarrely. Changing one vector modifies another one as well, and when we observe this strange behavior we have to find the error in our program. This is particularly difficult because there is no error in what we have written but in what we have omitted.

The reason is that we did not copy the data but only the address to it. Figure 2–1 illustrates this: when we copy v1 to v2 with the generated constructor, pointer v2.data will refer to the same data as v1.data.

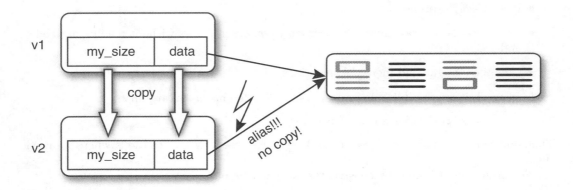

Figure 2–1: Generated vector copy

Another problem we would observe is that the run-time library will try to release the same memory twice.[1] For illustration purposes, we anticipated the destructor from Section 2.4.2 here: it deletes the memory addressed by data. Since both pointers contain the same memory address, the second destructor call will fail.

⇒ c++11/vector_unique_ptr.cpp

Since our vector is intended as the unique owner of its data, unique_ptr sounds like a better choice for data than the raw pointer:

C++11

```
class vector
{
    // ...
    std::unique_ptr<double[]>   data;
};
```

Not only would the memory be released automatically, the compiler could not generate the copy constructor automatically because the copy constructor is deleted in unique_ptr. This forces us to provide a user implementation.

Back to our question of why the argument of a copy constructor cannot be passed by value. You have certainly figured it out in the meantime. To pass an argument by value, we need the copy constructor which we are about to define. Thus, we create a self-dependency

---

1. This is an error message every programmer experiences at least once in his/her life (or he/she is not doing serious business). I hope I am wrong. My friend and proofreader Fabio Fracassi is optimistic that future programmers using modern C++ consequently will not run into such trouble. Let's hope that he is right.

that might lead compilers into an infinite loop. Fortunately, compilers do not stall on this and even give us a meaningful error message in this case (from the experience in the sense of Oscar Wilde that many programmers made this mistake before and some will in the future).

2.3.1.3 Conversion and Explicit Constructors

In C++, we distinguish between implicit and explicit constructors. Implicit constructors enable implicit conversion and assignment-like notation for construction. Instead of

```
complex c1{3.0};  // C++11 and higher
complex c1(3.0);  // all standards
```

we can also write:

```
complex c1= 3.0;
```

or

```
complex c1= pi * pi / 6.0;
```

This notation is more readable for many scientifically educated people, while current compilers generate the same code for both notations.

The implicit conversion kicks in when one type is needed and another one is given, e.g., a double instead of a complex. Assume we have a function:[2]

```
double inline complex_abs(complex c)
{
    return std::sqrt(real(c) * real(c) + imag(c) * imag(c));
}
```

and call this with a double, e.g.:

```
cout << "|7| = " << complex_abs(7.0) << '\n';
```

The literal 7.0 is a double but there is no function overload for complex_abs accepting a double. We have, however, an overload for a complex argument and complex has a constructor accepting double. So, the complex value is implicitly built from the double literal.

The implicit conversion can be disabled by declaring the constructor as explicit:

```
class complex { public:
    explicit complex(double nr= 0.0, double i= 0.0) : r(nr), i(i) {}
};
```

Then complex_abs would not be called with a double. To call this function with a double, we can write an overload for double or construct a complex explicitly in the function call:

```
cout << "|7| = " << complex_abs(complex{7.0}) << '\n';
```

The explicit attribute is really important for some classes, e.g., vector. There is typically a constructor taking the size of the vector as an argument:

```
class vector
{
  public:
    vector(int n) : my_size(n), data(new double[my_size]) {}
};
```

---

2. The definitions of real and imag will be given soon.

A function computing a scalar product expects two vectors as arguments:

```
double dot(const vector& v, const vector& w) { ... }
```

This function can be called with integer arguments:

```
double d= dot(8, 8);
```

What happens? Two temporary vectors of size 8 are created with the implicit constructor and passed to the function dot. This nonsense can be easily avoided by declaring the constructor explicit.

Which constructor will be explicit is in the end the class designer's decision. It is pretty obvious in the vector example: no right-minded programmer wants the compiler converting integers automatically into vectors.

Whether the constructor of the complex class should be explicit depends on the expected usage. Since a complex number with a zero imaginary part is mathematically identical to a real number, the implicit conversion does not create semantic inconsistencies. An implicit constructor is more convenient because a double value or literal can be used wherever a complex value is expected. Functions that are not performance-critical can be implemented only once for complex and used for double.

In C++03, the explicit attribute only mattered for single-argument constructors. From C++11 on, explicit is also relevant for constructors with multiple arguments due to uniform initialization, Section 2.3.4.

C++11 | **2.3.1.4 Delegation**

In the examples before, we had classes with multiple constructors. Usually such constructors are not entirely different and have some code in common; i.e., there is often some redundancy. In C++03, it was typically ignored when it only concerned the setup of primitive variables; otherwise the suitable common code fragments were outsourced into a method that was then called by multiple constructors.

C++11 offers *Delegating Constructors*; these are constructors that call other constructors. Our complex class could use this feature instead of default values:

```
class complex
{
  public:
    complex(double r, double i) : r{r}, i{i} {}
    complex(double r) : complex{r, 0.0} {}
    complex() : complex{0.0} {}
    ...
};
```

Obviously, the benefit is not impressive for this small example. Delegating constructors becomes more useful for classes where the initialization is more elaborate (more complex than our complex).

2.3.1.5   Default Values for Members

Another new feature in C++11 is default values for member variables. Then we only need to set values in the constructor that are different from the defaults:

```
class complex
{
  public:
    complex(double r, double i) : r{r}, i{i} {}
    complex(double r) : r{r} {}
    complex() {}
    ...
  private:
    double r= 0.0, i= 0.0;
};
```

Again, the benefit is certainly more pronounced for large classes.

2.3.2   Assignment

In Section 2.3.1.2, we have seen that we can copy objects of user classes without getters and setters—at least during construction. Now, we want to copy into existing objects by writing:

```
x= y;
u= v= w= x;
```

To this end, the class must provide an assignment operator (or refrain from stopping the compiler to generate one). As usual, we consider first the class complex. Assigning a complex value to a complex variable requires an operator like

```
complex& operator=(const complex& src)
{
    r= src.r; i= src.i;
    return *this;
}
```

Evidently, we copy the members r and i. The operator returns a reference to the object for enabling multiple assignments. this is a pointer to the object itself, and since we need a reference, we dereference the this pointer. The operator that assigns values of the object's type is called *Copy Assignment* and can be synthesized by the compiler. In our example, the generated code would be identical to ours and we could omit our implementation here.

What happens if we assign a double to a complex?

```
c= 7.5;
```

It compiles without the definition of an assignment operator for double. Once again, we have an implicit conversion: the implicit constructor creates a complex on the fly and assigns this one. If this becomes a performance issue, we can add an assignment for double:

```
complex& operator=(double nr)
{
    r= nr; i= 0;
```

```
        return *this;
    }
```

As before, vector's synthesized operator is not satisfactory because it only copies the address of the data and not the data itself. The implementation is very similar to the copy constructor:

```
1   vector& operator=(const vector& src)
2   {
3       if (this == &src)
4           return *this;
5       assert(my_size == src.my_size);
6       for (int i= 0; i < my_size; ++i)
7           data[i]= src.data[i];
8       return *this;
9   }
```

It is advised [45, p. 94] that copy assignment and constructor be consistent to avoid utterly confused users.

An assignment of an object to itself (source and target have the same address) can be skipped (lines 3 and 4). In line 5, we test whether the assignment is a legal operation by checking the equality of the vector sizes. Alternatively the assignment could resize the target if the sizes are different. This is a technically legitimate option but scientifically rather questionable. Just think of a context in mathematics or physics where a vector space all of a sudden changes its dimension.

C++11

2.3.3   Initializer Lists

C++11 introduces the *Initializer Lists* as a new feature—not to be confused with "member initialization list" (§2.3.1). To use it, we must include the header <initializer_list>. Although this feature is orthogonal to the class concept, the constructor and assignment operator of a vector are excellent use cases, making this a suitable location for introducing initializer lists. It allows us to set all entries of a vector at the same time (up to reasonable sizes).

Ordinary C arrays can be initialized entirely within their definition:

```
float v[]= {1.0, 2.0, 3.0};
```

This capability is generalized in C++11 so that any class may be initialized with a list of values (of the same type). With an appropriate constructor, we could write:

```
vector v= {1.0, 2.0, 3.0};
```

or

```
vector v{1.0, 2.0, 3.0};
```

We could also set all vector entries in an assignment:

```
v= {1.0, 2.0, 3.0};
```

Functions that take vector arguments could be called with a vector that is set up on the fly:

```
vector x= lu_solve(A, vector{1.0, 2.0, 3.0});
```

The previous statement solves a linear system for the vector $(1, 2, 3)^T$ with an LU factorization on A.

To use this feature in our vector class, we need a constructor and an assignment accepting initializer_list<double> as an argument. Lazy people can implement the constructor only and use it in the copy assignment. For demonstration and performance purposes, we will implement both. It also allows us to verify in the assignment that the vector size matches:

```cpp
#include <initializer_list>
#include <algorithm>

class vector
{
    // ...
    vector(std::initializer_list<double> values)
      : my_size(values.size()), data(new double[my_size])
    {
        std::copy(std::begin(values), std::end(values),
                  std::begin(data));
    }

    self& operator=(std::initializer_list<double> values)
    {
        assert(my_size == values.size());
        std::copy(std::begin(values), std::end(values),
                  std::begin(data));
        return *this;
    }
};
```

To copy the values within the list into our data, we use the function std::copy from the standard library. This function takes three iterators[3] as arguments. These three arguments represent the begin and the end of the input and the begin of the output. The free functions begin and end were introduced in C++11. In C++03, we have to use the corresponding member functions, e.g., values.begin().

2.3.4 Uniform Initialization

C++11

Braces {} are used in C++11 as universal notation for all forms of variable initialization by

- Initializer-list constructors,

- Other constructors, or

- Direct member setting.

The latter is only allowed for arrays and classes if all (non-static) variables are public and the class has no user-defined constructor.[4] Such types are called *Aggregates* and setting their values with braced lists accordingly *Aggregate Initialization*.

---

3. Which are kind of generalized pointers; see §4.1.2.
4. Further conditions are that the class has no base classes and no virtual functions (§6.1).

Assuming we would define a kind of sloppy `complex` class without constructors, we could initialize it as follows:

```
struct sloppy_complex
{
    double r, i;
};

sloppy_complex z1{3.66, 2.33},
               z2= {0, 1};
```

Needless to say, we prefer using constructors over the aggregate initialization. However, it comes in handy when we have to deal with legacy code.

The `complex` class from this section which contains constructors can be initialized with the same notation:

```
complex c{7.0, 8}, c2= {0, 1}, c3= {9.3}, c4= {c};
const complex cc= {c3};
```

The notation with = is not allowed when the relevant constructor is declared `explicit`.

There remain the initializer lists that we introduced in the previous section. Using a list as an argument of uniform initialization would actually require double braces:

```
vector v1= {{1.0, 2.0, 3.0}},
       v2{{3, 4, 5}};
```

To simplify our life, C++11 provides *Brace Elision* in a uniform initializer; i.e., braces can be omitted and the list entries are passed in their given order to constructor arguments or data members. So, we can shorten the declaration to

```
vector v1= {1.0, 2.0, 3.0},
       v2{3, 4, 5};
```

Brace elision is a blessing and a curse. Assume we integrated our `complex` class in the `vector` to implement a `vector_complex` which we can conveniently set up:

```
vector_complex v= {{1.5, -2}, {3.4}, {2.6, 5.13}};
```

However, the following example:

```
vector_complex v1d= {{2}};
vector_complex v2d= {{2, 3}};
vector_complex v3d= {{2, 3, 4}};

std::cout ≪ "v1d is " ≪ v1d ≪ std::endl; ...
```

might be a bit surprising:

```
v1d is [(2,0)]
v2d is [(2,3)]
v3d is [(2,0), (3,0), (4,0)]
```

In the first line, we have one argument so the vector contains one complex number which is initialized with the one-argument constructor (imaginary part is 0). The next statement creates a vector with one element whose constructor is called with two arguments. This scheme cannot continue obviously: `complex` has no constructor with three arguments. So, here we switch to multiple vector entries that are constructed with one argument each. Some more experiments are given for the interested reader in Appendix A.4.2.

Another application of braces is the initialization of member variables:

```
class vector
{
  public:
    vector(int n)
      : my_size{n}, data{new double[my_size]} {}
    ...
  private:
    unsigned my_size;
    double   *data;
};
```

This protects us from occasional sloppiness: in the example above we initialize an `unsigned` member with an `int` argument. This narrowing is denounced by the compiler and we will substitute the type accordingly:

```
vector(unsigned n) : my_size{n}, data{new double[my_size]} {}
```

We already showed that initializer lists allow us to create non-primitive function arguments on the fly, e.g.:

```
double d= dot(vector{3, 4, 5}, vector{7, 8, 9});
```

When the argument type is clear—when only one overload is available, for instance—the list can be passed typeless to the function:

```
double d= dot({3, 4, 5}, {7, 8, 9});
```

Accordingly, function results can be set by the uniform notation as well:

```
complex subtract(const complex& c1, const complex& c2)
{
    return {c1.r - c2.r, c1.i - c2.i};
}
```

The `return` type of this function is a `complex` and we initialize it with a two-argument braced list.

In this section, we demonstrated the possibilities of uniform initialization and illustrated some risks. We are convinced that it is a very useful feature but one that should be used with some care for tricky corner cases.

2.3.5 Move Semantics

C++11

Copying large amounts of data is expensive, and people use a lot of tricks to avoid unnecessary copies. Several software packages use shallow copy. That would mean for our `vector` example that we only copy the address of the data but not the data itself. As a consequence, after the assignment:

```
v= w;
```

the two variables contain pointers to the same data in memory. If we change v[7], then we also change w[7] and vice versa. Therefore, software with shallow copy usually provides a function for explicitly calling a deep copy:

```
copy(v, w);
```

This function must be used instead of the assignment every time variables are assigned. For temporary values—for instance, a vector that is returned as a function result—the shallow copy is not critical since the temporary is not accessible otherwise and we have no aliasing effects. The price for avoiding the copies is that the programmer must pay utter attention that in the presence of aliasing, memory is not released twice; i.e., reference counting is needed.

On the other hand, deep copies are expensive when large objects are returned as function results. Later, we will present a very efficient technique to avoid copies (see §5.3). Now, we introduce another feature from C++11 for it: *Move Semantics*. The idea is that variables (in other words all named items) are copied deeply and temporaries (objects that cannot be referred to by name) transfer their data.

This raises the question: How to tell the difference between temporary and persistent data? The good news is: the compiler does this for us. In the C++ lingo, the temporaries are called *Rvalues* because they can only appear on the right side in an assignment. C++11 introduces rvalue references that are denoted by two ampersands &&. Values with a name, so-called lvalues, cannot be passed to rvalue references.

C++11 ### 2.3.5.1 Move Constructor

By providing a move constructor and a move assignment, we can assure that rvalues are not expensively copied:

```
class vector
{
    // ...
    vector(vector&& v)
      : my_size(v.my_size), data(v.data)
    {
        v.data= 0;
        v.my_size= 0;
    }
};
```

The move constructor steals the data from its source and leaves it in an empty state.

An object that is passed as an rvalue to a function is considered expired after the function returns. This means that all data can be entirely random. The only requirement is that the destruction of the object (§2.4) must not fail. Utter attention must be paid to raw pointers (as usual). They must not point to random memory so that the deletion fails or some other user data is freed. If we would have left the pointer v.data unchanged, the memory would be released when v goes out of scope and the data of our target vector would be invalidated. Usually a raw pointer should be `nullptr` (0 in C++03) after a move operation.

Note that an rvalue reference like `vector&& v` is not an rvalue itself but an lvalue as it possesses a name. If we wanted to pass our v to another method that helps the move constructor with the data robbery, we would have to turn it into an rvalue again with the standard function `std::move` (see §2.3.5.4).

2.3.5.2   Move Assignment   C++11

The move assignment can be implemented in a simple manner by swapping the pointers to the data:

```cpp
class vector
{
    // ...
      vector& operator=(vector&& src)
      {
      assert(my_size == 0 || my_size == src.my_size);
    std::swap(data, src.data);
    return *this;
    }
};
```

This relieves us from releasing our own existing data because this is done when the source is destroyed.

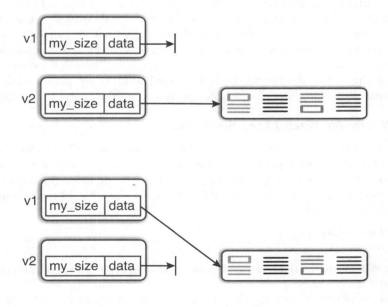

Figure 2–2: Moved data

Say we have an empty vector v1 and a temporarily created vector v2 within function f() as depicted in the upper part of Figure 2–2. When we assign the result of f() to v1:

```
v1= f();      // f returns v2
```

the move assignment will swap the data pointers so that v1 contains the values of v2 afterward while the latter is empty as in the lower part of Figure 2–2.

2.3.5.3   Copy Elision

If we add logging in these two functions, we might realize that our move constructor is not called as often as we thought. The reason for this is that modern compilers provide an even better optimization than stealing the data. This optimization is called *Copy Elision* where the compiler omits a copy of the data and modifies the generation of the data such that it is immediately stored to the target address of the copy operation.

Its most important use case is *Return Value Optimization (RVO)*, especially when a new variable is initialized with a function result like

```
inline vector ones(int n)
{
    vector v(n);
    for (unsigned i= 0; i < n; ++i)
        v[i]= 1.0;
    return v;
}
...
vector w(ones(7));
```

Instead of constructing v and copying (or moving) it to w at the end of the function, the compiler can create w immediately and perform all operations directly on it. The copy (or move) constructor is never called. We simply check this with a log output or a debugger.

Copy elision was already available in many compilers before move semantics. However, that should not mean that move constructors are useless. The rules for moving data are mandatory by the standard whereas the RVO optimization is not guaranteed. Often minor details can turn it off, for instance, if the function has multiple return statements.

C++11   2.3.5.4   Where We Need Move Semantics

One situation where a move constructor is definitely used is with the function std::move. Actually this function does not move, it only casts an lvalue to an rvalue. In other words, it pretends that the variable is a temporary; i.e., it makes it movable. As a consequence, subsequent constructors or assignments will call the overload for an rvalue reference, as in the following code snippet:

```
vector x(std::move(w));
v= std::move(u);
```

In the first line, x steals the data of w and leaves it as an empty vector. The second statement will swap v and u.

Our move constructor and assignment are not perfectly consistent when used with std::move. As long as we deal only with true temporaries, we would not see the difference.

However, for stronger consistency we can also leave the source of a move assignment in an empty state:

```
class vector
{
    // ...
    vector& operator=(vector&& src)
    {
        assert(my_size == src.my_size);
        delete[] data;
        data= src.data;
        src.data= nullptr;
        src.my_size= 0;
        return *this;
    }
};
```

Another take on this is that objects are considered expired after std::move. Phrased differently, they are not dead yet but retired, and it does not matter what value they have as long as they are in a legal state (i.e., the destructor must not crash).

A nice application of move semantics is the default implementation std::swap in C++11 and higher; see Section 3.2.3.

2.4 Destructors

A destructor is a function that is called every time when an object is destroyed, for example:

```
~complex()
{
    std::cout << "So long and thanks for the fish.\n";
}
```

Since the destructor is the complementary operation of the default constructor, it uses the notation for the complement ($\sim$). Opposed to the constructor, there is only one single overload and arguments are not allowed.

2.4.1 Implementation Rules

There are two very important rules:

1. **Never** throw an exception in a destructor! It is likely that your program will crash and the exception will never be caught. In C++11 or higher, it is always treated as a run-time error which aborts the execution (destructors are implicitly declared noexcept, §1.6.2.4). In C++03, what happens depends on the compiler implementation, but a program abortion is the most likely reaction.

2. If a class contains a virtual function, the destructor should be virtual, too. We come back to this in Section 6.1.3.

2.4.2   Dealing with Resources Properly

What we do in a destructor is our free choice; we have no limitations from the language. Practically, the main task of a destructor is releasing the resources of an object (memory, file handles, sockets, locks, ...) and cleaning up everything related to the object that is not needed any longer in the program. Because a destructor must not throw exceptions, many programmers are convinced that releasing resources should be the only activity of a destructor.

⇒ c++03/vector_test.cpp

In our example, there is nothing to do when a complex number is destroyed and we can omit the destructor. A destructor is needed when the object acquires resources like memory. In such cases, the memory or the other resource must be released in the destructor:

```
class vector
{
  public:
  // ...
    ~vector()
    {
        delete[] data;
    }
  // ...
  private:
    unsigned my_size;
    double   *data;
};
```

Note that delete already tests whether a pointer is nullptr (0 in C++03). Similarly, files that are opened with old C handles require explicit closing (and this is only one reason for not using them).

2.4.2.1   Resource Acquisition Is Initialization

Resource Acquisition Is Initialization (RAII) is a paradigm mainly developed by Bjarne Stroustrup and Andrew Koenig. The idea is tying resources to objects and using the mechanism of object construction and destruction to handle resources automatically in programs. Each time we want to acquire a resource, we do so by creating an object that owns it. Whenever the object goes out of scope, the resource (memory, file, socket, ...) is released automatically, as in our vector example above.

Imagine a program that allocates 37,186 memory blocks in 986 program locations. Can we be sure that all the memory blocks are freed? And how much time will we spend to get to this certainty or at least to an acceptable level of confidence? Even with tools like valgrind (§B.3), we can only test the absence of memory leaks for a single run but cannot guarantee in general that memory is always released. On the other hand, when all memory blocks are allocated in constructors and freed in destructors, we can be sure that no leaks exist.

2.4.2.2 Exceptions

Releasing all resources is even more challenging when exceptions are thrown. Whenever we detect a problem, we have to release all resources acquired so far before we throw the exception. Unfortunately, this is not limited to resources in the current scope but extends to those of surrounding scopes depending on where the exception is caught. This means that changing the error handling needs tedious adaption of the manual resource management.

2.4.2.3 Managed Resources

All the problems mentioned before can be solved by introducing classes that manage the resources. C++ already offers such managers in the standard library. File streams manage the file handles from C. `unique_ptr` and `shared_ptr` handle memory in a leak-free, exception-safe manner.[5] Also in our `vector` example, we can benefit from `unique_ptr` by not needing to implement a destructor.

2.4.2.4 Managing Ourselves

The smart pointers show that there can be different treatments of a resource type. However, when none of the existing classes handles a resource in the fashion we want, it is a great occasion to entertain ourselves writing a resource manager tailored to our needs.

When we do so, we should not manage more than one resource in a class. The motivation for this guideline is that exceptions can be thrown in constructors, and it is quite tedious to write the constructor in a way that guarantees that all resources acquired so far are released.

Thus, whenever we write a class that deals with two resources (even of the same type) we should introduce a class that manages one of the resources. Better yet, we should write managers for both resources and separate the resource handling entirely from the scientific content. Even in the case that an exception is thrown in the middle of the constructor, we have no problem with leaking resources since the destructors of their managers are called automatically and will take care of it.

The term "RAII" puts linguistically more weight on the initialization. However, the finalization is even more important technically. It is not mandatory that a resource is acquired in a constructor. This can happen later in the lifetime of an object. Fundamental is that one single object is responsible for the resource and releases it at the end of its lifetime. Jon Kalb calls this approach an application of the *Single Responsibility Principle* (SRP), and it is worthwhile to see his talk, which is available on the web.

2.4.2.5 Resource Rescue   C++11

In this section, we introduce a technique for releasing resources automatically even when we use a software package with explicit resource handling. We will demonstrate the technique with the Oracle C++ Call Interface (OCCI) [33] for accessing an Oracle database from a C++ program. This example allows us to show a realistic application, and we assume that many scientists and engineers have to deal with databases from time to time. Although the Oracle database is a commercial product, our example can be tested with the free Express edition.

---

5. Only cyclic references need special treatment.

Table 2–1: Herbert's Solutions

Problem	Worth an Award
Gauss circle	✓
Congruent numbers	?
Amicable numbers	✓
⋮	

OCCI is a C++ extension of the C library OCI and adds only a thin layer with some C++ features on top while keeping the entire software architecture in C style. Sadly, this applies to most inter-language interfaces of C libraries. Since C does not support destructors, one cannot establish RAII and resources must be released explicitly.

In OCCI, we first have to create an `Environment` which can be used to establish a `Connection` to the database. This in turn allows us to write a `Statement` that returns a `ResultSet`. All these resources are represented by raw pointers and must be released in reverse order.

As an example, we look at Table 2–1 where our friend Herbert keeps track of his solutions to (allegedly) unsolved mathematical problems. The second column indicates whether he is certain to deserve an award for his work. For size reasons, we cannot print the complete list of his tremendous discoveries here.

⇒ c++03/occi_old_style.cpp

From time to time, Herbert looks up his award-worthy discoveries with the following C++ program:

```cpp
#include <iostream>
#include <string>
#include <occi.h>

using namespace std;                    // import names (§3.2.1)
using namespace oracle::occi;

int main()
{
    string dbConn= "172.17.42.1", user= "herbert",
           password= "NSA_go_away";
    Environment *env = Environment::createEnvironment();
    Connection *conn = env->createConnection(user, password,
                                             dbConn);
    string query= "select problem from my_solutions"
                  "  where award_worthy != 0";
    Statement *stmt = conn->createStatement(query);
    ResultSet *rs = stmt->executeQuery();

    while (rs->next())
        cout << rs->getString(1) << endl;
```

```
    stmt->closeResultSet(rs);
    conn->terminateStatement(stmt);
    env->terminateConnection(conn);
    Environment::terminateEnvironment(env);
}
```

This time, we cannot blame Herbert for his old-style programming; it is forced by the library. Let us have a look at the code. Even for people not familiar with OCCI, it is evident what happens. First, we acquire the resources, then we iterate over Herbert's ingenious achievements, and finally we release the resources in reverse order. We highlighted the resource release operations as we will have to pay closer attention to them.

The release technique works reasonably well when our (or Herbert's) program is a monolithic block as above. The situation changes entirely when we try building functions with queries:

```
    ResultSet *rs = makes_me_famous();
    while (rs->next())
        cout ≪ rs->getString(1) ≪ endl;

    ResultSet *rs2 = needs_more_work();
    while (rs2->next())
        cout ≪ rs2->getString(1) ≪ endl;
```

Now we have result sets without the corresponding statements to close them; they were declared within the query functions and are out of scope now. Thus, for every object we have to keep additionally the object that was used for its generation. Sooner or later this becomes a nightmare of dependencies with an enormous potential for errors.

⇒ c++11/occi_resource_rescue.cpp

The question is: How can we manage resources that depend on other resources? The solution is to use deleters from unique_ptr or shared_ptr. They are called whenever managed memory is released. An interesting aspect of deleters is that they are not obliged to actually release the memory. We will explore this liberty to manage our resources. The Environment has the easiest handling because it does not depend on another resource:

```
struct environment_deleter {
    void operator()( Environment* env )
    { Environment::terminateEnvironment(env); }
};

shared_ptr<Environment> environment(
    Environment::createEnvironment(), environment_deleter{});
```

Now, we can create as many copies of the environment as we like and have the guarantee that the deleter executing terminateEnvironment(env) is called when the last copy goes out of scope.

A `Connection` requires an `Environment` for its creation and termination. Therefore, we keep a copy in connection_deleter:

```
struct connection_deleter
{
    connection_deleter(shared_ptr<Environment> env)
      : env(env) {}
    void operator()(Connection* conn)
    { env->terminateConnection(conn); }
    shared_ptr<Environment> env;
};


shared_ptr<Connection> connection(environment->createConnection(...),
                                  connection_deleter{environment});
```

Now, we have the guarantee that the `Connection` is terminated when it is not needed any longer. Having a copy of the `Environment` in the connection_deleter ensures that it is not terminated as long as a `Connection` exists.

We can handle the database more conveniently when we create a manager class for it:

```
class db_manager
{
  public:
    using ResultSetSharedPtr= std::shared_ptr<ResultSet>;

    db_manager(string const& dbConnection, string const& dbUser,
               string const& dbPw)
      : environment(Environment::createEnvironment(),
                    environment_deleter{}),
        connection(environment->createConnection(dbUser, dbPw,
                                                  dbConnection),
                   connection_deleter{environment} )
    {}
    // some getters ...
  private:
    shared_ptr<Environment> environment;
    shared_ptr<Connection>  connection;
};
```

Note that the class has no destructor since the members are managed resources now.

To this class, we can add a `query` method that returns a managed `ResultSet`:

```
struct result_set_deleter
{
    result_set_deleter(shared_ptr<Connection> conn,
                       Statement* stmt)
      : conn(conn), stmt(stmt) {}
    void operator()( ResultSet *rs )          // call op. like in (§3.8)
    {
        stmt->closeResultSet(rs);
        conn->terminateStatement(stmt);
    }
```

```
        shared_ptr<Connection> conn;
        Statement*              stmt;
    };

    class db_manager
    {
      public:
        // ...
        ResultSetSharedPtr query(const std::string& q) const
        {
            Statement *stmt= connection->createStatement(q);
            ResultSet *rs = stmt->executeQuery();
            auto deleter= result_set_deleter{connection, stmt};
            return ResultSetSharedPtr{rs, deleter};
        }
    };
```

Thanks to this new method and our deleters, the application becomes as easy as

```
    int main()
    {
        db_manager db("172.17.42.1", "herbert", "NSA_go_away");
        auto rs= db.query("select problem from my_solutions "
                          "    where award_worthy != 0");
        while (rs->next())
            cout ≪ rs->getString(1) ≪ endl;
    }
```

The more queries we have, the more our effort pays off. Not being ashamed to repeat ourselves: all resources are implicitly released.

The careful reader has realized that we violated the single-responsibility principle. To express our gratitude for this discovery we invite you to improve our design in Exercise 2.8.4.

2.5 Method Generation Résumé

C++ has six methods (four in C++03) with a default behavior:

- Default constructor

- Copy constructor

- Move constructor (C++11 or higher)

- Copy assignment

- Move assignment (C++11 or higher)

- Destructor

The code for those can be generated by the compiler—saving us from boring routine work and thus preventing oversights.

There is a fair amount of detail involved in the rules determining which method is generated implicitly. These details are covered in more detail in Appendix A, Section A.5. Here we only want to give you our final conclusions for C++11 and higher:

Rule of Six

Regarding the six operations above, implement as little as possible and declare as much as possible. Any operation not implemented shall be declared as `default` or `delete`.

2.6 Accessing Member Variables

C++ offers multiple ways to access the members of our classes. In this section, we present different options and discuss their advantages and disadvantages. Hopefully, you will get a feeling for how to design your classes in the future in a way that suits your domain best.

2.6.1 Access Functions

In §2.2.5, we introduced getters and setters to access the variables of the class `complex`. This becomes cumbersome when we want, for instance, to increment the `real` part:

```
c.set_r(c.get_r() + 5.);
```

This does not really look like a numeric operation and is not very readable either. A better way to realize this operation is writing a member function that returns a reference:

```
class complex {
  public:
    double& real() { return r; }
};
```

With this function we can write

```
c.real()+= 5.;
```

This already looks much better but is still a little bit weird. Why not increment the calculation like this:

```
real(c)+= 5.;
```

To this end, we write a free function:

```
inline double& real(complex& c) { return c.r; }
```

Unfortunately, this function accesses the private member `r`. We can modify the free function calling the member function:

```
inline double& real(complex& c) { return c.real(); }
```

Or alternatively declare the free function as `friend` of `complex` to access its `private` data:

```
class complex {
    friend double& real(complex& c);
};
```

Accessing the `real` part should also work when the `complex` number is constant. Thus, we further need a constant version of this function, regarding argument and result:

```
inline const double& real(const complex& c) { return c.r; }
```

This function requires a `friend` declaration, too.

In the last two functions we returned references, but those are guaranteed not to be out of date. The functions—in free as well as in member form—can evidently only be called when the referred object is already created. The references of the number's `real` part that we use in the statement

```
real(c)+= 5.;
```

exist only until the end of the statement in contrast to the referred variable `c` which lives longer: until the end of the scope in which it is defined. We can create a reference variable:

```
double &rr= real(c);
```

that lives till the end of the current scope. Even in the case that `c` is declared in the same scope, the reverse order of object destruction in C++ guarantees that `c` lives longer than `rr`.

Member references of temporary objects can safely be used within the same expression, e.g.:

```
double r2= real(complex(3, 7)) * 2.0;        // okay!
```

The temporary `complex` number lives only in the statement but at least longer than the reference of its `real` part so that this statement is correct. However, if we keep that reference to the `real` part, it will be outdated:

```
const double &rr= real(complex(3, 7));       // Really bad!!!
cout << "The real part is " << rr << '\n';
```

The complex variable is created temporarily and only exists until the end of the first statement. The reference to its `real` part lives till the end of the surrounding scope.

Rule

Do not keep references of temporary expressions!

They are invalid before we use them the first time.

2.6.2 Subscript Operator

To iterate over a `vector`, we could write a function like

```
class vector
{
  public:
    double at(int i)
    {
        assert(i >= 0 && i < my_size);
```

```
            return data[i];
        }
};
```

Summing the entries of vector v reads:

```
double sum= 0.0;
for (int i= 0; i < v.size(); ++i)
    sum+= v.at(i);
```

C++ and C access entries of (fixed-size) arrays with the subscript operator. It is, thus, only natural to do the same for (dynamically sized) vectors. Then we could rewrite the previous example as

```
double sum= 0.0;
for (int i= 0; i < v.size(); ++i)
    sum+= v[i];
```

This is more concise and shows more clearly what we are doing.

The operator overloading has the same syntax as the assignment operator and the implementation from function at:

```
class vector
{
  public:
    double& operator[](int i)
    {
        assert(i >= 0 && i < my_size);
        return data[i];
    }
};
```

With this operator, we can access vector elements with brackets but (in this form) only if the vector is mutable.

2.6.3 Constant Member Functions

This raises the more general question: How can we write operators and member functions that accept constant objects? In fact, operators are a special form of member functions and can be called like a member function:

```
    v[i];               // is syntactic sugar for:
    v.operator[](i);
```

Of course, the long form is almost never used, but it illustrates that operators are regular methods that only provide an additional call syntax.

Free functions allow qualifying the const-ness of each argument. Member functions do not even mention the processed object in the signature. How can we then specify that the current object must be const? There is a special notation to add qualifiers after the function header:

```
class vector
{
```

```
  public:
    const double& operator[](int i) const
    {
        assert(i >= 0 && i < my_size);
        return data[i];
    }
};
```

The const attribute is not just a casual indication that the programmer does not mind calling this member function with a constant object. The C++ compiler takes this constancy very seriously and will verify that the function does not modify the object (i.e., some of its members) and that the object is only passed as a const argument to other functions. Thus, when other methods are called they must be const, too.

This constancy guarantee also impedes returning non-constant pointers or references to data members. One can return constant pointers or references as well as objects. A returned value does not need to be constant (but it could) because it is a copy of the current object, of one of its member variables (or constants), or of a temporary variable. None of those copies bears the risk of modifying the current object.

Constant member functions can be called with non-constant objects as arguments (because C++ implicitly converts non-constant references into constant references when necessary). Therefore, it is often sufficient to provide only the constant member function. For instance, here is a function that returns the size of the vector:

```
class vector
{
  public:
    int size() const { return my_size; }
    // int size() { return my_size; } // futile
};
```

The non-constant size function does the same as the constant one and is therefore useless.

For our subscript operator, we need both the constant and the mutable version. If we only had the constant member function, we could use it to read the elements of both constant and mutable vectors but we could not modify the latter.

Data members can be declared mutable. Then they can even be changed in const methods. This is intended for internal states—like caches—that do not affect the observable behavior. We do not use this feature in this book and recommend that you apply it only when really necessary, as it undermines the language's data protection.

2.6.4 Reference-Qualified Members $\boxed{\text{C++11}}$

In addition to the constancy of an object (i.e., that of *this), we can also require in C++11 that an object be an lvalue or rvalue reference. Assume we have a vector addition (see §2.7.3). Its result will be a temporary object that is not constant. Thus we can assign values to its entries:

```
(v + w)[i]= 7.3; // nonsense
```

Admittedly, this is a quite artificial example, but it illustrates that there is room for improvement.

Assignments should only accept mutable lvalues on the left-hand side. This applies uncompromisingly to intrinsic types. This raises the question: Why is (v + w)[i] a mutable lvalue? The vector's bracket operator has two overloads: for mutable and constant objects. v+w is not constant so the overload for mutable vectors is preferred. Thus, we access a mutable reference to a mutable object's member which is legitimate.

The problem is that (v + w)[i] is an lvalue while v+w is not. What we are missing here is the requirement that the bracket operator can only be applied on lvalues:

```
class vector
{
  public:
    double&       operator[](int i) &       { ... }  // #1
    const double& operator[](int i) const&  { ... }  // #2
};
```

When we qualify one overload of a member with a reference, we have to qualify the other overloads as well. With this implementation, overload #1 cannot be used for temporary vectors, and overload #2 returns a constant reference to which no value can be assigned. As a consequence, we will see a compiler error for the nonsensical assignment above:

```
vector_features.cpp:167:15: error: read-only variable is not assignable
    (v + w)[i]= 3;
    ~~~~~~~~~~^
```

Likewise, we can *Ref-Qualify* the vector's assignment operators to disable them for temporary objects:

```
v + w= u; // nonsense, should be forbidden
```

As expected, two ampersands allow us to restrict a member function to rvalues; that is, the method should only be callable on temporaries:

```
class my_class
{
    something_good donate_my_data() && { ... }
};
```

Use cases could be conversions where huge copies (e.g., of matrices) should be avoided.

Multi-dimensional data structures like matrices can be accessed in different ways. First, we can use the application operator (§3.8) which allows us to pass multiple indices as arguments. The bracket operator unfortunately accepts only one argument, and we discuss some ways to deal with this in Appendix A.4.3 of which none is satisfying. An advanced approach to call the application operator from concatenated bracket operators will be presented later in Section 6.6.2.

2.7   Operator Overloading Design

With few exceptions (§1.3.10), most operators can be overloaded in C++. However, some operators make sense to overload only for specific purposes; e.g., the dereferred member selection p->m is useful for implementing new smart pointers. In a scientific or engineering context, it is much less obvious how to use this operator intuitively. Along the same lines, a customized meaning of the address operator &o needs a good reason.

2.7.1   Be Consistent!

As mentioned before, the language gives us a high degree of freedom in the design and implementation of operators for our classes. We can freely choose the semantics of every operator. However, the closer our customized behavior is to that of the standard types, the easier it is for others (co-developers, open-source users, ...) to understand what we do and to trust our software.

The overloading can of course be used to represent operations in a certain application domain concisely, i.e., to establish a *Domain-Specific Embedded Language* (DSEL). In this case, it can be productive to deviate from the typical meanings of the operators. Nonetheless, the DSEL should be consistent in itself. For instance, if the operators =, +, and += are user-defined, then the expressions a= a + b and a+= b should have the same effect.

Consistent Overloads

Define your operators consistently with each other and whenever appropriate provide semantics similar to those of standard types.

We are also free to choose the return type of each operator arbitrarily; e.g., x == y could return a string or a file handle. Again, the closer we stay to the typical return types in C++, the easier it is for everybody (including ourselves) to work with our customized operators.

The only predefined aspect of operators is their *Arity*: the number of arguments and the relative priority of the operators. In most cases this is inherent in the represented operation: a multiplication always takes two arguments. For some operators, one could imagine a variable arity. For instance, it would be nice if the subscription operator accepted two arguments in addition to the subscribed object so that we could access a matrix element like this: A[i, j]. The only operator allowing for an arbitrary arity (including variadic implementations, §3.10) is the application operator: operator().

Another freedom that the language provides us is the choice of the arguments' types. We can, for instance, implement a subscription operator for an unsigned (returning a single element), for a range (returning a sub-vector), and a set (returning a set of vector elements). This is indeed realized in MTL4. Compared to MATLAB, C++ offers fewer operators, but we have the unlimited opportunity of overloading them infinitely to create every amount of functionality we like.

2.7.2   Respect the Priority

When we redefine operators, we have to ascertain that the expected priority of the operation corresponds to the operator precedence. For instance, we might have the idea of using the LaTeX notation for exponentiation of matrices:

```
A= B^2;
```

A is *B* squared. So far so good. That the original meaning of ^ is a bitwise exclusive OR does not worry us as we never planned to implement bitwise operations on matrices.

Now we add *C* to B^2:

```
A= B^2 + C;
```

Looks nice. But it does not work (or does something weird). Why? Because + has a higher priority than ^. Thus, the compiler understands our expression as

```
A= B ^ (2 + C);
```

Oops. Although the operator notation gives a concise and intuitive interface, non-trivial expressions might not meet our expectations. Therefore:

Respect Priorities

Pay attention that the semantic/intended priority of your overloaded operators matches the priorities of C++ operators.

2.7.3 Member or Free Function

Most operators can be defined as members or as free functions. The following operators—any kind of assignment, operator[], operator->, and operator()—must be non-static methods to ensure that their first argument is an lvalue. We have shown examples of operator[] and operator() in Section 2.6. In contrast, binary operators with an intrinsic type as first argument can only be defined as free functions.

The impact of different implementation choices can be demonstrated with the addition operator for our complex class:

```
class complex
{
  public:
    explicit complex(double rn = 0.0, double in = 0.0) : r(rn), i(in) {}
    complex operator+(const complex& c2) const
    {
        return complex(r + c2.r, i + c2.i);
    }
    ...
  private:
    double r, i;
};

int main()
{
    complex cc(7.0, 8.0), c4(cc);
    std::cout << "cc + c4 is " << cc + c4 << std::endl;
}
```

Can we also add a complex and a double?

```
        std::cout << "cc + 4.2 is " << cc + 4.2 << std::endl;
```

Not with the implementation above. We can add an overload for the operator accepting a `double` as a second argument:

```
class complex
{
    ...
    complex operator+(double r2) const
    {
        return complex(r + r2, i);
    }
    ...
};
```

Alternatively, we can remove the `explicit` from the constructor. Then a `double` can be implicitly converted to a `complex` and we add two `complex` values.

Both approaches have pros and cons: the overloading needs only one addition operation, and the implicit constructor is more flexible in general as it allows for passing `double` values to `complex` function arguments. Or we do both the implicit conversion and the overloading, then we have the flexibility and the efficiency.

Now we turn the arguments around:

```
std::cout << "4.2 + c4 is " << 4.2 + c4 << std::endl;
```

This will not compile. In fact, the expression `4.2 + c4` can be considered as a short notion of

```
4.2.operator+(c4)
```

In other words, we are looking for an operator in `double` which is not even a class.

To provide an operator with a primitive type as a first argument, we must write a free function:

```
inline complex operator+(double d, const complex& c2)
{
    return complex(d + real(c2), imag(c2));
}
```

In the same manner, it is advisable to implement the addition of two complex values as free functions:

```
inline complex operator+(const complex& c1, const complex& c2)
{
    return complex(real(c1) + real(c2), imag(c1) + imag(c2));
}
```

To avoid an ambiguity, we have to remove the member function with the complex argument.

All this said, the main difference between a member and a free function is that the former allows the implicit conversion only for the second argument (here summand) and the latter for both arguments. If concise program sources are more important than performance, we could omit all the overloads with a `double` argument and rely on the implicit conversion.

Even if we keep all three overloads, it is more symmetric to implement them as free functions. The second summand is in any case subject to implicit conversion, and it is better to have the same behavior for both arguments. In short:

Binary Operators
Implement binary operators as free functions.

We have the same distinction for unary operands: only free functions, e.g.:

```
complex operator-(const complex& c1)
{ return complex(-real(c1), -imag(c1)); }
```

allow for implicit conversions, in contrast to members:

```
class complex
{
  public:
    complex operator-() const { return complex(-r, -i); }
};
```

Whether this is desirable depends on the context. Most likely, a user-defined dereference
operator* should not involve conversion.

Last but not least, we want to implement an output operator for streams. This operator
takes a mutable reference to std::ostream and a usually constant reference to the user type.
For simplicity's sake let us stick with our complex class:

```
std::ostream& operator≪(std::ostream& os, const complex& c)
{
    return os ≪ '(' ≪ real(c) ≪ ',' ≪ imag(c) ≪ ")";
}
```

As the first argument is ostream&, we cannot write a member function in complex, and adding
a member to std::ostream is not really an option. With this single implementation we provide
output on all standardized output streams, i.e., classes derived from std::ostream.

2.8   Exercises

2.8.1   Polynomial

Write a class for polynomials that should at least contain:

- A constructor giving the degree of the polynomial;
- A dynamic array/vector/list of double to store the coefficients;
- A destructor; and
- A output function for ostream.

Further members like arithmetic operations are optional.

2.8.2   Move Assignment

Write a move assignment operator for the polynomial in Exercise 2.8.1. Define the copy
constructor as default. To test whether your assignment is used write a function

polynomial f(double c2, double c1, double c0) that takes three coefficients and returns a polynomial. Print out a message in your move assignment or use a debugger to make sure your assignment is used.

2.8.3 Initializer List

Expand the program from Exercise 2.8.1 with a constructor and an assignment operator for a initializer list. The degree of the polynomial should be the length of the initializer list minus one afterward.

2.8.4 Resource Rescue

Refactor the implementation from Section 2.4.2.5. Implement a deleter for `Statement` and use managed statements in a managed `ResultSet`.

Chapter 3
Generic Programming

Templates are a feature of C++ to create functions and classes that operate on parametric (generic) types. As a result, a function or class can work with many different data types without being manually rewritten for each one.

Generic Programming is sometimes considered synonymous with template programming. But this is not correct. Generic programming is a programming paradigm aiming for maximal applicability while providing correctness. Its main tools are templates. Mathematically it is founded on *Formal Concept Analysis* [15]. In generic programming, the template programs are completed with documentation of sufficient conditions for correct usage. One could say that generic programming is the responsible fashion of template programming.

3.1   Function Templates

A *Function Template*—also called a generic function—is a blueprint to generate a potentially infinite number of function overloads. In everyday conversation, the term *Template Function* is more often used than function template, whereas the latter is the correct term from the standard. Within this book, we use both terms and they have the exact same meaning.

Suppose we want to write a function max(x, y) where x and y are variables or expressions of some type. Using function overloading, we can easily do this as follows:

```
int max (int a, int b)          double max (double a, double b)
{                               {
    if (a > b)                      if (a > b)
        return a;                       return a;
    else                            else
        return b;                       return b;
}                               }
```

Note that the function body is exactly the same for both int and double. With the template mechanism, we can write just one generic implementation:

```
template <typename T>
T max (T a, T b)
{
    if (a > b)
        return a;
```

```
    else
        return b;
}
```

This function template replaces the non-template overloads and we keep the name `max`. It can be used in the same fashion as the overloaded functions:

```
std::cout << "The maximum of 3 and 5 is " << max(3, 5) << '\n';
std::cout << "The maximum of 3l and 5l is " << max(3l, 5l) << '\n';
std::cout << "The maximum of 3.0 and 5.0 is " << max(3.0, 5.0) << '\n';
```

In the first case, 3 and 5 are literals of type `int` and the `max` function is *Instantiated* to

```
int max (int, int);
```

Likewise the second and third calls of `max` instantiate:

```
long max (long, long);
double max (double, double);
```

since the literals are interpreted as `long` and `double`. In the same way, the template function can be called with variables and expressions:

```
unsigned u1= 2, u2= 8;
std::cout << "The maximum of u1 and u2 is " << max(u1, u2) << '\n';
std::cout << "The maximum of u1*u2 and u1+u2 is "
          << max(u1*u2, u1+u2) << '\n';
```

Here the function is instantiated for `unsigned`.

    Instead of `typename`, one can also write `class` in this context, but we do not recommend this because `typename` expresses the intention of generic functions better.

3.1.1   Instantiation

What does *Instantiation* mean? For a non-generic function, the compiler reads its definition, checks for errors, and generates executable code. When the compiler processes a generic function's definition, it can only detect errors that are independent of the template parameters like parsing errors. For instance:

```
template <typename T>
inline T max (T a, T b)
{
    if a > b          // Error !
        return a;
    else
        return b;
}
```

would not compile because the `if`-statement without the parentheses is not a legal expression of the C++ grammar.

However, most errors we encounter depend on the substituted types. For instance, the following implementation would compile:

```
template <typename T>
inline T max(T x, T y)
{
    return x < y ? y.value : x.value;
}
```

We could not call it with any intrinsic type like `int` or `double`, but the function template might not be intended for intrinsic types and may work with the actual argument types.

The compilation of the function template itself does not generate any code in the binary. This only happens when we call it. In this case, we instantiate this function template. Only then the compiler performs a complete check of whether the generic function is correct for the given argument type(s). In our previous examples, we saw that `max` can be instantiated with `int` and `double`.

So far, we have seen the most implicit form: the template is instantiated when a call exists and the type parameter is deduced from the arguments. To be more explicit, we can declare the type that substitutes the template parameter, e.g.:

```
std::cout ≪ max<float>(8.1, 9.3) ≪ '\n';
```

Here, the template is explicitly instantiated with a given type. In the most explicit form, we force an instantiation without a function call:

```
template short max<short>(short, short);
```

This can be useful when we generate object files (§7.2.1.3) and must guarantee that certain instances are present, regardless of the function calls in the compile unit.

Definition 3–1. For conciseness, we call an instantiation with type deduction *Implicit Instantiation* and an instantiation with an explicit type declaration *Explicit Instantiation*.

In our experience, implicit instantiation works in most cases as expected. The explicit nomination of the instantiation type is mostly needed for disambiguation and special usages like `std::forward` (§3.1.2.4). For a deeper understanding of templates, it is very helpful to know how the compiler substitutes the types.

3.1.2 Parameter Type Deduction

⇒ c++11/template_type_deduction.cpp

In this section, we will have a closer look at how template parameters are substituted depending on whether the arguments are passed by value, lvalue, or rvalue reference. This knowledge is even more important when variables are declared with an automatic type via `auto` as shown in Section 3.4.1. However, the substitution rules are more intuitive with function parameters than with `auto` variables and we therefore discuss them here.

3.1.2.1   Value Parameters

In the previous example, we used the type parameter T directly as a function parameter in max:

```
template <typename T>
T max (T a, T b);
```

Like any other function parameter, those of function templates can be const- and reference-qualified as well:

```
template <typename T>
T max (const T& a, const T& b);
```

Let us denote this (without loss of generalization) for a unary void function f:

```
template <typename TPara>
void f(FPara p);
```

where FPara contains TPara. When we call f(arg), the compiler has to *Deduce* the type TPara such that parameter p can be initialized with arg. This is the whole story in a nutshell. But let us look at some cases to get a feeling for it. The easiest syntactical case is the equality of TPara and FPara:

```
template <typename TPara>
void f1(TPara p);
```

This means the function parameter is a local copy of the argument. We call f1 with an int literal, an int variable, and a mutable and constant int reference:

```
template <typename TPara>
void f1(TPara p) {}

int main ()
{
    int        i= 0;
    int&       j= i;
    const int& k= i;

    f1(3);
    f1(i);
    f1(j);
    f1(k);
    ...
}
```

In all four instantiations, TPara is substituted with int so that the type of the function parameter p is int as well. If TPara was substituted with int& or const int&, the arguments could be passed in as well. But then we would have no value semantics since a modification of p would affect the function argument (e.g., j). Thus, when the function parameter is a type parameter without qualification, TPara becomes the argument type where all qualifiers are removed. This template function accepts all arguments as long as their types are copyable.

For instance, `unique_ptr` has a deleted copy constructor and can only be passed to this function as an rvalue:

```
unique_ptr<int> up;
// f1(up);            // Error: no copy constructor
f1(move(up));         // Okay: use move constructor
```

3.1.2.2   Lvalue-Reference Parameters

To really accept every argument, we can use a constant reference as a parameter:

```
template <typename TPara>
void f2(const TPara& p) {}
```

TPara is again the argument type with all qualifiers stripped off. Thus, p is a constant reference of the unqualified argument type so we cannot modify p.

A more interesting case is the mutable reference as a parameter:

```
template <typename TPara>
void f3(TPara& p) {}
```

This function rejects all literals and temporaries as they are not referable.[1] We can phrase this also in terms of type substitution: the temporaries are refused because there exists no type for TPara such that TPara& becomes int&& (we will come back to this when we talk about reference collapsing in Section 3.1.2.3).

When we pass in an ordinary int variable like i, TPara is substituted by int so p has the type int& and refers to i. The same substitution can be observed when a mutable reference variable like j is passed. What happens when we pass a const int or const int& like k? Can this be matched with TPara&? Yes, it can, when TPara is substituted with const int. Accordingly, the type of p is const int&. Thus, the type pattern TPara& does not limit the arguments to mutable references. The pattern can match constant references. However, if the function modifies p, the instantiation would fail later.

3.1.2.3   Forward References   `C++11`

In Section 2.3.5.1, we introduced rvalue references that only accept rvalues as arguments. Rvalue references with a type parameter of the form T&& accept lvalues as well. For this reason, Scott Meyers coined the term *Universal Reference* for them. Here we stick with the standard term *Forward Reference*. We will show why they can accept both rvalues and lvalues. To this end, we look at the type substitution of the following unary function:

```
template <typename TPara>
void f4(TPara&& p) {}
```

When we pass an rvalue to this function, e.g.:

```
f4(3);
f4(move(i));
f4(move(up));
```

---

1. Formally, neither literals nor temporaries would be acceptable as const reference parameters for the same reason, but the language makes an exception here for the sake of programmers' convenience.

TPara is substituted by the unqualified argument type—here int and unique_ptr<int>—and the type of p is the corresponding rvalue reference.

When we call f4 with an lvalue like i or j, the compiler accepts these arguments as template rvalue-reference parameters. The type parameter TPara is substituted by int& and this is also the type of p. How is this possible? The explanation is found in Table 3–1, which shows how references of references are collapsed.

The résumé of Table 3–1 is that references are collapsed to an lvalue reference when at least one of them is an lvalue reference (loosely said, very loosely, we can take the minimal number of ampersands). This explains the handling of lvalues in f4. TPara is substituted by int& and an rvalue reference thereof is int&, too.

The lack of type substitution is the reason why the non-template rvalue references do not accept lvalues. The only reason why the function parameter can be an lvalue is that an lvalue reference is introduced by the substitution. Without this substitution, no lvalue reference is involved and references are not collapsed.

A more detailed and more dramatic telling of the whole type deduction story is found in [32, pages 9–35 and 157–214].

C++11 3.1.2.4 Perfect Forwarding

We have already seen that lvalues can be turned into rvalues with move (§2.3.5.4). This time we want to cast them conditionally. A forward reference parameter accepts both rvalue and lvalue arguments that are held by rvalue and lvalue references respectively. When we pass such a reference parameter to another function, we want the lvalue reference to be passed as an lvalue and the rvalue reference as an rvalue. However, the references themselves are lvalues in both cases (since they have names). We could cast a reference to an rvalue with move but this would also apply to an lvalue reference.

Here, we need a conditional cast. This is achieved by std::forward. It casts an rvalue reference into an rvalue and leaves an lvalue as it is. forward must be instantiated with the (unqualified) type parameter, e.g.:

```
template <typename TPara>
void f5(TPara&& p)
{
    f4(forward<TPara>(p));
}
```

The argument of f5 is passed with the same value category to f4. Whatever was passed as an lvalue to f5 is passed as an lvalue to f4; likewise for every rvalue. Like move, forward is a pure cast and does not generate a single machine operation. People have phrased this as: move does not move and forward does not forward. They rather cast their arguments to be moved or forwarded.

Table 3–1: Reference Collapsing

	·&	·&&
T&	T&	T&
T&&	T&	T&&

3.1.3 Dealing with Errors in Templates

Back to our max example that works for all numeric types. But what happens with types that provide no operator>, for instance, std::complex<T>? Let us try to compile the following snippet:[2]

```
std::complex<float>   z(3, 2), c(4, 8);
std::cout << "The maximum of c and z is " << ::max(c, z) << '\n';
```

Our compilation attempt will end in an error like this:

```
Error: no match for »operator>« in »a > b«
```

What happens when our template function calls another template function which in turn calls another one which ... and so on? Likewise, these functions are only parsed and the complete check is delayed until instantiation. Let us look at the following program:

```
int main ()
{
    vector<complex<float> >   v;
    sort(v.begin(), v.end());
}
```

Without going into detail, the problem is the same as before: we cannot compare complex numbers and thus we are unable to sort arrays of them. This time the missing comparison is discovered in an indirectly called function, and the compiler provides us the entire call and include stack so that we can trace back the error. Please try to compile this example on different compilers and see if you can make any sense out of the error messages.

If you run into such a lengthy error message,[3] **don't panic!** First, look at the error itself and take out what is useful for you: e.g., missing operator>, or something not assignable, or something that is const that should not be. Then find in the call stack the innermost code that is the part of your program, i.e., the location where you call a template function from the standard or a third-party library. Stare for a while at this code and its preceding lines because this is the most likely place where the error occurred (in our experience). Then ask yourself: Does a type of the function's template arguments miss an operator or a function according to the error message?

Do not get scared to the point that you decide not to use templates for the rest of your life. In most cases, the problem is much simpler than the never-ending error message makes us believe. In our experience, most errors in template functions can be found faster than run-time errors—with some training.

3.1.4 Mixing Types

Another question that we have not answered so far: What happens with our function max when we use two different types as arguments?

---

2. The double colons in front of max avoid ambiguities with the standard library's max which some compilers may include implicitly (e.g., g++).

3. The longest message we have heard of was 18MB which corresponds to about 9000 pages of text.

```
unsigned u1= 2;
int       i= 3;
std::cout ≪ "The maximum of u1 and i is " ≪ max(u1, i) ≪ '\n';
```

The compiler tells us—this time surprisingly briefly—something like

```
Error: no match for function call ≫max(unsigned int&, int)≪
```

Indeed, we assumed that both types are equal. But wait, does not C++ convert arguments implicitly when no exact match exists? Yes, it does, but not for template arguments. The template mechanism is supposed to provide enough flexibility on the type level. In addition, combining template instantiation with implicit conversion has such a high potential for ambiguities.

So far so bad. Can we write a function template with two template parameters? Of course we can. But this creates a new problem: What should be the return type of this template? There are different options. First, we could add a non-templated function overload like

```
int inline max (int a, int b) { return a > b ? a : b; }
```

This can be called with mixed types and the unsigned argument would be implicitly converted into an int. But what would happen if we also added another function overload for unsigned?

```
int max(unsigned a, unsigned b) { return a > b ? a : b; }
```

Will the int be converted into an unsigned or vice versa? The compiler does not know and will complain about this ambiguity.

At any rate, adding non-templated overloads to the template implementation is far from being elegant or productive. So, we remove all non-template overloads and look first at what we can do in the function call. We can explicitly convert one argument to the type of the other argument:

```
unsigned u1= 2;
int       i= 3;
std::cout ≪ "max of u1 and i is " ≪ max(int(u1), i) ≪ '\n';
```

Now, max is called with two ints. Yet another option is specifying the template type explicitly in the function call:

```
std::cout ≪ "max of u1 and i is " ≪ max<int>(u1, i) ≪ '\n';
```

Then both parameters are int and the function template's instance can be called when both arguments are either int or *implicitly* convertible to int.

After these less pleasant details on templates, some really good news: template functions perform as efficiently as their non-template counterparts! The reason is that C++ generates new code for every type or type combination that the function is called with. Java in contrast compiles templates only once and executes them for different types by casting them to the corresponding types. This results in faster compilation and shorter executables but takes more runtime.

Another price we have to pay for the fast templates is that we have longer executables because of the multiple instantiations for each type (combination). In extreme (and rare)

cases, larger binaries can lead to slower execution when the faster memory[4] is filled with
assembly instructions and the data must be loaded from and stored to slower memory instead.

However, in practice the number of a function's instances will not be that large, and it
only matters for large functions not inlined. For inlined functions, the binary code is at any
rate inserted directly in the executable at the location of the function call so the impact on
the executable length is the same for template and non-template functions.

3.1.5   Uniform Initialization

C++11

Uniform initialization (from §2.3.4) works with templates as well. However, in extremely rare
cases, the brace elimination can cause some astonishing behavior. If you are curious or have
already experienced some surprises, please read Appendix A, Section A.6.1.

3.1.6   Automatic `return` Type

C++14

C++11 introduced lambdas with automatic **return** types whereas the **return** type of functions
is still mandatory. In C++14, we can let the compiler deduce the **return** type:

```
template <typename T, typename U>
inline auto max (T a, U b)
{
    return a > b ? a : b;
}
```

The **return** type is deduced from the expression in the return statement in the same fashion
as parameters of function templates are deduced from the arguments. If the function contains
multiple return statements, their deduced types must all be equal. In template libraries,
sometimes simple functions have rather lengthy **return** type declarations—possibly even
longer than the function body—and it is then a great relief for the programmer not to have
to spell them out.

3.2   Namespaces and Function Lookup

Namespaces are not a sub-topic of generic programming (in fact they are orthogonal to it).
However, they become more important in the presence of function templates, so this is a
good place in the book to talk about them.

3.2.1   Namespaces

The motivation for namespaces is that common names like min, max, or abs can be defined
in different contexts so the names are ambiguous. Even names that are unique when the
function or class is implemented can collide later when more libraries are included or an
included library evolves. For instance, there is typically a class named window in a GUI
implementation, and there might be one in a statistics library. We can distinguish them by
namespaces:

---

4. L2 and L3 caches are usually shared between data and instructions.

```
namespace GUI {
    class window;
}

namespace statistics {
    class window;
}
```

One possibility to deal with name conflicts is using different names like max, my_abs, or library_name_abs. This is in fact what is done in C. Main libraries normally use short function names, user libraries longer names, and OS-related internals typically start with _. This decreases the probability of conflicts, but not sufficiently. Namespaces are very important when we write our own classes and even more so when they are used in function templates. They allow us to hierarchically structure the names in our software. This avoids name clashes and provides sophisticated access control of function and class names.

Namespaces are similar to scopes; i.e., we can see the names in the surrounding namespaces:

```
struct global {};
namespace c1 {
    struct c1c {};
    namespace c2 {
        struct c2c {};
        struct cc {
            global x;
            c1c    y;
            c2c    z;
        };
    } // namespace c2
} // namespace c1
```

Names that are redefined in an inner namespace hide those of the outer ones. In contrast to blocks, we can still refer to these names by *Namespace Qualification*:

```
struct same {};
namespace c1 {
    struct same {};
    namespace c2 {
        struct same {};
        struct csame {
            ::same     x;
            c1::same   y;
            same       z;
        };
    } // namespace c2
} // namespace c1
```

As you have guessed, ::same refers to the type from the global namespace and c1::same to the name in c1. The member variable z has type c1::c2::same since the inner name hides the outer ones. Namespaces are sought from inside out. If we add a namespace c1 in c2, this will hide the outer one with the same name and the type of y is incorrect:

```
struct same {};
namespace c1 {
    struct same {};
    namespace c2 {
        struct same {};
        namespace c1 {}    // hides ::c1
        struct csame {
            ::same     x;
            c1::same   y; // Error: c1::c2::c1::same not defined
            same       z;
        };
    } // namespace c2
} // namespace c1
```

Here, c1::same exists in the global namespace, but since c1 is hidden by c1::c2::c1, we cannot access it. We would observe similar hiding if we defined a class named c1 in namespace c2. We can avoid the hiding and be more explicit about the type of y by placing double colons in front of the namespace:

```
struct csame {
    ::c1::same    y; // this is unique
};
```

This makes clear that we mean the name c1 in the global namespace and not any other name c1. Names of functions or classes that are often needed can be imported with a using declaration:

```
void fun( ... )
{
    using c1::c2::cc;
    cc x;
    ...
    cc y;
}
```

This declaration works in functions and namespaces but not in classes (where it would collide with other using declarations). Importing a name into a namespace within header files considerably increases the danger of name conflicts because the name remains visible in all subsequent files of a compile unit. using within a function (even in header files) is less critical because the imported name is only visible till the end of the function.

Similarly, we can import an entire namespace with a using directive:

```
void fun( ... )
{
    using namespace c1::c2;
    cc x;
    ...
    cc y;
}
```

As before, it can be done within a function or another namespace but not in a class scope. The statement

```
using namespace std;
```

is often the first one in a main function or even the first after the includes. Importing std in the global namespace has good potential for name conflicts, for instance, when we also define a class named vector (in the global namespace). Really problematic is the using directive in header files.

When namespace names are too long for us, especially for nested namespaces, we can rename them with a *Namespace Alias*:

```
namespace lname=  long_namespace_name;
namespace nested= long_namespace_name::yet_another_name::nested;
```

As before, this should be done in an appropriate scope.

3.2.2   Argument-Dependent Lookup

Argument-Dependent Lookup, or ADL, expands the search of function names to the namespaces of their arguments—but not to their respective parent namespaces. This saves us from verbose namespace qualification for functions. Say we write the ultimate scientific library within the modest namespace rocketscience:

```
namespace rocketscience {
    struct matrix {};
    void initialize(matrix& A) { /* ... */ }
    matrix operator+(const matrix& A, const matrix& B)
    {
        matrix C;
        initialize(C); // not qualified, same namespace
        add(A, B, C);
        return C;
    }
}
```

Every time we use the function initialize, we can omit the qualification for all classes in namespace rocketscience:

```
int main ()
{
    rocketscience::matrix A, B, C, D;
    rocketscience::initialize(B); // qualified
    initialize(C);                // rely on ADL

    chez_herbert::matrix E, F, G;
    rocketscience::initialize(E); // qualification needed
    initialize(C);                // Error: initialize not found
}
```

Operators are also subject to ADL:

```
A= B + C + D;
```

Imagine the previous expression without ADL:

```
A= rocketscience::operator+(rocketscience::operator+(B, C), D);
```

Similarly ugly and even more cumbersome is streaming I/O when the namespace must be qualified. Since user code should not be in namespace std::, the operator≪ for a class is preferably defined in that class's namespace. This allows ADL to find the right overload for each type, e.g.:

```
std::cout ≪ A ≪ E ≪ B ≪ F ≪ std::endl;
```

Without ADL we would need to qualify the namespace of each operator in its verbose notation. This would turn the previous expression into

```
std::operator≪(chez_herbert::operator≪(
    rocketscience::operator≪(chez_herbert::operator≪(
        rocketscience::operator≪(std::cout, A), E), B),
    F), std::endl);
```

The ADL mechanism can also be used to select the right function template overload when the classes are distributed over multiple namespaces. The L_1 norm from linear algebra is defined for both matrices and vectors, and we want to provide a template implementation for both:

```
template <typename Matrix>
double one_norm(const Matrix& A) { ... }

template <typename Vector>
double one_norm(const Vector& x) { ... }
```

How can the compiler know which overload we want? One possible solution is to introduce a namespace for matrices and one for vectors so that the correct overload can be selected by ADL:

```
namespace rocketscience {
    namespace mat {
        struct sparse_matrix {};
        struct dense_matrix {};
        struct über_matrix⁵ {};        // Sadly, ü is not allowed in C++ ?

        template <typename Matrix>
        double one_norm(const Matrix& A) { ... }
    }
    namespace vec {
        struct sparse_vector {};
        struct dense_vector {};
        struct über_vector {};

        template <typename Vector>
```

---

5. Of course, we use the original German spelling of *uber*—sometimes even seen in American papers. Please note that special characters like *ü* are not allowed in names.

```
        double one_norm(const Vector& x) { ... }
    }
}
```

The ADL mechanism searches functions only in the namespaces of the arguments' type declarations but not in their respective parent namespaces:

```
namespace rocketscience {
    ...
    namespace vec {
        struct sparse_vector {};
        struct dense_vector {};
        struct über_vector {};
    }
    template <typename Vector>
    double one_norm(const Vector& x) { ... }
}

int main ()
{
    rocketscience::vec::über_vector x;
    double norm_x= one_norm(x);        // Error: not found by ADL
}
```

When we import a name within another namespace, the functions in that namespace are not subject to ADL either:

```
namespace rocketscience {
    ...
    using vec::über_vector;

    template <typename Vector>
    double one_norm(const Vector& x) { ... }
}

int main ()
{
    rocketscience::über_vector x;
    double norm_x= one_norm(x);        // Error: not found by ADL
}
```

Relying on ADL only for selecting the right overload has its limitations. When we use a third-party library, we may find functions and operators that we also implemented in our namespace. Such ambiguities can be reduced (but not entirely avoided) by using only single functions instead of entire namespaces.

The probability of ambiguities rises further with multi-argument functions, especially when parameter types come from different namespaces, e.g.:

```
namespace rocketscience {
    namespace mat {
        ...
        template <typename Scalar, typename Matrix>
        Matrix operator*(const Scalar& a, const Matrix& A) { ... }
    }
    namespace vec {
        ...
        template <typename Scalar, typename Vector>
        Vector operator*(const Scalar& a, const Vector& x) { ... }

        template <typename Matrix, typename Vector>
        Vector operator*(const Matrix& A, const Vector& x) { ... }
    }
}
int main (int argc, char* argv[])
{
    rocketscience::mat::über_matrix A;
    rocketscience::vec::über_vector x, y;
    y= A * x;                        // which overload is selected?
}
```

Here the intention is clear. Well, to human readers. For the compiler it is less so. The type of A is defined in `rocketscience::mat` and that of x in `rocketscience::vec` so that `operator*` is sought in both namespaces. Thus, all three template overloads are available and none of them is a better match than the others (although probably only one would compile).

Unfortunately, explicit template instantiation does not work with ADL. Whenever template arguments are explicitly declared in the function call, the function name is not sought in the namespaces of the arguments.[6]

Which function overload is called depends on the so-far discussed rules on

- Namespace nesting and qualification,

- Name hiding,

- ADL, and

- Overload resolution.

This non-trivial interplay must be understood for frequently overloaded functions to ascertain that no ambiguity occurs and the right overload is selected. Therefore, we give some examples in Appendix A.6.2. Feel free to postpone this discussion until you get baffled with unexpected overload resolutions or ambiguities when dealing with a larger code base.

---

6. The problem is that ADL is performed too late in the compilation and the opening angle bracket is already misinterpreted as less-than. To overcome this issue, the function must be made visible by namespace qualification or import via `using` (more details in §14.8.1.8 of the standard).

3.2.3 Namespace Qualification or ADL

Many programmers do not want to get into the complicated rules of how a compiler picks an overload or runs into ambiguities. They qualify the namespace of the called function and know exactly which function overload is selected (assuming the overloads in that namespace are not ambiguous within the overload resolution). We do not blame them; the name lookup is anything but trivial.

When we plan to write good generic software containing function and class templates instantiatable with many types, we should consider ADL. We will demonstrate this with a very popular performance bug (especially in C++03) that many programmers have run into. The standard library contains a function template called `swap`. It swaps the content of two objects of the same type. The old default implementation used copies and a temporary:

```
template <typename T>
inline void swap(T& x, T& y)
{
    T tmp(x); x= y; y= tmp;
}
```

It works for all types with copy constructor and assignment. So far, so good. Say we have two vectors, each containing 1GB of data. Then we have to copy 3GB and also need a spare gigabyte of memory when we use the default implementation. Or we do something smarter: we switch the pointers referring to the data and the size information:

```
template <typename Value>
class vector
{
    ...
    friend inline void swap(vector& x, vector& y)
    { std::swap(x.my_size, y.my_size); std::swap(x.data, y.data); }
  private:
    unsigned my_size;
    Value    *data;
};
```

Note that this example contains an `inline-friend` function. This declares a free function which is a `friend` of the contained class. Apparently, this is shorter than separate `friend` and function declarations.

Assume we have to swap data of a parametric type in some generic function:

```
template <typename T, typename U>
inline void some_function(T& x, T& y, const U& z, int i)
{
    ...
    std::swap(x, y); // can be expensive
    ...
}
```

We played it safe and used the standard `swap` function which works with all copyable types. But we copied 3GB of data. It would be much faster and memory-efficient to use our implementation that only switches the pointers. This can be achieved with a small change in a generic manner:

```
template <typename T, typename U>
inline void some_function(T& x, T& y, const U& z, int i)
{
    using std::swap;
    ...
    swap(x, y); // involves ADL
    ...
}
```

With this implementation, both swap overloads are candidates but the one in our class is prioritized by overload resolution as its argument type is more specific than that of the standard implementation. More generally, any implementation for a user type is more specific than std::swap. In fact, std::swap is already overloaded for standard containers for the same reason. This is a general pattern:

Use using

Do not qualify namespaces of function templates for which user-type overloads might exist. Make the name visible instead and call the function unqualified.

As an addendum to the default swap implementation: Since C++11, the default is to move the values between the two arguments and the temporary:

$\boxed{\text{C++11}}$

```
template <typename T>
inline void swap(T& x, T& y)
{
    T tmp(move(x));
    x= move(y);
    y= move(tmp);
}
```

As a result, types without user-defined swap can be swapped efficiently when they provide a fast move constructor and assignment. Only types without user implementation and move support are finally copied.

3.3 Class Templates

In the previous section, we described the use of templates to create generic functions. Templates can also be used to create generic classes. Analogous to generic functions, class template is the correct term from the standard whereas template class (or templated class) is more frequently used in daily life. In these classes, the types of data members can be parameterized.

This is in particular useful for general-purpose container classes like vectors, matrices, and lists. We could also extend the complex class with a parametric value type. However, we have already spent so much time with this class that it seems more entertaining to look at something else.

3.3.1　A Container Example

⇒ c++11/vector_template.cpp

Let us, for example, write a generic vector class, in the sense of linear algebra not like an STL vector. First, we implement a class with the most fundamental operators only:

Listing 3–1: Template vector class

```cpp
template <typename T>
class vector
{
  public:
    explicit vector(int size)
      : my_size(size), data( new Tmy_size] )
    {}

    vector(const vector& that)
      : my_size(that.my_size), data(new T[my_size])
    {
        std::copy(&that.data[0], &that.data[that.my_size], &data[0]);
    }

    int size() const { return my_size; }

    const T& operator[](int i) const
    {
        check_index(i);
        return data[i];
    }
    // ...

  private:
    int                 my_size;
    std::unique_ptr<T[]> data;
};
```

The template class is not essentially different from a non-template class. There is only the extra parameter T as a placeholder for the type of its elements. We have member variables like my_size and member functions size() that are not affected by the template parameter. Other functions like the bracket operator or the copy constructor are parameterized, still resembling their non-template equivalent: wherever we had double before, we put the type parameter T as for **return** types or in allocations. Likewise, the member variable data is just parameterized by T.

Template parameters can be defaulted. Assume that our vector class parameterizes not only the value type, but also orientation and location:

```cpp
struct row_major {}; // just for tagging
struct col_major {}; // ditto
struct heap {};
```

```
struct stack {};

template <typename T= double, typename Orientation= col_major,
          typename Where= heap>
class vector;
```

The arguments of a vector can be fully declared:

```
vector<float, row_major, heap>  v;
```

The last argument is equal to the default value and can be omitted:

```
vector<float, row_major>  v;
```

As for functions, only the final arguments can be omitted. For instance, if the second argument is the default and the last one is not, we must write them all:

```
vector<float, col_major, stack>  w;
```

When all template parameters are set to default values, we can of course omit them all. However, for grammar reasons not discussed here, the angle brackets still need to be written:

```
vector    x; // Error: it is considered a non-template class
vector<>  y; // looks a bit strange but is correct
```

Other than the defaults of function arguments, the template defaults can refer to preceding parameters:

```
template <typename T, typename U= T>
class pair;
```

This is a class for two values that might have different types. If not we can declare the type just once:

```
pair<int, float>  p1;  // object with an int and float value
pair<int>         p2;  // object with two int values
```

The default can even be expressions of preceding parameters as we will see in Chapter 5.

3.3.2 Designing Uniform Class and Function Interfaces

⇒ c++03/accumulate_example.cpp

When we write generic classes and functions, we can ask ourselves the chicken-and-egg question: what comes first? We have the choice to write function templates first and adapt our classes to them by realizing the corresponding methods. Alternatively, we can develop the interface of our classes first and implement generic functions against this interface.

The situation changes a little bit when our generic functions should be able to handle intrinsic types or classes from the standard library. These classes cannot be changed, and we should adapt our functions to their interface. There are other options that we will introduce later: specialization and meta-programming, which allow for type-dependent behavior.

As a case study, we use the function accumulate from the Standard Template Library, Section 4.1. It was developed at a time when programmers used pointers and ordinary arrays even more frequently than today. Thus, the STL creators Alex Stepanov and David Musser established an extremely versatile interface that works for pointers and arrays as well as on all containers of their library.

3.3.2.1   Genuine Array Summation

In order to sum the entries of an array generically, the first thing that comes to mind is probably a function taking the address and size of the array:

```
template <typename T>
T sum(const T* array, int n)
{
    T sum(0);
    for (int i= 0; i < n; ++i)
        sum+= array[i];
    return sum;
}
```

This function can be called as expected:

```
int    ai[]= {2, 4, 7};
double di[]= {2., 4.5, 7.};

cout << "sum ai is " << sum(ai, 3) << '\n';
cout << "sum ad is " << sum(ad, 3) << '\n';
```

However, we might wonder why we need to pass the size of the array. Could not the compiler deduce it for us? After all, it is known during compilation. In order to use compiler deduction, we introduce a template parameter for the size and pass the array by reference:

```
template <typename T, unsigned N> // more about non-type templates in §3.7
T sum(const T (&array)[N])
{
    T sum(0);
    for (int i= 0; i < N; ++i)
        sum+= array[i];
    return sum;
}
```

The syntax looks admittedly a bit strange: we need the parentheses to declare a reference of an array as opposed to an array of references. This function can be called with a single argument:

```
cout << "sum ai is " << sum(ai) << '\n';
cout << "sum ad is " << sum(ad) << '\n';
```

Now, the type and the size are deduced. This in turn means that if we sum over two arrays of the same type and different size, the function will be instantiated twice. Nonetheless, it should not affect the executable size since such small functions are usually inlined anyway.

3.3.2.2   Summing List Entries

A list is a simple data structure whose elements contain a value and a reference to the next element (and sometimes to the previous one, too). In the C++ standard library, the class template std::list is a double-linked list (§4.1.3.3), and a list without back-references was introduced in C++11 as std::forward_list. Here, we only consider forward references:

```
template <typename T>
struct list_entry
{
    list_entry(const T& value) : value(value), next(0) {}

    T               value;
    list_entry<T>* next;
};

template <typename T>
struct list
{
    list() : first(0), last(nullptr) {}
    ~list()
    {
        while (first) {
            list_entry<T> *tmp= first->next;
            delete first;
            first= tmp;
        }
    }
    void append(const T& x)
    {
        last= (first? last->next : first)= new list_entry<T>(x);
    }
    list_entry<T> *first, *last;
};
```

This list implementation is actually really minimalistic and a bit terse. With the interface at hand, we can set up a small list:

```
list<float>  l;
l.append(2.0f); l.append(4.0f); l.append(7.0f);
```

Please feel free to enrich our code with useful methods like the initializer_list construction.

A summation function for this list is straightforward:

Listing 3–2: Sum of list entries

```
template <typename T>
T sum(const list<T>& l)
{
    T sum= 0;
    for (auto entry= l.first; entry != nullptr; entry= entry->next)
        sum+= entry->value;
    return sum;
}
```

and can be called in the obvious way. We highlighted the details that differ from the array implementation.

3.3.2.3 Commonalities

When we are aiming for a common interface, we first have to ask ourselves: How similar are these two implementations of sum? At first glance not very:

- The values are accessed differently;

- The traversal of the entries is realized differently; and

- The termination criterion is different.

However, on a more abstract level, both functions perform the same tasks:

- Access of data

- Progress to the next entry

- Check for the end

The difference between the two implementations is how these tasks are realized with the given interfaces of the types. Thus, in order to provide a single generic function for both types, we have to establish a common interface.

3.3.2.4 Alternative Array Summation

In Section 3.3.2.1, we accessed the array in an index-oriented style that cannot be applied on lists arbitrarily dispersed in memory—at least not efficiently. Therefore, we reimplement the array summation here in a more sequential style with a stepwise traversal. We can achieve this by incrementing pointers until we pass the end of the array. The first address beyond the array is &a[n] or, more concisely with pointer arithmetic, a + n. Figure 3–1 illustrates that we start our traversal at the address of a and stop when we reach a+n. Thus, we specify the range of entries by a right-open interval of addresses.

When software is written for maximal applicability, right-open intervals turn out to be more versatile than closed intervals, especially for types like lists where positions are represented by memory addresses randomly allocated. The summation over a right-open interval can be implemented as shown in Listing 3–3.

Listing 3–3: Sum of array entries

```
template <typename T>
inline T accumulate_array(T* a, T* a_end)
{
    T sum(0);
    for (; a != a_end; ++a)
```

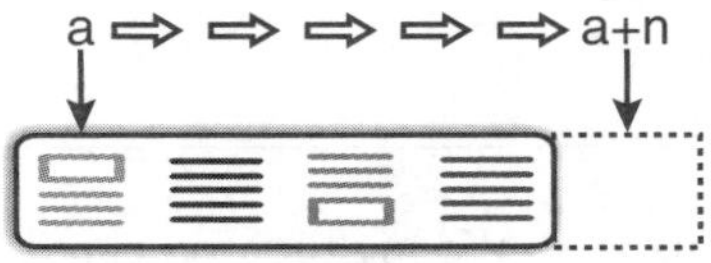

Figure 3–1: An array of length n with begin and end pointers

```
        sum+= *a;
    return sum;
}
```

and used as follows:

```
int main (int argc, char* argv[])
{
    int    ai[]= {2, 4, 7};
    double ad[]= {2., 4.5, 7.};

    cout << "sum ai is " << accumulate_array(ai, &ai[3]) << '\n';
    cout << "sum ad is " << accumulate_array(ad, ad+3) << '\n';
```

A pair of pointers representing a right-open interval as above is a *Range*: a very important concept in C++. Many algorithms in the standard library are implemented for ranges of pointer-like objects in a similar style to `accumulate_array`. To use such functions for new containers, we only need to provide this pointer-like interface. As an example, we will now demonstrate for our list how we can adapt its interface.

3.3.2.5 Generic Summation

The two summation functions in Listing 3–2 and Listing 3–3 look quite different because they are written for different interfaces. Functionally, they are not so different.

In Section 3.3.2.3, we stated about the `sum` implementations from Section 3.3.2.1 and Section 3.3.2.2:

- They both traverse the sequence from one element to the next.

- They both access the value of the current element and add it to `sum`.

- They both test whether the end of the sequence is reached.

The same holds for our revised array implementation in Section 3.3.2.4. However, the latter uses an interface with a more abstract notion of incrementally traversing a sequence. As a consequence, it is possible to apply it to another sequence like a `list` when it provides this sequential interface.

The ingenious idea of Alex Stepanov and David Musser in STL was to introduce a common interface for all container types and traditional arrays. This interface consisted of generalized pointers called *Iterators*. Then all algorithms were implemented for those iterators. We will discuss this more extensively in Section 4.1.2 and give only a little foretaste here.

⇒ c++03/accumulate_example.cpp

What we need now is an iterator for our `list` that provides the necessary functionality in a pointer-like syntax, namely:

- Traverse the sequence with ++it;

- Access a value with *it; and

- Compare iterators with == or !=.

The implementation is straightforward:

```
template <typename T>
struct list_iterator
{
    using value_type= T;

    list_iterator(list_entry<T>* entry) : entry(entry) {}

    T& operator*() { return entry->value; }

    const T& operator*operator*() const
    { return entry->value; }

    list_iterator<T> operator++()
    { entry= entry->next; return *this; }

    bool operator!=(const list_iterator<T>& other) const
    { return entry != other.entry; }

    list_entry<T>* entry;
};
```

and for convenience, to add a begin and end method to our list:

```
template <typename T>
struct list
{
    list_iterator<T> begin() { return list_iterator<T>(first); }
    list_iterator<T> end() { return list_iterator<T>(0); }
}
```

The list_iterator allows us to merge Listing 3–2 and Listing 3–3 together to accumulate:

Listing 3–4: Generic summation

```
template <typename Iter, typename T>
inline T accumulate(Iter it, Iter end, T init)
{
    for (; it != end; ++it)
        init+= *it;
    return init;
}
```

This generic sum can be used in the following form for both arrays and lists:

```
cout << "array sum = " << sum(a, a+10, 0.0) << '\n';
cout << "list sum = " << sum(l.begin(), l.end(), 0) << '\n';
```

As before, the key to success was finding the right abstraction: the iterator.

The `list_iterator` implementation is also a good opportunity to finally answer the question why iterators should be pre- and not post-incremented. We have already seen that the pre-increment updates the `entry` member and returns a reference to the iterator. The post-increment must return the old value and increment its internal state such that the following list entry is referred to when the iterator is used next time. Unfortunately, this can only be achieved when the post-increment operation copies the entire iterator before changing member data and returns this copy:

```
template <typename T>
struct list_iterator
{
    list_iterator<T> operator++(int)
    {
        list_iterator<T> tmp(*this);
        p= p->next;
        return tmp;
    }
};
```

Often we call the increment operation only to pass to the next entry and don't care about the value returned by the operation. Then it is just a waste of resources to create an iterator copy that is never used. A good compiler might optimize away the surplus operations but there is no point in taking chances. A funny detail of the post-increment definition is the fake `int` parameter that is only present for distinction from the pre-increment definition.

3.4 Type Deduction and Definition

C++ compilers already deduce types automatically in C++03 for arguments of function templates. Let `f` be a template function and we call

```
f(g(x, y, z) + 3 * x)
```

Then the compiler can deduce the type of `f`'s argument.

3.4.1 Automatic Variable Type C++11

When we assign the result of an expression like the preceding one to a variable, we need to know the type of this expression in C++03. On the other hand, if we assign to a type to which the result is not convertible, the compiler will let us know while providing the incompatible types. This shows that the compiler knows the type, and in C++11, this knowledge is shared with the programmer.

The easiest way to use the type information in the previous example is the `auto`-matic variable type:

```
auto a= f(g(x, y, z) + 3 * x);
```

This does not change the fact that C++ is strongly typed. The `auto` type is different from dynamic types in other languages like Python. In Python, an assignment to a can change the type of a, namely, to that of the assigned expression. In C++11, the variable a has the type of the expression's result, and this type will never change afterward. Thus, the `auto` type is not an automatic type that adapts to everything that is assigned to the variable but is determined once only.

We can declare multiple `auto` variables in the same statement as long as they are all initialized with an expression of the same type:

```
auto i= 2 * 7.5, j= std::sqrt(3.7); // okay: both are double
auto i= 2 * 4, j= std::sqrt(3.7);   // Error: i is int, j double
auto i= 2 * 4, j;                   // Error: j not initialized
auto v= g(x, y, z);                 // result of f
```

We can qualify `auto` with `const` and reference attributes:

```
auto&       ri= i;          // reference on i
const auto& cri= i;         // constant reference on i
auto&&      ur= g(x, y, z); // forward reference to result of f
```

The type deduction with `auto` variables works exactly like the deduction of function parameters, as described in Section 3.1.2. This means, for instance, that the variable v is not a reference even when g returns a reference. Likewise, the universal reference ur is either an rvalue or an lvalue reference depending on the result type of f being an rvalue or lvalue (reference).

C++11 ### 3.4.2 Type of an Expression

The other new feature in C++11 is `decltype`. It is like a function that returns the type of an expression. If f in the first `auto` example returns a value, we could also express it with `decltype`:

```
decltype(f(g(x, y, z) + 3 * x)) a= f(g(x, y, z) + 3 * x);
```

Obviously, this is too verbose and thus not very useful in this context.

The feature is very important in places where an explicit type is needed: first of all as a template parameter for class templates. We can, for instance, declare a vector whose elements can hold the sum of two other vectors' elements, e.g., the type of v1[0] + v2[0]. This allows us to express the appropriate `return` type for the sum of two vectors of different types:

```
template <typename Vector1, typename Vector2>
auto operator+(const Vector1& v1, const Vector2& v2)
  -> vector< decltype(v1[0] + v2[0]) >;
```

This code snippet also introduces another new feature: *Trailing Return Type*. In C++11, we are still obliged to declare the `return` type of every function. With `decltype`, it can be more handy to express it in terms of the function arguments. Therefore, we can move the declaration of the `return` type behind the arguments.

The two vectors may have different types and the resulting vector yet another one. With the expression `decltype(v1[0] + v2[0])` we deduce what type we get when we add elements of both vectors. This type will be the element type for our resulting vector.

An interesting aspect of `decltype` is that it only operates on the type level and does not evaluate the expression given as an argument. Thus, the expression from the previous example does not cause an error for empty vectors because `v1[0]` is not performed but only its type is determined.

The two features `auto` and `decltype` differ not only in their application; the type deduction is also different. While `auto` follows the rules of function template parameters and often drops reference and `const` qualifiers, `decltype` takes the expression type as it is. For instance, if the function `f` in our introductory example returned a reference, the variable `a` would be a reference. A corresponding `auto` variable would be a value.

As long as we mainly deal with intrinsic types, we get along without automatic type detection. But with advanced generic and meta-programming, we can greatly benefit from these extremely powerful features.

3.4.3 `decltype(auto)`

C++14

This new feature closes the gap between `auto` and `decltype`. With `decltype(auto)`, we can declare `auto` variables that have the same type as with `decltype`. The following two declarations are identical:

```
decltype(expr) v= expr;    // redundant + verbose when expr long
decltype(auto) v= expr;    // Ahh! Much better.
```

The first statement is quite verbose: everything we add to `expr` we have to add twice in the statement. And with every modification we must pay attention that the two expressions are still identical.

⇒ c++14/value_range_vector.cpp

The preservation of qualifiers is also important in automatic **return** types. As an example we introduce a view on vectors that tests whether the values are in a given range. The view will access an element of the viewed vector with `operator[]` and return it after the range test with exactly the same qualifiers. Obviously a job for `decltype(auto)`. Our example implementation of this view only contains a constructor and the access operator:

```
template <typename Vector>
class value_range_vector
{
    using value_type= typename Vector::value_type;
    using size_type=  typename Vector::size_type;
  public:
    value_range_vector(Vector& vref, value_type minv, value_type maxv)
      : vref(vref), minv(minv), maxv(maxv)
    {}

    decltype(auto) operator[](size_type i)
    {
```

```
        decltype(auto) value= vref[i];
        if (value < minv) throw too_small{};
        if (value > maxv) throw too_large{};
        return value;
    }
  private:
    Vector&     vref;
    value_type minv, maxv;
};
```

Our access operator caches the element from vref for the range checks before it is returned. Both the type of the temporary and the **return** type are deduced with decltype(auto). To test that vector elements are returned with the right type, we store one in a decltype(auto) variable and inspect its type:

```
int main ()
{
    using Vec= mtl::vector<double>;
    Vec v= {2.3, 8.1, 9.2};

    value_range_vector<Vec> w(v, 1.0, 10.0);
    decltype(auto) val= w[1];
}
```

The type of val is double& as wanted. The example uses decltype(auto) three times: twice in the view implementation and once in the test. If we replaced only one of them with auto, the type of val would become double.

C++11   3.4.4   Defining Types

There are two ways to define types: with typedef or with using. The former was introduced in C and existed in C++ from the beginning. This is also its only advantage: backward compatibility.[7] For writing new software without the need of compiling with pre-11 compilers, we highly recommend you

---

Advice
Use using instead of typedef.

It is more readable and more powerful. For simple type definitions, it is just a question of order:

```
typedef double value_type;
```

versus

```
using value_type= double;
```

---

7. This is the only reason why examples in this book sometimes still use typedef.

In a using declaration, the new name is positioned on the left while a typedef puts it on the right side. For declaring an array, the new type name is not the right-most part of a typedef and the type is split into two parts:

```
typedef double da1[10];
```

In contrast to it, within the using declaration, the type remains in one piece:

```
using da2= double[10];
```

The difference becomes even more pronounced for function (pointer) types—which you will hopefully never need in type definitions. std::function in §4.4.2 is a more flexible alternative. For instance, declaring a function with a float and an int argument that returns a float reads

```
typedef float float_fun1(float, int);
```

versus

```
using float_fun2= float (float, int);
```

In all these examples, the using declaration clearly separates the new type name from the definition.

In addition, the using declaration allows us to define *Template Aliases*. These are definitions with type parameters. Assume we have a template class for tensors of arbitrary order and parameterizable value type:

```
template <unsigned Order, typename Value>
class tensor { ... };
```

Now we like to introduce the type names vector and matrix for tensors of first and second order, respectively. This cannot be achieved with typedef but easily by template aliases via using:

```
template <typename Value>
using vector= tensor<1, Value>;

template <typename Value>
using matrix= tensor<2, Value>;
```

When we throw the output of the following lines:

```
std::cout << "type of vector<float> is "
          << typeid(vector<float>).name() << '\n';
std::cout << "type of matrix<float> is "
          << typeid(matrix<float>).name() << '\n';
```

into a name demangler, we will see

```
type of vector<float> is tensor<1u, float>
type of matrix<float> is tensor<2u, float>
```

Resuming, if you have experience with typedef, you will appreciate the new opportunities in C++11, and if you are new in the type definition business, you should start with using right away.

3.5   A Bit of Theory on Templates: Concepts

"Gray, dear friend, is all theory and green the life's golden tree."[8]

—Johann Wolfgang von Goethe

In the previous sections, you might have gotten the impression that template parameters can be substituted by any type. This is in fact not entirely true. The programmer of template classes and functions makes assumptions about the operations that can be performed on the template arguments.

Thus, it is very important to know which argument types are acceptable. We have seen, for instance, that `accumulate` can be instantiated with `int` or `double`. Types without addition like a solver class (on page 74) cannot be used for `accumulate`. What should be accumulated from a set of solvers? All the requirements for the template parameter `T` of function `accumulate` can be summarized as follows:

- `T` is copy-constructable: `T a(b);` is compilable when the type of `b` is `T`.

- `T` is plus-assignable: `a+= b;` compiles when the type of `a` and `b` is `T`.

- `T` can be constructed from `int`: `T a(0);` compiles.

Such a set of type requirements is called a *Concept*. A concept `CR` that contains all requirements of concept `C` and possibly additional requirements is called a *Refinement* of `C`. A type `t` that holds all requirements of concept `C` is called a *Model* of `C`. Plus-assignable types are, for instance, `int`, `float`, `double`, and even `string`.

A complete definition of a template function or class should contain the list of required concepts as is done for functions from the Standard Template Library; see `http://www.sgi.com/tech/stl/`.

Today such requirements are only documentation. Future C++ standards will most likely support concepts as a central language feature. A technical specification mainly by Andrew Sutton, "C++ Extensions for Concepts," [46] is in progress and may be part of C++17.

3.6   Template Specialization

On one hand, it is a great advantage that we can use the same implementation for many arguments types. For some argument types we may, however, know a more efficient implementation, and this can be realized in C++ with *Template Specialization*. In principle, we could even implement an entirely different behavior for certain types at the price of utter confusion. Thus, the specialization will be more efficient but behave the same. C++ provides enormous flexibility, and we as programmers are in charge of using this flexibility responsibly and of being consistent with ourselves.

---

8. Author's translation. Original: "Grau, teurer Freund, ist alle Theorie und grün des Lebens goldner Baum."

3.6.1 Specializing a Class for One Type

⇒ c++11/vector_template.cpp

In the following, we want to specialize our vector example from Listing 3.3.1 for bool. Our goal is to save memory by packing 8 bool values into one byte. Let us start with the class definition:

```
template <>
class vector<bool>
{
    // ..
};
```

Although our specialized class is not type-parametric anymore, we still need the template keyword and the empty triangle brackets. The name vector was declared to be a class template before, and we need this seemingly surplus template notation to show that the following definition is a specialization of the *Primary Template*. Thus, defining or declaring a template specialization before the primary template is an error. In a specialization, we must provide within the angle brackets a type for each template parameter. These values may be parameters themselves (or expressions thereof). For instance, if we specialize for one out of three parameters, the two others are still declared as template parameters:

```
template <template T1, template T3>
class some_container<T1, int, T3>
{
    // ..
};
```

Back to our boolean vector class: our primary template defines a constructor for an empty vector and one containing n elements. For the sake of consistency, we should define the same. With the non-empty vector, we have to round up the data size when the number of bits is not divisible by 8:

```
template <>
class vector<bool>
{
  public:
    explicit vector(int size)
      : my_size(size), data(new unsigned char*(my_size+7) / 8*)
    {}
    vector() : my_size(0) {}
  private:
    int                              my_size;
    std::unique_ptr<unsigned char[]> data;
};
```

You may have noticed that the default constructor is identical to that of the primary template. Unfortunately, the method is not "inherited" to the specialization. Whenever we write a specialization, we have to define everything from scratch or use a common base class.[9]

---

9. The author is trying to overcome this verbosity in future standards [16].

We are free to omit member functions or variables from the primary template, but for the sake of consistency we should do this only for good reasons, for *very good* reasons. For instance, we might omit the operator+ because we have no addition for bool. The constant access operator is implemented with shifting and bit masking:

```
template <> class vector<bool>
{
    bool operator[](int i) const
    { return (data[i/8] ≫ i%8) & 1; }
};
```

The mutable access is trickier because we cannot refer to a single bit. The trick is to return a *Proxy* which provides read and write operations for a single bit:

```
template <> class vector<bool>
{
    vector_bool_proxy operator[](int i)
    vector_bool_proxy operator[](int i)
    { return {data[i/8], i%8};    }
};
```

The return statement uses a braced list to call the two-argument constructor. Let us now implement our proxy to manage a specific bit within vector<bool>. Obviously, the class needs a reference to the containing byte and the position within this byte. To simplify further operations, we create a mask that has one bit on the position in question and zero bits on all other positions:

```
class vector_bool_proxy
{
  public:
    vector_bool_proxy(unsigned char& byte, int p)
      : byte(byte), mask(1 ≪ p) {}

  private:
    unsigned char& byte;
    unsigned char  mask;
};
```

The reading access is realized with a conversion to bool where we simply mask the referred byte:

```
class vector_bool_proxy
{
    operator bool() const { return byte & mask; }
};
```

Only when the considered bit is 1 in byte, the bitwise AND yields a non-zero value that is evaluated to true in the conversion from unsigned char to bool.

Setting a bit is realized by an assignment operator for bool:

```
class vector_bool_proxy
{
```

```
    vector_bool_proxy& operator=(bool b)
    {
        if (b)
            byte|= mask;
        else
            byte&= ~mask;
        return *this;
    }
};
```

The assignment is simpler to implement when we distinguish between the assigned values. When the argument is `true`, we apply an OR with the mask so that the bit in the considered position is switched on. All other positions remain unchanged since OR with 0 has no effect (0 is the identity element of bitwise OR). Conversely, with `false` as an argument, we first invert the mask and apply it with AND to the byte reference. Then the mask's zero bit on the active position turns the bit off. On all other positions, the AND with one bit conserves the old bit values.

With this specialization of `vector` for `bool`, we use only about an eighth of the memory. Nonetheless, our specialization is (mostly) consistent with the primary template: we can create vectors and read and write them in the same fashion. To be honest, the compressed vector is not perfectly identical to the primary template, e.g., when we take references of elements or when type deduction is involved. However, we made the specialization as similar as possible to the generic version and in most situations we will not realize the differences and it will work in the same way.

3.6.2   Specializing and Overloading Functions

In this section, we discuss and assess the advantages and disadvantages of template specialization for functions.

3.6.2.1   Specializing a Function to a Specific Type

Functions can be specialized in the same manner as classes. Unfortunately, they do not participate in overload resolution, and a less specific overload is prioritized over the more specific template specialization; see [44]. For that reason Sutter and Alexandrescu give in [45, Item 66] the following:

Advice

Do not use function template specialization!

To provide a special implementation for one specific type or type tuple as above, we can simply use overloading. This works better and is even simpler, e.g.:

```
#include <cmath>

template <typename Base, typename Exponent>
Base inline power(const Base& x, const Exponent& y) {  ...  }
```

```
double inline power(double x, double y)
{
    return std::pow(x, y);
}
```

Functions with many specializations are best implemented by means of class specialization. This allows for full and partial specialization without taking all overloading and ADL rules into consideration. We will show this in Section 3.6.4.

If you ever feel tempted to write hardware-specific specializations in assembler code, try to resist. If you cannot, please read first the few remarks in Appendix A.6.3.

3.6.2.2   Ambiguities

In the previous examples, we specialized all parameters of the function. It is also possible to specialize some of them in overloads and leave the remaining parameter(s) as template(s):

```
template <typename Base, typename Exponent>
Base inline power(const Base& x, const Exponent& y);

template <typename Base>
Base inline power(const Base& x, int y);

template <typename Exponent>
double inline power(double x, const Exponent& y);
```

The compiler will find all overloads that match the argument combination and select the most specific, which is supposed to provide the most efficient special-case implementation. For instance, power(3.0, 2u) will match for the first and third overload where the latter is more specific. To put it in terms of higher math:[10] type specificity is a partial order that forms a lattice, and the compiler picks the maximum of the available overloads. However, you do not need to dive deeply into algebra to see which type or type combination is more specific.

If we called power(3.0, 2) with the previous overloads, all three would match. However, this time we cannot determine the most specific overload. The compiler will tell us that the call is ambiguous and show us overloads 2 and 3 as candidates. As we implemented the overloads consistently and with optimal performance we might be happy with either choice but the compiler will not choose. To disambiguate, we must add a fourth overload:

```
double inline power(double x, int y);
```

The lattice experts will immediately say: "Of course, we were missing the join in the specificity lattice." But even without this expertise, most of us understand why the call was ambiguous with the three overloads and why the fourth one rescued us. In fact, the majority of C++ programmers get along without studying lattices.

---

10. For those who like higher mathematics. And only for those.

3.6.3 Partial Specialization

When we implement template classes, we will sooner or later run into situations where we want to specialize a template class for another template class. Suppose we have a template complex and vector and want to specialize the latter for all instances of complex. It would be quite annoying doing this one by one:

```
template <>
class vector<complex<float> >;

template <>
class vector<complex<double> >;        // again ??? :-/

template <>
class vector<complex<long double> >; // how many more ??? :-P
```

This is not only inelegant, it also destroys our ideal of universal applicability because the complex class supports all Real types and our specialization above only takes a limited number thereof into account. In particular, instances of complex with future user types cannot be considered for obvious reasons.

The solution that avoids the implementation redundancy and the ignorance of new types is *Partial Specialization*. We specialize our vector class for all complex instantiations:

```
template <typename Real>
class vector<complex<Real> >
{   ...   };
```

If you use a compiler without C++11 support, pay attention to put spaces between closing >; otherwise your compiler may interpret two subsequent > as shift operator ≫, leading to rather confusing errors. Although this book mainly addresses C++11 programming, we still keep the separating spaces for readability.

C++03

Partial specialization also works for classes with multiple parameters, for instance:

```
template <typename Value, typename Parameters>
class vector<sparse_matrix<Value, Parameters> >
{   ...   };
```

We can also specialize for all pointers:

```
template <typename T>
class vector<T*>
{   ...   };
```

Whenever the set of types is expressible by a *Type Pattern*, we can apply partial specialization on it.

Partial template specialization can be combined with regular template specialization from §3.6.1—let us call it *Full Specialization* for distinction. In this case, the full specialization is prioritized over the partial one. Between different partial specializations the most specific is selected. In the following example:

```
template <typename Value, typename Parameters>
class vector<sparse_matrix<Value, Parameters> >
{   ...   };
```

```
template <typename Parameters>
class vector<sparse_matrix<float, Parameters> > {    ...    };
```

the second specialization is more specific than the first one and picked when it matches. In fact, a full specialization is always more specific than any partial one.

3.6.4 Partially Specializing Functions

Function templates actually cannot be specialized partially. We can, however, as for the full specialization (§3.6.2.1), use overloading to provide special implementations. For that purpose, we write more specific function templates that are prioritized when they match. As an example, we overload the generic abs with an implementation for all complex instances:

```
template <typename T>
inline T abs(const T& x)
{
    return x < T(0) ? -x : x;
}

template <typename T>
inline T abs(const std::complex<T>& x)
{
    return sqrt(real(x)*real(x) + imag(x)*imag(x));
}
```

Overloading of function templates is easy to implement and works reasonably well. However, for massively overloaded functions or for overloads spread over many files of a large project, sometimes the intended overload is not called. The reason is the non-trivial interplay of the already challenging namespace resolution with the overload resolution of mixed template and non-template functions.

⇒ c++14/abs_functor.cpp

To ascertain a predictable specialization behavior, it is safest to implement it internally in terms of class template specialization and only provide a single function template as a user interface. The challenging part here is the return type of this single function when the return types for the specializations vary. As in our abs example: the general code returns the argument type while the more specific complex version returns the underlying value type. This can be handled in a portable way so that it works even with C++03. The newer standards, however, provide features to simplify this task.

C++14   We start with the easiest implementation by using C++14:

```
template <typename T> struct abs_functor;

template <typename T>
decltype(auto) abs(const T& x)
{
    return abs_functor<T>()(x);
}
```

Our generic abs function creates an anonymous object abs_functor<T>() and calls its operator() with the argument x. Thus, the corresponding specialization of abs_functor needs a default constructor (usually implicitly generated) and an operator() as a unary function accepting an argument of type T. The return type of operator() is automatically deduced. For abs, we could most likely deduce the return type with auto instead since all different specializations should return a value. Just for the unlikely case that some specialization might be const- or reference-qualified, we use decltype(auto) to pass on the qualifiers.

When we program with C++11, we have to declare the return type explicitly. At least, this declaration can apply type deduction: `C++11`

```
template <typename T>
auto abs(const T& x) -> decltype(abs_functor<T>()(x))
{
    return abs_functor<T>()(x);
}
```

It is admittedly redundant to repeat abs_functor<T>()(x) and any redundancy is a potential source of inconsistency.

Back in C++03, we cannot use type deduction at all for the return type. Thus, the functor must provide it, say, by a typedef named result_type: `C++03`

```
template <typename T>
typename abs_functor<T>::result_type
abs(const T& x)
{
    return abs_functor<T>()(x);
}
```

Here we have to rely on the implementor(s) of abs_functor that result_type is consistent with the return type of operator().

Finally, we implement the functor with a partial specialization for complex<T>:

```
template <typename T>
struct abs_functor
{
    typedef T result_type;

    T operator()(const T& x)
    {
        return x < T(0) ? -x : x;
    }
};

template <typename T>
struct abs_functor<std::complex<T> >
{
    typedef T result_type;

    T operator()(const std::complex<T>& x)
    {
```

```
        return sqrt(real(x)*real(x) + imag(x)*imag(x));
    }
};
```

This is a portable implementation working with all three implementations of abs. When we drop the support for C++03, we can omit the typedef in the templates. This abs_functor can be specialized further for any reasonable type pattern without the trouble we may run into with massively overloaded functions.

3.7   Non-Type Parameters for Templates

So far, we have used template parameters only for types. Values can be template arguments as well. Not all values but all integral types, i.e., integer numbers and bool. For completeness, pointers are also allowed but we will not explore this here.

$\Rightarrow$ c++11/fsize_vector.cpp

Very popular is the definition of short vectors and small matrices with the size as a template parameter:

```
template <typename T, int Size>
class fsize_vector
{
    using self= fsize_vector;
  public:
    using value_type= T;
    const static int      my_size= Size;

    fsize_vector(int s= Size) { assert(s == Size); }

    self& operator=(const self& that)
    {
        std::copy(that.data, that.data + Size, data);
        return *this;
    }

    self operator+(const self& that) const
    {
        self sum;
        for (int i= 0; i < my_size; ++i)
            sum[i]= data[i] + that[i];
        return sum;
    }
    // ...

  private:
    T      data[my_size];
};
```

Since the size is already provided as a template parameter, we do not need to pass it to the constructor. However, for establishing a uniform interface for vectors, we still accept a size argument at construction and check that it matches the template argument.

Comparing this implementation with the dynamically sized vector in Section 3.3.1, we will not see many differences. The essential distinction is that the size is now part of the type and that it can be accessed at compile time. As a consequence, the compiler can perform additional optimizations. When we add two vectors of size 3, for instance, the compiler can transform the loop into three statements like this:

```
self operator+(const self& that) const
{
    self sum;
    sum[0]= data[0] + that[0];
    sum[1]= data[1] + that[1];
    sum[2]= data[2] + that[2];
    return sum;
}
```

This saves the counter incrementation and the test for the loop end. Possibly the operations are performed in parallel on an SSE. We will talk more about loop unrolling in Section 5.4.

Which optimization is induced by additional compile-time information is of course compiler-dependent. One can only find out which transformation is actually done by reading the generated assembler code or indirectly by observing performance and comparing it with other implementations. Reading assembler is difficult, especially with a high optimization level. With less aggressive optimization, we might not see the benefit from the static size.

In the example above, the compiler will probably unroll the loop as shown for small sizes like 3 and keep the loop for larger sizes like 100. Therefore, these compile-time sizes are particularly interesting for small matrices and vectors, e.g., three-dimensional coordinates or rotations.

Another benefit of knowing the size at compile time is that we can store the values in an array so that our fsize_vector uses a single memory block. This makes the creation and destruction much easier compared to dynamically allocated memory that is expensive to manage.

We mentioned before that the size becomes part of the type. As a consequence, we do not need to check matching sizes for vectors of the same type.

We said that the size becomes part of the type. The careful reader might have realized that we omitted the checks for whether the vectors have the same size. We do not need these tests anymore. If an argument has the same class type, it has the same size implicitly. Consider the following program snippet:

```
fsize_vector<float, 3> v;
fsize_vector<float, 4> w;
vector<float>          x(3), y(4);

v= w;
x= y;
```

The last two lines are incompatible vector assignments. The difference is that the incompatibility in the second assignment x= y; is discovered at run time in our assertion. The assignment v= w; does not even compile because fixed-size vectors of dimension 3 only accept vectors of the same dimension as arguments.

If we want, we can declare default values for non-type template arguments. Living in our three-dimensional world, it makes sense to assume that many vectors have dimension 3:

```
template <typename T, int Size= 3>
class fsize_vector
{ /* ... */ };

fsize_vector<float>        v, w, x, y;

fsize_vector<float, 4>     space_time;
fsize_vector<float, 11>    string;
```

For relativity and string theory, we can afford the extra work of declaring their vector dimensions.

3.8 Functors

In this section, we introduce an extremely powerful feature: *Functors*, a.k.a. *Function Objects*. At first glance, they are just classes that provide an operator callable like a function. The crucial difference from ordinary functions is that function objects can be more flexibly applied to each other or to themselves, allowing us to create new function objects. These applications need some time to get used to, and reading this section is probably more challenging than the preceding ones. However, we reach here an entirely new quality of programming and every minute spent on this reading is worth it. This section also paves the way for lambdas (§3.9) and opens the door to meta-programming (Chapter 5).

As a study case, we develop a mathematical algorithm for computing the finite difference of a differentiable function f. The finite difference is an approximation of the first derivative by

$$f'(x) \approx \frac{f(x+h) - f(x)}{h}$$

where h is a small value also called spacing.

A general function for computing the finite difference is presented in Listing 3-5. We implement this in the function fin_diff, which takes an arbitrary function (from double to double) as an argument:

Listing 3–5: Finite differences with function pointers

```
double fin_diff(double f(double), double x, double h)
{
    return ( f(x+h) - f(x) ) / h;
}
```

```
double sin_plus_cos(double x)
{
    return sin(x) + cos(x);
}

int main() {
    cout << fin_diff(sin_plus_cos, 1., 0.001) << '\n';
    cout << fin_diff(sin_plus_cos, 0., 0.001) << '\n';
}
```

Here we approximated the derivative of sin_plus_cos at $x = 1$ and $x = 0$ with $h = 0.001$. sin_plus_cos is passed as a function pointer (functions can be implicitly converted to function pointers when necessary).

Now we want to compute the second-order derivative. It would make sense to call fin_diff with itself as an argument. Unfortunately, this is not possible since fin_diff has three parameters and does not match its own function pointer parameter with only one parameter.

We can solve this problem with *Functors* or *Function Objects*. These are classes that provide an application operator() so that objects thereof can be called like functions, explaining the term "function objects." Unfortunately, it is not obvious in many texts whether the term refers to a class or an object. This might not be problematic in those contexts but we need a sharp distinction between classes and objects. Therefore we prefer the word *functor* despite its other meaning in category theory. In this book, functor always refers to a class and an object thereof is accordingly called a functor object. Whenever we use the term function object it is synonymous with functor object.

Back to our example. The previously used function sin_plus_cos implemented as a functor reads as follows:

Listing 3–6: Function object

```
struct sc_f
{
    double operator() (double x) const
    {
        return sin(x) + cos(x);
    }
};
```

A great advantage of functors is the ability to hold parameters as internal states. So we could scale x with α in the sin function, i.e., $\sin \alpha x + \cos x$:

Listing 3–7: Function object with state

```
class psc_f
{
  public:
    psc_f(double alpha) : alpha(alpha) {}
```

```
    double operator() (double x) const
    {
        return sin(alpha * x) + cos(x);
    }
  private:
    double alpha;
};
```

Notation: In this section, we introduce a fair number of types and objects. For better distinction, we use the following naming conventions: Functor types are named with the suffix _f like psc_f and objects thereof have the suffix _o. An approximated derivative is prefixed with d_, the second derivative with dd_, and higher derivatives with d followed by its order, like d7_ for the seventh derivative. For brevity's sake, we will not state for each derivative that it is only approximated (the derivatives of orders around 20 are actually so incorrect that approximation is presumptuous).

3.8.1   Function-like Parameters

⇒ c++11/derivative.cpp

After defining our functor types, we have to find out how we can pass objects thereof to functions. Our previous definition of fin_diff had a function pointer as an argument which we cannot use for our functor objects. Furthermore, we cannot use a specific argument type when we want to support different functors, e.g., sc_f and psc_f. There are essentially two techniques for accepting arguments of different types: inheritance and templates. The inheritance version is postponed to Section 6.1.4 until we have actually introduced this feature. Right now, we have to mention that the generic approach is superior in applicability and performance. Thus, we use a type parameter for our functors and functions:

```
template <typename F, typename T>
T inline fin_diff(F f, const T& x, const T& h)
{
    return (f(x+h) - f(x)) / h;
}

int main()
{
    psc_f psc_o(1.0);
    cout << fin_diff(psc_o, 1., 0.001) << endl;
    cout << fin_diff(psc_f(2.0), 1., 0.001) << endl;
    cout << fin_diff(sin_plus_cos, 0., 0.001) << endl;
}
```

In this example, we create the functor object psc_o and pass it as a template argument to fin_diff. The next call passes the on-the-fly-created object psc_f(2.0) to the differentiation. In the last call of fin_diff, we demonstrate that we can still pass in an ordinary function as sin_plus_cos.

These three examples show that the parameter f is quite versatile. This raises the question of how versatile. From how we use f we deduce that it must be a function taking one argument. The STL (§4.1) introduces for these requirements the concept UnaryFunction:

- Let f be of type F.

- Let x be of type T, where T is the argument type of F.

- f(x) calls f with one argument and returns an object of the result type.

Since we perform all calculations with values of type T, we should add the requirement that the return type of f is T as well.

3.8.2 Composing Functors

So far, we have looked at different kinds of function parameters for our calculations. Unfortunately, we are not much closer to our goal of computing higher derivatives elegantly by passing fin_diff as an argument to itself. The problem is that fin_diff needs a unary function as an argument while being a ternary function itself. We can can overcome this discrepancy by defining a unary functor[11] that holds the the function to differentiate and the step size as internal states:

```
template <typename F, typename T>
class derivative
{
  public:
    derivative(const F& f, const T& h) : f(f), h(h) {}

    T operator()(const T& x) const
    {
        return ( f(x+h) - f(x) ) / h;
    }
  private:
    const F& f;
    T        h;
};
```

Then only x is still passed as a regular function argument to the differentiation. This functor can be instantiated with a functor representing[12] $f(x)$ and the result is a functor for the approximated $f'(x)$:

```
using d_psc_f= derivative<psc_f, double>;
```

Here the derivative of $f(x) = \sin(\alpha \cdot x) + \cos x$ is represented by the functor d_psc_f. We can now create a function object for the derivative with $\alpha = 1$:

```
psc_f          psc_o(1.0);
d_psc_f        d_psc_o(psc_o, 0.001);
```

---

11. For conciseness, we call a functor whose objects are unary functions a unary functor.
12. This is another abbreviating phrasing: when we say functor ft represents $f(x)$, we mean that an object of ft computes $f(x)$.

This allows us to calculate the differential quotient at $x = 0$:

```
cout ≪ "der. of sin(0) + cos(0) is " ≪ d_psc_o(0.0) ≪ '\n';
```

Well, we could do this before. The fundamental difference from our preceding solutions is the similarity of the original function and its derivative. They are both unary functions created from functors.

Thus, we have finally reached our goal: we can treat $f'(x)$ the same way we treated $f(x)$ and build $f''(x)$ from it. More technically phrased: we can instantiate `derivative` with the functor d_psc_f of the derived function:

```
using dd_psc_f= derivative<d_psc_f, double>;
```

Now we have indeed a functor for the second derivative. We demonstrate this by creating a function object of it and approximate $f''(0)$:

```
dd_psc_f              dd_psc_o(d_psc_o, 0.001);
cout ≪ "2nd der. of sin(0) + cos(0) is " ≪ dd_psc_o(0.0) ≪ '\n';
```

Since dd_psc_f is again a unary functor, we can create one for the third derivative and higher.

In case we need the second derivative from multiple functions we can invest some more effort in creating the second derivative directly without bothering the user to create the first derivative. The following functor creates a function object for the first derivative in the constructor and approximates $f''(x)$:

```
template <typename F, typename T>
class second_derivative
{
  public:
    second_derivative(const F& f, const T& h)
      : h(h), fp(f, h) {}

    T operator()(const T& x) const
    {
        return ( fp(x+h) - fp(x) ) / h;
    }
  private:
    T                   h;
    derivative<F, T> fp;
};
```

Now we can build a function object for f'' from f:

```
second_derivative<psc_f, double> dd_psc_2_o(psc_f(1.0), 0.001);
```

In the same fashion we could build a generator for each higher-order derivative. Better yet we will now realize a functor for approximating a derivative of arbitrary order.

3.8.3　Recursion

When we think of how we would implement the third, fourth, or in general the nth derivative, we realize that they would look much like the second one: calling the $(n-1)$th derivative on x+h and x. We can explore this repetitive scheme with a recursive implementation:

```
template <typename F, typename T, unsigned N>
class nth_derivative
{
    using prev_derivative= nth_derivative<F, T, N-1>;
  public:
    nth_derivative(const F& f, const T& h)
      : h(h), fp(f, h) {}

    T operator()(const T& x) const
    {
        return ( fp(x+h) - fp(x) ) / h;
    }
  private:
    T                 h;
    prev_derivative fp;
};
```

To rescue the compiler from infinite recursion, we must stop this mutual referring when we reach the first derivative. Note that we cannot use if or ?: to stop the recursion because both of its respective branches are eagerly evaluated and one of them still contains the infinite recursion. Recursive template definitions are terminated with a specialization like the following:

```
template <typename F, typename T>
class nth_derivative<F, T, 1>
{
  public:
    nth_derivative(const F& f, const T& h) : f(f), h(h) {}

    T operator()(const T& x) const
    {
        return ( f(x+h) - f(x) ) / h;
    }
  private:
    const F& f;
    T        h;
};
```

This specialization is identical to the class derivative that we now could throw away. Or we keep it and reuse its functionality by simply deriving from it (more about derivation in Chapter 6).

```
template <typename F, typename T>
class nth_derivative<F, T, 1>
  : public derivative<F, T>
{
    using derivative<F, T>::derivative;
};
```

Now we can compute any derivative like the 22nd:

```
nth_derivative<psc_f, double, 22> d22_psc_o(psc_f(1.0), 0.00001);
```

The new object `d22_psc_o` is again a unary function object. Unfortunately, it approximates so badly that we are too ashamed to present the results here. From Taylor series, we know that the error of the f'' approximation is reduced from $\mathcal{O}(h)$ to $\mathcal{O}(h^2)$ when a backward difference is applied to the forward difference. This said, maybe we can improve our approximation when we alternate between forward and backward differences:

```cpp
template <typename F, typename T, unsigned N>
class nth_derivative
{
    using prev_derivative= nth_derivative<F, T, N-1>;
  public:
    nth_derivative(const F& f, const T& h) : h(h), fp(f, h) {}

    T operator()(const T& x) const
    {
        return N & 1 ? ( fp(x+h) - fp(x) ) / h
                     : ( fp(x) - fp(x-h) ) / h;
    }
  private:
    T           h;
    prev_derivative fp;
};
```

Sadly, our 22nd derivative is still as wrong as before, well, slightly worse. Which is particularly frustrating when we become aware of the fact that we evaluate f over four million times. Decreasing h doesn't help either: the tangent better approaches the derivative but, on the other hand, the values of $f(x)$ and $f(x \pm h)$ approach each other and their differences remain only few meaningful bits. At least the second derivative improved by our alternating difference schemes as Taylor series teach us. Another consolidating fact is that we probably did not pay for the alteration. The template argument N is known at compile time and so is the result of the condition N&1. Thus, the compiler can shrink the if-statement to the accordingly active then- or else-branch.

If nothing else we learned something about C++ and we are confirmed in the

---

Truism

Not even the coolest programming can substitute for solid mathematics.

In the end, this book is primarily about programming. And the functors proved to be extremely expressive for generating new function objects. Nonetheless, if any reader has a good idea for a numerically better recursive computation, feel free to contact the author.

There is only one detail still disturbing us: the redundancy between the functor arguments and those of the constructors. Say we compute the seventh derivative of `psc_o`:

```cpp
nth_derivative<psc_f, double, 7> d7_psc_o(psc_o, 0.00001);
```

The first two arguments of nth_derivative are exactly the types of the constructor arguments. This is redundant and we preferred to deduce them. auto and decltype are no big help here:

```
auto d7_psc_o= nth_derivative<psc_f, double, 7>(psc_o, 0.00001);
nth_derivative<decltype(psc_o),
               decltype(0.00001), 7>   d7_psc_o(psc_o, 0.00001);
```

More promising is a make-function that takes the constructor arguments and deduces their types like this:

```
template <typename F, typename T, unsigned N> // Not clever
nth_derivative<F, T, N>
make_nth_derivative(const F& f, const T& h)
{
    return nth_derivative<F, T, N>(f, h);
}
```

This should deduce F and T, and we only need to declare N explicitly. Unfortunately, this doesn't work as expected. When we declare a certain template parameter, we are obliged to declare all preceding parameters:

```
auto d7_psc_o= make_nth_derivative<psc_f, double, 7>(psc_o, 0.00001);
```

Well, this is not particularly useful. We have to change the order of our make-function's template parameters: N must be declared and F and T can be deduced. Thus, we put N in front:

```
template <unsigned N, typename F, typename T>
nth_derivative<F, T, N>
make_nth_derivative(const F& f, const T& h)
{
    return nth_derivative<F, T, N>(f, h);
}
```

Now the compiler can deduce the functor and value type of the seventh derivative:

```
auto d7_psc_o= make_nth_derivative<7>(psc_o, 0.00001);
```

We have seen that the order of template parameters mattered for our make-function. In function templates where all parameters are deduced by the compiler, their order is irrelevant. Only when parameters or some of them are explicitly declared do we have to pay attention. The parameters not deduced must be located at the front of the parameter list. To remember this, imagine a template function call with partly deduced parameters: the explicitly declared parameters come first, left of the opening (, and the other parameters are deduced from the arguments to the right of (.

3.8.4 Generic Reduction

⇒ c++11/accumulate_functor_example.cpp

Recall the function accumulate from Section 3.3.2.5 that we used to illustrate generic programming. In this section, we will generalize this function to a generic reduction. We introduce a BinaryFunction implementing an operation on two arguments as a function or as a callable class object. Then we can perform any reduction applying the BinaryFunction on all elements of our sequence:

```
template <typename Iter, typename T, typename BinaryFunction>
T accumulate(Iter it, Iter end, T init, BinaryFunction op)
{
    for (; it != end; ++it)
    init= op(init, *it);
    return init;
}
```

To add values, we can realize a functor that is parameterized by the type of values:

```
template <typename T>
struct add
{
    T operator()(const T& x, const T& y) const { return x + y; }
};
```

Instead of the class, we can also parameterize the operator():

```
struct times
{
    template <typename T>
    T operator()(const T& x, const T& y) const { return x * y; }
};
```

This has the advantage that the compiler can deduce the value type:

```
vector v= {7.0, 8.0, 11.0};
double s= accumulate(v.begin(), v.end(), 0.0, add<double>{});
double p= accumulate(v.begin(), v.end(), 1.0, times{});
```

Here we computed the sum and the product of vector entries. The add functor requires instantiation with the vector's value type while the times functor is not a template class and the argument type is deduced in the application.

C++11 ## 3.9   Lambda

⇒ c++11/lambda.cpp

C++11 introduced lambda expressions. A λ-expression is simply shorthand for a functor. However, it makes programs more compact but often more comprehensible as well. Especially for simple calculation it is clearer to see their implementation at the place where they are used instead of calling a function whose code is somewhere else. Having seen classical functors before makes it quite easy to understand what lambdas are.

Listing 3–6 realizes a functor for $\sin x + \cos x$. The corresponding λ-expression is

Listing 3–8: Simple λ-expression

```
[](double x){ return sin(x) + cos(x); }
```

The lambda expression doesn't only define a functor but immediately creates an object thereof. Thus, we can pass it immediately to a function as an argument:

```
fin_diff([](double x){ return sin(x) + cos(x); }, 1., 0.001 )
```

Parameters can be incorporated directly in the lambda expression. So we can scale the sin argument as we did in functor psc_f (Listing 3–7) by just inserting the multiplication and still getting a unary function object:

```
fin_diff([](double x){ return sin(2.5*x) + cos(x); }, 1., 0.001)
```

We can also store it to a variable for reuse:

```
auto sc_l= [](double x){ return sin(x) + cos(x); };
```

The lambda expressions in the previous examples don't declare their return types. They are deduced by the compiler in such cases. In case it cannot be deduced or we prefer to declare it explicitly, we can provide the return type as a trailing argument:

```
[](double x)->double { return sin(x) + cos(x); };
```

⇒ c++11/derivative.cpp

Now that we can create function objects on the fly and are not particularly eager to bother with their types, we are glad that our derivative generator is able to deduce types. This allows us to create a function for the approximated seventh derivative of $\sin 2.5x + \cos x$ in one single expression:

```
auto d7_psc_l= make_nth_derivative<7>(
    [](double x){ return sin(2.5*x) + cos(x); }, 0.0001);
```

Sadly, the statement in a textbook is too long for a single line but not so in a real program (for the author's taste).

As soon as lambdas came out, many programmers were so excited about them that they implemented every function argument with a lambda—often over many lines and containing other lambdas inside. This might be an intriguing challenge for experienced programmers, but we are convinced that decomposing monstrous nested expressions into readable pieces helps everybody using and maintaining our software.

3.9.1 Capture

C++11

In the previous section, we parameterized a lambda by simply inserting an operation. This is not very productive for a multitude of parameters, however:

```
a= fin_diff([](double x){ return sin(2.5 * x); }, 1., 0.001);
b= fin_diff([](double x){ return sin(3.0 * x); }, 1., 0.001);
c= fin_diff([](double x){ return sin(3.5 * x); }, 1., 0.001);
```

Unfortunately, we cannot access variables or constants from the scope like this:

```
double phi= 2.5;
auto sin_phi= [](double x){ return sin(phi * x); }; // Error
```

The λ-expression can only use its own parameters or those *Captured* before.

3.9.2   Capture by Value

In order to use phi, we must capture it first:

```
double phi= 2.5;
auto sin_phi= [phi](double x){ return sin(phi * x); };
```

To capture multiple variables, we can give a comma-separated list:

```
double phi= 2.5, xi= 0.2;
auto sin2= [phi,xi](double x){ return sin(phi*x) + cos(x)*xi; };
```

These parameters are copied, but in contrast to function parameters passed by value it is forbidden to modify them. Written as a functor class, the previous λ corresponds to

```
struct lambda_f
{
    lambda_f(double phi, double xi) : phi(phi), xi(xi) {}
    double operator()(double x) const
    {
        return sin(phi * x) + cos(x) * xi;
    }
    const double phi, xi;
};
```

As a consequence, modifying the captured variables later has no effect on the lambda:

```
double phi= 2.5, xi= 0.2;
auto px= [phi,xi](double x){ return sin(phi * x) + cos(x) * xi; };
phi= 3.5; xi= 1.2;
a= fin_diff(px, 1., 0.001); // still uses phi= 2.5 and xi= 0.2
```

The variables are captured when the λ is defined, and thus the values at that time are used when the lambda is called.

Furthermore, we cannot modify the values inside the lambda function despite their being copies. The reason is that the lambda's function body corresponds to a const-qualified operator() as above in lambda_f. In the following lambda, for instance, it is illegal to increment the captured phi:

```
auto l_inc= [phi](double x) {phi+= 0.6; return phi; }; // Error
```

To allow the modification of the captured values, the lambda must be qualified as mutable:

```
auto l_mut= [phi](double x) mutable {phi+= 0.6; return phi; };
```

The functor class equivalent to this mutable lambda would not be const-qualified:

```
struct l_mut_f
{
    double operator()(double x); // not const
    // ...
    double phi, xi;                    // not const either
};
```

As a consequence, we cannot pass the lambda l_mut to const-parameters anymore. On the other hand, we don't really need the mutability here and could instead return phi+0.6 and drop the incrementation.

3.9.3   Capture by Reference   C++11

Variables can also be captured by reference:

```
double phi= 2.5, xi= 0.2;
auto pxr= [&phi,&xi](double x){ return sin(phi * x) + cos(x) * xi; };
phi= 3.5; xi= 1.2;
a= fin_diff(pxr, 1., 0.001); // now uses phi= 3.5 and xi= 1.2
```

In this example, the values of phi and xi at the time of the function call of λ are used—not those when the lambda was created. The corresponding functor class would look like this:

```
struct lambda_ref_type
struct lambda_f
{
    lambda_ref_type(double& phi, double& xi) : phi(phi), xi(xi) {}
    double operator()(double x)
    {
        return sin(phi * x) + cos(x) * xi;
    }
    double& phi;
    double& xi;
};
```

Another consequence of the reference semantics is the ability to modify the referred values. This is not only a possible source of side effects but can be used productively. Let's say we have different dense and sparse matrix classes. For all those classes, we provide the generic traversal function on_each_nonzero with the matrix as the first argument and a function object as the second (passed by value). This allows us to generically compute the Frobenius norm:

$$||A||_F = \sqrt{\sum_{i,j} |a_{ij}|^2}$$

Given this formula, we can apparently ignore all zero entries and process the non-zeros only:

```
template <typename Matrix>
typename Matrix::value_type
frobenius_norm(const Matrix& A)
{
    using std::abs; using std::sqrt;
    using value_type= typename Matrix::value_type;
    value_type ss= 0;
    on_each_nonzero(A, [&ss](value_type x) { ss+= abs(x) * abs(x); });
    return sqrt(ss);
}
```

For simplicity's sake, we assume here that the types of A(0,0) and abs(A(0,0)) are identical. Note that the λ-expression doesn't return a value since its purpose is to sum up the squared matrix values in the referred variable ss. Here the lack of a return statement implies the void return type.

There are shortcuts for capturing all variables:

- [=]: capture all by copy;

- [&]: capture all by reference;

- [=,&a,&b,&c]: capture all by copy but a, b, c by reference; and

- [&,a,b,c]: capture all by reference but a, b, c by copy.

Scott Meyers advises not using the capture-all feature as it increases the danger of stale references and of ignoring static or member variables; see [32, Item 31].

 ### 3.9.4 Generalized Capture

The generalization of capturing is brought in by *Init Capture*. It allows us to move variables into a closure and to give new names to context variables or expressions thereof. Say we have a function returning a Hilbert matrix as unique_ptr:

```
auto F= make_unique<Mat>(Mat{{1., 0.5},{0.5,1./3.}});
```

We can capture a reference to the pointer, but we risk a stale reference when the closure outlives the pointer. On the other hand, a unique_ptr cannot be copied. For assuring that our matrix lives as long as the closure, we have to move the data into a unique_ptr owned by the closure:

```
auto apply_hilbert= [F= move(F)](const Vec& x){ return Vec(*F * x); };
```

The init capture allows us further to introduce new names for existing variables and to evaluate expressions and associate a name with the result:

```
int x= 4;
auto y=
    [&r= x, x= x + 1]()
    {
        r+= 2;            // increment r, a reference to outer x
        return x + 2;     // return x + 2 where x is the outer x + 1
    }();
```

This example from the standard defines a nullary closure returning an int. The closure introduces two local variables: r is a reference to the context's x and the local value x is initialized with the outer x + 1.

In the example, we can see that an init capture has the form var= expr. An interesting fact (which you have probably noticed) is that var and expr are defined in different scopes. var is defined in the scope of the closure and expr in its context. Therefore, the same name can appear on both sides of =. Conversely, the following capture list:

```
int x= 4;
auto y= [&r= x, x= r + 1](){ ... }; // Error: no r in context
```

is not allowed because r only exists in the closure and can therefore not be used on the right-hand side of a capture.

3.9.5   Generic Lambdas   `C++14`

Lambdas in C++11 determined the **return** type but the arguments needed to be declared
explicitly. This restriction was lifted in C++14. In contrast to function templates, the
arguments are not declared in the somewhat verbose template-typename notation but by the
keyword auto. For instance, a function that sorts elements of a (random-access) container in
descending order is implemented as simply as

```
template <typename C>
void reverse_sort(C& c)
{
    sort(begin(c), end(c), [](auto x, auto y){ return x > y; });
}
```

In the same fashion, we can simplify our frobenius_norm from Section 3.9.3. The lambda
summing the squared magnitudes can simply instantiate the argument type:

```
template <typename Matrix>
inline auto frobenius_norm(const Matrix& A)
{
    using std::abs; using std::sqrt;
    decltype(abs(A[0][0])) ss= 0;
    on_each_nonzero(A, [&ss](auto x) { ss+= abs(x) * abs(x); });
    return sqrt(ss);
}
```

In this little function, we used more type deduction mechanisms and liberated ourselves
entirely from declaring value_type. We can now also handle the fact that abs might return a
type different from value_type.

3.10   Variadic Templates   `C++11`

Function and class templates are called *Variadic* when their arity can vary; i.e., they work
for an arbitrary number of arguments. More precisely, there may be a minimal number
of arguments but not a maximal. Furthermore, the template arguments are allowed to be
different types (or integral constants).

At the time of this writing, the programmer community is still on the journey of
discovering this powerful feature. Use cases are, for instance, type-safe printf implementations,
different kinds of reduction, and all forms of generic forwarding functions. Hopefully, our
examples will contribute a little to more frequent variadic template implementations in
applications.

We will illustrate the feature with a sum function for mixed types:

```
template <typename T>
inline T sum(T t) { return t; }

template <typename T, typename ...P>
inline T sum(T t, P ...p)
```

```
{
    return t + sum(p...);
}
```

Variadic templates are handled by recursion. We break down the so-called *Parameter Pack* and deal with subsets thereof. Usually, one element is split off and combined with the result of the remainder.

Variadic templates introduce the new ellipsis operator denoted by .... The operator on the left side means packing and on the right side unpacking. The different interpretations of the ellipsis are the following:

- typename ...P: pack multiple type arguments into the type pack P;

- <P...>: unpack P when instantiating a class or function template (comes later);

- P ...p: pack multiple function arguments into the variable pack p; and

- sum(p...): unpack variable pack p and call sum with multiple arguments.

Thus, our sum function computes the addition of the first entry with the sum of the others. This sum in turn is computed recursively as well. To terminate the recursion, we write an overload for a single argument. We could have also written an overload for a nullary function (one without arguments) returning 0 as int.

Our implementation has a significant disadvantage: the **return** type is the type of the first argument. This might work more or less in some cases:

```
auto s= sum(-7, 3.7f, 9u, -2.6);
std::cout ≪ "s is " ≪ s
          ≪ " and its type is " ≪ typeid(s).name() ≪ '\n';
```

yields

```
s is 2 and its type is int
```

The correct result of 3.1 cannot be stored as int,[13] the type of our first argument -7.

This is not really satisfying but it can be much worse as in the following computation:

```
auto s2= sum(-7, 3.7f, 9u, -42.6);
std::cout ≪ "s2 is " ≪ s2 ≪ " and its type is " ≪ typeid(s2).name() ≪ '\n';
```

which also returns an int:

```
s2 is -2147483648 and its type is int
```

The first intermediate result is $9 - 42.6 = -33.6$, which yields a very large number when converted to unsigned and is later turned into a very small int value. On the other hand, the calculation

```
auto s= -7 + 3.7f + 9u + -42.6;
```

computes the correct result and stores it as double. But before we condemn variadic templates, we have to admit to ourselves that we chose inappropriate types for intermediate values and the final result. We will correct this in Section 5.2.7 with a better suited return type.

---

13. The output of typeid must be demangled with tools like c++filt.

For counting the number of arguments in a parameter pack at compile time, we can use the function-like expression `sizeof...`:

```
template <typename ...P>
void count(P ...p)
{
    cout << "You have " << sizeof...(P) << " parameters.\n";
    ...
}
```

The binary I/O from Section A.2.7 is revised in Section A.6.4 to allow arbitrary numbers of arguments in the write and read operations.

As the `sum` example already indicated, the full power of variadic templates will only be unleashed in combination with meta-programming (Chapter 5).

3.11 Exercises

3.11.1 String Representation

Write a generic function `to_string` that takes an argument of an arbitrary type (as `const&`) and generates a string by piping it to a `std::stringstream` and returning the resulting string.

3.11.2 String Representation of Tuples

Write a variadic template function that represents an arbitrary number of arguments as a tuple in a string. That is, the function call `to_tuple_string(x, y, z)` returns a string of the form (x, y, z) by printing each element to a string stream.

Hint: Use a helper function `to_tuple_string_aux` that is overloaded for different arities.

3.11.3 Generic Stack

Write a stack implementation for a generic value type. The maximal size of the stack is defined in the class (hard-wired). Provide the following functions:

- Constructor;

- Destructor if necessary;

- `top`: show last element;

- `pop`: remove last element (without returning);

- `push`: insert new element;

- `clear`: delete all entries;

- `size`: number of elements;

- `full`: whether stack is full;

- `empty`: whether stack is empty.

Stack over- or underflow must throw an exception.

3.11.4   Iterator of a Vector

Add the methods `begin()` and `end()` for returning a begin and end iterator to class `vector`. Add the types `iterator` and `const_iterator` to the class as well. Note that pointers are models of the concept of random-access iterators.

Use the STL function `sort` for ordering vector entries to demonstrate that your iterators work as they should.

3.11.5   Odd Iterator

Write an iterator class for odd numbers named `odd_iterator`. The class must model (realize) the `ForwardIterator` concept (`http://www.sgi.com/tech/stl/ForwardIterator.html`). That means it must provide the following members:

- Default and copy constructor;

- `operator++` to the next odd element, as pre-increment and post-increment;

- `operator*` as dereference which returns an (odd) `int`;

- `operator==` and `operator!=`; and

- `operator=`.

with the obvious semantics. In addition, the class should contain a constructor that accepts an `int` value. This value will be returned in the dereference operator (as long as the iterator is not incremented). This constructor should throw an exception if the value is even. Likewise the default constructor should initialize the internal value with 1 to provide a legal state.

3.11.6   Odd Range

Write a class for a range of odd numbers. The member or free functions `begin` and `end` should return an `odd_iterator` as defined in Exercise 3.11.5.

The following code should print the odd numbers $\{7, 9, \ldots, 25\}$:

```
for (int i : odd_range(7, 27))
    std::cout << i << "\n";
```

3.11.7   Stack of `bool`

Specialize your `stack` implementation from Exercise 3.11.3 for `bool`. Use an unsigned char for 8 `bool` as in Section 3.6.1.

3.11.8 Stack with Custom Size

Revise your stack implementation from Exercise 3.11.3 (and optionally that of Exercise 3.11.7) with a user-defined size. The size is passed as the second template argument. The default should be 4096.

3.11.9 Deducing Non-type Template Arguments

We have seen that the type of a template argument can be deduced in a function call. Non-type template arguments are in most cases declared explicitly, but they can be deduced as well when they are part of the argument type. As illustration: write a function array_size that accepts a C array of arbitrary type and size as a reference and returns the size of that array. The actual function argument can be omitted since we are only interested in its type. Do you remember? We threatened this exercise in Section 1.8.7.1. On the other hand, we revealed the trickiest part of it in the meantime.

3.11.10 Trapezoid Rule

A simple method for computing the integral of a function is the trapezoid rule. Suppose we want to integrate the function f over the interval $[a, b]$. We split the interval in n small intervals $[x_i, x_{i+1}]$ of the same length $h = (b - a)/n$ and approximate f by a piecewise linear function. The integral is then approximated by the sum of the integrals of that function. This leads to the following formula:

$$I = \frac{h}{2} f(a) + \frac{h}{2} f(b) + h \sum_{j=1}^{n-1} f(a + jh) \tag{3.1}$$

In this exercise, we develop a function for the trapezoid rule, with a functor argument. For comparison, implement this using inheritance and generic programming. As a test case, integrate:

- $f = \exp(-3x)$ for $x \in [0, 4]$. Try trapezoid with the following arguments:

```
double exp3f(double x) {
  return std::exp(3.0 * x);
}

struct exp3t {
  double operator() (double x) const {
    return std::exp(3.0 * x);
  }
};
```

- $f = \sin(x)$ if $x < 1$ and $f = \cos(x)$ if $x \geqslant 1$ for $x \in [0, 4]$.

- Can we call trapezoid(std::sin, 0.0, 2.0); ?

As a second exercise, develop a functor for computing the finite difference. Then integrate the finite difference to verify that you get the function value back.

3.11.11   Functor

Write a functor for $2\cos x + x^2$ and compute the first and second derivatives with the functor from Section 3.8.1.

3.11.12   Lambda

Compute the same derivatives as in Exercise 3.11.11 but this time with a lambda expression.

3.11.13   Implement `make_unique`

Implement your own `make_unique`. Use `std::forward` to pass parameter packs to the `new`.

Chapter 4

Libraries

"God, grant me the serenity to accept the things I cannot change,
The courage to change the things I can,
And the wisdom to know the difference"

—Reinhold Niebuhr

We as programmers need similar strengths. We have great visions of what our software should accomplish, and we need very strong *Courage* to make this happen. Nonetheless, a day has only 24 hours and even hardcore geeks eat and sleep sometimes. As a consequence, we cannot program everything we dream of (or are paid for) by ourselves and have to rely on existing software. Then we have to *Accept* what this software provides us by implementing interfaces with appropriate pre- and post-processing. The decision whether to use existing software or write a new program requires all our *Wisdom*.

Actually, it even requires some prophetic powers to rely on software without having years of experience with it. Sometimes, packages work well at the beginning, and once we build a larger project on top of it, we may experience some serious problems that cannot be compensated for easily. Then we might realize painfully that another software package or an implementation from scratch would have been the better option.

The C++ standard library might not be perfect, but it is designed and implemented very carefully so that we can prevent such bad surprises. The components of the standard library pass the same thorough evaluation process as the features of the core language and guarantee the highest quality. The library standardization also assures that its classes and functions are available on every compliant compiler. We already introduced some library components before, like initializer lists in §2.3.3 or I/O streams in §1.7. In this chapter, we will present more library components that can be very useful for the programming scientist or engineer.

A comprehensive tutorial and reference for the standard library in C++11 is given by Nicolai Josuttis [26]. The fourth edition of Bjarne Stroustrup's book [43] covers all library components as well, although in a little less detail.

Furthermore, there are many scientific libraries for standard domains like linear algebra or graph algorithms. We will briefly introduce some of them in the last section.

4.1 Standard Template Library

The *Standard Template Library* (STL) is the fundamental generic library for containers and algorithms. Every programmer should know it and use it when appropriate instead of reinventing the wheel. The name might be a bit confusing: most parts of the STL as created by Alex Stepanov and David Musser became part of the C++ standard library. On the other hand, other components of the standard library are also implemented with templates. To make the confusion perfect, the C++ standard associates a library name with each library-related chapter. In the 2011 and 2014 standards, the STL is contained in three such chapters: Chapter 23 Containers library, Chapter 24 Iterators library, and Chapter 25 Algorithms library (the latter also contains part of the C library).

The Standard Template Library doesn't only provide useful functionality but also laid the foundation of a programming philosophy that is incomparably powerful in its combination of reusability and performance. The STL defines generic container classes, generic algorithms, and iterators. Online documentation is provided under **www.sgi.com/tech/stl**. There are also entire books written about the usage of STL, so we can keep it short here and refer to these books. For instance, Matt Austern—an STL core implementer—wrote an entire book exclusively on it: [3]. Josuttis's library tutorial dedicates around 500 pages to the STL only.

4.1.1   Introductory Example

Containers are classes whose purpose is to contain objects (including containers and containers of containers and so on). The classes `vector` and `list` are examples of STL containers. Each of these class templates is parameterized by an element type. For example, the following statements create a `double` and an `int` vector:

```
std::vector<double> vec_d;
std::vector<int>    vec_i;
```

Note that the STL vectors are not vectors in the mathematical sense as they don't provide arithmetic operations. Therefore, we created our own vector class in various evolving implementations.

The STL also includes a large collection of algorithms that manipulate the containers' data. The before-mentioned `accumulate` algorithm, for example, can be used to compute any reduction—such as sum, product, or minimum—on a list or vector in the following way:

```
std::vector<double> vec ; // fill the vector...
std::list<double>   lst ; // fill the list...

double vec_sum = std::accumulate(begin(vec), end(vec), 0.0);
double lst_sum = std::accumulate(begin(lst), end(lst), 0.0);
```

The functions `begin()` and `end()` return iterators representing right-open intervals as before. C++11 introduced the free-function notation for them while we have to use the corresponding member functions in C++03.

4.1.2   Iterators

The central abstraction of the STL is *Iterators*. Simply put, iterators are generalized pointers: one can dereference and compare them and change the referred location as we have already demonstrated with our own `list_iterator` in Section 3.3.2.5. However, this simplification does not do justice to the iterators given their importance. Iterators are a **Fundamental Methodology to Decouple the Implementation of Data Structures**

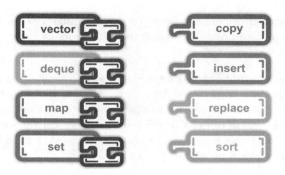

Figure 4–1: Interoperability between STL containers and algorithms

and Algorithms. In STL, every data structure provides an iterator for traversing it, and all algorithms are implemented in terms of iterators as illustrated in Figure 4–1.

To program m algorithms on n data structures, one needs in classical C and Fortran programming

$$m \cdot n \text{ implementations.}$$

Expressing algorithms in terms of iterators decreases the number to only

$$m + n \text{ implementations!}$$

4.1.2.1   Categories

Not all algorithms can be used with every data structure. Which algorithm works on a given data structure (e.g., linear find or binary search) depends on the kind of iterator provided by the container. Iterators can be distinguished by the form of access:

> **InputIterator:**   an iterator concept for reading the referred entries (but only once).

> **OutputIterator:**   an iterator concept for writing to the referred entries (but only once).

Note that the ability to write doesn't imply readability; e.g., an `ostream_iterator` is an STL interface used for writing to output streams like `cout` or output files. Another differentiation of iterators is the form of traversal:

> **ForwardIterator:**   a concept for iterators that can pass from one element to the next, i.e., types that provide an `operator++`. It is a refinement[1] of `InputIterator` and `OutputIterator`. In contrast to those, `ForwardIterator` allows for reading values twice and for traversing multiple times.

> **BidirectionalIterator:**   a concept for iterators with step-wise forward and backward traversal, i.e., types with `operator++` and `operator--`. It refines `ForwardIterator`.

---

1. In the sense of §3.5.

RandomAccessIterator: a concept for iterators to which an arbitrary positive or negative offset can be added, i.e., types that additionally provide operator[]. It refines BidirectionalIterator.

Algorithm implementations that only use a simple iterator interface (like that of InputIterator) can be applied to more data structures. Also, data structures that provide a richer iterator interface (e.g., modeling RandomAccessIterator) can be used in more algorithms.

A clever design choice of all iterator interfaces was that their operations are also provided by pointers. Every pointer models RandomAccessIterator so that all STL algorithms can be applied on old-style arrays via pointers.

C++11 ### 4.1.2.2 Working with Iterators

All standard container templates provide a rich and consistent set of iterator types. The following very simple example shows a typical use of iterators:

```
using namespace std;
std::list<int> l= {3, 5, 9, 7};                    // C++11
for (list<int>::iterator it= l.begin(); it != l.end(); ++it) {
    int i= *it;
    cout << i << endl;
}
```

In this first example, we limited ourselves to C++03 features (apart from the list initialization) to demonstrate that the work with iterators is nothing new to C++11. In the remainder of the section, we will use more C++11 features but the principle remains the same.

As illustrated in the code snippet, iterators are typically used in pairs, where one handles the actual iteration and the second one marks the end of the container. The iterators are created by the corresponding container class using the standard methods begin() and end(). The iterator returned by begin() points to the first element whereas end() yields an iterator pointing past the end of elements. The end iterator is only used for comparison since the attempt to access the value fails in most cases. All algorithms in STL are implemented with right-open intervals $[b, e)$ operating on the value referred to by b until $b = e$. Therefore, intervals of the form $[x, x)$ are regarded as empty.

The member functions begin() and end() preserve the constancy of the container:

- If the container object is mutable, then the methods return an iterator type referring to mutable container entries.

- For constant containers the methods return const_iterator which accesses the container entries by constant references.

Often iterator is implicitly convertible into const_iterator but you should not count on this.

Back to modern C++. We first incorporate type deduction for the iterator:

```
std::list<int> l= {3, 5, 9, 7};
for (auto it = begin(l), e= end(l); it != e; ++it) {
    int i= *it;
    std::cout << i << std::endl;
}
```

We also switched to the more idiomatic notation of free functions for begin and end that were introduced in C++11. As they are inline functions, this change doesn't affect the performance. Speaking of performance, we introduced a new temporary to hold the end iterator since we cannot be 100 % sure that the compiler can optimize the repeated calls for the end function.

Where our first snippet used const_iterator, the deduced iterator allows us to modify the referred entries. Here we have multiple possibilities to assure that the list is not modified inside the loop. One thing that doesn't work is const auto:

```
for (const auto it = begin(l), e= end(l); ...)   // Error
```

This doesn't deduce a const_iterator but a const iterator. This is a small but important difference: the former is a (mutable) iterator referring to constant data while the second is a constant itself so it cannot be incremented. As mentioned before, begin() and end() return const_iterator for constant lists. So we can declare our list to be constant with the drawback that it can only be set in the constructor. Or we define a const reference to this list:

```
const std::list<int>& lr= l;
for (auto it = begin(lr), e= end(lr); it != e; ++it) ...
```

or cast the list to a const reference:

```
for (auto it = begin(const_cast<const std::list<int>&>(l)),
          e= end(const_cast<const std::list<int>&>(l));
     it != e; ++it) ...
```

Needless to say, both versions are rather cumbersome. Therefore, C++11 introduced the member functions cbegin and cend returning const_iterator for both constant and mutable containers. The corresponding free functions were introduced in C++14:

```
for (auto it = cbegin(l); it != cend(l); ++it) // C++14
```

That this begin-end-based traversal pattern is so common was the motivation for introducing the range-based for (§1.4.4.3). So far, we have only used it with anachronistic C arrays and are glad now to finally apply it to real containers:

```
std::list<int> l= {3, 5, 9, 7};
for (auto i : l)
    std::cout << i << std::endl;
```

The loop variable i is a dereferenced (hidden) iterator traversing the entire container. Thus, i refers successively to each container entry. Since all STL containers provide begin and end functions, we can traverse them all with this concise for-loop.

More generally, we can apply this for-loop to all types with begin and end functions returning iterators: like classes representing sub-containers or helpers returning iterators for reverse traversal. This broader concept including all containers is called *Range*, and this is not surprisingly where the name range-based for-loop originates from. Although we only use it on containers in this book it is worth mentioning it since ranges are gaining importance in the evolution of C++. To avoid the overhead of copying the container entries into i, we can create a type-deduced reference:

```
for (auto& i : l)
    std::cout ≪ i ≪ std::endl;
```

The reference i has the same constancy as l: if l is a mutable/constant container (range), then the reference is mutable/constant as well. To assure that the entries cannot be changed, we can declare a const reference:

```
for (const auto& i : l)
    std::cout ≪ i ≪ std::endl;
```

The STL contains both simple and complex algorithms. They all contain (often somewhere deep inside) loops that are essentially equivalent to the examples above.

4.1.2.3 Operations

The <iterator> library provides two basic operations: advance and distance. The operation advance(it, n) increments n times the iterator it. This might look like a cumbersome way to say it+n but there are two fundamental differences: the second notation doesn't change the iterator it (which is not necessarily a disadvantage) and it works only with a RandomAccessIterator. The function advance can be used with any kind of iterator. In that sense, advance is like an implementation of += that also works for iterators that can only step one by one.

To be efficient, the function is internally dispatched for different iterator categories. This implementation is often used as an introduction for *Function Dispatching*, and we cannot resist sketching a typical implementation of advance:

Listing 4–1: Function dispatching in advance

```
template <typename Iterator, typename Distance>
inline void advance_aux(Iterator& i, Distance n, input_iterator_tag)
{
    assert(n >= 0);
    for (; n > 0; --n)
        ++i;
}


template <typename Iterator, typename Distance>
inline void advance_aux(Iterator& i, Distance n,
                        bidirectional_iterator_tag)
{
    if (n >= 0)
        for (; n > 0; --n) ++i;
    else
        for (; n < 0; ++n) --i;
}


template <typename Iterator, typename Distance>
inline void advance_aux(Iterator& i, Distance n,
                        random_access_iterator_tag)
```

```
{
    i+= n;
}

template <typename Iterator, typename Distance>
inline void advance(Iterator& i, Distance n)
{
    advance(i, n, typename iterator_category<Iterator>::type());
}
```

When the function advance is instantiated with an iterator type, the category of that iterator is determined by a type trait (§5.2.1). An object of that *Tag Type* determines which overload of the helper function advance_aux is called. Thus the run time of advance is constant when Iterator is a random-access iterator and linear otherwise. Negative distances are allowed for bidirectional and random-access iterators.

Modern compilers are smart enough to realize that the third argument in each overload of advance_aux is unused and that the tag types are empty classes. As a consequence, the argument passing and construction of the tag type objects are optimized out. Thus, the extra function layer and the tag dispatching don't cause any run-time overhead. For instance, calling advance on a vector iterator boils down to generating the code of i+= n only.

The dual counterpart of advance is distance:

```
int i= distance(it1, it2);
```

It computes the distance between two iterators, i.e., how often the first iterator must be incremented to be equal to the second one. It goes without saying that the implementation is tag-dispatched as well so that the effort for random-access iterators is constant and linear otherwise.

4.1.3 Containers

The containers in the standard library cover a broad range of important data structures, are easy to use, and are quite efficient. Before you write your own containers, it is definitely worth trying the standard ones.

4.1.3.1 Vectors

std::vector is the simplest standard container and the most efficient for storing data contiguously, similar to C arrays. Whereas C arrays up to a certain size are stored on the stack, a vector always resides on the heap. Vectors provide a bracket operator and array-style algorithms can be used:

```
std::vector<int> v= {3, 4, 7, 9};
for (int i= 0; i < v.size(); ++i)
    v[i]*= 2;
```

Alternatively, we can use the iterators: directly or hidden in range-based for:

```
for (auto& x : v)
    x*= 2;
```

Figure 4–2: Memory layout of vector

The different forms of traversal should be similarly efficient. Vectors can be enlarged by adding new entries at the end:

```
std::vector<int> v;
for (int i= 0; i < 100; ++i)
    v.push_back(my_random());
```

where my_random() returns random numbers like a generator in Section 4.2.2. The STL vector often reserves extra space as illustrated in Figure 4–2 to accelerate push_back.

Therefore, appending entries can be

- Either pretty fast by just filling already reserved space;

- Or rather slow when more memory must be allocated and all data copied.

The available space is given by the member function capacity. When the vector data is enlarged, the amount of extra space is usually proportional to the vector size, so push_back takes asymptotically constant time. Typical implementations perform two memory allocations when the vector is doubled in size (i.e., enlarged from s to $\sqrt{2}s$ at each reallocation). Figure 4–3 illustrates this: the first picture is a completely filled vector where the addition of a new entry requires a new allocation as in the second picture. After that, we can add further entries until the extra space is filled as well, as in picture three. Then new memory has to be allocated and all entries must be copied as in the fourth picture; only then a new entry can be added.

The method resize(n) shrinks or expands the vector to size n. New entries are default-constructed (or set to 0 for built-in types). Shrinking vectors with resize doesn't release memory. This can be done in C++11 with shrink_to_fit which reduces the capacity to the actual vector size.

⇒ c++11/vector_usage.cpp

The following simple program illustrates how a vector is set up and modified with C++11 features:

C++11

```
#include <iostream>
#include <vector>
#include <algorithm>

int main ()
{
```

```
    using namespace std;
    vector<int> v= {3, 4, 7, 9};
    auto it= find(v.begin(), v.end(), 4);
    cout ≪ "After " ≪ *it ≪ " comes " ≪ *(it+1) ≪ '\n';
    auto it2= v.insert(it+1, 5); // insert value 5 at pos. 2
    v.erase(v.begin());          // delete entry at pos. 1
    cout ≪ "Size = " ≪ v.size() ≪ ", capacity = "
        ≪ v.capacity() ≪ '\n';
    v.shrink_to_fit();           // drop extra entries
    v.push_back(7);
    for (auto i : v)
        cout ≪ i ≪ ",";
    cout ≪ '\n';
}
```

Section A.7 shows how the same can be achieved in old C++03.

It is possible to add and remove entries in arbitrary positions, but these operations are expensive since all entries behind have to be shifted. However, it is not as expensive as many of us would expect.

Other new methods in vector are emplace and emplace_back, e.g.: C++11

```
vector<matrix> v;
v.push_back(matrix(3, 7)); // add 3 by 7 matrix, built outside
v.emplace_back(7, 9);      // add 7 by 9 matrix, built in place
```

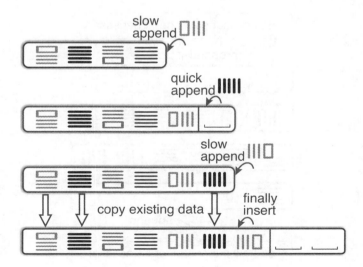

Figure 4–3: Appending vector entries

With push_back, we have to construct an object first (like the 3×7 matrix in the example) and then it is copied or moved to a new entry in the vector. In contrast, emplace_back constructs a new object (here a 7×9 matrix) directly in the vector's new entry. This saves the copy or move operation and possibly some memory allocation/deallocation. Similar methods are also introduced in other containers.

If the size of a vector is known at compile time and not changed later, we can take the C++11 container array instead. It resides on the stack and is therefore more efficient (except for shallow-copy operations like move and swap).

C++11

4.1.3.2 Double-Ended Queue

The deque (quasi-acronym for **D**ouble-**E**nded **QUE**ue) can be approached from several angles:

- As a FIFO (First-In First-Out) queue;

- As a LIFO (Last-In First-Out) stack; or

- As a generalization of a vector with fast insertion at the beginning.

This container has very interesting properties thanks to its memory layout. Internally, it consists of multiple sub-containers as depicted in Figure 4–4. When a new item is appended, it is inserted at the end of the last sub-container, and if that one is full, a new sub-container is allocated. In the same manner, a new entry can be prepended.

The benefit of this design is that the data is mostly sequential in memory and access almost as fast as for vector [41]. At the same time, deque entries are never relocated. This

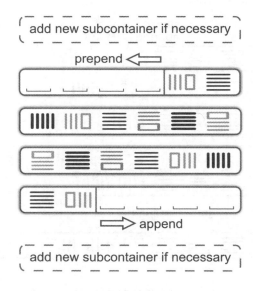

Figure 4–4: deque

doesn't only save the cost of copy or move, it also allows us to store types that are neither copyable nor movable as we will show in the following.

⇒ c++11/deque_emplace.cpp

Pretty advanced: With the emplace methods, we can even create containers of non-copyable, non-movable classes. Say we have a solver class that contains neither copy nor move constructors (e.g., due to an atomic member; for atomic see §4.6): C++11

```cpp
struct parameters {};
struct solver
{
    solver(const mat& ref, const parameters& para)
      : ref(ref), para(para) {}
    solver(const solver&) = delete;
    solver(solver&&) = delete;

    const mat&       ref;
    const parameters& para;
};
```

Several objects of this class are stored in a deque. Later, we iterate over those solvers:

```cpp
void solve_x(const solver& s) { ... }

int main ()
{
    parameters   p1, p2, p3;
    mat          A, B, C;
    deque<solver> solvers;

    // solvers.push_back(solver(A, p1)); // would not compile
    solvers.emplace_back(B, p1);
    solvers.emplace_back(C, p2);
    solvers.emplace_front(A, p1);

    for (auto& s : solvers)
        solve_x(s);
}
```

Please note that the solver class can only be used in container methods without data motion or copy. For instance, vector::emplace_back potentially copies or moves data and the corresponding code wouldn't compile due to the deleted constructors in solver. Even with deque, we cannot use all member functions: insert and erase, for instance, need to move data. We must also use a reference for our loop variable s to avoid a copy there.

4.1.3.3 Lists

The list container (in <list>) is a doubly-linked list as shown in Figure 4–5 so that it can be traversed forward and backward (i.e., its iterators model BidirectionalIterator). In contrast to the preceding containers, we cannot access the *n*-th entry directly. An advantage over vector and deque is that insertion and deletion in the middle are less expensive.

List entries are never moved when others are inserted or deleted. Thus, only references and iterators of deleted entries are invalidated while all others keep their validity.

```
int main ()
{
    list<int> l= {3, 4, 7, 9};
    auto it= find(begin(l), end(l), 4), it2= find(begin(l), end(l), 7);
    l.erase(it);
    cout << "it2 still points to " << *it2 << '\n';
}
```

The dynamic memory handling on each individual entry scatters them in the memory as illustrated in Figure 4–6 so that unfortunate cache behavior causes poorer performance than for vector and deque. Lists are more efficient for some operations but slower for many others so the overall performance is seldom better for list; compare, for instance, [28] or [52]. Fortunately, such performance bottlenecks can be quickly overcome in generically programmed applications by just changing the container types.

An entry of our list<int> takes 20 bytes on a typical 64-bit platform: two times 8 bytes for the 64-bit pointers and 4 bytes for int. When the backward iteration is not needed, we can save the space for one pointer and use a forward_list (in <forward_list>).

C++11

4.1.3.4   Sets and Multisets

The purpose of a set container is to store the information that a value belongs to the set. The entries in the set are internally sorted as a tree so that they can be accessed with logarithmic complexity. The presence of a value in a set can be tested by the member functions find and

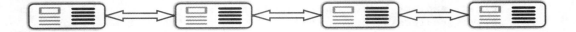

Figure 4–5: Doubly-linked list (in theory)

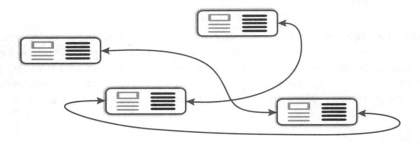

Figure 4–6: Doubly-linked list in practice

count. find returns an iterator referring to the value or if not found to the end iterator. If we don't need the iterator, count is more convenient. In this case, it is more convenient to use count:

```
set<int> s= {1, 3, 4, 7, 9};
s.insert(5);
for (int i= 0; i < 6; ++i)
    cout ≪ i ≪ " appears " ≪ s.count(i) ≪ " times.\n";
```

yielding the expected output:

```
0 appears 0 time(s).
1 appears 1 time(s).
2 appears 0 time(s).
3 appears 1 time(s).
4 appears 1 time(s).
5 appears 1 time(s).
```

Multiple insertions of the same value have no impact; i.e., count always returns 0 or 1.

The container multiset additionally counts how often a value is inserted:

```
multiset<int> s= {1, 3, 4, 7, 9, 1, 1, 4};
s.insert(4);
for (int i= 0; i < 6; ++i)
    cout ≪ i ≪ " appears " ≪ s.count(i) ≪ " time(s).\n";
```

yielding:

```
0 appears 0 time(s).
1 appears 3 time(s).
2 appears 0 time(s).
3 appears 1 time(s).
4 appears 3 time(s).
5 appears 0 time(s).
```

For only checking whether a certain value is present in the multiset, find is more efficient as it doesn't need to traverse replicated values.

Please note that there is no header file named multiset but the class multiset is also defined in <set>.

4.1.3.5 Maps and Multimaps

⇒ c++11/map_test.cpp

A map is an associative container; i.e., values are associated with a *Key*. The key can have any type with an ordering: either provided by operator < (via the less functor) or by a functor establishing a strict weak ordering. The map provides a bracket operator for a concise access notation. The following program illustrates its usage:

```
map<string, double> constants=
    {{"e", 2.7}, {"pi", 3.14}, {"h", 6.6e-34}};
cout ≪ "The Planck constant is " ≪ constants["h"] ≪ '\n';
constants["c"]= 299792458;
cout ≪ "The Coulomb constant is "
    ≪ constants["k"] ≪ '\n';       // Access missing entry!
cout ≪ "The value of pi is "
    ≪ constants.find("pi")->second ≪ '\n';
auto it_phi= constants.find("phi");
if (it_phi != constants.end())
    cout ≪ "Golden ratio is " ≪ it_phi->second ≪ '\n';
cout ≪ "The Euler constant is "
    ≪ constants.at("e") ≪ "\n\n";
for (auto& c : constants)
    cout ≪ "The value of " ≪ c.first ≪ " is "
        ≪ c.second ≪ '\n';
```

This yields:

```
The Planck constant is 6.6e-34
The Coulomb constant is 0
The circle's circumference pi is 3.14
The Euler constant is 2.7

The value of c is 2.99792e+08
The value of e is 2.7
The value of h is 6.6e-34
The value of k is 0
The value of pi is 3.14
```

The map is here initialized by a list of key-value pairs. Note that the value_type of the map is not double but pair<const string, double>. In the next two lines, we use the bracket operator for finding the value with key h and for inserting a new value for c. The bracket operator returns a reference to the value of that key. If the key is not found, a new entry is inserted with a default-constructed value. The reference to this value is then returned. In case of c, we assign a value to this reference and set up the key-value pair. Then we ask for the non-existing Coulomb constant and accidentally create an entry with a zero value.

To avoid inconsistencies between the mutable and the constant overload of [], the creators of STL omitted the constant overload altogether (a design choice we are not really happy with). To search keys in a constant map, we can use the classical method find or the C++11 method at. find is less elegant than [] but it saves us from accidentally inserting entries. It returns a const_iterator which refers to a key-value pair. If the key is not found, the end iterator is returned to which we should compare when the presence of the key is uncertain.

When we are sure that a key exists in the map, we can use at. It returns a reference to the value like []. The key difference is that an out_of_range exception is thrown when the the key is not found—even when the map is mutable. Thus, it cannot be used to insert new entries but provides a compact interface for finding entries.

When we iterate over the container, we get pairs of keys and associated values (as the values on their own would be meaningless).

⇒ c++11/multimap_test.cpp

When a key can be associated with multiple values, we need a multimap. The entries with the same key are stored next to each other so we can iterate over them. The iterator range is provided by the methods lower_bound and upper_bound. In the next example we iterate over all entries with key equals 3 and print their values:

```
multimap<int, double> mm=
    {{3, 1.3}, {2, 4.1}, {3, 1.8}, {4, 9.2}, {3, 1.5}};
for (auto it= mm.lower_bound(3),
        end= mm.upper_bound(3); it != end; ++it)
    cout << "The value is " << it->second << '\n';
```

This yields:

```
The value is 1.3
The value is 1.8
The value is 1.5
```

The last four containers—set, multiset, map, and multimap—are all realized as some kind of tree and have logarithmic complexity for the access. In the following section, we introduce containers with faster access regarding average complexity.

4.1.3.6 Hash Tables

C++11

⇒ c++11/unordered_map_test.cpp

Hash tables are containers with very efficient search. In contrast to the preceding containers, hash maps have a constant complexity for a single access (when the hash function is reasonably good). To avoid name clashes with existing software, the standards committee refrained from names with "hash" and prepended "unordered" to the names of the ordered containers.

Unordered containers can be used in the same manner as their ordered counterparts:

```
unordered_map<string, double> constants=
    {{"e", 2.7}, {"pi", 3.14}, {"h", 6.6e-34}};
cout << "The Planck constant is " << constants["h"] << '\n';
constants["c"]= 299792458;
cout << "The Euler constant is " << constants.at("e") << "\n\n";
```

yielding the same results as map. If desired, a user-defined hash function can be provided.

Further reading: All containers provide a customizable allocator that allows us to implement our own memory management or to use platform-specific memory. The allocator interface is given, for instance, in [26], [43].

4.1.4   Algorithms

General-purpose STL algorithms are defined in the header <algorithm> and those primarily for number crunching in <numeric>.

4.1.4.1   Non-modifying Sequence Operations

find   takes three arguments: two iterators that define the right-open interval of the search space, and a value to search for in that range. Each entry referred to by first is compared with value. When a match is found, the iterator pointing to it is returned; otherwise the iterator is incremented. If the value is not contained in the sequence, an iterator equal to last is returned. Thus, the caller can test whether the search was successful by comparing its result with last.

This is actually not a particularly difficult task and we could implement this by ourselves:

```
template <typename InputIterator, typename T>
InputIterator find(InputIterator first, InputIterator last,
                   const T& value)
{
    while (first != last && *first != value)
        ++first;
    return first;
}
```

This program snippet is indeed the standard way find is realized whereas specialized overloads for special iterators may exist.

⇒ c++11/find_test.cpp

As a demonstration we consider a sequence of integer values containing the number 7 twice. We want to write the sub-sequence that starts with the first and ends with the second 7. In other words, we have to find the two occurrences and print out a closed interval—whereas STL always works on right-open intervals. This requires a little extra work:

```
vector<int> seq= {3, 4, 7, 9, 2, 5, 7, 8};
auto it= find(seq.begin(), seq.end(), 7);       // first 7
auto end= find(it+1, seq.end(), 7);             // second 7
for (auto past= end+1; it != past; ++it)
    cout << *it << ' ';
cout << '\n';
```

After we find the first 7, we restart the search from the succeeding position (so as not to find the same 7 again). In the for-loop, we increment the end iterator, so as not to include the second 7 in the printing. In the example above, we relied on the fact that 7 appears twice in the sequence. For robustness we throw user-defined exceptions when 7 isn't found or is found only once.

To be more robust, we can check whether our search succeeded:

```
if (it == seq.end())
    throw no_seven{};
    ...
if (end == seq.end())
    throw one_seven{};
```

⇒ c++11/find_test2.cpp

The implementation above would not work for a `list` since we used the expressions `it+1` and `end+1`. This requires that the iterators be random-access iterators. However, we can lift this requirement by copying one iterator and using an increment operation:

```
list<int> seq= {3, 4, 7, 9, 2, 5, 7, 8};
auto it= find(seq.begin(), seq.end(), 7), it2= it; // first 7
++it2;
auto end= find(it2, seq.end(), 7);                 // second 7
++end;
for (; it != end; ++it)
    std::cout << *it << ' ';
```

This iterator usage is not that different from the preceding implementation but it is more generic by avoiding the random-access operations. We can now use `list`, for instance. More formally: our second implementation only requires `ForwardIterator` for `it` and `end` while the first one needed `RandomAccessIterator`.

⇒ c++11/find_test3.cpp

In the same style, we can write a generic function to print the interval that works with all STL containers. Let's go one step further: we also want to support classical arrays. Unfortunately, arrays have no member `begin` and `end`. (Right, they have no members at all.) C++11 donated them and all STL containers free functions named `begin` and `end` which allow us to be even more generic:

Listing 4–2: Generic function for printing a closed interval

```
struct value_not_found {};
struct value_not_found_twice {};

template <typename Range, typename Value>
void print_interval(const Range& r, const Value& v,
                    std::ostream& os= std::cout)
{
    using std::begin; using std::end;
    auto it= std::find(begin(r), end(r), v), it2= it;
    if (it == end(r))
        throw value_not_found();
    ++it2;
    auto past= std::find(it2, end(r), v);
    if (past == end(r))
        throw value_not_found_twice();
    ++past;
    for (; it != past; ++it)
            os << *it << ' ';
    os << '\n';
}

int main ()
{
```

```
std::list<int> seq= {3, 4, 7, 9, 2, 5, 7, 8};
print_interval(seq, 7);

int array[]= {3, 4, 7, 9, 2, 5, 7, 8};
std::stringstream ss;
print_interval(array, 7, ss);
std::cout << ss.str();
}
```

We also parameterized the output stream for not being restricted to std::cout. Please note the harmonic mixture of static and dynamic polymorphism in the function arguments: the types of the range r and the value v are instantiated during compilation while the output operator << of os is selected at run time depending on the type that was actually referred to by os.

At this point, we want to draw your attention to the way we dealt with namespaces. When we use a lot of standard containers and algorithms, we can just declare

```
using namespace std;
```

directly after including the header files and don't need to write std:: any longer. This works fine for small programs. In larger projects, we run sooner or later into name clashes. They can be laborious and annoying to fix (preventing is better than healing here). Therefore, we should import as little as possible—especially in header files. Our implementation of print_interval doesn't rely on preceding name imports and can be safely placed in a header file. Even within the function, we don't import the entire std namespace but limit ourselves to those functions that we really use.

Note that we did not qualify the namespace in some function calls, e.g., std::begin(r). This would work in the example above, but we would not cover user types that define a function begin in the namespace of the class. The combination of using std::begin and begin(r) guarantees that std::begin is found. On the other hand, a begin function for a user type is found by ADL (§3.2.2) and would be a better match than std::begin. The same applies to end. In contrast, for the function find we didn't want to call possible user overloads and made sure that it is taken from std.

find_if   generalizes find by searching for the first entry that holds a general criterion. Instead of comparing with a single value it evaluates a *Predicate*—a function returning a bool. Say we search the first list entry larger than 4 and smaller than 7:

```
bool check(int i) { return i > 4 && i < 7; }

int main ()
{
    list<int> seq= {3, 4, 7, 9, 2, 5, 7, 8};
    auto it= find_if(begin(seq), end(seq), check);
    cout << "The first value in range is " << *it << '\n';
}
```

C++11 Or we create the predicate in place:

```
auto it= find_if(begin(seq), end(seq),
                 [](int i){ return i > 4 && i < 7; } );
```

The searching and counting algorithms can be used similarly and the online manuals provide good documentation.

`for_each`: An STL function whose usefulness remains a mystery to us today is `for_each`. Its purpose is to apply a function on each element of a sequence. In C++03, we had to define a function object upfront or compose it with functors or pseudo-lambdas. A simple for-loop was easier to implement and much clearer to understand. Today we can create the function object on the fly with lambdas, but we also have a more concise range-based for-loop so the loop implementation is again simpler to write and to read. However, if you find `for_each` useful in some context, we do not want to discourage you. While `for_each` allows for modifying sequence elements according to the standard, it is still classified as non-mutable for historical reasons.

4.1.4.2 Modifying Sequence Operations

`copy`: The modifying operations have to be used with care because the modified sequence is usually only parameterized by the starting iterator. It is therefore our responsibility as programmers to make sure enough space is available. For instance, before we `copy` a container we can `resize` the target to the source's size:

```
vector<int> seq= {3, 4, 7, 9, 2, 5, 7, 8}, v;
v.resize(seq.size());
copy(seq.begin(), seq.end(), v.begin());
```

A nice demonstration of the iterators' flexibility is printing a sequence by means of `copy`:

```
copy(seq.begin(), seq.end(), ostream_iterator<int>(cout, ", "));
```

The `ostream_iterator` builds a minimalistic iterator interface for an output stream: the ++ and * operations are void, comparison is not needed here, and an assignment of a value sends it to the referred output stream together with the delimiter.

unique is a function that is quite useful in numeric software: it removes the duplicated entries in a sequence. As a precondition the sequence must be sorted. Then `unique` can be used to rearrange the entries such that unique values are at the front and the replications at the end. An iterator to the first repeated entry is returned and can be used to remove the duplicates:

```
std::vector<int> seq= {3, 4, 7, 9, 2, 5, 7, 8, 3, 4, 3, 9};
sort(seq.begin(), seq.end());
auto it= unique(seq.begin(), seq.end());
seq.resize(distance(seq.begin(), it));
```

If this is a frequent task, we can encapsulate the preceding operations in a generic function parameterized with a sequence/range:

```
template <typename Seq>
void make_unique_sequence(Seq& seq)
{
    using std::begin; using std::end; using std::distance;
```

```
        std::sort(begin(seq), end(seq));
        auto it= std::unique(begin(seq), end(seq));
        seq.resize(distance(begin(seq), it));
}
```

There are many more mutating sequence operations that follow the same principles.

4.1.4.3 Sorting Operations

The sorting functions in the standard library are quite powerful and flexible and can be used in almost all situations. Earlier implementations were based on quick sort with $\mathcal{O}(n \log n)$ average but quadratic worst-case complexity.[2] Recent versions use intro-sort whose worst-case complexity is $\mathcal{O}(n \log n)$, too. In short, there is very little reason to bother with our own implementation.

By default, sort uses the < operator but we can customize the comparison, e.g., to sort sequences in descending order:

```
vector<int> seq= {3, 4, 7, 9, 2, 5, 7, 8, 3, 4, 3, 9};
sort(seq.begin(), seq.end(), [](int x, int y){return x > y;});
```

Lambdas come in handy again. Sequences of complex numbers cannot be sorted unless we define a comparison, for instance, by magnitude:

```
using cf= complex<float>;
vector<cf> v= {{3, 4}, {7, 9}, {2, 5}, {7, 8}};
sort(v.begin(), v.end(), [](cf x, cf y){return abs(x)<abs(y);});
```

Although not particularly meaningful here, a lexicographic order is also quickly defined with a lambda:

```
auto lex= [](cf x, cf y){return real(x)<real(y)
                           || real(x)==real(y)&&imag(x)<imag(y);};
sort(v.begin(), v.end(), lex);
```

Many algorithms require a sorted sequence as a precondition as we have seen with unique. Set operations can also be performed on sorted sequences and do not necessarily need a set type.

4.1.4.4 Numeric Operation

The numeric operations from STL are found in header/library <numeric>. iota generates a sequence starting with a given value successively incremented by 1 for all following entries. accumulate evaluates by default the sum of a sequence and performs an arbitrary reduction when a binary function is provided by the user. inner_product performs by default a dot product whereby the general form allows for specifying a binary function object substituting the addition and multiplication respectively. partial_sum and adjacent_difference behave as their names suggest. The following little program shows all numeric functions at once:

```
vector<float> v= {3.1, 4.2, 7, 9.3, 2, 5, 7, 8, 3, 4},
              w(10), x(10), y(10);
iota(w.begin(), w.end(), 12.1);
```

---

2. Lower worst-case complexity was already provided at that time by stable_sort and partial_sort.

```
partial_sum(v.begin(), v.end(), x.begin());
adjacent_difference(v.begin(), v.end(), y.begin());

float alpha= inner_product(w.begin(), w.end(), v.begin(), 0.0f);
float sum_w= accumulate(w.begin(), w.end(), 0.0f),
      product_w= accumulate(w.begin(), w.end(), 1.0f,
                            [](float x, float y){return x * y;});
```

The function iota was not part of C++03 but is integrated in the standard since C++11.

4.1.4.5 Complexity

Bjarne Stroustrup summarized the complexities of all STL algorithms in a concise table (Table 4–1) that we share with you.

4.1.5 Beyond Iterators

Iterators undoubtedly made an important contribution to modern programming in C++. Nonetheless, they are quite dangerous and lead to inelegant interfaces.

Let's start with the dangers. Iterators appear in pairs and only the programmer can assure that the two iterators used for the termination criterion really relate to each other. This offers us an unattractive repertoire of failures:

- The end iterator comes first.

- The iterators are from different containers.

- The iterator makes larger steps (over multiple entries) and doesn't hit the end iterator.

In all these cases, the iteration can run over arbitrary memory and might only stop when the program leaves the accessible address space. A program crash is probably still our best option because we see where we failed. An execution that at some point stops the iteration has most likely already ruined a lot of data so the program can cause serious damage before ending in a crash or in an alleged success.

Similarly, STL functions on multiple containers only take a pair of iterators from one container[3] and solely the beginning iterator from the other containers, e.g.:

```
copy(v.begin(), v.end(), w.begin());
```

Table 4–1: Complexity of STL Algorithms

Algorithmic Complexities	
$\mathcal{O}(1)$	swap, iter_swap
$\mathcal{O}(\log n)$	lower_bound, upper_bound, equal_range, binary_search, push_heap, pop_heap
$\mathcal{O}(n \log n)$	inplace_merge, stable_partition, all sorting algorithms
$\mathcal{O}(n^2)$	find_end, find_first_of, search, search_n
$\mathcal{O}(n)$	All other algorithms

From [43, page 931]

---

3. A pair of iterators does not necessarily represent an entire container. It can also refer to a part of a container or some more general abstraction. Considering entire containers only is already enough to demonstrate catastrophic consequences of even little errors.

Thus, it cannot be tested whether the target of the copy provides enough space and random memory can be overwritten.

Finally, the interface of iterator-based functions is not always elegant. Consider

```
x= inner_product(v.begin(), v.end(), w.begin());
```

versus

```
x= dot(v, w);
```

The example speaks for itself. Plus, the second notion allows us to check that v and w match in size.

C++17 may introduce *Ranges*. These are all types providing a begin and an end function which return iterators. This includes all containers but is not limited to it. A range can also represent a sub-container, the reverse traversal of a container, or some transformed view. The ranges will trim the function interface nicely and will also allow size checks.

In the meantime, we do ourselves a favor by adding functions on top of those with an iterator interface. There is nothing wrong with using iterator-based functions on low or intermediate levels. They are excellent to provide the most general applicability. But in most cases we don't need this generality because we operate on complete containers, and size-checking functions with a concise interface allow us to write more elegant and more reliable applications. On the other hand, existing iterator-based functions can be called internally as we did for print_interval in Listing 4–2. Likewise, we could realize a concise dot function from inner_product. Thus:

Iterator-Based Functions
If you write iterator-based functions, provide a user-friendly interface on top of them.

Final remark: This section only scratches the surface of STL and is intended as a mere appetizer.

4.2   Numerics

In this section we illustrate how the complex numbers and the random-number generators of C++ can be used. The header <cmath> contains a fair number of numeric functions whose usage is straightforward, not needing further illustration.

4.2.1   Complex Numbers

We already demonstrated how to implement a non-templated complex class in Chapter 2 and used the complex class template in Chapter 3. To not repeat the obvious again and again, we illustrate the usage with a graphical example.

4.2.1.1 Mandelbrot Set

The Mandelbrot set—named after its creator, Benoît B. Mandelbrot—is the set of `complex` numbers that don't reach infinity by successive squaring and adding the original value:

$$M = \{c \in \mathbb{C}: \lim_{n \to \infty} z_n(c) \neq \infty\}$$

where

$$z_0(c) = c$$
$$z_{n+1}(c) = z_n^2 + c$$

It can be shown that a point is outside the Mandelbrot set when $|z_n(c)| > 2$. The most expensive part of computing the magnitude is the square root at the end. C++ provides a function `norm` which is the square of `abs`, i.e., the calculation of `abs` without the final `sqrt`. Thus, we replace the continuation criterion `abs(z) <= 2` with `norm(z) <= 4`.

$\Rightarrow$ c++11/mandelbrot.cpp

The visualization of the Mandelbrot set is a color coding of the iterations needed to reach that limit. To draw the fractal, we used the cross-platform library Simple DirectMedia Layer (SDL 1.2). The numeric part is realized by the class `mandel_pixel` that computes for each pixel on the screen how many iterations are needed until `norm(z) > 4` and which color that represents:

```cpp
class mandel_pixel
{
  public:
    mandel_pixel(SDL_Surface* screen, int x, int y,
                 int xdim, int ydim, int max_iter)
      : screen(screen), max_iter(max_iter), iter(0), c(x, y)
    {
        // scale y to [-1.2,1.2] and shift -0.5+0i to the center
        c*= 2.4f / static_cast<float>(ydim);
        c-= complex<float>(1.2 * xdim / ydim + 0.5, 1.2);
        iterate();
    }
    int iterations() const { return iter; }
    uint32_t color() const { ... }

  private:
    void iterate()
    {
        complex<float> z= c;
        for (; iter < max_iter && norm(z) <= 4.0f; iter++)
        z= z * z + c;
    };
    // ...
```

```
    int iter;
    complex<float> c;
};
```

The complex numbers are scaled such that their imaginary parts lie between -1.2 and 1.2 and are shifted by 0.5 to the left. We have omitted the code lines for the graphics, as they are beyond the scope of this book. The complete program is found on GitHub, and the resulting picture in Figure 4–7.

In the end, our core computation is realized in three lines and the other ≈ 50 lines are needed to draw a nice picture, despite our having chosen a very simple graphics library. This is unfortunately not an uncommon situation: many real-world applications contain far more code for file I/O, database access, graphics, web interfaces, etc., than for the scientific core functionality.

4.2.1.2   Mixed Complex Calculations

As demonstrated before, complex numbers can be built from most numeric types. In this regard, the library is quite generic. For its operations it is not so generic: a value of type complex<T> can only be added (subtracted, etc.) with a value of type complex<T> or T. As a consequence, the simple code

```
complex<double> z(3, 5), c= 2 * z;
```

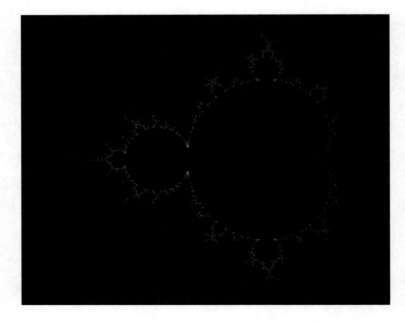

Figure 4–7: Mandelbrot set

doesn't compile since no multiplication is defined for int and complex<double>. The problem is easily fixed by replacing 2 with 2.0. However, the issue is more annoying in generic functions, e.g.:

```
template <typename T>
inline T twice(const T& z)
{    return 2 * z; }

int main ()
{
    complex<double> z(3, 5), c;
    c= twice(z);
}
```

The function twice will not compile for the same reason as before. If we wrote 2.0 * z it would compile for complex<double> but not for complex<float> or complex<long double>. The function

```
template <typename T>
complex<T> twice(const complex<T>& z)
{    return T{2} * z; }
```

works with all complex types—but only with complex types. In contrast, the following:

```
template <typename T>
inline T twice(const T& z)
{    return T{2} * z; }
```

compiles with complex and non-complex types. However, when T is a complex type, 2 is unnecessarily converted into a complex and four multiplications plus two additions are performed where only half of them are needed. A possible solution is to overload the last two implementations. Alternatively, we can write type traits to deal with it.

The programming becomes more challenging when multiple arguments of different types are involved, some of them possibly complex numbers. The Matrix Template Library (MTL4, Section 4.7.3) provides mixed arithmetic for complex numbers. We are committed to incorporate this feature into future standards.

4.2.2 Random Number Generators

C++11

Many application domains—like computer simulation, game programming, or cryptography—use random numbers. Every serious programming language thus offers generators for them. Such generators produce sequences of numbers that appear random. A random generator may depend on physical processes like quantum phenomena. However, most generators are based on pseudo-random calculations. They have an internal state—called a *Seed*—that is transformed by deterministic computation each time a pseudo-random number is requested. Thus, a pseudo-random number generator (PRNG) always emits the same sequence when started with the same seed.

Before C++11, there were only the rand and srand functions from C with very limited functionality. More problematic is that there are no guarantees for the quality of generated numbers and it is indeed quite low on some platforms. Therefore, a high-quality <random>

library was added in C++11. It was even considered to deprecate rand and srand altogether in C++. They are still around but should really be avoided where the quality of random numbers is important.

4.2.2.1 Keep It Simple

The random number generators in C++11 provide a lot of flexibility which is very useful for experts but somewhat overwhelming for beginners. Walter Brown proposed a set of novice-friendly functions [6]. Slightly adapted,[4] they are:

```cpp
#include <random>

std::default_random_engine& global_urng()
{
    static std::default_random_engine u{};
    return u;
}

void randomize()
{
    static std::random_device rd{};
    global_urng().seed(rd());
}

int pick(int from, int thru)
{
    static std::uniform_int_distribution<> d{};
    using parm_t= decltype(d)::param_type;
    return d(global_urng(), parm_t{from, thru});
}

double pick(double from, double upto)
{
    static std::uniform_real_distribution<> d{};
    using parm_t= decltype(d)::param_type;
    return d(global_urng(), parm_t{from, upto});
}
```

To start with random numbers, you could just copy these three function into the project and look at the details later. Walter's interface is pretty simple and nonetheless sufficient for many practical purposes like code testing. We only need to remember the following three functions:

- randomize: Make the following numbers really random by initializing the generator's seed.

- pick(int a, int b): Give me an int in the interval $[a, b]$ when a and b are int.

- pick(double a, double b): Give me an double in the right-open interval $[a, b)$ when a and b are double.

---

4. Walter used return type deduction of non-lambda functions which is only available in C++14 and higher. We further shortened the function name from pick_a_number to pick.

Without calling randomize, the sequence of generated numbers is equal each time which is desirable in certain situations: finding bugs is much easier with reproducible behavior. Note that pick includes the upper bound for int but not for double to be consistent with standard functions. global_urng can be considered as an implementation detail for the moment.

With those functions, we can easily write loops for rolling dice:

```
randomize();
cout ≪ "Now, we roll dice:\n";
for (int i= 0; i < 15; ++i)
    cout ≪ pick(1, 6) ≪ endl;

cout ≪ "\nLet's roll continuous dice now: ;-)\n";
for (int i= 0; i < 15; ++i)
    cout ≪ pick(1.0, 6.0) ≪ endl;
```

In fact, this is even simpler than the old C interface. Apparently it is too late for C++14, but the author would be glad to see these functions in future standards. In the following section, we will use this interface for testing.

4.2.2.2 Randomized Testing

⇒ c++11/random_testing.cpp

Say we want to test whether our complex implementation from Chapter 2 is distributive:

$$a(b + c) = ab + ac \qquad \text{for } \forall a, b, c. \tag{4.1}$$

The multiplication is canonically implemented as

```
inline complex operator*(const complex& c1, const complex& c2)
{
    return complex(real(c1) * real(c2) - imag(c1) * imag(c2),
                   real(c1) * imag(c2) + imag(c1) * real(c2));
}
```

To cope with rounding errors we introduce a function similar that checks relative difference:

```
#include <limits>

const double eps= 10 * numeric_limits<double>::epsilon();

inline bool similar(complex x, complex y)
{
    double sum= abs(x) + abs(y);
    if (sum < 1000 * numeric_limits<double>::min())
        return true;
    return abs(x - y) / sum <= eps;
}
```

To avoid divisions by zero we treat two complex numbers as similar if their magnitudes are both very close to zero (the sum of magnitudes smaller than 1000 times the minimal value representable as double). Otherwise, we relate the difference of the two values to the sum of their magnitudes. This should not be larger than 10 times epsilon, the difference between

1 and the next value representable as `double`. This information is provided by the `<limits>` library later introduced in Section 4.3.1.

Next, we need a test that takes a triplet of `complex` numbers for the variables in (4.1) and that checks the similarity of the terms on both sides thereafter:

```
struct distributivity_violated {};

inline void test(complex a, complex b, complex c)
{
    if (!similar(a * (b + c), a * b + a * c)) {
    cerr ≪ "Test detected that " ≪ a ≪ ...
    throw distributivity_violated();
    }
}
```

If a violation is detected, the critical values are reported on the error stream and a user-defined exception is thrown. Finally, we implement the random generation of `complex` numbers and the loops over test sets:

```
const double from= -10.0, upto= 10.0;

inline complex mypick()
{    return complex(pick(from, upto), pick(from, upto)); }

int main ()
{
    const int max_test= 20;
    randomize();
    for (int i= 0; i < max_test; ++i) {
        complex a= mypick();
        for (int j= 0; j < max_test; j++) {
            complex b= mypick();
            for (int k= 0; k < max_test; k++) {
                complex c= mypick();
                test(a, b, c);
            }
        }
    }
}
```

Here we only tested with random numbers from $[-10, 10)$ for the real and the imaginary parts; whether this is sufficient to reach good confidence in the correctness is left open. In large projects it definitely pays off to build a reusable test framework. The pattern of nested loops containing random value generation and a test function in the innermost loop is applicable in many situations. It could be encapsulated in a class which might be variadic to handle properties involving different numbers of variables. The generation of a random value could also be provided by a special constructor (e.g., marked by a tag), or a sequence could be generated upfront. Different approaches are imaginable. The loop pattern in this section was chosen for the sake of simplicity.

To see that the distributivity doesn't hold precisely, we can decrease eps to 0. Then, we see an (abbreviated) error message like

```
Test detected that (-6.21,7.09) * ((2.52,-3.58) + (-4.51,3.91))
    != (-6.21,7.09) * (2.52,-3.58) + (-6.21,7.09) * (-4.51,3.91)
terminate called after throwing 'distributivity_violated'
```

Now we go into the details of random number generation.

4.2.2.3 Engines

The library <random> contains two kinds of functional objects: generators and distributions. The former generate sequences of unsigned integers (the precise type is provided by each class's typedef). Every value should have approximately the same probability. The distribution classes map these numbers to values whose probability corresponds to the parameterized distribution.

Unless we have special needs, we can just use the default_random_engine. We have to keep in mind that the random number sequence depends deterministically on its seed and that each engine is initialized with the same seed whenever an object is created. Thus, a new engine of a given type always produces the same sequence, for instance:

```
void random_numbers()
{
    default_random_engine re;
    cout << "Random numbers: ";
    for (int i= 0; i < 4; i++)
        cout << re << (i < 3 ? ", " : "");
    cout << '\n';
}

int main ()
{
    random_numbers();
    random_numbers();
}
```

yielded on the author's machine:

```
Random numbers: 16807, 282475249, 1622650073, 984943658
Random numbers: 16807, 282475249, 1622650073, 984943658
```

To get a different sequence in each call of random_numbers, we have to create a persistent engine by declaring it static:

```
void random_numbers()
{
    static default_random_engine re;
    ...
}
```

Still, we have the same sequence in every program run. To overcome this, we must set the seed to an almost truly random value. Such a value is provided by random_device:

```
void random_numbers()
{
    static random_device rd;
    static default_random_engine re(rd());
    ...
}
```

random_device returns a value that depends on measurements of hardware and operating system events and can be considered virtually random (i.e., a very high *Entropy* is achieved). In fact, random_device provides the same interface as an engine except that the seed cannot be set. So, it can be used to generate random values as well, at least when performance doesn't matter. On our test machine, it took 4–13 ms to generate a million random numbers with the default_random_engine and 810–820 ms with random_device. In applications that depend on high-quality random numbers, like in cryptography, the performance penalty can still be acceptable. In most cases, it should suffice to generate only the starting seed with random_device.

Among the generators there are primary engines, parameterizable adapters thereof, and predefined adapted engines:

- **Basic engines** that generate random values:

  - linear_congruential_engine,
  - mersenne_twister_engine, and
  - subtract_with_carry_engine.

- **Engine adapters** to create a new engine from another one:

  - discard_block_engine: ignores n entries from the underlying engine each time;
  - independent_bits_engine: map the primary random number to w bits;
  - shuffle_order_engine: modifies the order of random numbers by keeping an internal buffer of the last values.

- **Predefined adapted engines** build from basic engines by instantiation or adaption:

  - knuth_b
  - minstd_rand
  - minstd_rand0
  - mt19937
  - mt19937_64
  - ranlux24
  - ranlux24_base
  - ranlux48
  - ranlux48_base

The predefined engines in the last group are just type definitions, for instance:

```
typedef shuffle_order_engine <minstd_rand0,256> knuth_b;
```

4.2.2.4 Distribution Overview

As mentioned before, the distribution classes map the unsigned integers to the parameterized distributions. Table 4–2 summarizes the distributions defined in C++11. Due to space limits, we used some abbreviated notations. The result type of a distribution can be specified as an argument of the class template where I represents an integer and R a real type. When different symbols are used in the constructor (e.g., m) and the describing formula (e.g., μ), we denoted the equivalence in the precondition (like $m \equiv \mu$). For consistency's sake, we used the same notation in the log-normal and the normal distribution (in contrast to other books, online references, and the standard).

Table 4–2: Distribution Overview

Name	Distributions		
	Preconditions	**Defaults**	**Result**
uniform_int_distribution<I>(a,b)	$a \leqslant b$ $$p(x\|a,b) = \frac{1}{b-a+1}$$	$(0, \max)$	$[a,b] \subseteq \mathbb{N}$
uniform_real_distribution<I>(a,b)	$a \leqslant b$ $$p(x\|a,b) = \frac{1}{b-a}$$	$(0.0, 1.0)$	$[a,b) \subseteq \mathbb{R}$
bernoulli_distribution(p)	$0 \leqslant p < 1$ $$P(b\|p) = \begin{cases} p & \text{if } b = \text{true} \\ 1-p & \text{if } b = \text{false} \end{cases}$$	0.5	$\{\text{true,false}\}$
binomial_distribution<I>(t,p)	$0 \leqslant p \leqslant 1$ and $0 \leqslant t$ $$P(i\|t,p) = \binom{t}{i}p^i(1-p)^{t-i}$$	$(1, 0.5)$	$\mathbb{N}$
geometric_distribution<I>(p)	$0 < p < 1$ $$P(i\|p) = p(1-p)^i$$	0.5	$\mathbb{N}$
negative_binomial_distribution<I> (k,p)	$0 < p < 1$ and $0 < k$ $$P(i\|k,p) = \binom{k+i-1}{i}p^k(1-p)^i$$	$(1, 0.5)$	$\mathbb{N}$
poisson_distribution<I>(m)	$0 < m \equiv \mu$ $$p(i\|\mu) = \frac{e^{-\mu}\mu^i}{i!}$$	1.0	$\mathbb{N}$
exponential_distribution<R>(l)	$1 < l \equiv \lambda$ $$p(x\|\lambda) = \lambda e^{-\lambda x}$$	1.0	$x \geqslant 0 \subset \mathbb{R}$
gamma_distribution<R,R>(a,b)	$0 < a \equiv \alpha$ and $0 < b \equiv \beta$ $$p(x\|\alpha,\beta) = \frac{e^{-x/\beta}}{\beta^\alpha \Gamma(\alpha)}x^{\alpha-1}$$	$(1.0, 1.0)$	$x \geqslant 0 \subset \mathbb{R}$
weibull_distribution<R>(a,b)	$0 < a$ and $0 < b$ $$p(x\|a,b) = \frac{a}{b}\left(\frac{x}{b}\right)^{a-1}\exp-\left(\frac{x}{b}\right)^a$$	$(1.0, 1.0)$	$x \geqslant 0 \subset \mathbb{R}$
extreme_value_distribution<R>(a,b)	$0 < b$	$(0.0, 1.0)$	$\mathbb{R}$

(continues)

Table 4–2: Distribution Overview (Continued)

Name	Distributions		
	Preconditions	**Defaults**	**Result**
	$p(x\vert a,b) = \frac{1}{b}\exp\left(\frac{a-x}{b} - \exp\left(\frac{a-x}{b}\right)\right)$		
normal_distribution<R>(m,s)	$0 < s \equiv \sigma,\ m \equiv \mu$	$(0.0, 1.0)$	$\mathbb{R}$
	$p(x\vert\mu,\sigma) = \frac{1}{\sigma\sqrt{2\pi}}\exp-\frac{(x-\mu)^2}{2\sigma^2}$		
lognormal_distribution<R>(m,s)	$0 < s \equiv \sigma,\ m \equiv \mu$	$(0.0, 1.0)$	$x > 0 \subset \mathbb{R}$
	$p(x\vert\mu,\sigma) = \frac{1}{x\sigma\sqrt{2\pi}}\exp-\frac{(\ln x-\mu)^2}{2\sigma^2}$		
chi_squared_distribution<R>(n)	$0 < n$	1	$x > 0 \subset \mathbb{R}$
	$p(x\vert n) = \frac{x^{(n/2)-1}e^{-x/2}}{\Gamma(n/2)2^{n/2}}$		
cauchy_distribution<R>(a,b)	$0 < b$	$(0.0, 1.0)$	$\mathbb{R}$
	$p(x\vert a,b) = \left(\pi b\left(1+\left(\frac{x-a}{b}\right)^2\right)\right)^{-1}$		
fisher_f_distribution<R>(m,n)	$0 < m$ and $0 < n$	$(1,1)$	$x \geqslant 0 \subset \mathbb{R}$
	$p(x\vert m,n) = \frac{\Gamma((m+n)/2)}{\Gamma(m/2)\Gamma(n/2)}\left(\frac{m}{n}\right)^{\frac{m}{2}}x^{\frac{m}{2}-1}\left(1+m\frac{x}{n}\right)^{-\frac{m+n}{2}}$		
student_t_distribution<R>(n)	$0 < n$	1	$\mathbb{R}$
	$p(x\vert m) = \frac{1}{\sqrt{n\pi}}\frac{\Gamma((n+1)/2)}{\Gamma(n/2)}\left(1+\frac{x^2}{n}\right)^{\frac{n+1}{2}}$		
discrete_distribution<I>(b,e)	$0 \leqslant b[i]$	none	$[0, e-b) \subset \mathbb{N}$
	$P(i\vert w_0,\ldots,w_{n-1}) = \frac{w_i}{s},\ 0 \leqslant i < n,\ s = \sum_{k=0}^{n-1} w_k$		
piece_constant_distribution<R> (b,e,b2,e2)	$b[i] < b[i+1]$	none	$[{}^*b, {}^*(e-1)) \subseteq \mathbb{R}$
	$P(x\vert b,w) = \frac{w_i}{s},\ b_i \leqslant x < b_{i+1},\ s = \sum_k w_k(b_{k+1}-b_k)$		
piece_linear_distribution<R> (b,e,b2,e2)	$b[i] < b[i+1]$	none	$[{}^*b, {}^*(e-1)) \subseteq \mathbb{R}$
	$P(x\vert b,w) = \frac{w_i(b_{i+1}-x)+w_{i+1}(x-b_i)}{s(b_{i+1}-b_i)},\ b_i \leqslant x < b_{i+1}$		
	with $s = \sum_{k=0}^{n-1}\frac{w_k+w_{k+1}}{2}(b_{k+1}-b_k)$		

4.2.2.5   Using a Distribution

Distributions are parameterized with a random number generator, for instance:

```
default_random_engine re(random_device{}());
normal_distribution<> normal;

for (int i= 0; i < 6; ++i)
    cout << normal(re) << endl;
```

Here we created an engine—randomized in the constructor—and a normal distribution of type double with default parameters $\mu = 0.0$ and $\sigma = 1.0$. In each call of the distribution-based generator, we pass the random engine as an argument. The following is an example of the program's output:

```
-0.339502
0.766392
-0.891504
0.218919
2.12442
-1.56393
```

It will of course be different each time we call it.

Alternatively, we can use the `bind` function from the `<functional>` header (§4.4.2) to bind the distribution to the engine:

```
auto normal= bind(normal_distribution<>{},
                  default_random_engine(random_device{}()));

for (int i= 0; i < 6; ++i)
    cout ≪ normal() ≪ endl;
```

The function object `normal` can now be called without arguments. In this situation, `bind` is more compact than a lambda—even with init capture (§3.9.4):

`C++14`

```
auto normal= [re= default_random_engine(random_device{}()),
              n= normal_distribution<>{}]() mutable
             { return n(re); };
```

In most other scenarios, lambdas lead to more readable program sources than `bind` but the latter seems more suitable for binding random engines to distributions.

4.2.2.6 Stochastic Simulation of Share Price Evolution

With the normal distribution we can simulate possible developments of a stock's share price in the Black-Scholes model by Fischer Black and Myron Scholes. The mathematical background is for instance discussed in Jan Rudl's lecture [36, pages 94–95] (in German, unfortunately) and in other quantitative finance publications like [54]. Starting with an initial price of $s_0 \equiv S_0^1$ with an expected yield of μ, a variation of σ, a normally distributed random value Z_i, and a time step Δ, the share price at $t = i \cdot \Delta$ is simulated with respect to the preceding time step by

$$S_{i \cdot \Delta}^1 \sim S_{(i-1) \cdot \Delta}^1 \cdot e^{\sigma \cdot \sqrt{\Delta} \cdot Z_i + \Delta \cdot (\mu - \sigma^2 / 2)}.$$

Subsuming $a = \sigma \cdot \sqrt{\Delta}$ and $b = \Delta \cdot (\mu - \sigma^2 / 2)$, the equation simplifies to

$$S_{i \cdot \Delta}^1 \sim S_{(i-1) \cdot \Delta}^1 \cdot e^{a \cdot Z_i + b}. \tag{4.2}$$

⇒ c++11/black_scholes.cpp

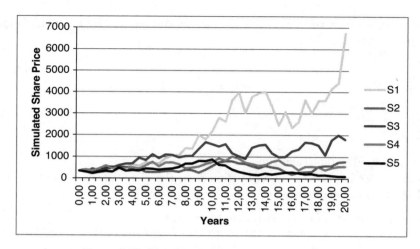

Figure 4–8: Simulated share price over 20 years

The development of S^1 with the parameters $\mu = 0.05, \sigma = 0.3, \Delta = 1.0, t = 20$ as constants according to (4.2) can now be programmed in a few lines:

```
default_random_engine re(random_device{}());
normal_distribution<> normal;

const double mu= 0.05, sigma= 0.3, delta= 0.5, years= 20.01,
             a= sigma * sqrt(delta),
             b= delta * (mu - 0.5 * sigma * sigma);
vector<double>  s= {345.2};      // Start with initial price

for (double t= 0.0; t < years; t+= delta)
    s.push_back( s.back() * exp(a * normal(re) + b) )
```

Figure 4–8 depicts five possible developments of the share price for the parameters from the previous code.

We hope that this introduction to random numbers will give you a smooth start to the exploration of this powerful library.

4.3   Meta-programming

In this section, we will give you a foretaste of meta-programming. Here, we will focus on the library support and in Chapter 5 we will provide more background.

4.3.1   Limits

A very useful library for generic programming is <limits> which provides important information on types. It can also prevent surprising behavior when the source is compiled on another platform and some types are implemented differently. The header `<limits>` contains the class template `numeric_limits` that delivers type-specific information on intrinsic types. This is especially important when dealing with numeric type parameters.

In Section 1.7.5, we demonstrated that only some digits of floating-point numbers are written to the output. Especially when the numbers are written to files, we want to be able to read back the correct value. The number of decimal digits is given in `numeric_limits` as a compile-time constant. The following program prints 1/3 in different floating-point formats with one extra digit:

```cpp
#include <iostream>
#include <limits>

using namespace std;

template <typename T>
inline void test(const T& x)
{
    cout << "x = " << x << " (";
    int oldp= cout.precision(numeric_limits<T>::digits10 + 1);
    cout << x << ")" << endl;
    cout.precision(oldp);
}

int main ()
{
    test(1.f/3.f);
    test(1./3.0);
    test(1./3.0l);
}
```

This yields

```
x = 0.333333 (0.3333333)
x = 0.333333 (0.3333333333333333)
x = 0.333333 (0.3333333333333333333)
```

Another example is computing the minimum value of a container. When the container is empty we want the identity element of the minimum operation, which is the maximal representable value of the corresponding type:

```cpp
template <typename Container>
typename Container::value_type
inline minimum(const Container& c)
{
    using vt= typename Container::value_type;
    vt min_value= numeric_limits<vt>::max();
    for (const vt& x : c)
        if (x < min_value)
            min_value= x;
    return min_value;
}
```

The method max is static and can be called for the type directly without the need of an object. Likewise, the static method min yields the minimal value—more precisely the minimal representable value for int types and the minimal value larger than 0 for floating-point types. Therefore, C++11 introduces the member lowest which yields the smallest value for

all fundamental types.

Termination criteria in fixed-point computations should be type-dependent. When they are too large, the result is unnecessarily imprecise. When they are too small, the algorithm might not terminate (i.e., it may only finish when two consecutive values are identical). For a floating-point type, the static method epsilon yields the smallest value to be added to 1 for a number larger than 1, in other words, the smallest possible increment (with respect to 1), also called *Unit of Least Precision* (ULP). We already used it in Section 4.2.2.2 for determining the similarity of two values.

The following generic example computes the square root iteratively. The termination criterion is that the approximated result of $\sqrt{x}$ should be in an ε-environment of x. To ascertain that our environment is large enough, we scale it with x and double it afterward:

```cpp
template <typename T>
T square_root(const T& x)
{
    const T my_eps= T{2} * x * numeric_limits<T>::epsilon();
    T r= x;

    while (std::abs((r * r) - x) > my_eps)
        r= (r + x/r) / T{2};
    return r;
}
```

The complete set of numeric_limits's members is available in online references like www.cppreference.com or www.cplusplus.com.

4.3.2 Type Traits

⇒ c++11/type_traits_example.cpp

The type traits that many programmers have already used for several years from the Boost library were standardized in C++11 and provided in <type_traits>. We refrain at this point from enumerating them completely and refer you instead to the before-mentioned online manuals. Some of the type traits—like is_const (§5.2.3.3)—are very easy to implement by partial template specialization. Establishing domain-specific type traits in this style (e.g., is_matrix) is not difficult and can be quite useful. Other type traits that reflect the existence of functions or properties thereof—such as is_nothrow_assignable—are quite tricky to implement. Providing type traits of this kind requires a fair amount of expertise (if not black magic).

⇒ c++11/is_pod_test.cpp

With all the new features, C++11 did not forget its roots. There are type traits that allow us to check the compatibility with C. is_pod tells us whether a type is a *Plain Old Data type*

(POD). These are all intrinsic types and "simple" classes that can be used in a C program. In case we need a class that is used in C and C++ programs, it is best to define it only once in a C-compatible fashion: as struct and with no or conditionally compiled methods. It should not contain virtual functions and static data members. In sum, the memory layout of the class must be compatible with C and the default and copy constructor must be *Trivial*: they are either declared as default or compiler-generated in a default manner. For instance, the following class is POD:

```
struct simple_point
{
# ifdef __cplusplus
    simple_point(double x, double y) : x(x), y(y) {}
    simple_point() = default;
    simple_point(initializer_list<double> il)
    {
        auto it= begin(il);
        x= *it;
        y= *next(it);
    }
# endif

    double x, y;
};
```

We can check this as follows:

```
cout << "simple_point is pod = " << boolalpha
     << is_pod<simple_point>::value << endl;
```

All C++-only code is conditionally compiled: the macro __cplusplus is predefined in all C++ compilers. Its value reveals which standard the compiler supports (in the current translation). The class above can be used with an initializer list:

```
simple_point p1= {3.0, 7.0};
```

and is nonetheless compilable with a C compiler (unless some clown defined __cplusplus in the C code). The CUDA library implements some classes in this style. However, such hybrid constructs should only be used when really necessary to avoid surplus maintenance effort and inconsistency risks.

⇒ c++11/memcpy_test.cpp

Plain old data is stored contiguously in memory and can be copied as raw data without calling a copy constructor. This is achieved with the traditional functions memcpy or memmove. However, as responsible programmers we check upfront with is_trivially_copyable whether we can really call these low-level copy functions:

```
simple_point p1{3.0, 7.1}, p2;

static_assert(std::is_trivially_copyable<simple_point>::value,
              "simple_point is not as simple as you think "
              "and cannot be memcpyd!");
std::memcpy(&p2, &p1, sizeof(p1));
```

Unfortunately, the type trait was implemented late in several compilers. For instance, g++ 4.9 and clang 3.4 don't provide it while g++ 5.1 and clang 3.5 do.

This old-style copy function should only be used in the interaction with C. Within pure C++ programs it is better to rely on STL copy:

```
copy(&x, &x + 1, &y);
```

This works regardless of our class's memory layout and the implementation of copy uses memmove internally when the types allow for it.

C++14 adds some template aliases like

```
conditional_t<B, T, F>
```

as a shortcut for

```
typename conditional<B, T, F>::type
```

Likewise, enable_if_t is an abbreviation for the type of enable_if.

4.4   Utilities

C++11 adds new libraries that make modern programming style easier and more elegant. For instance, we can return multiple results more easily, refer to functions and functors more flexibly, and create containers of references.

4.4.1   Tuple

When a function computes multiple results, they used to be passed as mutable reference arguments. Assume we implement an LU factorization with pivoting taking a matrix A and returning the factorized matrix LU and the permutation vector p:

```
void lu(const matrix& A, matrix& LU, vector& p) { ... }
```

We could also return either LU or p as function results and pass the other object by reference. This mixed approach is even more confusing.

⇒ c++11/tuple_move_test.cpp

To return multiple results without implementing a new class, we can bundle them into a *Tuple*. A tuple (from <tuple>) differs from a container by allowing different types. In contrast to most containers, the number of objects must be known at compile time. With a tuple we can return both results of our LU factorization at once:

```
tuple<matrix, vector> lu(const matrix& A)
{
    matrix LU(A);
    vector p(n);

    // ... some computations
    return tuple<matrix, vector>(LU, p);
}
```

The **return** statement can be simplified with the helper function make_tuple deducing the type parameters:

```
tuple<matrix, vector> lu(const matrix& A)
{
    ...
    return make_tuple(LU, p);
}
```

make_tuple is especially convenient in combination with auto variables:

```
auto t= make_tuple(LU, p, 7.3, 9, LU*p, 2.0+9.0i);
```

The caller of our function lu will probably extract the matrix and the vector from the tuple with the function get:

```
tuple<matrix, vector> t= lu(A);
matrix LU= get<0>(t);
vector p= get<1>(t);
```

Here, all types can be deduced as well:

```
auto t= lu(A);
auto LU= get<0>(t);
auto p= get<1>(t);
```

The function get takes two arguments: a tuple and a position therein. The latter is a compile-time parameter. Otherwise the type of the result would not be known. If the index is too large, the error is detected during compilation:

```
auto t= lu(A);
auto am_i_stupid= get<2>(t); // Error during compilation
```

In C++14, the tuple entries can also be accessed by their type if this is unambiguous: `C++14`

```
auto t= lu(A);
auto LU= get<matrix>(t);
auto p= get<vector>(t);
```

Then we are not obliged any longer to memorize the internal order in the tuple. Alternatively, we can use the function tie to separate the entries in the tuple. This is often more elegant. In this case, we have to declare compatible variables beforehand:

```
matrix LU;
vector p;
tie(LU, p)= lu(A);
```

tie looks quite mysterious at first but its implementation is surprisingly simple: it creates an object with references to function arguments. Assigning a tuple to that object performs assignments of each tuple member to the respective reference.

The implementation with tie has a performance advantage over the implementation with get. When we pass the result of function lu directly to tie, it is still an rvalue (it has no name) and we can move the entries. With an intermediate variable, it becomes an lvalue (it has a name) and the entries must be copied. To avoid the copies, we can also move the tuple entries explicitly:

```
auto t=  lu(A);
auto LU= get<0>(move(t));
auto p=  get<1>(move(t));
```

Here, we step on rather thin ice. In principle, an object is considered expired after move is applied on it. It is allowed to be in any state as long as the destructor doesn't crash. In our example, we read t again after using move upon it. This is correct in this special situation. move turns t into an rvalue and we can do whatever we want to its data. But we don't. When LU is created, we only take the data of the tuple's entry 0 and don't touch entry 1. Conversely, we only steal the data from t's entry 1 in p's creation and don't access the expired data in entry 0. Thus, the two operations move entirely disjoint data. Nonetheless, multiple occurrences of move on the same data item are very dangerous and must be analyzed carefully (like we did).

After discussing the efficient data handling on the caller side, we should take another look at the function lu. The resulting matrix and vector are copied into the tuple when returned from the function. Within a return statement it is safe to move all data from the function[5] as it is going to be destroyed anyway. Here is the revised function excerpt:

```
tuple<matrix, vector> lu(const matrix& A)
{
    ...
    return make_tuple(move(LU), move(p));
}
```

Now that we have avoided all copies, the implementation returning a tuple is as efficient as the code with mutable references, at least when the result is used to initialize variables. When the result is assigned to existing variables, we still have the overhead of allocating and releasing memory.

The other heterogeneous class in C++ is pair. It already existed in C++03 and still does. pair is equivalent to a tuple with two arguments. Conversions from one to another exist so pair and two-argument tuple can be exchanged with each other and even mixed. The examples in this section could all be implemented with pair. Instead of get<0>(t) we could also write t.first (and t.second for get<1>(t)).

⇒ c++11/boost_fusion_example.cpp

Further reading: The library Boost::Fusion is designed for fusing meta-programming with classical (run-time) programming. Using this library, we can write code that iterates over tuples. The following program implements a generic functor printer that is called for each entry of tuple t:

```
struct printer
{
    template <typename T>
    void operator()(const T& x) const
```

---

5. Unless an object appears twice in the tuple.

```
    {    std::cout << "Entry is " << x << std::endl;    }
};

int main ()
{
    auto t= std::make_tuple(3, 7u, "Hallo", std::string("Hi"),
                            std::complex<float>(3, 7));
    boost::fusion::for_each(t, printer{});
}
```

The library further offers more powerful features for traversing and transforming hetero-geneous type composites (boost::fusion::for_each is in our opinion way more useful than std::for_each). Especially when functionality at compile and run time interferes in non-trivial fashion, Boost Fusion is indispensable.

The widest functionality in the area of meta-programming is supplied by the Boost Meta-Programming Library (MPL) [22]. The library implements most of the STL algorithms (§4.1) and also provides similar data types: for instance, vector and map are realized as compile-time containers. Especially, the combination of MPL and Boost Fusion is extremely powerful when functionality at compile and run time interferes in a non-trivial fashion. A new library at the time of this writing is Hana [11] which addresses compile- and run-time calculations with a more functional approach. It leads to significantly more compact programs while heavily relying on C++14 features.

4.4.2 function

C++11

⇒ c++11/function_example.cpp

The function class template in <functional> is a generalized function pointer. The function type specification is passed as a template argument like this:

```
double add(double x, double y)
{    return x + y;   }

int main ()
{
    using bin_fun= function<double(double, double)>;

    bin_fun f= &add;
    cout << "f(6, 3) = " << f(6, 3) << endl;
}
```

The function wrapper can hold functional entities of different kinds with the same return type and the same list of parameter types.[6] We can even build containers of compatible functional objects:

```
vector<bin_fun> functions;
functions.push_back(&add);
```

---

6. Thus, they may have different signatures since equal function names aren't required. In contrast, the equality of signatures doesn't impose the same return types.

When a function is passed as an argument, its address is taken automatically. Just as arrays are implicitly decayed to pointers, functions are decayed to pointer pointers. So, we can omit the address operator &:

```
functions.push_back(add);
```

When a function is declared `inline`, its code should be inserted in the calling context. Nonetheless, each `inline` function gets a unique address when needed which can be stored as a `function` object as well:

```
inline double sub(double x, double y)
{    return x - y;   }

functions.push_back(sub);
```

Again, the address is taken implicitly. Functors can be stored as well:

```
struct mult {
    double operator()(double x, double y) const { return x * y; }
};

functions.push_back(mult{});
```

Here we constructed an anonymous object with the default constructor. Class templates are not types so we cannot create objects thereof:

```
template <typename Value>
struct power {
    Value operator()(Value x, Value y) const { return pow(x, y); }
};

functions.push_back(power()); // Error
```

We can only construct objects from instantiated templates:

```
functions.push_back(power<double>{});
```

On the other hand, we can create objects from classes that contain function templates:

```
struct greater_t {
    template <typename Value>
    Value operator()(Value x, Value y) const { return x > y; }
} greater_than;

functions.push_back(greater_than);
```

In this context, the template call operator must be instantiatable for `function` type. As a counter-example, the following statement doesn't compile as we cannot instantiate it to a `function` with different argument types:

```
function<double(float, double)> ff= greater_than; // Error
```

Last but not least, lambdas with matching return and argument types can be stored as `function` objects:

```
functions.push_back([](double x, double y){ return x / y; });
```

Each entry of our container can be called like a function:

```
for (auto& f : functions)
    cout << "f(6, 3) = " << f(6, 3) << endl;
```

yielding the expected output:

```
f(6, 3) = 9
f(6, 3) = 3
f(6, 3) = 18
f(6, 3) = 216
f(6, 3) = 1
f(6, 3) = 2
```

Needless to say, this function wrapper is preferable to function pointers in terms of flexibility and clarity (which we pay for with some overhead).

4.4.3 Reference Wrapper

⇒ c++11/ref_example.cpp

Assume we want to create a list of vectors or matrices—possibly large ones. In addition, suppose that some entries appear multiple times. Therefore, we don't want to store the actual vectors or matrices. We could create a container of pointers, but we want to avoid all the danger related to them (§1.8.2).

Unfortunately, we cannot create a container of references:

```
vector<vector<int>&> vv; // Error
```

C++11 provides for this purpose a reference-like type called reference_wrapper that can be included with the header <functional>:

```
vector<reference_wrapper<vector<int> > > vv;
```

The vectors can be inserted:

```
vector<int> v1= {2, 3, 4}, v2= {5, 6}, v3= {7, 8};

vv.push_back(v1);
vv.push_back(v2);
vv.push_back(v3);
vv.push_back(v2);
vv.push_back(v1);
```

They are implicitly converted into reference wrappers (reference_wrapper<T> contains a constructor for T& that is not explicit).

The class contains a method get to get a reference to the actual object so that we can, for instance, print our vector:

```
for (const auto& vr : vv) {
    copy(begin(vr.get()), end(vr.get()),
        ostream_iterator<int>(cout, ", "));
    cout << endl;
}
```

Here, the type of vr is const reference_wrapper<vector<int> >&. The wrapper also provides an implicit conversion to the underlying reference type T& that can be used more conveniently:

```
for (const vector<int>& vr : vv) {
    copy(begin(vr), end(vr), ostream_iterator<int>(cout, ", "));
    cout ≪ endl;
}
```

The wrapper is complemented by two helpers: ref and cref, found in the same header. ref yields for an lvalue of type T an object of type reference_wrapper<T> referring to the former. If the argument of ref is already a reference_wrapper<T>, then it is just copied. Likewise, cref yields an object of type reference_wrapper<const T>. These functions are used in several places in the standard library.

We will use them for creating a std::map of references:

```
map<int, reference_wrapper<vector<int> > > mv;
```

Given the length of the wrapper's type name, it is shorter to declare it with type deduction like this:

```
map<int, decltype(ref(v1))> mv;
```

The usual bracket notation of maps:

```
mv[4]= ref(v1); // Error
```

cannot be applied since the wrapper has no default constructor which is called internally in the expression mv[4] before the assignment takes place. Instead of the bracket notation, we should use insert or emplace:

```
mv.emplace(make_pair(4, ref(v1)));
mv.emplace(make_pair(7, ref(v2)));
mv.insert(make_pair(8, ref(v3)));
mv.insert(make_pair(9, ref(v2)));
```

To iterate over the entries, it is again easier to apply type deduction:

```
for (const auto& vr : mv) {
    cout ≪ vr.first ≪ ": ";
    for (int i : vr.second.get())
        cout ≪ i ≪ ", ";
    cout ≪ endl;
}
```

As the bracket operator of our map doesn't compile, searching for a specific entry is performed with find:

```
auto& e7= mv.find(7)->second;
```

This yields a reference to the vector associated with the key 7.

4.5   The Time Is Now

⇒ c++11/chrono_example.cpp

The <chrono> library supplies type-safe features for clocks and timers. The two main entities are

- time_point, representing a point in time relative to a clock; and

- duration with the obvious meaning.

They can added, subtracted, and scaled (where meaningful). We can, for instance, add a duration to a time_point to send a message that we will be home in two hours:

```
time_point<system_clock> now= system_clock::now(),
                         then= now + hours(2);
time_t then_time= system_clock::to_time_t(then);
cout << "Darling, I'll be with you at " << ctime(&then_time);
```

Here we computed the time_point two hours from now. For the string output, C++ recycled the C-library <ctime>. The time_point is converted with to_time_t into a time_t. ctime generates a string (more precisely a char[]) with the local time:

```
Darling, I'll be with you at Wed Feb 11 22:31:31 2015
```

The string is terminated by a newline which we had to cut off to keep the output on the same line.

Very often we need to know how long a certain calculation took with our well-tuned implementation, for instance, a square root computation with the Babylonian method:

```
inline double my_root(double x, double eps= 1e-12)
{
    double sq= 1.0, sqo;
    do {
        sqo= sq;
        sq= 0.5 * (sqo + x / sqo);
    } while (abs(sq - sqo) > eps);
    return sq;
}
```

On one hand, it contains an expensive operation: the division (which usually flushes the floating-point pipeline). On the other hand, the algorithm has quadratic convergence. So, we need precise measurement:

```
time_point<steady_clock> start= steady_clock::now();
for (int i= 0; i < rep; ++i)
    r3= my_root(3.0);
auto end= steady_clock::now();
```

For not polluting our benchmarks with the clock overhead, we run multiple computations and scale down our time interval accordingly:

```
cout << "my_root(3.0) = " << r3 << ", the calculation took "
     << ((end - start) / rep).count() << " ticks\n";
```

yielding on the test machine:

```
my_root(3.0) = 1.73205, the calculation took 54 ticks
```

Thus, we should know how long a tick is. We will figure this out later. First, we convert the duration into something more tangible like microseconds:

```
duration_cast<microseconds>((end - start) / rep).count()
```

Our new output is

```
my_root(3.0) = 1.73205, the calculation took 0 µs
```

count returns an integer value and our computation took apparently less than a microsecond. For printing the duration with three decimal places, we convert it to nanoseconds and divide this by the double value 1000.0:

```
duration_cast<nanoseconds>((end - start) / rep).count() / 1000.
```

Note the dot at the end; if we divided by an int, we would cut off the fractional part:

```
my_root(3.0) = 1.73205, the calculation took 0.054 micros
```

The resolution of a clock is given by a ratio of a second in the clock's internal typedef period:

```
using P= steady_clock::period;        // type of time unit
cout << "Resolution is " << double{P::num} / P::den << "s.\n";
```

The output on the test machine was

```
Resolution is 1e-09s.
```

Thus, the resolution of the clock is one nanosecond. The library distinguishes three clocks:

- The system_clock represents the native wall clock on the system. It is compatible with <ctime> as needed in our first example.

- The high_resolution_clock has the maximal resolution possible on the underlying system.

- steady_clock is a clock with guaranteed increasing time points. The other two clocks might be adjusted (e.g., at midnight) on some platforms so that later time points might have lower values. This can lead to negative durations and other nonsense. Therefore, steady_clock is the most convenient for a timer (when the resolution is sufficient).

People knowing <ctime> might find <chrono> somewhat complicated at the beginning, but we don't need to deal with seconds, milliseconds, microseconds, and nanoseconds in different interfaces. The C++ library offers a uniform interface, and many errors can be detected at the type level—making the programs much safer.

4.6 Concurrency

C++11

Every general-purpose processor sold these days contains multiple cores. However, exploring the compute power of multi-core platforms is still a challenge for many programmers. In addition to keeping several cores busy, multi-threading can also be useful on a single core for using it more efficiently, e.g., loading data from the web while the received data is processed. Finding the right abstractions to provide maximal clarity and expressiveness on one hand and optimal performance on the other is one of the most important challenges of the C++ evolution.

The first concurrent features were introduced in C++11. Currently, the fundamental components of concurrent programming are:

- `thread`: class for a new path of execution;

- `async`: calls a function asynchronously;

- `atomic`: class template for non-interleaved value access;

- `mutex`: facility class to steer mutually exclusive execution;

- `future`: class template to receive a result from a `thread`; and

- `promise`: template to store values for a `future`.

As a use case, we want to implement an asynchronous and interruptible iterative solver. Such a solver will offer the scientist or engineer more productivity:

- Asynchrony: We can already work on the next model while the solver is running.

- Interruptibility: If we are convinced that our new model is much better, we can as well stop the solution of the old model.

Unfortunately, a `thread` cannot be killed. Well, it can but this aborts the entire application. To stop threads properly, they must cooperate by supplying well-defined interruption points. The most natural occasion to stop an iterative solver is in the termination test at the end of each iteration. This doesn't allow us to stop the solver immediately. For typical real-world applications where very many reasonably short iterations are performed, this approach offers a good benefit for relatively little work.

Thus, the first step toward an interruptible solver is an interruptible iteration control class. For the sake of brevity, we build our control class on top of `basic_iteration` from MTL4 [17], and we apologize that the complete code for this example is not publicly available. An iteration object is initialized with an absolute and relative epsilon plus a maximal number of iterations—or a subset thereof. An iterative solver computes after each iteration a certain error estimation—typically a norm of the residuum—and checks with the iteration control object whether the calculation should be `finished`. Our job is now to incorporate there a test for possibly submitted interruptions:

```
class interruptible_iteration
{
  public:
```

```
    interruptible_iteration(basic_iteration<double>& iter)
      : iter(iter), interrupted(false) {}
    bool finished(double r)
    {  return iter.finished(r) || interrupted.load(); }
    void interrupt() { interrupted= true; }
    bool is_interrupted() const { return interrupted.load(); }
  private:
    basic_iteration<double>&  iter;
    std::atomic<bool>         interrupted;
};
```

The interruptible_iteration contains a **bool** to indicate whether it is interrupted. This **bool**
is atomic to avoid interfering with access by different threads. Calling the method interrupt
causes the termination of the solver at the end of the iteration.

    In a purely single-thread program, we cannot take any advantage of our interruptible_
iteration: once a solver is started, the next command is only executed after the solver is finished.
Therefore, we need an asynchronous execution of the solver. To avoid the reimplementation of
all sequential solvers, we implement an async_executor that runs the solver in an extra thread
and gives back the control over the execution after the solver is started:

```
template <typename Solver>
class async_executor
{
  public:
    async_executor(const Solver& solver)
      : my_solver(solver), my_iter{}, my_thread{} {}

    template <typename VectorB, typename VectorX,
              typename Iteration>
    void start_solve(const VectorB& b, VectorX& x,
                     Iteration& iter) const
    {
        my_iter.set_iter(iter);
        my_thread= std::thread(
            [this, &b, &x](){
                return my_solver.solve(b, x, my_iter);}
        );
    }
    int wait() {
        my_thread.join();
        return my_iter.error_code();
    }
    int interrupt() {
        my_iter.interrupt();
        return wait();
    }

    bool finished() const { return my_iter.iter->finished(); }
```

```
  private:
    Solver                                my_solver;
    mutable interruptible_iteration my_iter;
    mutable std::thread                   my_thread;
};
```

After a solver is started with the async_executor, we can work on something else and check from time to time whether the solver is finished(). If we realize that the result has become irrelevant, we can interrupt() the execution. For both the complete solution and the interrupted execution, we must wait() until the thread is properly finished with join.

The following pseudo-code illustrates how the asynchronous execution could be used by scientists:

```
while ( !happy(science_foundation) ) {
    discretize_model();
    auto my_solver= itl::make_cg_solver(A, PC);
    itl::async_executor<decltype(my_solver)> async_exec(my_solver);
    async_exec.start_solve(x, b, iter);

    play_with_model();
    if ( found_better_model )
        async_exec.interrupt();
    else
        async_exec.wait();
}
```

For the engineering version, replace science_foundation with client.

We could also use the asynchronous solvers for systems that are numerically challenging and we don't know a priori which solver might converge. To this end, we'd start all solvers with a chance to succeed in parallel and wait until one of them completes and interrupt the others. For clarity's sake, we should store the executors in a container. Especially when the executors are neither copyable nor movable, we can use the container from Section 4.1.3.2.

This section is far from being a comprehensive introduction to concurrent C++ programming. It is merely an inspiration for what we can do with the new features. Before writing serious concurrent applications, we strongly advise that you read dedicated publications on the topic that also discuss the theoretical background. In particular, we recommend *C++ Concurrency in Action* [53] by Antony Williams who was the main contributor to the concurrent features in C++11.

4.7 Scientific Libraries Beyond the Standard

In addition to the standard libraries, there are many third-party libraries for scientific applications. In this section, we will present some open-source libraries briefly. The selection is a purely subjective choice of the author at the time of writing. Thus, the absence of a library should not be overrated; neither should its presence—even more so since some time has passed since then writing. Moreover, since open-source software is changing more rapidly than the foundations of the underlying programming language, and many libraries quickly add new features, we refrain from detailed presentations and refer to the respective manuals.

4.7.1 Other Arithmetics

Most computations are performed on real, complex, and integer numbers. In our math classes we also learned about rational numbers. Rational numbers are not supported by standard C++[7] but there are open-source libraries for it. Some of them are:

`Boost::Rational` is a template library that provides the usual arithmetic operations in a natural operator notation. The rational numbers are always normalized (denominator always positive and and co-prime to numerator). Using the library with integers of unlimited precision overcomes the problems of precision loss, overflow, and underflow.

GMP offers such unlimited/arbitrary precision integers. It also provides rationals based upon its own integers and arbitrary precision floating-point numbers. The C++ interface introduces classes and operator notation for those operations.

ARPREC is another library for ARbitrary PRECision offering integers and real and complex numbers with a customizable number of decimals.

4.7.2 Interval Arithmetic

The idea of this arithmetic is that input data items are not exact values in practice but approximations of the modeled entities. To take this inaccuracy into account, each data item is represented by an interval that is guaranteed to contain the correct value. The arithmetic is realized with appropriate rounding rules such that the resulting interval contains the exact result; i.e., the value is achieved with perfectly correct input data and computations without imprecision. However, when the intervals for the input data are already large or the algorithm is numerically unstable (or both), the resulting interval can be large—in the worst case $[-\infty, \infty]$. This is not satisfying but at least it is evident that something went wrong, whereas the quality of calculated floating-point numbers is entirely unclear and extra analysis is necessary.

`Boost::Interval` provides a template class to represent intervals as well as the common arithmetic and trigonometric operations. The class can be instantiated with each type for which the necessary policies are established, e.g., those of the preceding paragraphs.

4.7.3 Linear Algebra

This is a domain where many open-source as well as commercial software packages are available. Here we only present a small fraction thereof.

Blitz++ is the first scientific library using expression templates (Section 5.3) created by Todd Veldhuizen, one of the two inventors of this technique. It allows for defining vectors, matrices, and higher-order tensors of customizable scalar types.

---

7. It was proposed several times and may appear in the future.

uBLAS   is a more recent C++ template library initially written by Jörg Walter and Mathias Koch. It became part of the Boost collection where it is maintained by its community.

MTL4   is a template library from the author for vectors and a wide variety of matrices. In addition to standard linear-algebra operations, it provides the latest iterative linear solvers. The basic version is open source. GPU support is provided with CUDA. The Supercomputing edition can run on thousands of processors. More versions are in progress.

4.7.4   Ordinary Differential Equations

odeint   by Karsten Ahnert and Mario Mulansky solves Ordinary Differential Equations (ODE) numerically. Thanks to its generic design, the library doesn't only work with a variety of standard containers but also cooperates with external libraries. Therefore, the underlying linear algebra can be performed with MKL, the CUDA library Thrust, MTL4, VexCL, and ViennaCL. The advanced techniques used in the library are explaned by Mario Mulansky in Section 7.1.

4.7.5   Partial Differential Equations

The number of software packages for solving Partial Differential Equations (PDE) is enormous. Here, we only mention two of them which are in our opinion very broadly applicable and make good use of modern programming techniques.

FEniCS   is a software collection for solving PDEs by the Finite Element Method (FEM). It provides a user API in Python and C++ in which the weak form of the PDE is denoted. FEniCS can generate from this formulation a C++ application that solves the PDE problem.

FEEL++   is a FEM library from Christophe Prud'homme that similarly allows the notation of the weak form. In contrast to FEniCS, FEEL++ doesn't use external code generators but the power of the C++ compiler to transform code.

4.7.6   Graph Algorithms

Boost Graph Library   (BGL), mainly written by Jeremy Siek, provides a very generic approach so that the library can be applied on a variety on data formats [37]. It contains a considerable number of graph algorithms. Its parallel extension runs efficiently on hundreds of processors.

4.8   Exercises

4.8.1   Sorting by Magnitude

Create a vector of `double` and initialize it with the values -9.3, -7.4, -3.8, -0.4, 1.3, 3.9, 5.4, 8.2. You can use an initializer list. Sort the values by magnitude. Write

- A functor and
- A lambda expression for the comparison.

Try both solutions.

4.8.2 STL Container

Create a `std::map` for phone numbers; i.e., map from a string to an `unsigned long`. Fill the map with at least four entries. Search for an existing and a non-existing name. Also search for an existing and a non-existing number.

4.8.3 Complex Numbers

Implement a visualization of the Julia set (of a quadratic polynomial) similar to the Mandelbrot set. The mere difference is that the constant added to the square function is independent of the pixel position. Essentially, you have to introduce a constant k and modify `iterate` a little.

- Start with $k = -0.6 + 0.6i$ (Figure 4–9) which is a complex Cantor dust, also known as Fatou dust.

- Try other values for k, like $0.353 + 0.288i$ (compare `http://warp.povusers.org/ Mandelbrot`). Eventually you may want to change the color scheme to come up with a cooler visualization.

- The challenge in software design is to write an implementation for both Mandelbrot and Julia sets with minimal code redundancy. (The algorithmic challenge is probably finding colors that look good for all k. But this goes beyond the scope of this book.)

Figure 4–9: Julia for $k = -0.6 + 0.6i$ yielding a complex Cantor dust

- Advanced: Both fractals can be combined in an interactive manner. For this, one has to provide two windows. The first one draws the Mandelbrot set as before. In addition, it can enable mouse input so that the complex value under the mouse cursor is used as k for the Julia set in the second window.

- Pretty advanced: If the calculation of the Julia set is too slow, one can use thread parallelism or even GPU acceleration with CUDA or OpenGL.

Chapter 5

Meta-Programming

Meta-Programs are programs on programs. Reading a program as a text file and performing certain transformations on it is certainly feasible in most programming languages. In C++, we can even write programs that compute during compilation or transform themselves. Todd Veldhuizen showed that the template type system of C++ is Turing-complete [49]. This means that everything computable can be calculated in C++ at compile time.

We will discuss this intriguing asset thoroughly in this chapter. In particular, we will look at three major applications of it:

- Compile-time calculations (§5.1);

- Information about and transformations of types (§5.2); and

- Code generation (§5.3–§5.4).

These techniques allow us to make the examples from the preceding chapters more reliable, more efficient, and more broadly applicable.

5.1 Let the Compiler Compute

Meta-programming in its full extent was probably discovered thanks to a bug. Erwin Unruh wrote in the early 90s a program that printed prime numbers as *Error Messages* and thus demonstrated that C++ compilers are able to compute. This program is certainly the most famous C++ code that does not compile. The interested reader will find it in Appendix A.9.1. Please take this as testimony of exotic behavior and not as inspiration for your future programs.

Compile-time computations can be realized in two ways: backward compatible with template *Meta-Functions* or more easily with constexpr. The last feature was introduced in C++11 and extended in C++14.

5.1.1 Compile-Time Functions

C++11

⇒ c++11/fibonacci.cpp

Even in modern C++, it is not trivial to implement a prime-number test and we therefore start with something simpler: Fibonacci numbers. They can be computed recursively:

```
constexpr long fibonacci(long n)
{
    return n <= 2 ? 1 : fibonacci(n - 1) + fibonacci(n - 2);
}
```

A constexpr in C++11 is in most cases a single return statement. We are further allowed to include certain statements without computation: empty ones, (certain) static_assert, type definitions, and using declarations and directives. Compared to a regular function, a constexpr is rather restrictive:

- It cannot read or write anything outside the function. That is, no side effects!
- It cannot contain variables.[1]
- It cannot contain control structures like if or for.[1]
- It can only contain a single computational statement.[1]
- It can only call functions that are constexpr as well.

In comparison to template meta-functions (§5.2.5), on the other hand, a constexpr is perceivably more flexible:

- We can pass in floating-point types.
- We can even process user types (if they can be handled at compile time).
- We can use type detection.
- We can define member functions.
- We can use conditionals (which are simpler than specializations).
- We can call the functions with run-time arguments.

An easy function for floating-point numbers is square:

```
constexpr double square(double x)
{
    return x * x;
}
```

Floating-point types are not allowed as template arguments, and before C++11 it was not possible at all to perform compile-time calculations with floating points. We can generalize the preceding function with a template parameter to all suitable numeric types:

```
template <typename T>
constexpr T square(T x)
{
    return x * x;
}
```

The generalized function even accepts user types under certain conditions. Whether a type is suitable for constexpr functions depends on subtle details. Simply put, the type definition

---

1. Only in C++11. This limitation was lifted in C++14. We come to this in Section 5.1.2.

does not impede the creation of compile-time objects by containing, for instance, volatile members or arrays sized at run time.

The language standard tried to define conditions under which a type is usable in a constexpr function. It turned out that this is not definable as a type property because it depends on how the type is used—more precisely which constructor is called in the considered constexpr function. Accordingly, the respective type trait is_literal_type was doomed to be useless and declared deprecated in C++14.[2] A new definition is expected in C++17.

A really nice feature of constexpr functions is their usability at compile and run time, for instance:

```
long n= atoi(argv[1]);
cout ≪ "fibonacci(" ≪ n ≪ ") = " ≪ fibonacci(n) ≪ '\n';
```

Here we passed the first argument from the command line (which is definitely not known during compilation). Thus, whenever one or more arguments are only known at run time, the function cannot be evaluated at compile time. Only when all function arguments are available at compile time can the function be computed during compilation.

The hybrid applicability of constexpr functions implies in turn that their parameters can only be passed to constexpr functions. Passing a parameter to a regular function would impede the usage at compile time. Conversely, we cannot pass a function parameter to a compile-time evaluation like static_assert as it prevents run-time calls. As a consequence, we cannot express assertions within constexpr functions in C++11. Recent compilers provide assert as constexpr in C++14 mode so it can be used for parameters.

The language standard regulates which functions from the standard library must be realized as constexpr. Some library implementations realize additional functions as constexpr. For instance, the following function:

```
constexpr long floor_sqrt(long n)
{
    return floor(sqrt(n));
}
```

is supported by g++ in versions 4.7–4.9. In contrast, floor and sqrt are not constexpr functions in earlier and later versions (or other compilers) so the code above does not compile there.

5.1.2 Extended Compile-Time Functions

C++14

The restrictions on compile-time functions are relaxed as far as is reasonable in C++14. Now, we can use:

- Void functions, e.g.:

```
constexpr void square(int &x) { x *= x; }
```

---

2. Nonetheless, attention was paid that the useless result is well defined.

- Local variables, as long as they

  - Are initialized;
  - Have neither static nor thread storage duration; and
  - Have a literal type.

- Control structures, except

  - goto (which we do not want to use anyway);
  - Assembler code, i.e., an asm block; and
  - try-blocks.

The following example is allowed in C++14 but not in C++11 (for multiple reasons):

```cpp
template <typename T>
constexpr T power(const T& x, int n)
{
    T r(1);
    while (--n > 0)
        r *= x;
    return r;
}
```

⇒ c++14/popcount.cpp

With these extensions, compile-time functions are almost as expressive as regular functions. As a more technical example we will also realize popcount (short for population count) which counts the number of 1-bits in binary data:

```cpp
constexpr size_t popcount(size_t x)
{
    int count= 0;
    for (; x != 0; ++count)
        x&= x - 1;
    return count;
}
```

Analyzing this algorithm will also contribute to a better understanding of binary arithmetic. The key idea here is that x&= x - 1 sets the least significant bit to zero and leaves all other bits unaltered.

⇒ c++11/popcount.cpp

C++11 The function can be expressed in C++11 constexpr as well and is even shorter in the recursive formulation:

```cpp
constexpr size_t popcount(size_t x)
{
    return x == 0 ? 0 : popcount(x & x-1) + 1;
}
```

This stateless, recursive computation might be less comprehensible for some readers, and maybe clearer to others. It is said that finding iterative or recursive programs easier to understand depends on the order in which they are introduced to a programmer. Fortunately, C++ let us implement both.

5.1.3 Primeness

C++14

We have already mentioned that prime numbers were the topic of the first serious meta-program, although not compilable. Now we want to demonstrate that we can compute them in (compilable) modern C++. More precisely, we will implement a function that tells us at compile time whether a given number is prime. You may ask: "Why on earth do I need this information during compilation?" Fair question. Actually, the author used this compile-time function once in his research for categorizing cyclic groups with semantic concepts (§3.5). When the size of the group is a prime number, it is a field, otherwise a ring. An experimental compiler (ConceptGCC [21]) enabled such algebraic concepts in C++, and their model declarations contained the compile-time check for primeness (unfortunately before constexpr was available).

⇒ c++14/is_prime.cpp

Our algorithmic approach is that 1 is not prime, even numbers are not prime except 2, and for all other numbers we check that they are not divisible by any odd number larger than 1 and smaller than itself:

```
constexpr bool is_prime(int i)
{
    if (i == 1)
        return false;
    if (i % 2 == 0)
        return i == 2;
    for (int j= 3; j < i; j+= 2)
        if (i % j == 0)
            return false;
    return true;
}
```

Actually, we only need to test the divisibility by odd numbers smaller than the square root of the parameter i:

```
constexpr bool is_prime(int i)
{
    if (i == 1)
        return false;
    if (i % 2 == 0)
        return i == 2;
    int max_check= static_cast<int>(sqrt(i)) + 1;
    for (int j= 3; j < max_check; j+= 2)
        if (i % j == 0)
            return false;
    return true;
}
```

Unfortunately, this version only works with standard libraries where sqrt is a constexpr (g++ 4.7–4.9 as before). Otherwise we have to provide our own constexpr implementation. For instance, we can use the fixed-point algorithm from Section 4.3.1:

```
constexpr int square_root(int x)
{
    double r= x, dx= x;
    while (const_abs((r * r) - dx) > 0.1) {
        r= (r + dx/r) / 2;
    }
    return static_cast<int>(r);
}
```

As you can see, we performed the iterative approach as double and only converted it to int when the result is returned. This leads to a (sufficiently) efficient and portable implementation:

```
constexpr bool is_prime(int i)
{
    if (i == 1)
        return false;
    if (i % 2 == 0)
        return i == 2;
    int max_check= square_root(i) + 1;
    for (int j= 3; j < max_check; j+= 2)
        if (i % j == 0)
            return false;
    return true;
}
```

⇒ c++11/is_prime.cpp

At the end, we like taking the challenge to implement this (well, the first version of it) with the restricted constexpr in C++11:

```
constexpr bool is_prime_aux(int i, int div)
{
    return div >= i ? true :
        (i % div == 0 ? false : is_prime_aux(i, div + 2));
}

constexpr bool is_prime(int i)
{
    return i == 1 ? false :
        (i % 2 == 0 ? i == 2 : is_prime_aux(i, 3));
}
```

Here we need two functions: one for the special cases and one for checking the divisibility by odd numbers from 3.

In theory, we can implement every calculation with a C++11 constexpr. It provides all features of μ-recursive functions: constant and successor function, projection, and recursion. In computability theory, it is further proved that the μ-recursive functions are equivalent to a Turing machine so that every computable function can be implemented with μ-recursive functions and in turn with C++11 constexpr. So much for theory. In practice, the effort (and pain) it takes to realize really complicated calculations with that restricted expressiveness is a different kettle of fish.

Backward compatibility: Before `constexpr` was introduced, compile-time calculations were realized with template *Meta-Functions*. They are more limited in their applicability (no float or user types) and harder to implement. If you cannot use C++11 features for some reason or are just interested in historic programming, you are welcome to read the meta-function section in Appendix 5.2.5.

5.1.4   How Constant Are Our Constants?

Declaring a (non-member) variable to be `const`:

```
const int i= something;
```

can establish two levels of constancy:

1. The object cannot be changed during program execution (always the case).

2. The value is already known at compile time (sometimes the case).

Whether the value of `i` is available during compilation depends on the expression that is assigned to it. If `something` is a literal:

```
const long i= 7, j= 8;
```

then we can use it during compilation, e.g., as a template parameter:

```
template <long N>
struct static_long
{
    static const long value= N;
};

static_long<i>   si;
```

Simple expressions of compile-time constants are usually available during compilation:

```
const long k= i + j;
static_long<k>   sk;
```

When we assign a variable to a `const` object, it is definitely not available during compilation:

```
long ll;
cin >> ll;

const long cl= ll;
static_long<cl>   scl;    // Error
```

The constant `cl` cannot be changed in the program. On the other hand, it cannot be used during compilation as it depends on a run-time value.

There are scenarios where we cannot say from the program sources what kind of constant we have, for instance:

```
const long        ri= floor(sqrt(i));
static_long<ri>   sri;                    // compiles with g++ 4.7-4.9
```

Here, ri is known during compilation when sqrt and floor are both constexpr in the implementation of the standard library (e.g., in g++ 4.7–4.9); otherwise it is an error when used as a template argument.

To ensure that a constant has a compile-time value, we have to declare it constexpr:

```
constexpr long ri= floor(sqrt(i)); // compiles with g++ 4.7-4.9
```

This guarantees that ri is known during compilation; otherwise this line does not compile.

Note that constexpr is stricter for variables than for functions. A constexpr variable accepts only compile-time values while a constexpr function accepts both compile-time and run-time arguments.

5.2   Providing and Using Type Information

In Chapter 3, we saw the expressive power of function and class templates. However, all those functions and classes contained exactly the same code for all possible argument types. To increase the expressiveness of templates further, we will introduce smaller or larger code variations depending on the argument types. Thus, we first need information on types to dispatch on. Such type information can be technical—like is_const or is_reference—or semantic/domain-specific—like is_matrix or is_pressure. For most technical type information, we will find library support in the headers <type_traits> and <limits> as illustrated in Section 4.3. Domain-specific type properties are waiting for us to be implemented.

5.2.1   Type Traits

⇒ c++11/magnitude_example.cpp

In the function templates we have written so far, the types of temporaries and the return values were equal to one of the function arguments. Unfortunately, this does not always work. Imagine we implement a function that returns out of two values the one with the minimal magnitude:

```
template <typename T>
T inline min_magnitude(const T& x, const T& y)
{
    using std::abs;
    T ax= abs(x), ay= abs(y);
    return ax < ay ? x : y;
}
```

We can call this function for int, unsigned, or double values:

```
double          d1= 3., d2= 4.;
cout << "min |d1, d2| = " << min_magnitude(d1, d2) << '\n';
```

If we call this function with two `complex` values:

```
std::complex<double> c1(3.), c2(4.);
cout ≪ "min |c1, c2| = " ≪ min_magnitude(c1, c2) ≪ '\n';
```

we will see an error message like this:

```
no match for ≫operator< ≪ in ≫ax < ay≪
```

The problem is that `abs` returns `double` values here which provide the comparison operator, but we store the results as `complex` values in the temporaries.

   We now have different possibilities to solve this problem. For instance, we could avoid the temporaries altogether by comparing the two magnitudes without storing them. In C++11 or higher, we could leave it to the compiler to deduce the type of the temporaries:

C++11

```
template <typename T>
T inline min_magnitude(const T& x, const T& y)
{
    using std::abs;
    auto ax= abs(x), ay= abs(y);
    return ax < ay ? x : y;
}
```

In this section, we choose a more explicit approach for demonstration's sake: the magnitude type for possible argument types is provided by the user. Explicit type information is less important in newer standards but not entirely superfluous. Furthermore, knowing the basic mechanisms helps us understand tricky implementations.

   Type properties are supplied in C++ by *Type Traits*. These are essentially meta-functions with type arguments. For our example, we will write a type trait to provide the magnitude's type (for C++03 just replace each `using` with a traditional `typedef`). This is implemented by template specialization:

```
template <typename T>
struct Magnitude {};

template <>
struct Magnitude<int>
{
    using type= int;
};

template <>
struct Magnitude<float>
{
    using type= float;
};

template <>
struct Magnitude<double>
{
```

```
    using type= double;
};

template <>
struct Magnitude<std::complex<float> >
{
    using type= float;
};

template <>
struct Magnitude<std::complex<double> >
{
    using type= double;
};
```

Admittedly, this code is quite clumsy. We can abbreviate the first definitions by postulating "if we don't know better, we assume that T's Magnitude type is T itself."

```
template <typename T>
struct Magnitude
{
    using type= T;
};
```

This is true for all intrinsic types and we handle them all correctly with one definition. A slight disadvantage of this definition is that it incorrectly applies to all types without a specialized trait. Classes for which we know that the definition above is not correct are all instantiations of the class template complex. So we define specializations like this:

```
template <>
struct Magnitude<std::complex<double> >
{
    using type= double;
};
```

Instead of defining them individually for complex<float>, complex<double>, and so on, we can use partial specialization for all complex types:

```
template <typename T>
struct Magnitude<std::complex<T> >
{
    using type= T;
};
```

Now that the type traits are defined, we can use them in our function:

```
template <typename T>
T inline min_magnitude(const T& x, const T& y)
{
    using std::abs;
    typename Magnitude<T>::type ax= abs(x), ay= abs(y);
    return ax < ay ? x : y;
}
```

We can also extend this definition to (mathematical) vectors and matrices, to determine, for instance, the **return** type of a norm. The specialization reads:

```
template <typename T>
struct Magnitude<vector<T> >
{
    using type= T;                // not really perfect
};
```

However, when the value type of the vector is complex its norm will not be complex. Thus, we do not need the value type itself but its respective Magnitude:

```
template <typename T>
struct Magnitude<vector<T> >
{
    using type= typename Magnitude<T>::type;
};
```

Implementing type traits requires some perceivable programming effort, but it pays off by enabling much more powerful programming afterward.

5.2.2 Conditional Exception Handling

⇒ c++11/vector_noexcept.cpp

C++11

In Section 1.6.2.4, we introduced the qualifier noexcept which indicates that a function is not allowed to throw an exception (i.e., exception-handling code is not generated and eventual exceptions would kill the program or lead to undefined behavior). For function templates, it may depend on the type argument whether it is exception-free.

For example, a clone function does not throw an exception when the argument type has an exception-free copy constructor. The standard library provides a type trait for this property:

```
std::is_nothrow_copy_constructible
```

This allows us to express the exception freedom of our clone function:

```
#include <type_traits>

template <typename T>
inline T clone(const T& x)
    noexcept(std::is_nothrow_copy_constructible<T>::value)
{    return T{x}; }
```

You might feel that this implementation is somewhat disproportionate: the function head is many times the size of the body. Honestly, we share this feeling and think that such verbose declarations are only necessary for heavily used functions under the highest coding standards.

Another use case for conditional noexcept is the generic addition of two vectors that will be exception-free when the bracket operator of the vector class does not throw:

```
template <typename T>
class my_vector
```

```
{
    const T& operator[](int i) const noexcept;
};

template <typename Vector>
inline Vector operator+(const Vector& x, const Vector& y)
                                    noexcept(noexcept(x[0]))
{   ... }
```

The double noexcept certainly needs some familiarization. Here the outer one is a conditional declaration and the inner one the corresponding condition on an expression. This condition holds when a noexcept declaration is found for the respective expression—here for the bracket operator of the type of x. For instance, if we added two vectors of type my_vector, the addition would be declared noexcept.

5.2.3   A const-Clean View Example

⇒ c++11/trans_const.cpp

In this section, we will use type traits to solve technical problems of *Views*. These are small objects that provide a different perspective on another object. A prototypical use case is the transposition of a matrix. One way to provide a transposed matrix is of course to create a new matrix object with corresponding interchanged values. This is a quite expensive operation: it requires memory allocation and deallocation and copying all data of the matrix with switched values. A view is more efficient as we will see.

5.2.3.1   Writing a Simple View Class

In contrast to constructing an object with new data, a view only refers to an existing object and adapts its interface. This works very well for matrix transposition: we only have to switch the roles of rows and columns in the interface:

Listing 5–1: Simple view implementation

```
template <typename Matrix>
class transposed_view
{
  public:
    using value_type= typename Matrix::value_type;
    using size_type=  typename Matrix::size_type;

    explicit transposed_view(Matrix& A) : ref(A) {}

    value_type& operator()(size_type r, size_type c)
    { return ref(c, r); }
    const value_type& operator()(size_type r, size_type c) const
    { return ref(c, r); }

  private:
    Matrix& ref;
};
```

Here we assume that the `Matrix` class supplies an `operator()` accepting two arguments for the row and column index and returns a reference to the corresponding entry a_{ij}. We further suppose that type traits are defined for `value_type` and `size_type`. This is all we need to know about the referred matrix in this mini-example (ideally we would specify a concept for a simple matrix). Real template libraries like MTL4 of course provide larger interfaces. However, this small example is good enough to demonstrate the usage of meta-programming in certain views.

An object of class `transposed_view` can be treated like a regular matrix; e.g., it can be passed to all function templates expecting a matrix. The transposition is achieved on the fly by calling the referred object's `operator()` with switched indices. For every matrix object, we can define a transposed view that behaves like a matrix:

```
mtl::dense2D<float> A= {{2, 3, 4},
                        {5, 6, 7},
                        {8, 9, 10}};
transposed_view<mtl::dense2D<float> >  At(A);
```

When we access `At(i, j)`, we will get `A(j, i)`. We also define a non-`const` access so that we can even change entries:

```
At(2, 0)= 4.5;
```

This operation sets `A(0, 2)` to `4.5`.

The definition of a transposed view object does not lead to particularly concise programs. For convenience, we add a function that returns the transposed view:

```
template <typename Matrix>
inline transposed_view<Matrix> trans(Matrix& A)
{
    return transposed_view<Matrix>(A);
}
```

Now we can use the `trans` elegantly in our scientific software, for instance, in a matrix-vector product:

```
v= trans(A) * q;
```

In this case, a temporary view is created and used in the product. Since most compilers will inline the view's `operator()`, computations with `trans(A)` will be as fast as with `A`.

5.2.3.2 Dealing with `const`-ness

So far, our view works nicely. Problems arise when we build the transposed view of a constant matrix:

```
const mtl::dense2D<float> B(A);
```

We still can create the transposed view of `B` but we cannot access its elements:

```
cout << "trans(B)(2, 0) = " << trans(B)(2, 0) << '\n'; // Error
```

The compiler will tell us that it cannot initialize a `float&` from a `const float`. When we look at the location of the error, we realize that this happens in the non-constant overload of the operator. This raises the question of why the constant overload is not used which returns a constant reference and fits our needs perfectly.

First of all, we should check whether the `ref` member is really constant. We never used the `const` declarator in the class definition or the function `trans`. Help is provided from the *Run-Time Type Identification (RTTI)*. We add the header `<typeinfo>` and print the type information:

```
#include <typeinfo>
...

cout ≪ "trans(A) is " ≪ typeid(tst::trans(A)).name() ≪ '\n';
cout ≪ "trans(B) is = " ≪ typeid(tst::trans(B)).name() ≪ '\n';
```

This will produce the following output with g++:

```
typeid of trans(A) = N3tst15transposed_viewIN3mtl6matrix7dense2DIfNS2_10
  parametersINS1_3tag9row_majorENS1_5index7c_indexENS1_9non_fixed10
  dimensionsELb0EEEEEEE
typeid of trans(B) = N3tst15transposed_viewIKN3mtl6matrix7dense2DIfNS2_10
  parametersINS1_3tag9row_majorENS1_5index7c_indexENS1_9non_fixed10
  dimensionsELb0EEEEEEE
```

The output is not particularly readable. The types that are printed by RTTI are name-mangled. When we look very carefully, we can see the extra K in the second line that tells us that the view is instantiated with a constant matrix type. Nonetheless, we recommend you not waste your time with mangled names. An easy (and portable!) trick to achieve readable type names is provoking an error message like this:

```
int ta= trans(A);
int tb= trans(B);
```

A better way is using a *Name Demangler*. For instance, the GNU compiler comes with a tool called c++filt. By default it only demangles function names and we have to add the flag -t as in the following command pipe: const_view_test|c++filt -t. Then we will see:

```
typeid of trans(A) = transposed_view<mtl::matrix::dense2D<float,
      mtl::matrix::parameters<mtl::tag::row_major, mtl::index::c_index,
         mtl::non_fixed::dimensions, false, unsigned long> > >
typeid of trans(B) = transposed_view<mtl::matrix::dense2D<float,
      mtl::matrix::parameters<mtl::tag::row_major, mtl::index::c_index,
         mtl::non_fixed::dimensions, false, unsigned long> > const>
```

Now we can clearly see that `trans(B)` returns a `transposed_view` with template parameter `const dense2D<...>` (not `dense2D<...>`). Accordingly, the member `ref` has the type `const dense 2D<...>&`.

When we go one step back it now makes sense. We passed an object of type `const dense2D<...>` to the function `trans` which takes a template argument of type parameter `Matrix&`. Thus, `Matrix` is substituted by `const dense2D<...>` and the **return** type is accordingly `transposed_view <const dense2D<...> >`. After this short excursion into type introspection, we are certain that the member `ref` is a constant reference. The following happens:

- When we call `trans(B)`, the function's template parameter is instantiated with `const dense2D<float>`.

- Thus, the **return** type is `transposed_view<const dense2D<float> >`.

- The constructor parameter has type `const dense2D<float>&`.

- Likewise, the member `ref` is a `const dense2D<float>&`.

There remains the question why the non-`const` version of the operator is called despite our referring to a constant matrix. The answer is that the constancy of `ref` does not matter for the choice but whether or not the view object itself is constant. To ascertain that the view is also constant, we could write:

```
const transposed_view<const mtl::dense2D<float> > Bt(B);
cout << "Bt(2, 0) = " << Bt(2, 0) << '\n';
```

This works but is pretty clumsy. A brutal possibility to get the view compiled for constant matrices is to cast away the constancy. The undesired result would be that mutable views on constant matrices enable the modification of the allegedly constant matrix. This violates our principles so heavily that we do not even show what the code would look like.

Rule

Consider casting away `const` only as the very last resort.

In the following, we will empower you with very strong methodologies for handling constancy correctly. Every `const_cast` is an indicator of a severe design error. As Herb Sutter and Andrei Alexandrescu phrased it, "If you go const you never go back." The only situation where we need `const_cast` is when we deal with `const`-incorrect third-party software, i.e., where read-only arguments are passed as mutable pointers or references. That is not our fault and we have no choice. Unfortunately, there are still many packages around that are entirely ignorant of the `const` qualifier. Some of them are too large for a quick rewrite. The best we can do about it is add an appropriate API on top of it and avoid working with the original API. This saves us from spoiling our applications with `const_cast`s and restricts the unspeakable `const_cast` to the interface. A good example of such a layer is *Boost::Bindings* [30] that provides a const-correct high-quality interface to BLAS, LAPACK, and other libraries with similarly old-fashioned interfaces (to phrase it diplomatically). Conversely, as long as we only use our own functions and classes we are able to avoid every `const_cast` with more or less extra work.

To handle constant matrices correctly, we could implement a second view class especially for constant matrices and overload the `trans` function to return this view for constant arguments:

```
template <typename Matrix>
class const_transposed_view
{
  public:
```

```
      using value_type= typename Matrix::value_type;
      using size_type=  typename Matrix::size_type;

      explicit const_transposed_view(const Matrix& A) : ref(A) {}

      const value_type& operator()(size_type r, size_type c) const
      { return ref(c, r); }
    private:
      const Matrix& ref;
};

template <typename Matrix>
inline const_transposed_view<Matrix> trans(const Matrix& A)
{
      return const_transposed_view<Matrix>(A);
}
```

With this extra class, we solved our problem. But we added a fair amount of code for it. And what is even worse than the code length is the redundancy: our new class const_transposed_view is almost identical to transposed_view except for not containing a non-const operator(). Let's look for a more productive and less redundant solution. To this end, we introduce in the following two new meta-functions.

5.2.3.3   Check for Constancy

Our problem with the view in Listing 5–1 is that it cannot handle constant types as template arguments correctly in all methods. To modify the behavior for constant arguments, we first need to find out whether an argument is constant. The meta-function is_const that provides this information is very simple to implement by partial template specialization:

```
template <typename T>
struct is_const
{
      static const bool value= false;
};

template <typename T>
struct is_const<const T>
{
      static const bool value= true;
};
```

Constant types match both definitions, but the second one is more specific and therefore picked by the compiler. Non-constant types match only the first one. Note that we only look at the outermost type: the constancy of template parameters is not considered. For instance, view<const matrix> is not regarded as constant because the view itself is not const.

5.2.3.4 Compile-Time Branching

The other tool we need for our view is a type selection depending on a logical condition. This technology was introduced by Krzysztof Czarnecki and Ulrich W. Eisenecker [8]. The *Compile-Time If* is named `conditional` in the standard library. It can be realized by a rather simple implementation:

Listing 5–2: `conditional` a.k.a. compile-time `if`

```cpp
template <bool Condition, typename ThenType, typename ElseType>
struct conditional
{
    using type= ThenType;
};


template <typename ThenType, typename ElseType>
struct conditional<false, ThenType, ElseType>
{
    using type= ElseType;
};
```

When this template is instantiated with a logical expression and two types, only the primary template (on top) matches when the first argument evaluates to `true` and ThenType is used in the type definition. If the first argument evaluates to `false`, then the specialization (below) is more specific so that ElseType is used. Like many ingenious inventions it is very simple once it is found. This meta-function is part of C++11 in header `<type_traits>`.[3]

This meta-function allows us to define funny things like using `double` for temporaries when our maximal iteration number is larger than 100, otherwise float:

```cpp
using tmp_type=
    typename conditional<(max_iter > 100), double, float>::type;
cout << "typeid = " << typeid(tmp_type).name() << '\n';
```

Needless to say, `max_iter` must be known at compile time. Admittedly, the example does not look extremely useful and the meta-if is not so important in small isolated code snippets. In contrast, for the development of large generic software packages, it becomes extremely important.

Please note that the comparison is surrounded by parentheses; otherwise the greater-than symbol > would be interpreted as the end of the template arguments. Likewise, expressions containing right shift ≫ must be surrounded by parentheses in C++11 or higher for the same reason.

---

3. With C++03, you can use `boost::mpl::if_c` from Boost's Meta-Programming Library (MPL). If you program with both the standard type traits and Boost, pay attention to the sometimes deviating naming conventions.

To relieve us from typing `typename` and `::type` when referring to the resulting type, C++14 introduces a template alias:

```
template <bool b, class T, class F>
using conditional_t= typename conditional<b, T, F>::type;
```

If the standard library of your compiler does not provide this alias, you can quickly add it—maybe with a different name or in another namespace to avoid name conflicts later on.

5.2.3.5 The Final View

Now we have all we need to revise the view from Listing 5–1. The problem was that we returned an entry of a constant matrix as a mutable reference. To avoid this, we can try to make the mutable access operator disappear in the view when the referred matrix is constant. This is possible but more complicated. We will come back to this approach in Section 5.2.6.

An easier solution is to keep both the mutable and the constant access operator but choose the **return** type of the former depending on the type of the template argument:

Listing 5–3: const-safe view implementation

```
 1   template <typename Matrix>
 2   class transposed_view
 3   {
 4     public:
 5       using value_type= Collection<Matrix>::value_type;
 6       using size_type=  Collection<Matrix>::size_type;
 7     private:
 8       using vref_type= conditional_t<is_const<Matrix>::type,
 9                                      const value_type&,
10                                      value_type&>;
11     public:
12       transposed_view(Matrix& A) : ref(A) {}
13
14       vref_type operator()(size_type r, size_type c)
15       { return ref(c, r); }
16
17       const value_type& operator()(size_type r, size_type c) const
18       { return ref(c, r); }
19
20     private:
21       Matrix& ref;
22   };
```

This implementation differentiates the `return` type of mutable views between constant and mutable referred matrices. This establishes the desired behavior as the following case study will show.

When the referred matrix is mutable, the **return** type of operator() depends on the constancy of the view object:

- If the view object is mutable, then operator() in line 14 returns a mutable reference (line 10); and

- If the view object is constant, then operator() in line 17 returns a constant reference.

This is the same behavior as in Listing 5–1.

If the matrix reference is constant, then a constant reference is always returned:

- If the view object is mutable, then operator() in line 14 returns a constant reference (line 9); and

- If the view object is constant, then operator() in line 17 returns a constant reference.

Altogether, we implemented a view class that supplies write access only when the view object and the referred matrix are both mutable.

5.2.4 Standard Type Traits

Note: The type traits in the standard originate from the Boost library collection. If you are moving from the Boost type traits to those of the standard, be aware that some names are different. There are also slight differences in the behavior: whereas meta-functions in Boost expect a type and implicitly read its boolean value implicitly, the meta-function with the same name in the standard expects a boolean value as an argument. Whenever possible prefer the standard type traits sketched in Section 4.3.

5.2.5 Domain-Specific Type Properties

Now that we have seen how the type traits in the standard library are realized, we can use this knowledge for ourselves and realize domain-specific type properties. Not surprisingly, we pick linear algebra as the domain and implement the property is_matrix. To be on the safe side, a type is only considered as a matrix when we explicitly declare it as such. Thus, types are by default declare as not being a matrix:

```
template <typename T>
struct is_matrix
{
    static const bool value= false;
};
```

The standard library supplies a false_type containing just this static constant.[4] We can save ourselves some typing by deriving from this meta-function and inheriting (See Chapter 6) value from false_type:

```
template <typename T>
struct is_matrix
  : std::false_type
{};
```

---

4. In C++03 you can resort to boost::mpl::false_.

Now we specialize the meta-predicate for all known matrix classes:

```
template <typename Value, typename Para>
struct is_matrix<mtl::dense2D<Value, Para> >
  : std::true_type
{};
// more matrix classes ...
```

The predicate can also depend on the template arguments. For instance, we might have a transposed_view class applicable to matrices and vectors (certainly tricky to implement but this is a different question). Certainly, a transposed vector is not a matrix whereas a transposed matrix is:

```
template <typename Matrix>
struct is_matrix<transposed_view<Matrix> >
  : is_matrix<Matrix>
{};
// more views ...
```

More likely, we will realize separate views for transposing matrices and vectors, e.g.:

```
template <typename Matrix>
struct is_matrix<matrix::transposed_view<Matrix> >
  : std::true_type
{};
```

C++11 To ascertain that our view is used correctly, we verify with static_assert that the template argument is a (known) matrix:

```
template <typename Matrix>
class transposed_view
{
    static_assert(is_matrix<Matrix>::value,
                  "Argument of this view must be a matrix!");
    // ...
};
```

If the view is instantiated with a type that is not a matrix (or not declared as such), the compilation aborts and the user-defined error message is printed. Since static_assert does not create run-time overhead, it should be used wherever errors can be detected at the type level or regarding compile-time constants. Up to C++14, the error message must be a literal. Later C++ versions will probably allow us to compose messages with type information.

When we try to compile our test with the static assertion, we will see that trans(A) compiles but not trans(B). The reason is that const dense2D<> is considered different from dense2D<> in template specialization so it is still not considered as a matrix. The good news is that we do not need to double our specializations for mutable and constant types, but we can write a partial specialization for all constant arguments:

```
template <typename T>
struct is_matrix<const T>
  : is_matrix<T> {};
```

Thus, whenever a type T is a matrix, then const T is as well.

5.2.6 enable_if

C++11

A very powerful mechanism for meta-programming is enable_if, discovered by Jaakko Järvi and Jeremiah Wilcock. It is based on a convention for compiling function templates called *SFINAE: Substitution Failure Is Not An Error.* It means that function templates whose header cannot be substituted with the argument types are just ignored and do not cause an error.

Such substitution errors can happen when the **return** type of a function is a meta-function on a template argument, e.g.:

```
template <typename T>
typename Magnitude<T>::type
inline min_abs(const T& x, const T& y)
{
    using std::abs;
    auto ax= abs(x), ay= abs(y);
    return ax < ay ? ax : ay;
}
```

Here our **return** type is the Magnitude of T. When Magnitude<T> contains no member type for the type of x and y, the substitution fails and the function template is ignored. The benefit of this approach is that a function call can be compiled when for multiple overloads exactly one of them can be successfully substituted. Or when multiple function templates can be substituted and one of them is more specific than all others. This mechanism is exploited in enable_if.

Here we will use enable_if to select function templates based on domain-specific properties. As a showcase, we realize the L_1 norm. It is defined for vector spaces and linear operators (matrices). Although these definitions are related, the practical real-world implementation for finite-dimensional vectors and matrices is different enough to justify multiple implementations. Of course, we could implement L_1 norm for every matrix and vector type so that the call one_norm(x) would select the appropriate implementation for this type.

⇒ c++03/enable_if_test.cpp

To be more productive, we like to have one single implementation for all matrix types (including views) and one single implementation for all vector types. We use the meta-function is_matrix and implement is_vector accordingly. Further, we need the meta-function Magnitude to handle the magnitude of complex matrices and vectors. For convenience, we further provide a template alias Magnitude_t to access contained type information.

Next, we implement the meta-function enable_if that allows us to define function overloads that are only viable when a given condition holds:

```
template <bool Cond, typename T= void>
struct enable_if {
    typedef T type;
};

template <typename T>
struct enable_if<false, T> {};
```

It defines a type only when the condition holds. Our realization is compatible with <type_traits> from C++11. The program snippet here serves as illustration while we use the standard meta-function in production software.

As in C++14, we want to add a template alias for making the notation more concise:

```
template <bool Cond, typename T= void>
using enable_if_t= typename enable_if<Cond, T>::type;
```

As before, it saves us from writing the typename-::type pair. Now we have all we need to implement the L_1 norm in the generic fashion we aimed for:

```
1   template <typename T>
2   enable_if_t<is_matrix<T>::value, Magnitude_t<T> >
3   inline one_norm(const T& A)
4   {
5       using std::abs;
6       Magnitude_t<T> max{0};
7       for (unsigned c= 0; c < num_cols(A); c++) {
8           Magnitude_t<T> sum{0};
9           for (unsigned r= 0; r < num_cols(A); r++)
10          sum+= abs(A[r][c]);
11          max= max < sum ? sum : max;
12      }
13      return max;
14  }
15
16  template <typename T>
17  enable_if_t<is_vector<T>::value, Magnitude_t<T> >
18  inline one_norm(const T& v)
19  {
20      using std::abs;
21      Magnitude_t<T> sum{0};
22      for (unsigned r= 0; r < size(v); r++)
23          sum+= abs(v[r]);
24      return sum;
25  }
```

The selection is now driven by enable_if in lines 2 and 17. Let us look at line 2 in detail for a matrix argument:

1. is_matrix<T> is evaluated to (i.e., inherited from) true_type.

2. enable_if_t< > becomes Magnitude_t<T>.

3. This is the **return** type of the function overload.

Here is what happens in this line when the argument is not a matrix type.

1. is_matrix<T> is evaluated to false_type.

2. enable_if_t< > cannot be substituted because enable_if< >::type does not exist in this case.

3. The function overload has no **return** type and is erroneous.

4. It is therefore ignored.

In short, the overload is only enabled if the argument is a matrix—as the names of the meta-functions say. Likewise the second overload is only available for vectors. A short test demonstrates this:

```
matrix A= {{2, 3, 4},
           {5, 6, 7},
           {8, 9, 10}};

dense_vector<float> v= {3, 4, 5}; // from MTL4

cout << "one_norm(A) is " << one_norm(A) << "\n";
cout << "one_norm(v) is " << one_norm(v) << "\n";
```

For types that are neither matrix nor vector, there will be no overload of one_norm available, and there should not be. Types that are considered both matrix and vector would cause an ambiguity and indicate a design flaw.

Limitations: The mechanism of enable_if is quite powerful but can complicate debugging. Especially with old compilers, error messages caused by enable_if are usually rather verbose and at the same time not very meaningful. When a function match is missing for a given argument type, it is hard to determine the reason because no helpful information is provided to the programmer; he/she is only told that no match is found, period. Newer compilers (clang++ $\geqslant$ 3.3 or gcc $\geqslant$ 4.9) inform the programmer that an appropriate overload was found which is disabled by enable_if.

Furthermore, the enabling mechanism cannot select the most specific condition. For instance, we cannot specialize implementation for, say, is_sparse_matrix. This can be achieved by avoiding ambiguities in the conditions:

```
template <typename T>
enable_if<is_matrix<T>::value && !is_sparse_matrix<T>::value,
          Magnitude_t<T> >
inline one_norm(const T& A);

template <typename T>
enable_if<is_sparse_matrix<T>::value, Magnitude_t<T> >
inline one_norm(const T& A);
```

Evidently, this becomes quite error-prone when too many hierarchical conditions are considered.

The SFINAE paradigm only applies to template arguments of the function itself. Member functions cannot apply enable_if on the class's template argument. For instance, the mutable access operator in line 9 of Listing 5–1 cannot be hidden with enable_if for views on constant matrices because the operator itself is not a template function.

In the previous examples, we used SFINAE to invalidate the **return** type. This does not work for functions without a **return** type like constructors. In this case, we can introduce a dummy argument with a default value that can be invalidated as well when our condition does not hold. Problematic are functions without optional arguments and customizable **return** types like conversion operators.

Several of these issues can be addressed with *Anonymous Type Parameters*. Since this feature is not frequently used in daily programming, we put it into Section A.9.4.

5.2.7   Variadic Templates Revised

In Section 3.10, we implemented a variadic sum that accepted an arbitrary number of arguments of mixed types. The problem in this implementation was that we did not know an appropriate return type and used that of the first argument. And failed miserably.

In the meantime, we have seen more features and want to re-attack the problem. Our first approach is to use decltype to determine the result type:

```cpp
template <typename T>
inline T sum(T t) { return t; }

template <typename T, typename ...P>
auto sum(T t, P ...p) -> decltype( t + sum(p...) ) // Error
{
    return t + sum(p...);
}
```

Unfortunately, this implementation does not compile for more than two arguments. To determine the **return** type for n arguments, the **return** type for the last $n-1$ arguments is needed which is only available after the function is completely defined but not yet for the trailing **return** type. The function above is recursively called but not instantiated recursively.

5.2.7.1   Variadic Class Template

Thus, we have to determine the result type first. This can be done recursively by a variadic type trait:

```cpp
// Forward declaration
template <typename ...P> struct sum_type;

template <typename T>
struct sum_type<T>
{
    using type= T;
};

template <typename T, typename ...P>
struct sum_type<T, P...>
{
    using type= decltype(T() + typename sum_type<P...>::type());
};

template <typename ...P>
using sum_type_t= typename sum_type<P...>::type;
```

Variadic class templates are also declared recursively. For the sake of visibility, we first need the general form as a declaration before we can write the definition. The definition always consists of two parts:

- The composite part—how we define the class with n parameters in terms of $n-1$ parameters; and

- The base case for usually zero or one argument.

The example above uses an expression that did not appear in the variadic function template before: P... unpacks the type pack.

   Please note the different compilation behaviors of recursive functions and classes: the latter are instantiated recursively and the former are not. That is the reason why we can use decltype recursively in the variadic class but not in the variadic function.

5.2.7.2 Decoupling Return Type Deduction and Variadic Computation

C++11

Using the previous type trait, we can realize the variadic function with a reasonable **return** type:

```
template <typename T>
inline T sum(T t) { return t; }

template <typename T, typename ...P>
inline sum_type_t<T, P...> sum(T t, P ...p)
{
    return t + sum(p...);
}
```

This function yields the correct results for the previous examples:

```
auto s= sum(-7, 3.7f, 9u, -2.6);
cout ≪ "s is " ≪ s ≪ " and its type is "
    ≪ typeid(s).name() ≪ '\n';

auto s2= sum(-7, 3.7f, 9u, -42.6);
cout ≪ "s2 is " ≪ s2 ≪ " and its type is "
    ≪ typeid(s2).name() ≪ '\n';
```

which are:

```
s is 3.1 and its type is d
s2 is -36.9 and its type is d
```

5.2.7.3 Common Type

C++11

The standard library provides a type trait similar to sum_type named std::common_type in <type_traits> (plus the alias common_type_t in C++14). The motivation of this type trait is that intrinsic C++ types have implicit conversion rules so that the result type of an expression is independent of the operation; it only depends on the argument types. Thus, x + y + z, x - y - z, x * y * z, and x * y + z all have the same type when the variables are intrinsics. For intrinsic types, the following meta-predicate always evaluates to the true_type:

```
is_same<decltype(x + y + z),
        common_type<decltype(x), decltype(y), decltype(z)>
```

Likewise for other expressions.

User-defined types are not guaranteed to return the same types in all operations. Therefore, it can make sense to provide operation-dependent type traits.

The standard library contains a minimum function. This function is limited to two arguments of the same type. Using common_type and variadic templates, we can easily write a generalization:

```
template <typename T>
inline T minimum(const T& t) { return t; }

template <typename T, typename ...P>
typename std::common_type<T, P...>::type
minimum(const T& t, const P& ...p)
{
    typedef typename std::common_type<T, P...>::type res_type;
    return std::min(res_type(t), res_type(minimum(p...)));
}
```

To avoid confusion, we called the function minimum. It takes an arbitrary number of arguments with arbitrary types as long as std::common_type and comparison are defined for it. For instance, the expression

```
minimum(-7, 3.7f, 9u, -2.6)
```

returns a double with the value -7. In C++14, the variadic overload of minimum simplifies to

```
template <typename T, typename ...P>
inline auto minimum(const T& t, const P& ...p)
{
    using res_type= std::common_type_t<T, P...>;
    return std::min(res_type(t), res_type(minimum(p...)));
}
```

by using the template alias and return type deduction.

5.2.7.4   Associativity of Variadic Functions

Our variadic implementations of sum added the first argument to the sum of the remaining. That is, the right-most + is computed first. On the other hand, the + operator in C++ is defined left-associative; the left-most + is first calculated in summations. Unfortunately, the corresponding left-associative implementation:

```
template <typename T>
inline T sum(T t) { return t; }

template <typename ...P, typename T>
```

```
typename std::common_type<P..., T>::type
sum(P ...p, T t)
{
    return sum(p...) + t;
}
```

does not compile. The language does not support splitting off the last argument.

Integer numbers are associative (i.e., the order of calculation does not matter). Floating-point numbers are not due to rounding errors. Thus, we have to pay attention that changes in evaluation order due to the use of variadic templates do not cause numeric instabilities.

5.3   Expression Templates

Scientific software usually has strong performance requirements—especially when C++ is involved. Many large-scale simulations of physical, chemical, or biological processes run for weeks or months and everybody is glad when at least a part of this very long execution time can be saved. The same can be said about engineering, e.g., for static and dynamic analysis of large constructions. Saving execution time often comes at the price of program sources' readability and maintainability. In Section 5.3.1, we will show a simple implementation of an operator and discuss why this is not efficient, and in the remainder of Section 5.3 we will demonstrate how to improve performance without sacrificing the natural notation.

5.3.1   Simple Operator Implementation

Assume we have an application with vector addition. We want, for instance, to write the following vector expression:

```
w = x + y + z;
```

Say we have a vector class like in Section 3.3:

```
template <typename T>
class vector
{
  public:
    explicit vector(int size) : my_size(size), data(new T[my_size])    {}

    const T& operator[](int i) const { check_index(i); return data[i]; }
    T& operator[](int i) { check_index(i); return data[i];    }
    // ...
};
```

We can of course provide an operator for adding such vectors:

Listing 5–4: Naïve addition operator

```
1  template <typename T>
2  inline vector<T> operator+(const vector<T>& x, const vector<T>& y)
3  {
```

```
4          x.check_size(size(y));
5          vector<T> sum(size(x));
6          for (int i= 0; i < size(x); ++i)
7              sum[i] = x[i] + y[i];
8          return sum;
9    }
```

A short test program checks that everything works properly:

```
vector<float> x= {1.0, 1.0, 2.0, -3.0},
              y= {1.7, 1.7, 4.0, -6.0},
              z= {4.1, 4.1, 2.6, 11.0},
              w(4);

cout ≪ "x = " ≪ x ≪ std::endl;
cout ≪ "y = " ≪ y ≪ std::endl;
cout ≪ "z = " ≪ z ≪ std::endl;

w= x + y + z;
cout ≪ "w= x + y + z = " ≪ w ≪ endl;
```

If this works as expected, what is wrong with it? From the software engineering perspective: nothing. From the performance perspective: a lot.

The following list shows which operation is performed in which line of operator+ when the statement is executed:

1. Create a temporary variable sum for the addition of x and y (line 5).

2. Perform a loop reading x and y, adding it element-wise, and writing the result to sum (lines 6+7).

3. Copy sum to a temporary variable, say, t_xy, in the return statement (line 8).

4. Delete sum with the destructor when it goes out of scope (line 9).

5. Create a temporary variable sum for the addition of t_xy and z (line 5).

6. Perform a loop reading t_xy and z, adding it element-wise, and writing the result to sum (lines 6+7).

7. Copy sum to a temporary variable, say, t_xyz, in the return statement (line 8).

8. Delete sum (line 9).

9. Delete t_xy (after second addition).

10. Perform a loop reading t_xyz and writing to w (in assignment).

11. Delete t_xyz (after assignment).

This is admittedly the worst-case scenario; however, it really happened with old compilers. Modern compilers perform more optimizations by static code analysis and optimize return values (§2.3.5.3), thus avoiding the copies into temporaries t_xy and t_xyz.

The optimized version performs still:

1. Create a temporary variable sum for the addition of x and y (for distinction we call it sum_xy) (line 5).

2. Perform a loop reading x and y, adding it element-wise, and writing the result to sum (lines 6+7).

3. Create a temporary variable sum (for distinction, sum_xyz) for the addition of sum_xy and z (line 5).

4. Perform a loop reading sum_xy and z, adding it, and writing the result to sum_xyz (lines 6+7).

5. Delete sum_xy (after second addition).

6. Perform a loop reading sum_xyz and writing it element-wise to w (in assignment).

7. Delete sum_xyz (after assignment).

How many operations did we perform? Say our vectors have dimension n, then we have in total:

- $2n$ additions
- $3n$ assignments
- $5n$ reads
- $3n$ writes
- 2 memory allocations
- 2 memory deallocations

By comparison, if we could write a single loop or an inline function:

```
template <typename T>
void inline add3(const vector<T>& x, const vector<T>& y,
                 const vector<T>& z, vector<T>& sum)
{
    x.check_size(size(y));
    x.check_size(size(z));
    x.check_size(size(sum));
    for (int i= 0; i < size(x); ++i)
        sum[i] = x[i] + y[i] + z[i];
}
```

This function performs

- $2n$ additions
- n assignments
- $3n$ reads
- n writes

The call of this function:

```
add3(x, y, z, w);
```

is of course less elegant than the operator notation. It is also a little bit more prone to errors: we need to look at the documentation to see whether the first or the last argument contains the result. With operators, the semantics are evident.

In high-performance software, programmers tend to implement a hard-coded version of every important operation instead of freely composing them from smaller expressions. The reason is obvious; our operator implementation performed additionally

- $2n$ assignments
- $2n$ reads
- $2n$ writes
- 2 memory allocations
- 2 memory deallocations

The good news is we have not performed additional arithmetic. The bad news is that the operations above are more expensive. On modern computers, it takes much more time to read large amounts of data from or to write to the memory than executing fixed or floating-point operations.

Unfortunately, vectors in scientific applications tend to be rather long, often larger than the caches of the platform, and the vectors must really be transferred to and from main memory. In Figure 5–1, we depict the memory hierarchy symbolically. The chip on top represents the processor, the blue chips beneath it the L1 cache, the disks L2, the floppies the main memory, and the cassettes the virtual memory. The hierarchy consists of small fast memory close to the processor and large slow memory. When a data item from slow memory is read (marked in the second (blue) cassette), a copy is held in every faster memory (second floppy, first disk, first blue L1 cache chip).

In case of shorter vectors, the data might reside in L1 or L2 cache and the data transfer is less critical. But in this case, the allocation and deallocation become serious slow-down factors.

5.3.2   An Expression Template Class

The purpose of *Expression Templates* (ET) is to keep the original operator notation without introducing the overhead induced by temporaries. The technique was independently discovered by Todd Veldhuizen and Daveed Vandevoorde.

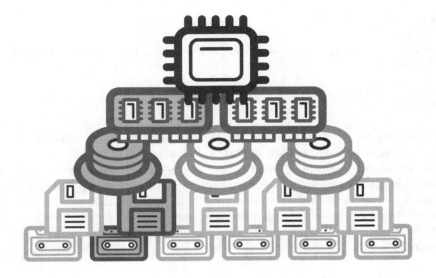

Figure 5–1: Memory hierarchy

⇒ c++11/expression_template_example.cpp

The solution to the dilemma of elegance versus performance is the introduction of a class for intermediate objects keeping references to the vectors and allowing us to perform all computations later in one sweep. The addition does not return a vector any longer but an object referring to the arguments:

```cpp
template <typename T>
class vector_sum
{
  public:
    vector_sum(const vector<T>& v1, const vector<T>& v2)
      : v1(v1), v2(v2) {}
  private:
    const vector<T> &v1, &v2;
};

template <typename T>
vector_sum<T> operator+(const vector<T>& x, const vector<T>& y)
{
    return {x, y};
}
```

Now we can write x + y but not w= x + y yet. It is not only that the assignment is not defined; we have not yet provided vector_sum with enough functionality to perform something useful in the assignment. Thus, we first extend vector_sum so that it looks like a vector itself:

```cpp
template <typename T>
class vector_sum
{
```

```
public:
  // ...
  friend int size(const vector_sum& x) { return size(x.v1); }
  T operator[](int i) const { return v1[i] + v2[i]; }
private:
  const vector<T> &v1, &v2;
};
```

The most interesting function in this class is the bracket operator: when the i-th entry is accessed, we compute the sum of the operands' i-th entries on the fly.

The drawback of computing element-wise sums in the bracket operator is the repeated calculation when the entries are accessed multiple times. This happens, for instance, in matrix vector multiplication when we compute A * (x+y). Thus, it can be beneficial for some operations to evaluate the vector sum upfront instead of doing so element-wise in the access operator.

To evaluate w= x + y, we also need an assignment operator for vector_sum:

```
template <typename T> class vector_sum; // forward declaration

template <typename T>
class vector
{   // ...
    vector& operator=(const vector_sum<T>& that)
    {
        check_size(size(that));
        for (int i= 0; i < my_size; ++i)
            data[i]= that[i];
        return *this;
    }
};
```

The assignment iterates over the data from the current object and over that of the parameter that. Since the latter is a vector_sum, the expression that[i] computes an element-wise sum, here x[i] + y[i]. Thus, in contrast to what the naïve implementation from Listing 5–4 would perform, the evaluation of w= x + y has now

- Only one loop;

- No temporary vector;

- No additional memory allocation and deallocation; and

- No additional data reads and writes.

In fact, the same operations are performed as in the loop:

```
for (int i= 0; i < size(w); ++i)
    w[i] = x[i] + y[i];
```

The cost to create a `vector_sum` object is negligible. The object will be kept on the stack and does not require memory allocation. Even this little effort for creating the object is normally optimized away by most compilers with decent static code analysis.

What happens when we add three vectors? The naïve implementation from Listing 5–4 returns a vector, and this vector can be added to another vector. Our approach returns a `vector_sum`, and we have no addition for `vector_sum` and `vector`. Thus, we would need another expression template class and a corresponding operation:

```
template <typename T>
class vector_sum3
{
  public:
    vector_sum3(const vector<T>& v1, const vector<T>& v2,
                const vector<T>& v3)
      : v1(v1), v2(v2), v3(v3)
    { ... }

    T operator[](int i) const { return v1[i] + v2[i] + v3[i]; }
  private:
    const vector<T> &v1, &v2, &v3;
};

template <typename T>
vector_sum3<T> inline operator+(const vector_sum<T>& x,
                                const vector<T>& y)
{
    return {x.v1, x.v2, y};
}
```

Furthermore, `vector_sum` must declare our new plus operator as **friend** to access its private members, and `vector` needs an assignment for `vector_sum3`. This becomes increasingly annoying. Also, what happens if we perform the second addition first: `w= x + (y + z)`? Then we need another plus operator. What if some of the vectors are multiplied with a scalar like `w= x + dot(x, y) * y + 4.3 * z`, and this scalar product is also implemented by an ET? Our implementation effort runs into combinatorial explosion and we need a more flexible solution that we introduce in the next section.

5.3.3 Generic Expression Templates

⇒ c++11/expression_template_example2.cpp

So far, we have started from a specific class (`vector`) and generalized the implementation gradually. Although this can help us understand the mechanism, we now go directly to the general version working for arbitrary vector types and views thereof:

```
template <typename V1, typename V2>
inline vector_sum<V1, V2> operator+(const V1& x, const V2& y)
{
    return {x, y};
}
```

We now need an expression class with arbitrary arguments:

```
template <typename V1, typename V2>
class vector_sum
{
  public:
    vector_sum(const V1& v1, const V2& v2) : v1(v1), v2(v2) {}

    ???? operator[](int i) const { return v1[i] + v2[i]; }

  private:
    const V1& v1;
    const V2& v2;
};
```

This is rather straightforward. The only issue is what type to return in `operator[]`. For this we must define `value_type` in each class (an external type trait would be more flexible but we want to keep it as simple as possible here). In `vector_sum`, we could take the `value_type` of the first argument, which can itself be taken from another class. This is an acceptable solution as long as the scalar types are identical in the entire application. However, we have seen in Section 3.10 that we can get completely absurd results with mixed arguments when we do not pay attention to the result types. To be prepared for mixed arithmetic, we take the `common_type_t` of the arguments' value types:

```
template <typename V1, typename V2>
class vector_sum
{
    // ...
    using value_type= std::common_type_t<typename V1::value_type,
                                         typename V2::value_type>;

    value_type operator[](int i) const { return v1[i] + v2[i]; }
};
```

If our class `vector_sum` does not need the explicit declaration of a `value_type`, we can use `decltype(auto)` in C++14 as a `return` type and leave the type deduction entirely to the compiler. In contrast, trailing `return` types do not work when the template is instantiated with `vector_sum` itself as this creates a dependency on itself.

To assign different kinds of expressions to a vector class, we should also generalize the assignment operator:

```
template <typename T>
class vector
{
  public:
    template <typename Src>
    vector& operator=(const Src& that)
    {
        check_size(size(that));
        for (int i= 0; i < my_size; ++i)
```

```
          data[i]= that[i];
      return *this;
    }
};
```

This assignment operator accepts every type except vector<T> for which we need a dedicated copy-assignment operator. To avoid code redundancy, we could implement a method that performs the actual copy and is called from both the general and the copy assignment.

Advantages of expression templates: Although the availability of operator overloading in C++ resulted in notationally nicer code, the scientific community refused to give up programming in Fortran or to implement the loops directly in C/C++. The reason was that the traditional operator implementations were too expensive. Due to the overhead of creating temporary variables and of copying vector and matrix objects, C++ could not compete with the performance of programs written in Fortran. This problem has been resolved with the introduction of generics and expression templates. Now we can write extremely efficient scientific programs in a notationally convenient manner.

5.4 Meta-Tuning: Write Your Own Compiler Optimization

Compiler technology is progressing, and more and more optimization techniques are provided. Ideally, we all write software in the easiest and most readable way, and the compiler generates the optimal executable out of it. We would only need a newer and better compiler for our programs to become faster and faster. Unfortunately, this only sometimes really works.

In addition to general-purpose optimizations like copy elision (§2.3.5.3), compilers provide numeric optimization techniques like *Loop Unrolling*: the loop is transformed such that multiple iterations are performed in one. This decreases the overhead of loop control and increases the potential for concurrent execution. Many compilers apply this technique only on the inner loop whereas unrolling multiple loops often enables even better performance. Several iterative calculations benefit from the introduction of additional temporaries which in turn can require semantic information that is not available for user types or operations.

Some compilers are particularly tuned for specific operations—especially those used in benchmarks and even more specifically for the LINPACK benchmark used to rate the 500 fastest computers in the world (www.top500.org). For instance, they can use pattern matching to recognize the typical three-nested loop in canonical dense-matrix multiplication and replace this code with a highly tuned assembler implementation that can be one or more orders of magnitude faster. These programs use seven or nine loops with platform-dependent block size to squeeze out the last bit of every cache level, transpose sub-matrices, run on multiple threads, perform a filigree register choreography, and so on.[5]

---

5. One could sometimes get the impression that the High-Performance Computing (HPC) community believes that multiplying dense matrices at near-peak performance solves all performance issues of the world or at least demonstrates that everything can be computed at near-peak performance if only one tries hard enough. Fortunately, more and more people in the supercomputer centers realize that their machines are not only running dense-matrix operations and that real-world applications are in most cases limited by memory bandwidth and latency.

Having a simple loop implementation replaced with code running at almost peak performance is definitely a great achievement. Unfortunately, this makes many programmers believe that most calculations can be similarly accelerated. Often small changes suffice to fall out of the pattern and the performance is much less spectacular than expected. No matter how generally the patterns are defined, their applicability will always be limited. An algorithmic change (e.g., multiplying triangular instead of rectangular matrices) that does not impede the blocking and unrolling optimizations will probably fall out of the compiler's special-case optimization.

To make a long story short: compilers can do a lot but not everything. Regardless of how many special cases are tuned by a compiler, there will always be a need for domain-specific optimizations. Alternatively to the techniques in compilers, there are tools like ROSE [35] that allow you to transform source code (including C++) with user-defined transformations on the abstract syntax tree (AST, the compiler-internal representation of programs).

A major roadblock for compiler optimization is that certain transformations require semantic knowledge. This is only available for types and operations known to the compiler implementers. The interested reader might also look at a deeper discussion of the topic in [19]. Research is going on to provide user-defined transformations with concept-based optimization [47]. Unfortunately, it will take time for this to become mainstream; even the new *Concepts Lite* extension planned for C++17 can only be a step toward optimization driven by user semantics since it will only deal with syntax at first.

In the remainder of this chapter, we will show user-defined code transformations with meta-programming in the domain of linear algebra. The goal is that the user writes operations as clearly as possible and the function and class templates reach for the maximal achievable performance. Given the Turing completeness of the template system, we can provide any desirable user interface while realizing an implementation underneath that behaves equivalently to the most efficient code, as we will demonstrate in this section. Writing well-tuned templates is a significant programming, testing, and benchmarking effort. For this to pay off, the templates should be contained in well-maintained libraries that are available to a broad user community (at least within the research team or company).

5.4.1 Classical Fixed-Size Unrolling

⇒ c++11/fsize_unroll_test.cpp

The easiest form of compile-time optimization can be realized for fixed-size data types, in particular for math vectors like those in Section 3.7. Similar to the default assignment, we can write a generic vector assignment:

```
template <typename T, int Size>
class fsize_vector
{
  public:
    const static int      my_size= Size;

    template <typename Vector>
    self& operator=(const self& that)
    {
```

```
            for (int i= 0; i < my_size; ++i)
                data[i]= that[i];
        }
};
```

A state-of-the-art compiler will recognize that all iterations are independent from each other; e.g., data[2]= that[2]; is independent of data[1]= that[1];. The compiler will also determine the size of the loop during compilation. As a consequence, the generated binary for an fsize_vector of size 3 will be equivalent to

```
    template <typename T, int Size>
    class fsize_vector
    {
        template <typename Vector>
        self& operator=(const self& that)
        {
            data[0]= that[0];
            data[1]= that[1];
            data[2]= that[2];
        }
    };
```

The right-hand-side vector that might be an expression template (§5.3) for, say, alpha * x + y and its evaluation will be also inlined:

```
    template <typename T, int Size>
    class fsize_vector
    {
        template <typename Vector>
        self& operator=(const self& that)
        {
            data[0]= alpha * x[0] + y[0];
            data[1]= alpha * x[1] + y[1];
            data[2]= alpha * x[2] + y[2];
        }
    };
```

To make the unrolling more explicit and for the sake of introducing meta-tuning step by step, we develop a functor that performs the assignment:

```
    template <typename Target, typename Source, int N>
    struct fsize_assign
    {
        void operator()(Target& tar, const Source& src)
        {
            fsize_assign<Target, Source, [*N-1>()(tar, src);
            std::cout ≪ "assign entry " ≪ N ≪ '\n';
            tar[N]= src[N];
        }
    };
```

```
template <typename Target, typename Source>
struct fsize_assign<Target, Source, 0>
{
    void operator()(Target& tar, const Source& src)
    {
        std::cout << "assign entry " << 0 << '\n';
        tar[0]= src[0];
    }
};
```

The printouts will show us the execution. To save ourselves from explicitly instantiating the argument types, we parameterize the operator() instead of the class:

```
template <int N>
struct fsize_assign
{
    template <typename Target, typename Source>
    void operator()(Target& tar, const Source& src)
    {
        fsize_assign<N-1>()(tar, src);
        std::cout << "assign entry " << N << '\n';
        tar[N]= src[N];
    }
};

template <>
struct fsize_assign<0>
{
    template <typename Target, typename Source>
    void operator()(Target& tar, const Source& src)
    {
        std::cout << "assign entry " << 0 << '\n';
        tar[0]= src[0];
    }
};
```

Then the vector types can be deduced by the compiler when the operator is called. Instead of a loop implementation, we call the recursive assignment functor in the operator:

```
template <typename T, int Size>
class fsize_vector
{
    static_assert(my_size > 0, "Vector must be larger than 0.");

    self& operator=(const self& that)
    {
        fsize_assign<my_size-1>{}(*this, that);
        return *this;
    }
```

```
    template <typename Vector>
    self& operator=(const Vector& that)
    {
        fsize_assign<my_size-1>{}(*this, that);
        return *this;
    }
};
```

The execution of the following code fragment:

```
fsize_vector<float, 4> v, w;
v[0]= v[1]= 1.0; v[2]= 2.0; v[3]= -3.0;
w= v;
```

shows the expected behavior:

```
assign entry 0
assign entry 1
assign entry 2
assign entry 3
```

In this implementation, we replaced the loop with a recursion—counting on the compiler to inline the operations and the loop control. Otherwise the recursive function calls would be even slower than an ordinary loop.

This technique is only beneficial for small loops that run in L1 cache. Larger loops are dominated by loading the data from memory and the loop overhead is irrelevant. To the contrary, unrolling all operations with very large vectors usually decreases the performance because a lot of instructions need to be loaded, so the transfer of the data must wait. As mentioned before, compilers can unroll such operations by themselves and hopefully contain heuristics to decide when it is better not to. We have observed that the automatic unrolling of single loops is sometimes faster than explicit implementations like that above.

One would think that the implementation should be simpler with constexpr at least with the C++14 extensions. Unfortunately, it is not because we would mix compile-time arguments—the size—with run-time arguments—the vector references. Thus, the constexpr would degrade to an ordinary function.

5.4.2   Nested Unrolling

In our experience, most compilers unroll non-nested loops. Even good compilers that can handle certain nested loops will not be able to optimize every program kernel, in particular those with many template arguments that are instantiated with user-defined types. We will demonstrate here how to unroll nested loops at compile time with matrix vector multiplication as an example.

⇒ c++11/fsize_unroll_test.cpp

For this purpose, we introduce a simplistic fixed-size matrix type:

```cpp
template <typename T, int Rows, int Cols>
class fsize_matrix
{
    static_assert(Rows > 0, "Rows must be larger than 0.");
    static_assert(Cols > 0, "Cols must be larger than 0.");

    using self= fsize_matrix;
  public:
    using value_type= T;
    const static int     my_rows= Rows, my_cols= Cols;

    fsize_matrix(const self& that) { ... }

    // Cannot check column index here!
    const T* operator[](int r) const { return data[r]; }
    T* operator[](int r) { return data[r]; }

    mat_vec_et<self, fsize_vector<T, Cols> >
    operator*(const fsize_vector<T, Cols>& v) const
    {
        return {*this, v};
    }

  private:
    T       data[Rows][Cols];
};
```

The bracket operator returns a pointer for the sake of simplicity whereas a good implementation should return a proxy that allows for checking the column index (see §A.4.3.3). The multiplication with a vector is realized by means of an expression template to avoid copying the result vector. Then the vector assignment is overloaded for our expression template type:

```cpp
template <typename T, int Size>
class fsize_vector
{
    template <typename Matrix, typename Vector>
    self& operator=(const mat_vec_et<Matrix, Vector>& that)
    {
        using et= mat_vec_et<Matrix, Vector>;
        using mv= fsize_mat_vec_mult<et::my_rows-1, et::my_cols-1>;
        mv{}(that.A, that.v, *this);
        return *this;
    }
};
```

The functor `fsize_mat_vec_mult` computes the matrix vector product with respect to the three arguments. The general implementation of the functor reads:

```cpp
template <int Rows, int Cols>
struct fsize_mat_vec_mult
```

```
{
    template <typename Matrix, typename VecIn, typename VecOut>
    void operator()(const Matrix& A, const VecIn& v_in, VecOut& v_out)
    {
        fsize_mat_vec_mult<Rows, Cols-1>()(A, v_in, v_out);
        v_out[Rows]+= A[Rows][Cols] * v_in[Cols];
    }
};
```

Again, the functor only takes the size arguments as explicit parameters whereas the types of the containers are deduced. The operator assumes that all smaller column indices are already handled and that we can increment v_out[Rows] by A[Rows][Cols] * v_in[Cols]. In particular, we assume that the first operation on v_out[Rows] initializes the value. Thus, we need a (partial) specialization for Cols = 0:

```
template <int Rows>
struct fsize_mat_vec_mult<Rows, 0>
{
    template <typename Matrix, typename VecIn, typename VecOut>
    void operator()(const Matrix& A, const VecIn& v_in, VecOut& v_out)
    {
        fsize_mat_vec_mult<Rows-1, Matrix::my_cols-1>()(A, v_in, v_out);
        v_out[Rows]= A[Rows][0] * v_in[0];
    }
};
```

The careful reader will have noticed the substitution of += with =. We also have to call the computation for the preceding row with all columns and inductively for all smaller rows. For the sake of simplicity, the number of matrix columns is taken from an internal definition in the matrix type.[6] We further need a (full) specialization to terminate the recursion:

```
template <>
struct fsize_mat_vec_mult<0, 0>
{
    template <typename Matrix, typename VecIn, typename VecOut>
    void operator()(const Matrix& A, const VecIn& v_in, VecOut& v_out)
    {
        v_out[0]= A[0][0] * v_in[0];
    }
};
```

With the inlining, our program will execute the operation w= A * v for vectors of size 4 as if we computed

```
w[0]=  A[0][0] * v[0];
w[0]+= A[0][1] * v[1];
w[0]+= A[0][2] * v[2];
w[0]+= A[0][3] * v[3];
w[1]=  A[1][0] * v[0];
```

---

6. Passing this as an extra template argument or taking type traits would have been more general because we would not depend on the my_cols definition in the class.

```
w[1]+= A[1][1] * v[1];
w[1]+= A[1][2] * v[2];
            ⋮
```

Our tests have shown that such an implementation is really faster than the compiler optimization on loops.

5.4.2.1 Increasing Concurrency

A disadvantage of the preceding implementation is that all operations on an entry of the target vector are performed in one sweep. Therefore, the second operation must wait for the first one, the third for the second, and so on. The fifth operation can be done in parallel with the fourth, the ninth with the eighth, et cetera. However, this is a quite limited concurrency. We like having more parallelism in our program so that parallel pipelines in super-scalar processors or even SSEs are enabled. Again, we can twiddle our thumbs and hope that the compiler will reorder the statements into our favorite order or take it in our own hands. More concurrency is provided when we traverse the result vector and the matrix rows in the "inner" loop:

```
w[0]=  A[0][0] * v[0];
w[1]=  A[1][0] * v[0];
w[2]=  A[2][0] * v[0];
w[3]=  A[3][0] * v[0];
w[0]+= A[0][1] * v[1];
w[1]+= A[1][1] * v[1];
            ⋮
```

We only need to restructure our functor. The general template now reads:

```
template <int Rows, int Cols>
struct fsize_mat_vec_mult_cm
{
    template <typename Matrix, typename VecIn, typename VecOut>
    void operator()(const Matrix& A, const VecIn& v_in, VecOut& v_out)
    {
        fsize_mat_vec_mult_cm<Rows-1, Cols>()(A, v_in, v_out);
        v_out[Rows]+= A[Rows][Cols] * v_in[Cols];
    }
};
```

Now, we need a partial specialization for row 0 that goes to the next column:

```
template <int Cols>
struct fsize_mat_vec_mult_cm<0, Cols>
{
    template <typename Matrix, typename VecIn, typename VecOut>
    void operator()(const Matrix& A, const VecIn& v_in, VecOut& v_out)
    {
```

```
            fsize_mat_vec_mult_cm<Matrix::my_rows-1,
                Cols-1>()(A, v_in, v_out);
            v_out[0]+= A[0][Cols] * v_in[Cols];
    }
};
```

The partial specialization for column 0 must also initialize the entry of the output vector:

```
template <int Rows>
struct fsize_mat_vec_mult_cm<Rows, 0>
{
    template <typename Matrix, typename VecIn, typename VecOut>
    void operator()(const Matrix& A, const VecIn& v_in, VecOut& v_out)
    {
        fsize_mat_vec_mult_cm<Rows-1, 0>()(A, v_in, v_out);
        v_out[Rows]= A[Rows][0] * v_in[0];
    }
};
```

Finally, we still need a specialization for row and column 0 to terminate the recursion. This can be reused from the previous functor:

```
template <>
struct fsize_mat_vec_mult_cm<0, 0>
    : fsize_mat_vec_mult<0, 0> {};
```

Note that we perform the same operation on different data from which *SIMD* architectures can benefit. SIMD stands for *Single Instruction, Multiple Data*. Modern processors contain *SSE* units that perform arithmetic operations simultaneously on multiple floating-point numbers. To use these SSE commands, the processed data must be aligned and contiguous in memory and the compiler must be aware of it. In our examples, we did not address the alignment issue, but the unrolled code makes it clear that identical operations are executed on contiguous memory.

5.4.2.2 Using Registers

Another feature of modern processors that we should keep in mind is cache coherency. Processors are nowadays designed to share memory while retaining consistency in their caches. As a result, every time we write a data structure in memory like our vector w, a cache invalidation signal is sent to other cores and processors. Regrettably, this slows down computation perceivably.

Fortunately, the cache invalidation bottleneck can be avoided in many cases, simply by introducing temporaries in functions that reside in registers when the types allow for it. We can rely on the compiler to make good decisions where temporaries are located. C++03 had the keyword register. However, it was a mere hint and the compiler was not obliged to store variables in registers. Especially when a program is compiled for a target platform that was not considered in the development process, it would do more harm than good if the register use was mandatory. Thus, the keyword was deprecated in C++11 given that compilers have pretty good heuristics to locate variables platform-dependently without help from the programmer.

The introduction of temporaries requires two classes: one for the outer and one for the inner loop. Let us start with the outer loop:

```
1   template <int Rows, int Cols>
2   struct fsize_mat_vec_mult_reg
3   {
4       template <typename Matrix, typename VecIn, typename VecOut>
5       void operator()(const Matrix& A, const VecIn& v_in, VecOut& v_out)
6       {
7           fsize_mat_vec_mult_reg<Rows-1, Cols>()(A, v_in, v_out);
8
9           typename VecOut::value_type tmp;
10          fsize_mat_vec_mult_aux<Rows, Cols>()(A, v_in, tmp);
11          v_out[Rows]= tmp;
12      }
13  };
```

We assume that fsize_mat_vec_mult_aux is defined or declared before this class. The first statement in line 7 calls the computations on the preceding rows. A temporary is defined in line 9 assuming that it will be located in a register by a decent compiler. Then we start the computation for this matrix row. The temporary is passed as a reference to an inline function so that the summation will be performed in a register. In line 10, we write the result back to v_out. This still causes the invalidation signal on the bus but only once for each entry. The functor must be specialized for row 0 to avoid infinite loops:

```
template <int Cols>
struct fsize_mat_vec_mult_reg<0, Cols>
{
    template <typename Matrix, typename VecIn, typename VecOut>
    void operator()(const Matrix& A, const VecIn& v_in, VecOut& v_out)
    {
        typename VecOut::value_type tmp;
        fsize_mat_vec_mult_aux<0, Cols>()(A, v_in, tmp);
        v_out[0]= tmp;
    }
};
```

Within each row, we iterate over the columns and increment the temporary (within a register hopefully):

```
template <int Rows, int Cols>
struct fsize_mat_vec_mult_aux
{
    template <typename Matrix, typename VecIn, typename ScalOut>
    void operator()(const Matrix& A, const VecIn& v_in, ScalOut& tmp)
    {
        fsize_mat_vec_mult_aux<Rows, Cols-1>()(A, v_in, tmp);
        tmp+= A[Rows][Cols] * v_in[Cols];
    }
};
```

To terminate the computation for the matrix column, we write a specialization:

```
template <int Rows>
struct fsize_mat_vec_mult_aux<Rows, 0>
{
    template <typename Matrix, typename VecIn, typename ScalOut>
    void operator()(const Matrix& A, const VecIn& v_in, ScalOut& tmp)
    {
        tmp= A[Rows][0] * v_in[0];
    }
};
```

In this section, we showed different ways to optimize a two-dimensional loop (with fixed sizes). There are certainly more possibilities: for instance, we could try an implementation with good concurrency and register usage at the same time. Another optimization would be the agglomeration of the write-backs to minimize the cache invalidation signals further.

5.4.3 Dynamic Unrolling–Warm-up

⇒ c++11/vector_unroll_example.cpp

As important as the fixed-size optimization is, acceleration for dynamically sized containers is needed even more. We start here with a simple example and some observations. We will reuse the vector class from Listing 3–1. To show the implementation more clearly, we write the code without operators and expression templates. Our test case will compute

$$u = 3v + w$$

for three short vectors of size 1000. The wall clock time will be measured with <chrono>. The vectors v and w will be initialized, and to make absolutely sure that the data is in cache, we will run some additional operations before the timing. For conciseness, we moved the benchmarking code to Appendix A.9.5.

We compare the straightforward loop with one that performs four operations in each iteration:

```
for (unsigned j= 0; j < rep; j++)
    for (unsigned i= 0; i < s; i+= 4) {
        u[i]=    3.0f * v[i]    + w[i];
        u[i+1]= 3.0f * v[i+1] + w[i+1];
        u[i+2]= 3.0f * v[i+2] + w[i+2];
        u[i+3]= 3.0f * v[i+3] + w[i+3];
    }
```

This code will obviously only work when the vector size is divisible by 4. To avoid errors we can add an assertion on the vector size but this is not really satisfying. Instead, we generalize this implementation to arbitrary vector sizes:

Listing 5–5: Unrolled computation of $u = 3v + w$

```
for (unsigned j= 0; j < rep; j++) {
    unsigned sb= s / 4 * 4;
```

```
        for (unsigned i= 0; i < sb; i+= 4) {
            u[i]=    3.0f * v[i]    + w[i];
            u[i+1]= 3.0f * v[i+1] + w[i+1];
            u[i+2]= 3.0f * v[i+2] + w[i+2];
            u[i+3]= 3.0f * v[i+3] + w[i+3];
        }
        for (unsigned i= sb; i < s; ++i)
            u[i]= 3.0f * v[i] + w[i];
    }
```

Sadly, we see the largest benefit with the oldest compilers. Using gcc 4.4 with the flags -O3 -ffast-math -DNDEBUG running on an Intel i7-3820 3.6 GHz resulted in

```
Compute time native loop is 0.801699 μs.
Compute time unrolled loop is 0.600912 μs.
```

Measured timings in this chapter are averages over at least 1000 runs, so the accumulated execution time was more than 10s and the clock provides sufficient resolution.

Alternatively or in addition to our hand-coded unrolling, we can use the compiler flag -funroll-loops. This resulted in the following execution time on the test machine:

```
Compute time native loop is 0.610174 μs.
Compute time unrolled loop is 0.586364 μs.
```

Thus, the compiler flag supplied us with a similar performance gain.

The compiler is able to apply more optimizations when the vector size is already known at compile time:

```
const unsigned s= 1000;
```

Then it can be easier to transform the loop or to determine that a transformation is beneficial:

```
Compute time native loop is 0.474725 μs.
Compute time unrolled loop is 0.471488 μs.
```

With g++ 4.8, we observed run times around $0.42\,\mu s$ and with clang 3.4 even $0.16\,\mu s$. Investigating the generated assembler revealed that the main difference was how the data is moved from the main memory to the floating-point registers and back.

It also demonstrated that 1D loops are very well optimized by modern compilers, often better than by our hand tuning. Nonetheless, we will show the meta-tuning technique first in one dimension as preparation for higher dimensions where it still supplies significant accelerations.

Assuming that loop unrolling is beneficial for a given calculation on a platform in question, we ask ourselves next: "What is the optimal block size for the unrolling?"

- Does it depend on the expression?

- Does it depend on the types of the arguments?

- Does it depend on the computer architecture?

The answer is yes. All of them. The main reason (but not the only one) is that different processors have different numbers of registers. How many registers are needed in one iteration depends on the expression and on the types (a `complex` value needs more registers than a `float`).

In the following section, we will address both issues: how to encapsulate the transformation so that it does not show up in the application and how we can change the block size without rewriting the loop.

5.4.4 Unrolling Vector Expressions

For easier understanding, we discuss the abstraction in meta-tuning step by step. We start with the previous loop example $u = 3v + w$ and implement it as a tunable function. The function's name is `my_axpy`, and it has a template argument for the block size so we can write, for instance:

```
for (unsigned j= 0; j < rep; j++)
    my_axpy<2>(u, v, w);
```

This function contains an unrolled main loop with customizable block size and a clean-up loop at the end:

```
template <unsigned BSize, typename U, typename V, typename W >
void my_axpy(U& u, const V& v, const W & w)
{
    assert(u.size() == v.size() && v.size() == w.size());
    unsigned s= u.size(), sb= s / BSize * BSize;

    for (unsigned i= 0; i < sb; i+= BSize)
        my_axpy_ftor<0, BSize>()(u, v, w, i);

    for (unsigned i= sb; i < s; ++i)
        u[i]= 3.0f * v[i] + w[i];
}
```

As mentioned before, deduced template types, like the vector types in our case, must be defined at the end of the parameter list and the explicitly given arguments, in our case the block size, must be passed to the first template parameters. The implementation of the block statement in the first loop can be implemented similarly to the functor in Section 5.4.1. We deviate a bit from this implementation by using two template parameters where the first one is increased until it is equal to the second. We observed that this approach yielded faster binaries on `gcc` than using only one argument and counting it down to zero. In addition, the two-argument version is more consistent with the multi-dimensional implementation in Section 5.4.7. As for fixed-size unrolling, we need a recursive template definition. Within each operator, a single operation is performed and the following called:

```
template <unsigned Offset, unsigned Max>
struct my_axpy_ftor
{
    template <typename U, typename V, typename W >
    void operator()(U& u, const V& v, const W & w, unsigned i)
```

```
        {
            u[i+Offset]= 3.0f * v[i+Offset] + w[i+Offset];
            my_axpy_ftor<Offset+1, Max>()(u, v, w, i);
        }
    };
```

The only difference from fixed-size unrolling is that the indices are relative to the index i. The operator() is first called with Offset equal to 0, then with 1, 2, and so on. Since each call is inlined, the functor call behaves like one monolithic block of operations without loop control and function call. Thus, the call of my_axpy_ftor<0, 4>()(u, v, w, i) performs the same operations as one iteration of the first loop in Listing 5–5.

Of course, this compilation would end in an infinite loop without the specialization for Max:

```
    template <unsigned Max>
    struct my_axpy_ftor<Max, Max>
    {
        template <typename U, typename V, typename W>
        void operator()(U& u, const V& v, const W& w, unsigned i) {}
    };
```

Performing the considered vector operation with different unrolling parameters yields

```
Compute time unrolled<2> loop is 0.667546 μs.
Compute time unrolled<4> loop is 0.601179 μs.
Compute time unrolled<6> loop is 0.565536 μs.
Compute time unrolled<8> loop is 0.570061 μs.
```

Now we can call this operation for any block size we like. On the other hand, it is an unacceptable programming effort to provide such functors for each vector expression. Therefore, we will now combine this technique with expression templates.

5.4.5   Tuning an Expression Template

⇒ c++03/vector_unroll_example2.cpp

In Section 5.3.3, we implemented expression templates for vector sums (without unrolling). In the same manner we could implement a scalar-vector product, but we leave this as Exercise 5.5.4 for the motivated reader and consider expressions with addition only, for example:

$$u = v + v + w$$

Our baseline performance is

```
Compute time is 1.72 μs.
```

To incorporate meta-tuning into expression templates, we only need to modify the actual assignment because this is where all loop-based vector operations are performed. The other operations (addition, subtraction, scaling, ...) solely return small objects containing references. We can split the loop in operator= as before into the unrolled part at the beginning and the completion at the end:

```
template <typename T>
class vector
{
    template <typename Src>
    vector& operator=(const Src& that)
    {
    check_size(size(that));
    unsigned s= my_size, sb= s / 4 * 4;

    for (unsigned i= 0; i < sb; i+= 4)
        assign<0, 4>()(*this, that, i);

    for (unsigned i= sb; i < s; ++i)
        data[i]= that[i];
    return *this;
    }
};
```

The assign functor is realized analogously to my_axpy_ftor:

```
template <unsigned Offset, unsigned Max>
struct assign
{
    template <typename U, typename V>
    void operator()(U& u, const V& v, unsigned i)
    {
        u[i+Offset]= v[i+Offset];
        assign<Offset+1, Max>()(u, v, i);
    }
};

template <unsigned Max>
struct assign<Max, Max>
{
    template <typename U, typename V>
    void operator()(U& u, const V& v, unsigned i) {}
};
```

Computing the expression above yields

```
Compute time is 1.37 μs.
```

With this rather simple modification we now accelerated all vector expression templates. In comparison to the previous implementation, however, we lost the flexibility to customize the loop unrolling. The functor assign has two arguments, thus allowing for customization. The problem is the assignment operator. In principle we can define an explicit template argument here:

```
template <unsigned BSize, typename Src>
vector& operator=(const Src& that)
{
    check_size(size(that));
```

```
        unsigned s= my_size, sb= s / BSize * BSize;

        for (unsigned i= 0; i < sb; i+= BSize)
            assign<0, BSize>()(*this, that, i);

        for (unsigned i= sb; i < s; ++i)
            data[i]= that[i];
        return *this;
    }
```

The drawback is that we cannot use the symbol = as a natural infix operator any longer. Instead we must write:

```
    u.operator=<4>(v + v + w);
```

This has indeed a certain geeky charm, and one could also argue that people did, and still do, much more painful things for performance. Nonetheless, it does not meet our ideals of intuitiveness and readability.

Alternative notations are

```
    unroll<4>(u= v + v + w);
```

or

```
    unroll<4>(u)= v + v + w;
```

Both versions are implementable but we find the latter more readable. The former expresses more correctly what we are doing, while the latter is easier to implement and the structure of the computed expression retains better visibility. Therefore we show the realization of the second form.

The function unroll is simple to implement: it just returns an object of type unroll_vector (see below) with a reference to the vector and type information for the unroll size:

```
    template <unsigned BSize, typename Vector>
    unroll_vector<BSize, Vector> inline unroll(Vector& v)
    {
        return unroll_vector<BSize, Vector>(v);
    }
```

The class unroll_vector is not complicated either. It only needs to take a reference of the target vector and to provide an assignment operator:

```
    template <unsigned BSize, typename V>
    class unroll_vector
    {
      public:
        unroll_vector(V& ref) : ref(ref) {}

        template <typename Src>
        V& operator=(const Src& that)
        {
            assert(size(ref) == size(that));
```

```
            unsigned s= size(ref), sb= s / BSize * BSize;

            for (unsigned i= 0; i < sb; i+= BSize)
                assign<0, BSize>()(ref, that, i);

            for (unsigned i= sb; i < s; ++i)
                ref[i]= that[i];
            return ref;
        }
    private:
        V&      ref;
};
```

Evaluating the considered vector expressions for some block sizes yields

```
Compute time unroll<1>(u)= v + v + w is 1.72 μs.
Compute time unroll<2>(u)= v + v + w is 1.52 μs.
Compute time unroll<4>(u)= v + v + w is 1.36 μs.
Compute time unroll<6>(u)= v + v + w is 1.37 μs.
Compute time unroll<8>(u)= v + v + w is 1.4 μs.
```

These few benchmarks are consistent with the previous results; i.e., unroll<1> is equal to the canonical implementation and unroll<4> is as fast as the hard-wired unrolling.

5.4.6   Tuning Reduction Operations

The techniques in this section are applicable in similar fashion to a variety of vector and matrix norms. They can also be used for dot products and tensor reductions.

5.4.6.1   Reducing on a Single Variable

⇒ c++03/reduction_unroll_example.cpp

In the preceding vector operations, the i-th entry of each vector was handled independently of any other entry. For reduction operations, they are related by one or more temporary variables. And these temporary variables can become a serious bottleneck.

First, we test whether a reduction operation, say, the discrete L_1 norm (also known as the Manhattan norm), can be accelerated by the techniques from Section 5.4.4. We implement the one_norm function in terms of a functor for the iteration block:

```
template <unsigned BSize, typename Vector>
typename Vector::value_type
inline one_norm(const Vector& v)
{
    using std::abs;
    typename Vector::value_type sum(0);
    unsigned s= size(v), sb= s / BSize * BSize;

    for (unsigned i= 0; i < sb; i+= BSize)
        one_norm_ftor<0, BSize>()(sum, v, i);
    for (unsigned i= sb; i < s; ++i)
```

```
        sum+= abs(v[i]);
    return sum;
}
```

The functor is also implemented in the same manner as before:

```
template <unsigned Offset, unsigned Max>
struct one_norm_ftor
{
    template <typename S, typename V>
    void operator()(S& sum, const V& v, unsigned i)
    {
        using std::abs;
        sum+= abs(v[i+Offset]);
        one_norm_ftor<Offset+1, Max>()(sum, v, i);
    }
};

template <unsigned Max>
struct one_norm_ftor<Max, Max>
{
    template <typename S, typename V>
    void operator()(S& sum, const V& v, unsigned i) {}
};
```

For reductions, we can see a tuning benefit with more recent compilers like gcc 4.8:

```
Compute time one_norm<1>(v) is 0.788445 µs.
Compute time one_norm<2>(v) is 0.43087 µs.
Compute time one_norm<4>(v) is 0.436625 µs.
Compute time one_norm<6>(v) is 0.43035 µs.
Compute time one_norm<8>(v) is 0.461095 µs.
```

This corresponds to a speedup of 1.8. Let us try some alternative implementations.

5.4.6.2   Reducing on an Array

⇒ c++03/reduction_unroll_array_example.cpp

When we look at the previous computation, we see that a different entry of v is used in each iteration. But every computation accesses the same temporary variable sum, and this limits the concurrency. To provide more concurrency, we can use multiple temporaries[7] in an array, for instance. The modified function then reads:

```
template <unsigned BSize, typename Vector>
typename Vector::value_type
```

---

7. Strictly speaking, this is not true for every possible scalar type we can think of. The addition of the sum type must be a commutative monoid because we change the evaluation order. This holds of course for all intrinsic numeric types and certainly for almost all user-defined arithmetic types. However, we are free to define an addition that is not commutative or not monoidal. In this case, our transformation would be wrong. To deal with such exceptions, we need semantic concepts which will hopefully become part of C++ at some point. (Especially since the author has already spent a lot of time with them.)

```
inline one_norm(const Vector& v)
{
    using std::abs;
    typename Vector::value_type sum[BSize];
    for (unsigned i= 0; i < BSize; ++i)
        sum[i]= 0;

    unsigned s= size(v), sb= s / BSize * BSize;
    for (unsigned i= 0; i < sb; i+= BSize)
        one_norm_ftor<0, BSize>()(sum, v, i);

    for (unsigned i= 1; i < BSize; ++i)
        sum[0]+= sum[i];
    for (unsigned i= sb; i < s; ++i)
        sum[0]+= abs(v[i]);

    return sum[0];
}
```

Now, each instance of one_norm_ftor operates on another entry of the sum array:

```
template <unsigned Offset, unsigned Max>
struct one_norm_ftor
{
    template <typename S, typename V>
    void operator()(S* sum, const V& v, unsigned i)
    {
        using std::abs;
        sum[Offset]+= abs(v[i+Offset]);
        one_norm_ftor<Offset+1, Max>()(sum, v, i);
    }
};

template <unsigned Max>
struct one_norm_ftor<Max, Max>
{
    template <typename S, typename V>
    void operator()(S* sum, const V& v, unsigned i) {}
};
```

Running this implementation on the test machine yielded

```
Compute time one_norm<1>(v) is 0.797224 µs.
Compute time one_norm<2>(v) is 0.45923 µs.
Compute time one_norm<4>(v) is 0.538913 µs.
Compute time one_norm<6>(v) is 0.467529 µs.
Compute time one_norm<8>(v) is 0.506729 µs.
```

This is even a bit slower than the version with one variable. Maybe an array is more expensive to pass as an argument even in an inline function. Let us try something else.

5.4.6.3 Reducing on a Nested Class Object

⇒ c++03/reduction_unroll_nesting_example.cpp

To avoid arrays, we can define a class for n temporary variables where n is a template parameter. Then the class design is more consistent with the recursive scheme of the functors:

```
template <unsigned BSize, typename Value>
struct multi_tmp
{
    typedef multi_tmp<BSize-1, Value> sub_type;

    multi_tmp(const Value& v) : value(v), sub(v) {}

    Value      value;
    sub_type   sub;
};

template <typename Value>
struct multi_tmp<0, Value>
{
    multi_tmp(const Value& v) {}
};
```

An object of this type can be recursively initialized so that we do not need a loop as for the array. A functor can operate on the value member and pass a reference to the sub member to its successor. This leads us to the implementation of our functor:

```
template <unsigned Offset, unsigned Max>
struct one_norm_ftor
{
    template <typename S, typename V>
    void operator()(S& sum, const V& v, unsigned i)
    {
        using std::abs;
        sum.value+= abs(v[i+Offset]);
        one_norm_ftor<Offset+1, Max>()(sum.sub, v, i);
    }
};

template <unsigned Max>
struct one_norm_ftor<Max, Max>
{
    template <typename S, typename V>
    void operator()(S& sum, const V& v, unsigned i) {}
};
```

The unrolled function that uses this functor reads:

```
template <unsigned BSize, typename Vector>
typename Vector::value_type
inline one_norm(const Vector& v)
```

```
{
    using std::abs;
    typedef typename Vector::value_type value_type;
    multi_tmp<BSize, value_type> multi_sum(0);

    unsigned s= size(v), sb= s / BSize * BSize;
    for (unsigned i= 0; i < sb; i+= BSize)
        one_norm_ftor<0, BSize>()(multi_sum, v, i);

    value_type sum= multi_sum.sum();
    for (unsigned i= sb; i < s; ++i)
        sum+= abs(v[i]);

    return sum;
}
```

There is still one piece missing: we must reduce the partial sums in multi_sum at the end. Unfortunately, we cannot write a loop over the members of multi_sum. So, we need a recursive function that dives into multi_sum which is easiest to implement as a member function with the corresponding specialization:

```
template <unsigned BSize, typename Value>
struct multi_tmp
{
    Value sum() const { return value + sub.sum(); }
};

template <typename Value>
struct multi_tmp<0, Value>
{
    Value sum() const { return 0; }
};
```

Note that we started the summation with the empty multi_tmp, not the innermost value member. Otherwise we would need an extra specialization for multi_tmp<1, Value>. Likewise, we could implement a general reduction as in accumulate, but this would require the presence of an initial element:

```
template <unsigned BSize, typename Value>
struct multi_tmp
{
    template <typename Op>
    Value reduce(Op op, const Value& init) const
    { return op(value, sub.reduce(op, init)); }
};

template <typename Value>
struct multi_tmp<0, Value>
{
    template <typename Op>
    Value reduce(Op, const Value& init) const { return init; }
};
```

The compute times of this version are

```
Compute time one_norm<1>(v) is 0.786668 μs.
Compute time one_norm<2>(v) is 0.442476 μs.
Compute time one_norm<4>(v) is 0.441455 μs.
Compute time one_norm<6>(v) is 0.410978 μs.
Compute time one_norm<8>(v) is 0.426368 μs.
```

Thus, in our test environment, the performance of the different implementations is similar.

5.4.6.4 Dealing with Abstraction Penalty

⇒ c++03/reduction_unroll_registers_example.cpp

In the previous sections, we introduced temporaries for enabling more independent operations. These temporaries are only beneficial, however, when they are assigned to registers. Otherwise they can even slow down the entire execution due to extra memory traffic and cache invalidation signals. With certain old compilers, arrays and nested classes were located in main memory and the run time of the unrolled code was even longer than that of the sequential one.

This is a typical example of *Abstraction Penalty*: semantically equivalent programs running slower due to a more abstract formulation. To quantify the abstraction penalty, Alex Stepanov wrote in the early 90s a benchmark for measuring the impact of wrapper classes on the performance of the accumulate function [40]. The idea was that compilers able to run all versions of the test with the same speed should be able to perform STL algorithms without overhead.

At that time, one could observe significant overhead for more abstract codes whereas modern compilers can easily deal with the abstractions in that benchmark. That does not imply that they can handle every level of abstraction, and we always have to check whether our performance-critical kernels could be faster with a less abstract implementation. For instance, in MTL4, the matrix vector product is generically implemented in an iterator-like fashion for all matrix types and views. This operation is specialized for important matrix classes and tuned for those data structures, partially with raw pointers. Generic, high-performance software needs a good balance of generic reusability and targeted tuning to avoid perceivable overhead on one hand and combinatorial code explosion on the other.

In our special case of register usage, we can try to help the compiler optimization by transferring the complexity away from the data structure. Our best chances that temporaries are stored in registers is to declare them as function-local variables:

```
inline one_norm(const Vector& v)
{
    typename Vector::value_type s0(0), s1(0), s2(0), ...
}
```

The question is now how many we should declare. The number cannot depend on the template parameter but must be fixed for all block sizes. Furthermore, the number of temporaries limits our ability to unroll the loop.

How many temporaries are actually used in the iteration block depends on the template parameter BSize. Unfortunately, we cannot change the number of arguments in a function call depending on a template parameter, i.e., passing fewer arguments for smaller values of BSize. Thus, we have to pass all variables to the iteration block functor:

```
for (unsigned i= 0; i < sb; i+= BSize)
    one_norm_ftor<0, BSize>()(s0, s1, s2, s3, s4, s5, s6, s7, v, i);
```

The first calculation in each block accumulates on s0, the second on s1, and so on. Unfortunately, we cannot select the temporary argument-dependently (unless we specialize for every value).

Alternatively, each computation is performed on its first function argument and subsequent functors are called without the first argument:

```
one_norm_ftor<1, BSize>()(s1, s2, s3, s4, s5, s6, s7, v, i);
one_norm_ftor<2, BSize>()(s2, s3, s4, s5, s6, s7, v, i);
one_norm_ftor<3, BSize>()(s3, s4, s5, s6, s7, v, i);
```

This is not realizable with templates either.

The solution is to rotate the references:

```
one_norm_ftor<1, BSize>()(s1, s2, s3, s4, s5, s6, s7, s0, v, i);
one_norm_ftor<2, BSize>()(s2, s3, s4, s5, s6, s7, s0, s1, v, i);
one_norm_ftor<3, BSize>()(s3, s4, s5, s6, s7, s0, s1, s2, v, i);
```

This rotation is achieved by the following functor implementation:

```cpp
template <unsigned Offset, unsigned Max>
struct one_norm_ftor
{
    template <typename S, typename V>
    void operator()(S& s0, S& s1, S& s2, S& s3, S& s4, S& s5, S& s6,
                    S& s7, const V& v, unsigned i)
    {
        using std::abs;
        s0+= abs(v[i+Offset]);
        one_norm_ftor<Offset+1, Max>()(s1, s2, s3, s4, s5, s6, s7,
                                       s0, v, i);
    }
};

template <unsigned Max>
struct one_norm_ftor<Max, Max>
{
    template <typename S, typename V>
    void operator()(S& s0, S& s1, S& s2, S& s3, S& s4, S& s5, S& s6,
                    S& s7, const V& v, unsigned i) {}
};
```

The corresponding one_norm function based on this functor is straightforward:

```cpp
template <unsigned BSize, typename Vector>
typename Vector::value_type
```

```
inline one_norm(const Vector& v)
{
  using std::abs;
  typename Vector::value_type s0(0), s1(0), s2(0), s3(0), s4(0),
      s5(0), s6(0), s7(0);
  unsigned s= size(v), sb= s / BSize * BSize;
  for (unsigned i= 0; i < sb; i+= BSize)
      one_norm_ftor<0, BSize>()(s0, s1, s2, s3, s4, s5, s6, s7, v, i);
  s0+= s1 + s2 + s3 + s4 + s5 + s6 + s7;

  for (unsigned i= sb; i < s; ++i)
      s0+= abs(v[i]);

  return s0;
}
```

A slight disadvantage is the overhead for very small vectors: all registers must be accumulated after the block iterations even when there are none. A great advantage, on the other hand, is that the rotation allows for block sizes larger than the number of temporaries. They are reused without corrupting the result. Nonetheless, the actual concurrency will not be larger.

The execution of this implementation took on the test machine:

```
Compute time one_norm<1>(v) is 0.793497 µs.
Compute time one_norm<2>(v) is 0.500242 µs.
Compute time one_norm<4>(v) is 0.443954 µs.
Compute time one_norm<6>(v) is 0.441819 µs.
Compute time one_norm<8>(v) is 0.430749 µs.
```

This performance is comparable to the nested-class implementation for compilers that handle the latter properly (i.e., data members in registers); otherwise the rotation code is clearly faster.

5.4.7   Tuning Nested Loops

⇒ c++11/matrix_unroll_example.cpp

The most used (and abused) example in performance discussions is dense-matrix multiplication. We do not claim to compete with hand-tuned assembler codes, but we show the power of meta-programming to generate code variations from a single implementation. As a starting point, we use a template implementation of the matrix class from Section A.4.3. In the following, we use this simple test case:

```
const unsigned s= 128;          // s= 4 in testing, 128 in timing
matrix<float> A(s, s), B(s, s), C(s, s);

for (unsigned i= 0; i < s; ++i)
    for (unsigned j= 0; j < s; j++) {
        A(i, j)= 100.0 * i + j;
        B(i, j)= 200.0 * i + j;
    }
mult(A, B, C);
```

A matrix multiplication is easily implemented with three nested loops. One of the six possible ways of nesting is a dot-product-like calculation for each entry from C:

$$c_{ik} = A_i \cdot B^k$$

where A_i is the i-th row of A and B^k the k-th column of B. We use a temporary in the innermost loop to decrease the cache-invalidation overhead of writing to C's elements in each operation:

```cpp
template <typename Matrix>
inline void mult(const Matrix& A, const Matrix& B, Matrix& C)
{
    assert(A.num_rows() == B.num_rows()); // ...

    typedef typename Matrix::value_type   value_type;
    unsigned s= A.num_rows();

    for (unsigned i= 0; i < s; ++i)
        for (unsigned k= 0; k < s; k++) {
            value_type tmp(0);
            for (unsigned j= 0; j < s; j++)
                tmp+= A(i, j) * B(j, k);
            C(i, k)= tmp;
        }
}
```

For this implementation, we provide a backward-compatible benchmark in Appendix A.9.6. The run time and performance of our canonical implementation (with 128×128 matrices) are:

```
Compute time mult(A, B, C) is 1980 µs. These are 2109 MFlops.
```

This implementation is our reference regarding performance and results. For the development of the unrolled implementation, we go back to 4×4 matrices. In contrast to Section 5.4.6, we do not unroll a single reduction but perform multiple reductions in parallel. Regarding the three loops, this means that we unroll the two outer loops and perform block operations in the inner loop; i.e., multiple i and j values are handled in each iteration. This block is realized by a size-parameterizable functor.

   As in the canonical implementation, the reduction is not performed directly on elements of C but in temporaries. For this purpose, we use the class multi_tmp from §5.4.6.3. For the sake of simplicity, we limit ourselves to matrix sizes that are multiples of the unroll parameters (a full implementation for arbitrary matrix sizes is realized in MTL4). The unrolled matrix multiplication is shown in the following function:

```cpp
template <unsigned Size0, unsigned Size1, typename Matrix>
inline void mult(const Matrix& A, const Matrix& B, Matrix& C)
{
    using value_type= typename Matrix::value_type;
    unsigned s= A.num_rows();
    mult_block<0, Size0-1, 0, Size1-1> block;
```

```
        for (unsigned i= 0; i < s; i+= Size0)
            for (unsigned k= 0; k < s; k+= Size1) {
                multi_tmp<Size0 * Size1, value_type> tmp(value_type(0));
                for (unsigned j= 0; j < s; j++)
                    block(tmp, A, B, i, j, k);
                block.update(tmp, C, i, k);
            }
    }
```

We still have to implement the functor mult_block. The techniques are essentially the same as in the vector operations, but we have to deal with more indices and their respective limits:

```
    template <unsigned Index0, unsigned Max0, unsigned Index1,
              unsigned Max1>
    struct mult_block
    {
        typedef mult_block<Index0, Max0, Index1+1, Max1>  next;

        template <typename Tmp, typename Matrix>
        void operator()(Tmp & tmp, const Matrix& A, const Matrix& B,
                        unsigned i, unsigned j, unsigned k)
        {
            tmp.value+= A(i + Index0, j) * B(j, k + Index1);
            next()(tmp.sub, A, B, i, j, k);
        }

        template <typename Tmp, typename Matrix>
        void update(const Tmp & tmp, Matrix& C, unsigned i, unsigned k)
        {
            C(i + Index0, k + Index1)= tmp.value;
            next().update(tmp.sub, C, i, k);
        }
    };

    template <unsigned Index0, unsigned Max0, unsigned Max1>
    struct mult_block<Index0, Max0, Max1, Max1>
    {
        typedef mult_block<Index0+1, Max0, 0, Max1>  next;

        template <typename Tmp, typename Matrix>
        void operator()(Tmp & tmp, const Matrix& A, const Matrix& B,
                        unsigned i, unsigned j, unsigned k)
        {
            tmp.value+= A(i + Index0, j) * B(j, k + Max1);
            next()(tmp.sub, A, B, i, j, k);
        }

        template <typename Tmp, typename Matrix>
        void update(const Tmp & tmp, Matrix& C, unsigned i, unsigned k)
        {
```

```
        C(i + Index0, k + Max1)= tmp.value;
        next().update(tmp.sub, C, i, k);
    }
};

template <unsigned Max0, unsigned Max1>
struct mult_block<Max0, Max0, Max1, Max1>
{
    template <typename Tmp, typename Matrix>
    void operator()(Tmp & tmp, const Matrix& A, const Matrix& B,
                    unsigned i, unsigned j, unsigned k)
    {
        tmp.value+= A(i + Max0, j) * B(j, k + Max1);
    }

    template <typename Tmp, typename Matrix>
    void update(const Tmp & tmp, Matrix& C, unsigned i, unsigned k)
    {
        C(i + Max0, k + Max1)= tmp.value;
    }
};
```

With appropriate logging, we can show that the same operations are performed for each entry of C as in the canonical implementation. We can also see that calculations regarding the entries are interleaved. In the following logging, we multiply 4×4 matrices and unroll 2×2 blocks. From the four temporaries, we observe two:

```
tmp.4+= A[1][0] * B[0][0]
tmp.3+= A[1][0] * B[0][1]
tmp.4+= A[1][1] * B[1][0]
tmp.3+= A[1][1] * B[1][1]
tmp.4+= A[1][2] * B[2][0]
tmp.3+= A[1][2] * B[2][1]
tmp.4+= A[1][3] * B[3][0]
tmp.3+= A[1][3] * B[3][1]
C[1][0]= tmp.4
C[1][1]= tmp.3
tmp.4+= A[3][0] * B[0][0]
tmp.3+= A[3][0] * B[0][1]
tmp.4+= A[3][1] * B[1][0]
tmp.3+= A[3][1] * B[1][1]
tmp.4+= A[3][2] * B[2][0]
tmp.3+= A[3][2] * B[2][1]
tmp.4+= A[3][3] * B[3][0]
tmp.3+= A[3][3] * B[3][1]
C[3][0]= tmp.4
C[3][1]= tmp.3
```

In temporary number 4, we accumulate $A_1 \cdot B^0$ and store the result to $c_{1,0}$. This is interleaved with the accumulation of $A_1 \cdot B^1$ in temporary 3, allowed for using multiple pipelines of super-scalar processors. We can also see that

$$c_{ik} = \sum_{j=0}^{3} a_{ij} b_{jk} \quad \forall i, k.$$

The implementation above can be simplified. The first functor specialization only differs from the general functor in the way the indices are incremented. We can factor this out with an additional loop2 class:

```
template <unsigned Index0, unsigned Max0, unsigned Index1,
          unsigned Max1>
struct loop2
{
    static const unsigned next_index0= Index0,
        next_index1= Index1 + 1;
};

template <unsigned Index0, unsigned Max0, unsigned Max1>
struct loop2<Index0, Max0, Max1, Max1>
{
    static const unsigned next_index0= Index0 + 1, next_index1= 0;
};
```

Such a general class has a high potential for reuse. With this class, we can fuse the functor template and the first specialization:

```
template <unsigned Index0, unsigned Max0, unsigned Index1,
          unsigned Max1>
struct mult_block
{
    typedef loop2<Index0, Max0, Index1, Max1> l;
    typedef mult_block<l::next_index0, Max0,
                       l::next_index1, Max1>  next;

    template <typename Tmp, typename Matrix>
    void operator()(Tmp& tmp, const Matrix& A, const Matrix& B,
                    unsigned i, unsigned j, unsigned k)
    {
        tmp.value+= A(i + Index0, j) * B(j, k + Index1);
        next()(tmp.sub, A, B, i, j, k);
    }

    template <typename Tmp, typename Matrix>
    void update(const Tmp& tmp, Matrix& C, unsigned i, unsigned k)
    {
        C(i + Index0, k + Index1)= tmp.value;
        next().update(tmp.sub, C, i, k);
    }
};
```

The other specialization remains unaltered.

Last but not least, we want to see the impact of our not-so-simple matrix product implementation. The benchmark yielded on our test machine:

```
Time mult<1, 1> is 1968 μs. These are 2122 MFlops.
Time mult<1, 2> is 1356 μs. These are 3079 MFlops.
Time mult<1, 4> is 1038 μs. These are 4022 MFlops.
Time mult<1, 8> is 871 μs. These are 4794 MFlops.
Time mult<1, 16> is 2039 μs. These are 2048 MFlops.
Time mult<2, 1> is 1394 μs. These are 2996 MFlops.
Time mult<4, 1> is 1142 μs. These are 3658 MFlops.
Time mult<8, 1> is 1127 μs. These are 3705 MFlops.
Time mult<16, 1> is 2307 μs. These are 1810 MFlops.
Time mult<2, 2> is 1428 μs. These are 2923 MFlops.
Time mult<2, 4> is 1012 μs. These are 4126 MFlops.
Time mult<2, 8> is 2081 μs. These are 2007 MFlops.
Time mult<4, 4> is 1988 μs. These are 2100 MFlops.
```

We can see that mult<1, 1> has the same performance as the original implementation, which in fact is performing the operations in exactly the same order (so far the compiler optimization does not change the order internally). We also see that most unrolled versions are faster, up to a factor of 2.3.

With double matrices, the performance is slightly lower in general:

```
Time mult is 1996 μs. These are 2092 MFlops.
Time mult<1, 1> is 1989 μs. These are 2099 MFlops.
Time mult<1, 2> is 1463 μs. These are 2855 MFlops.
Time mult<1, 4> is 1251 μs. These are 3337 MFlops.
Time mult<1, 8> is 1068 μs. These are 3908 MFlops.
Time mult<1, 16> is 2078 μs. These are 2009 MFlops.
Time mult<2, 1> is 1450 μs. These are 2880 MFlops.
Time mult<4, 1> is 1188 μs. These are 3514 MFlops.
Time mult<8, 1> is 1143 μs. These are 3652 MFlops.
Time mult<16, 1> is 2332 μs. These are 1791 MFlops.
Time mult<2, 2> is 1218 μs. These are 3430 MFlops.
Time mult<2, 4> is 1040 μs. These are 4014 MFlops.
Time mult<2, 8> is 2101 μs. These are 1987 MFlops.
Time mult<4, 4> is 2001 μs. These are 2086 MFlops.
```

This shows that other parameterizations yield more acceleration and that the performance could be doubled.

Which configuration is the best and why is—as mentioned before—not the topic of this book; we only show programming techniques. The reader is invited to try this program on his/her own computer. The techniques in this section are intended for best L1 cache usage. When matrices are larger, we should use more levels of blocking. A general-purpose methodology for locality on L2, L3, main memory, local disk, ... is recursion. This avoids reimplementation for each cache size and performs even reasonably well in virtual memory; see, for instance, [20].

5.4.8   Tuning Résumé

Software tuning including benchmarking [25] is an art of its own with advanced compiler optimization. The tiniest modification in the source can change the run-time behavior of an examined computation. In our example, it should not have mattered whether the size was known at compile time or not. But it did. Especially when the code is compiled without -DNDEBUG, the compiler might omit the index check in some situations and perform it in others. It is also important to print out computed values because the compiler might omit an entire computation when it is obvious that the result is not needed.

In addition, we must verify that repeated execution—for better clock resolution and amortized measuring overhead—is really repeated. When the result is independent on the number of repetitions, clever compilers might perform the code only once (we observed this in the unrolled reduction with clang 3.4 and block size 8). Such optimizations happen in particular when the results are intrinsic types while computations on user-defined types are usually not subject to such omissions (but we cannot count on it). Especially, the CUDA compiler performs an intensive static code analysis and rigorously drops all calculations without impact—leaving the benchmarking programmer utterly bewildered (and often prematurely excited about allegedly extremely fast calculations that were actually never performed or not as often as intended).

The goal of this section was not to implement the ultimate matrix or scalar product. In the presence of the new GPU and many-core processors with hundreds and thousands of cores and millions of threads, our exploration of super-scalar pipelining seems like a drop in the ocean. But it is not. The tuned implementations can be combined with multi-threading techniques like that of Section 4.6 or with OpenMP. The template-parameterized blocking is also an excellent preparation for SSE acceleration.

More important than the exact performance values is for us to illustrate the expressive and generative power of C++. We can generate any execution that we like from any syntactic representation that pleases us. The best-known code generation project in high-performance computing is ATLAS [51]. For a given dense linear-algebra function, it generates different implementations from C and assembler snippets and compares their performance on a target platform. After a training phase, an efficient implementation of the BLAS library [5] is available for the targeted platform.

In C++, we can use any compiler to generate every possible implementation without the need of external code generators. Programs can be tuned by simply changing template arguments. Tuning parameters can be easily set in configuration files platform-dependently, leading to significantly different executables on various platforms without the need of massive reimplementation.

Performance tuning is, however, shooting at moving targets: what yields a great benefit today might be irrelevant or even detrimental tomorrow. Therefore, it is important that performance improvements are not hard-wired deep inside an application but that we are able to configure our tuning parameters conveniently.

The examples in this section demonstrated that meta-tuning is quite elaborate, and to our disappointment, the benefit of the transformations is not as pronounced as it used to be when we first investigated them in 2006. We have also seen in several examples that compilers are very powerful to apply general-purpose optimizations and often yield better results with less effort. Effort-wise, it is also advisable not to compete with highly tuned libraries in popular domains like dense linear algebra. Such libraries as MKL or Goto-BLAS are extremely efficient, and our chances of outperforming them after enormous work are tiny. All this said, we shall focus our efforts on the most important targets: domain-specific optimizations of fundamental kernels with strong impact on our applications' overall run time.

5.5 Exercises

5.5.1 Type Traits

Write type traits for removing and adding references. Add a domain-specific type trait for the meta-predicate is_vector and assume that the only known vectors are so far my_vector<Value> and vector_sum<E1, E2>.

5.5.2 Fibonacci Sequence

Write a meta-template that generates the Fibonacci sequence at compile-time. The Fibonacci sequence is defined by the following recursion:

$$x_0 = 0$$
$$x_1 = 1$$
$$x_n = x_{n-1} + x_{n-2} \quad \text{for} \quad n \geqslant 2 .$$

5.5.3 Meta-Program for Greatest Common Divisor

Write a meta-program for the GCD (greatest common divisor) of two integers. The algorithm is as follows: Write a generic function for an integer type I that computes the GCD.

```
1   function gcd(a, b):
2       if b = 0 return a
3       else return gcd(b, a mod b)
```

```cpp
template <typename I>
I gcd( I a, I b ) { ... }
```

Then write an integral meta-function that executes the same algorithm but at compile time. Your meta-function should be of the following form:

```cpp
template <int A, int B>
struct gcd_meta {
    static int const value = ... ;
} ;
```

i.e., gcd_meta<a,b>::value is the GCD of a and b. Verify whether the results correspond to your C++ function gcd().

5.5.4 Vector Expression Template

Implement a vector class (you can use `std::vector<double>` internally) that contains at least
the following members:

```cpp
class my_vector {
  public:
    typedef double value_type ;

    my_vector( int n );

    // Copy Constructor from type itself
    my_vector( my_vector& );

    // Constructor from generic vector
    template <typename Vector>
    my_vector( Vector& );

    // Assignment operator
    my_vector& operator=( my_vector const& v );

    // Assignment for generic Vector
    template <typename Vector>
    my_vector& operator=( Vector const& v );

    value_type& operator() ( int i );

    int size() const;
    value_type operator() ( int i ) const;
};
```

Make an expression for a scalar multiplied with a vector:

```cpp
template <typename Scalar, typename Vector>
class scalar_times_vector_expression
{};

template <typename Scalar, typename Vector>
scalar_times_vector_expressions<Scalar, Vector>
operator*( Scalar const& s, Vector const& v )
{
    return scalar_times_vector_expressions<Scalar, Vector>( s, v );
}
```

Put all classes and functions in the namespace `math`. You can also create an expression
template for the addition of two vectors.

  Write a small program, e.g.:

```cpp
int main() {
  math::my_vector v( 5 );
  ... Fill in some values of v ...
```

```
  math::my_vector w( 5 );
  w = 5.0 * v;

  w = 5.0 * (7.0 * v );
  w = v + 7.0*v; // (If you have added the operator+)
}
```

Use the debugger to see what happens.

5.5.5 Meta-List

Create a list of types. Implement the meta-functions insert, append, erase, and size.

Chapter 6

Object-Oriented Programming

C++ is a multi-paradigm language, and the paradigm that is most strongly associated with C++ is *Object-Oriented Programming* (OOP). As a result, we find all these beautiful dog-cat-mouse examples in books and tutorials. Experience shows, however, that most real software packages do not contain such deep class hierarchies as the literature makes us believe.

It is furthermore our experience that generic programming is the superior paradigm in scientific and engineering programming because

- It is more flexible: polymorphism is not limited to sub-classes; and

- It provides better performance: no overhead in function calls.

We will explain this in more detail within this chapter.

On the other hand, inheritance can help us to increase productivity when multiple classes share data and functionality. Accessing inherited data is free of overhead, and even calling inherited methods has no extra cost when they are not `virtual`.

The great benefit of object-oriented programming is the run-time polymorphism: which implementation of a method is called can be decided at run time. We can even select class types during execution. The before-mentioned overhead of `virtual` functions is only an issue when very fine-grained methods (like element access) are `virtual`. Conversely, when we implement only coarse-grained methods (like linear solvers) as `virtual`, the extra execution cost is negligible.

OOP in combination with generic programming is a very powerful way to provide as a form of reusability that neither of the paradigms can provide on its own (§6.2–§6.6).

6.1 Basic Principles

The basic principles of OOP related to C++ are:

- *Abstraction*: Classes (Chapter 2) define the attributes and methods of an object. The class can also specify invariants of attributes; e.g., numerator and denominator shall be co-prime in a class for rational numbers. All methods must preserve these invariants.

- *Encapsulation* denotes the hiding of implementation details. Internal attributes cannot be accessed directly for not violating the invariants but only via the class's methods. In return, `public` data members are not internal attributes but part of the class interface.

- *Inheritance* means that derived classes contain all data and function members of their base class(es).

- *Polymorphism* is the ability of an identifier to be interpreted depending on context or parameters. We have seen polymorphism in terms of function overloading and template instantiation. In this chapter, we will see another form that is related to inheritance.

  - *Late Binding* is the selection of the actually called function at run time.

We have already discussed abstraction, encapsulation, and some kinds of polymorphism. In this chapter, we will introduce inheritance and the related polymorphism.

To demonstrate the classical usage of OOP, we will use a simple example that has only a tangential relation to science and engineering but allows us to study the C++ features in a comprehensible fashion. Later, we will provide examples from science and introduce more sophisticated class hierarchies.

6.1.1   Base and Derived Classes

⇒ c++03/oop_simple.cpp

A use case for all kinds of OOP principles is a database of different types of people. We start with a class that will be the basis of all other classes in this section:

```
class person
{
  public:
    person() {}
    explicit person(const string& name) : name(name) {}

    void set_name(const string& n) { name= n; }
    string get_name() const { return name; }
    void all_info() const
    { cout << "[person]   My name is " << name << endl; }

  private:
    string name;
};
```

For the sake of simplicity, we only use one member variable for the name and refrain from splitting it into first, middle, and last names.

Typical OOP classes often contain getter and setter methods for member variables (which some IDEs insert automatically in the class whenever a new variable is added). Nonetheless, introducing a getter and a setter unconditionally for each member is considered bad practice nowadays because it contradicts the idea of encapsulation. Many even consider this an *Anti-Pattern* since we are directly reading and writing the internal states to perform tasks with the object. Instead the object should provide methods that perform their respective tasks without uncovering internal states.

The method all_info is intended to be *Polymorphic* in the sense that it depends on the person's actual class type which information we get about a person.

Our first type of person is student:

```
class student
  : public person
{
  public:
    student(const string& name, const string& passed)
      : person(name), passed(passed) {}
    void all_info() const {
    cout << "[student]  My name is " << get_name() << endl;
    cout << "I passed the following grades: " << passed << endl;
    }
  private:
    string passed;
};
```

The class student is *Derived* from person. As a consequence, it contains all members of person: both methods and data members; that is, it *Inherits* them from its base (person). Figure 6–1 shows the public and private members (denoted by +/- respectively) of person and student. A student can access them all and a (mere) person only its own. Accordingly, if we added a member to person like a method get_birthday(), it would be added to student as well.

In other words, a student *Is-A* person. Therefore, student can be used wherever person can: as an argument, in assignments, etc. Just as in real life, if we allow that a person can open a bank account, so can a student (we're sorry for all the hard-up students with different experiences). We will later see how this is expressed in C++.

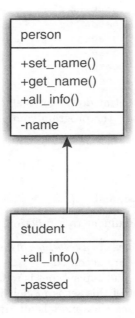

Figure 6–1: Derived class

Regarding the visibility of names, the derived class is similar to an inner scope: in addition to the class's members, we see those of its base class (and their base classes as well). When a derived class contains a variable or function with the same name, those of the base class are hidden, similarly again to a scope. In contrast, we can still access members of the derived class by name qualification like `person::all_info`. Even a function (overload) with an equal name and a different signature is hidden in the derived class—C++ hides names not signatures. They can be made visible in the derived class with a **using** declaration like `using base::fun`. Then those function overloads with a signature different from all overloads in the derived class are accessible without qualification.

When we use our two classes in the following way:

```cpp
person mark("Mark Markson");
mark.all_info();

student tom("Tom Tomson", "Algebra, Analysis");
tom.all_info();

person  p(tom);
person& pr= tom;        // or pr(tom)  or pr{tom}
person* pp= &tom;       // or pp(&tom) or pp{tom}

p.all_info();
pr.all_info();
pp->all_info();
```

we might be surprised if not disappointed by the result:

```
[person]   My name is Mark Markson
[student]  My name is Tom Tomson
    I passed the following grades: Algebra, Analysis
[person]   My name is Tom Tomson
[person]   My name is Tom Tomson
[person]   My name is Tom Tomson
```

Only when the variable has type `student` do we get the grading information. When we try to handle a `student` as a regular `person`, the program compiles and runs but we do not see the additional `student` information.

Nonetheless, we are allowed to

- Copy a `student` to a `person`;

- Refer to a `student` as a `person`; and

- Pass a `student` as a `person` argument to a function.

More formally phrased: a derived class is a *Sub-type* of its base class, and wherever the base class is required its derived classes are accepted.

A good way to understand sub- and super-types is to think of sub- and super-sets. A class models a certain set, and a sub-set of this set is modeled by a sub-class that constrains the super-class by invariants. Our `person` class models all kind of people, and we model groups of people with classes that are sub-classes of `person`.

The paradox of this picture is that the derived classes may contain additional member variables, and the number of possible objects is larger than that of its super-class. This paradox can be resolved by considering appropriate invariants to model the sub-set properly. For instance, the invariant of the student class would be that no two objects with the same name and different grades exist. This would guarantee that the cardinality of the student set is not larger than that of the person set. Unfortunately, the before-mentioned invariant is hard to verify (even for those languages with automatic invariant check) and must be implicitly established by well-designed program logic.

When we derive from a base class, we can specify how restrictive the access to the members inherited from that class is. In the preceding example we derived publicly so that all inherited members have the same accessibility in the base and derived classes. If we derive a class as protected, public base class members are protected in the derived class while the others preserve their accessibility. Members of privately derived classes are all private (this form of inheritance is only used in advanced OOP applications). When we do not specify how the base class is accessed, the derivation is by default private when we define a class and public for a struct.

6.1.2 Inheriting Constructors

⇒ c++11/inherit_constructor.cpp

C++11

One method that is not inherited implicitly from the base class is the constructor. Therefore, the following program does not compile:

```
class person
{
  public:
    explicit person(const string& name) : name(name) {}
    // ...
};

class student
  : public person
{};                      // No constructor for string defined

int main ()
{
    student tom("Tom Tomson"); // Error: no string constructor
}
```

The class student inherits all methods from person except the string constructor. C++11 allows us to inherit all constructors from a base class with a using declaration:

```
class student
  : public person
{
    using person::person;
};
```

When constructors with the same signature exist in both classes, that from the derived class is preferred.

So far, we have applied three of the four before-mentioned basic principles: encapsulation, inheritance, and sub-typing. But there is still something missing and we will introduce it now.

6.1.3   Virtual Functions and Polymorphic Classes

⇒ c++03/oop_virtual.cpp

The full potential of object-oriented programming is only unleashed with virtual functions. Their presence changes the behavior of a class fundamentally, leading to the following:

> **Definition 6–1 (Polymorphic Types).** Classes containing one or more **virtual** functions are called *Polymorphic Types*.

We continue with the preceding implementation and only add the attribute virtual to the method all_info():

```
class person
{
    virtual void all_info() const { cout << "My name is " << name << endl; }
    ...
};

class student
  : public person
{
    virtual void all_info() const {
        person::all_info();                     // call all_info() from person
        cout << "I passed the following grades: " << passed << endl;
    }
    ...
};
```

The double colons :: that we have seen as namespace qualifications (§3.2) can similarly qualify a class from which we call a method. This requires of course that the method is accessible: we cannot call a private method from another class, not even a base class.

Printing the information with the polymorphic class yields a completely different result all of a sudden:

```
[person]   My name is Mark Markson
[student]  My name is Tom Tomson
    I passed the following grades: Algebra, Analysis
[person]   My name is Tom Tomson
[student]  My name is Tom Tomson
    I passed the following grades: Algebra, Analysis
[student]  My name is Tom Tomson
    I passed the following grades: Algebra, Analysis
```

Printing the information on the objects behaves as before. The big difference is getting information on references and pointers to objects: `pr.all_info()` and `pp->all_info()`. In this case, the compiler goes through the following steps:

1. What is the static type of `pr` or `pp`? That is, how is `pr` or `pp` declared?

2. Is there a function named `all_info` in that class?

3. Can it be accessed? Or is it `private`?

4. Is it a `virtual` function? Otherwise just call it.

5. What is the dynamic type of `pr` or `pp`? That is, what is the type of the object referred to by `pr` or `pp`?

6. Call `all_info` from that dynamic type.

To realize these dynamic function calls, the compiler maintains *Virtual Function Tables* (a.k.a. *Virtual Method Tables*) or *Vtables*. They contain function pointers through which each `virtual` method of the actual object is called. The reference `pr` has the type `person&` and refers to an object of type `student`. Through the vtable of `pr`, the call of `all_info()` is directed to `student::all_info`. This indirection over function pointers adds some extra cost to `virtual` functions which is significant for tiny functions and negligible for sufficiently large functions.

Definition 6–2 (Late Binding and Dynamic Polymorphism). Selecting the executed method during run time is called *Late Binding* or *Dynamic Binding*. It also represents *Dynamic Polymorphism*—as opposed to static polymorphism with templates.

Analogously to the reference `pr`, the pointer `pp` points to a `student` object, and `student::all_info` is called by late binding for `pp->all_info()`. We can also introduce a free function `spy_on()`:

```
void spy_on(const person& p)
{
    p.all_info();
}
```

that provides Tom's complete information thanks to late binding even when we pass a reference to the base class.

The benefit of dynamic selection is that the code exists only once in the executable no matter for how many sub-classes of `person` it is called. Another advantage over function templates is that only the declaration (i.e., the signature) must be visible when the function is called but not necessarily the definition (i.e., the implementation). This not only saves significant compile time but also allows us to hide our clever (or dirty) implementation from users.

The only entity originating from Tom that calls `person::all_info()` is `p`. `p` is an object of type `person` to which we can copy a `student` object. But when we copy a derived to a base class, we lose all extra data of the derived class and only the data members of the base class are really copied. Likewise, the `virtual` function calls perform those of the base class (here `person::all_info()`). That is, a base class object does not behave differently when it is constructed by copy from a derived class: all the extra members are gone and the vtable does not refer to any method from the derived class.

In the same way, passing arguments by value to function:

```
void glueless(person p)
{
    p.all_info();
}
```

disables late binding and thus impedes calling virtual functions from derived classes. This is a very frequent (not only) beginners' error in OOP called *Slicing*. Thus, we must obey the following rule:

Passing Polymorphic Types
Polymorphic types must always be passed by reference or (smart) pointer!

C++11 ### 6.1.3.1 Explicit Overriding

Another popular trap that even advanced programmers fall into from time to time is a slightly different signature in the overridden method, like this:

```
class person
{
    virtual void all_info() const { ... }
};

class student
  : public person
{
    virtual void all_info() { ... }
};

int main ()
{
    student tom("Tom Tomson", "Algebra, Analysis");
    person& pr= tom;
    pr.all_info();
}
```

In this example, person::all_info() is not lately bound to person::all_info() because the signatures are different. This difference is admittedly not obvious, starting with the question of what the method's const qualification has to do with the signature at all. We can think of a member function as having an implicit hidden argument referring to the object itself:

```
void person::all_info_impl(const person& me= *this) { ... }
```

Now it becomes clear that the const qualifier of the method qualifies this hidden reference in person::all_info(). The corresponding hidden reference in student::all_info() is not const-qualified and the method is not considered as an override due to the distinct signature. The compiler will not warn us, just taking student::all_info() as new overload. And you can believe us that this little nasty mistake can keep you busy for a while, when classes are large and stored in different files.

We can easily protect ourselves against such trouble with the attribute override added to C++11:

```
class student
  : public person
{
    virtual void all_info() override { ... }
};
```

Here the programmer declares that this function overrides a **virtual** function of the base class (with the exact same signature). If there is no such function, the compiler will complain:[1]

```
...: error: 'all_info' marked 'override' but doesn't override
           any member functions
    virtual void all_info() override {
                 ^
...: warning: 'student::all_info' hides overloaded virtual fct.
...: note: hidden overloaded virtual function 'person::all_info'
           declared here: different qualifiers (const vs none)
    virtual void all_info() const { ... }
                 ^
```

Here, we also get the hint from clang that the qualifiers are different. Using override for non-virtual functions is an error:

```
...: error: only virtual member fct. can be marked 'override'
    void all_info() override {
         ^~~~~~~~~
```

override does not add exciting new functionality to our software, but it can save us from tediously searching for slips of the pen (keyboard). It is advisable to use override everywhere, unless backward compatibility is needed. The word is quickly typed (especially with auto-completion) and renders our programs more reliable. It also communicates our intentions to other programmers or even to ourselves after not having looked at the code for some years.

Another new attribute in C++11 is final. It declares that a **virtual** member function cannot be overridden. This allows the compiler to replace certain indirect vtable calls with direct function calls. Unfortunately, we have no experience so far with how much final actually accelerates a virtual function. However, we can also use final to protect against surprising behavior of function overriding. Even entire classes can be declared final to prevent somebody from deriving from them.

Compared to each other, override is a statement regarding the super-classes while final refers to sub-classes. Both are contextual keywords; i.e., they are only reserved in a certain

---

1. Messages have been reformatted to fit on the page.

context: as qualifiers of member functions. Everywhere else the words could be freely used, for instance, as variable names. However, it is advisable to refrain from doing this for the sake of clarity.

6.1.3.2 Abstract Classes

So far we have looked only at examples where a virtual function was defined in a base class and then expanded in derived classes. Sometimes we find ourselves in a situation where we have an ensemble of classes with a common function and need a common super-class to select the classes dynamically. For instance, in Section 6.4, we will introduce solvers that provide the same interface: a solve function. To select them at run time, they need to share a super-class with a solve function. However, there is no universal solve algorithm that we can override later. For that purpose, we need a new feature to state: "I have a **virtual** function in this class without implementation; this will come later in sub-classes."

> **Definition 6–3 (Pure Virtual Function and Abstract Class).** A virtual function is a *Pure Virtual Function* when it is declared with $= 0$. A class containing a pure virtual function is called an *Abstract Class*.

$\Rightarrow$ c++11/oop_abstract.cpp

To be more specific, we expand our person example with an abstract super-class creature:

```
class creature
{
    virtual void all_info() const= 0; // pure virtual
};

class person
  : public creature
{ ... };

int main ()
{
    creature some_beast;    // Error: abstract class

    person mark("Mark Markson");
    mark.all_info();
}
```

The creation of a creature object fails with a message like this:

```
...: error: variable type 'creature' is an abstract class
    creature some_biest;
             ^
...: note: unimplemented pure method 'all_info' in 'creature'
    virtual void all_info() const= 0;
                 ^
```

The object mark behaves as before when we override all_info so that person contains no pure **virtual** functions.

Abstract classes can be considered as interfaces: we can declare references and pointers thereof but no objects. Note that C++ allows us to mix pure and regular **virtual** functions. Objects of sub-classes can only be built[2] when all pure **virtual** functions are overridden.

Side note to Java programmers: In Java, all member functions are by nature virtual (i.e., methods cannot be non-virtual[3]). Java provides the language feature interface where methods are only declared but not defined (unless they have the attribute default which allows for an implementation). This corresponds to a C++ class where all methods are pure **virtual**.

Large projects often establish multiple levels of abstraction:

- Interface: no implementations;

- Abstract class: default implementations;

- Specific classes.

This helps to keep a clear mental picture for an elaborate class system.

6.1.4 Functors via Inheritance

In Section 3.8, we discussed functors and mentioned that they can be implemented in terms of inheritance as well. Now, we keep our promise. First we need a common base class for all functors to be realized:

```
struct functor_base
{
    virtual double operator() (double x) const= 0;
};
```

This base class can be abstract since it only serves us as an interface, for instance, to pass a functor to finite_difference evaluation:

```
double finite_difference(functor_base const& f,
                         double x, double h)
{
    return (f(x+h) - f(x)) / h;
}
```

Evidently, all functors to be differentiated must be derived from functor_base, for instance:

```
class para_sin_plus_cos
  : public functor_base
{
  public:
```

---

2. We refrain here from the term *Instantiation* to avoid confusion. The term is used in Java for saying that an object is built from a class (whereas some authors even call objects specific classes). In C++, instantiation almost always names the process of creating a specific class/function from a class/function template. We have occasionally seen the term "class instantiation" for the creation of an object from a class but this is not common terminology and we refrain from it.

3. However, declaring them final enables the compiler to remove the overhead of late binding.

```
        para_sin_plus_cos(double p) : alpha(p) {}

        virtual double operator() (double x) const override
        {
            return sin(alpha * x) + cos(x);
        }

    private:
        double alpha;
};
```

We reimplemented `para_sin_plus_cos` so that we can approximate the derivative of $\sin(\alpha x) + \cos x$ with finite differences:

```
para_sin_plus_cos sin_1(1.0);
cout ≪ finite_difference( sin_1, 1., 0.001 ) ≪ endl;
double df1= finite_difference(para_sin_plus_cos(2.), 1., 0.001),
       df0= finite_difference(para_sin_plus_cos(2.), 0., 0.001);
```

The object-oriented approach allows us as well to realize functions with states. If we like, we could also implement the finite differences as OOP functors and combine them similarly as the generic functors.

The disadvantages of the OOP approach are:

- Performance: `operator()` is always called as a **virtual** function.

- Applicability: Only classes that are derived from `functor_base` are allowed as arguments. A template parameter allows for traditional functions and any kind of functors including those from Section 3.8.

Thus, functors should be implemented whenever possible with the generic approach from Section 3.8. Only when functions are selected at run time does the use of inheritance provide a benefit.

6.2   Removing Redundancy

By using inheritance and implicit up-casting, we can avoid the implementation of redundant member and free functions. The fact that classes are implicitly casted to super-classes allows us to implement common functionality once and reuse it in all derived classes. Say we have several matrix classes (dense, compressed, banded, triangle, ...) that share member functions like `num_rows` and `num_cols`.[4] Those can be easily outsourced into a common super-class—including the corresponding data members:

```
class base_matrix
{
  public:
    base_matrix(size_t nr, size_t nc) : nr(nr), nc(nc) {}
```

---

4. The terminology used is from MTL4.

```
      size_t num_rows() const { return nr; }
      size_t num_cols() const { return nc; }
   private:
      size_t nr, nc;
};

class dense_matrix
  : public base_matrix
{ ... };

class compressed_matrix
  : public base_matrix
{ ... };

class banded_matrix
  : public base_matrix
{ ... };

...
```

All matrix types now provide the member functions from base_matrix by inheritance. Having the common implementations in one place not only saves typing but also ensures that modifications apply in all relevant classes at once. This is not an issue in this toy example (especially as there is not much to change anyway), but keeping all redundant code snippets consistent becomes pretty laborious in large projects.

Free functions can be reused in the same manner, for instance:

```
inline size_t num_rows(const base_matrix& A)
{    return A.num_rows(); }

inline size_t num_cols(const base_matrix& A)
{    return A.num_cols(); }

inline size_t size(const base_matrix& A)
{    return A.num_rows() * A.num_cols(); }
```

These free functions can be called for all matrices derived from base_matrix thanks to implicit up-casting. This form of common base class functionality does not cost run time.

We can also consider the implicit up-cast of free functions' arguments as a special case of a more general concept: the *is-a* relation; for instance, compressed_matrix *is-a* base_matrix and we can pass a compressed_matrix value to every function that expects a base_matrix.

6.3   Multiple Inheritance

C++ provides multiple inheritance which we will illustrate now with some examples.

6.3.1   Multiple Parents

⇒ c++11/oop_multi0.cpp

A class can be derived from multiple super-classes. For more figurative descriptions and for a less clumsy discussion of base classes' base classes we occasionally use the terms parents and grandparents which are intuitively understood. With two parents, the class hierarchy looks like a V (and with many like a bouquet). The members of the sub-class are the union of all super-class members. This bears the danger of ambiguities:

```cpp
class student
{
    virtual void all_info() const {
        cout << "[student]  My name is " << name << endl;
        cout << "    I passed the following grades: " << passed << endl;
    }
    ...
};

class mathematician
{
    virtual void all_info() const {
        cout << "[mathman]  My name is " << name << endl;
        cout << "    I proved: " << proved << endl;
    }
    ...
};

class math_student
  : public student, public mathematician
{
    // all_info not defined -> ambiguously inherited
};

int main ()
{
    math_student bob("Robert Robson", "Algebra", "Fermat's Last Theorem");
    bob.all_info();
}
```

math_student inherits all_info from student and from mathematician and there is no priority for one or another. The only way to disambiguate all_info for math_student is to define the method in the class math_student appropriately.

This ambiguity allows us to illustrate a subtlety of C++ that we should be aware of. public, protected, and private modify accessibility, not visibility. This becomes painfully clear when we try to disambiguate member functions by inheriting one or more super-classes as private or protected:

```cpp
class student { ... };
class mathematician { ... };
```

```
class math_student
  : public student, private mathematician
{ ... };
```

Now the methods of student are public and those of mathematician private. Calling math_student::all_info we hope to see now the output of student::all_info. Instead we get two error messages: first that math_student::all_info is ambiguous and in addition that mathematician::all_info is inaccessible.

6.3.2 Common Grandparents

It is not rare that multiple base classes share their base classes as well. In the previous section, mathematician and student had no super-classes. From the sections before, it would be more natural to derive them both from person. Depicting this inheritance configuration builds a diamond shape as in Figure 6–2. We will implement this in two slightly different ways.

6.3.2.1 Redundancy and Ambiguity

⇒ c++11/oop_multi1.cpp

First, we implement the classes in a straightforward way:

```
class person { ... }  // as before
class student { ... }  // as before

class mathematician
  : public person
```

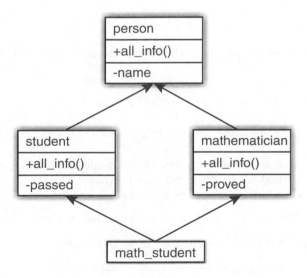

Figure 6–2: Diamond-shaped class hierarchy

```cpp
{
  public:
    mathematician(const string& name, const string& proved)
      : person(name), proved(proved) {}
    virtual void all_info() const override {
    person::all_info();
    cout << "    I proved: " << proved << endl;
    }
  private:
    string proved;
};

class math_student
  : public student, public mathematician
{
  public:
    math_student(const string& name, const string& passed,
                 const string& proved)
      : student(name, passed), mathematician(name, proved) {}
    virtual void all_info() const override {
        student::all_info();
        mathematician::all_info();
    }
};

int main ()
{
    math_student bob("Robert Robson", "Algebra", "Fermat's Last Theorem");
    bob.all_info();
}
```

The program works properly except for the redundant name information:

```
[student]  My name is Robert Robson
    I passed the following grades: Algebra
[person]   My name is Robert Robson
    I proved: Fermat's Last Theorem
```

You as reader now have two choices: accept this sub-optimal method and keep reading or jump to Exercise 6.7.1 and try to solve it on your own.

As a consequence of deriving person twice, this code is

- **Redundant:** The name is stored twice as illustrated in Figure 6–3.

- **Error-prone:** The two values of name can be inconsistent.

- **Ambiguous:** when accessing person::name in math_student.

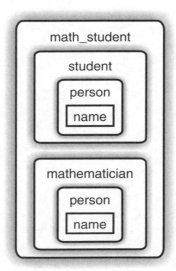

Figure 6–3: Memory layout of math_student

⇒ c++11/oop_multi2.cpp

To illustrate the before-mentioned ambiguity, we call person::all_info within math_student:

```
class math_student : ...
{
    virtual void all_info() const override {
    person::all_info();
    }
};
```

This causes the following (reformatted) complaint:

```
...: error: ambiguous conversion from derived class
          'const math_student' to base class 'person':
    class math_student -> class student -> class person
    class math_student -> class mathematician -> class person
        person::all_info();
        ^^^^^^^^^
```

with clang 3.4. We will of course encounter the same problem with every function or data member of super-classes inherited via multiple paths.

6.3.2.2 Virtual Base Classes

⇒ c++11/oop_multi3.cpp

Virtual Base Classes allow us to store members in common super-classes only once and thus help overcome related problems. However, it requires a basic understanding of the internal implementation to not introduce new problems. In the following example, we just denote person as a virtual base class:

```
class person { ... };

class student
  : public virtual person
{ ... };

class mathematician
  : public virtual person
{ ... };

class math_student
  : public student, public mathematician
{
  public:
    math_student(const string& name, const string& passed, const string&
      proved) : student(name, passed), mathematician(name, proved) {}
  ...
};
```

and get the following output that might surprise some of us:

```
[student]  My name is
      I passed the following grades: Algebra
      I proved: Fermat's Last Theorem
```

We lost the value of name despite both student and mathematician calling the person constructor which initializes name. To understand this behavior, we need to know how C++ handles virtual base classes. We know that it is a derived class's responsibility to call the base-class constructor (or else the compiler will generate a call to the default constructor). However, we have only one copy of the person base class. Figure 6–4 illustrates the new memory layout: mathematician and student do not contain the person data any longer but only refer to a common object that is part of the most derived class: math_student.

When creating a student object, its constructor must call the person constructor. And likewise when we create a mathematician object, its constructor will call the person constructor. Now we create a math_student object. The math_student constructor must call the constructors of both mathematician and student. But we know that those constructors should both call the person constructor and thus the shared person part would be constructed twice.

To prevent that, it has been defined that in the case of virtual base classes, it is the responsibility of the *Most Derived Class* (in our case: math_student) to call the shared base-class constructor (in our case: person). In return, the person constructor calls in mathematician and student are disabled when they are indirectly called from a derived class.

⇒ c++11/oop_multi4.cpp

With this in mind, we modify our constructors accordingly:

```
class student
  : public virtual person
{
  protected:
    student(const string& passed) : passed(passed) {}
```

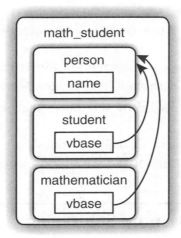

Figure 6–4: `math_student`'s memory with `virtual` base classes

```
  ...
};

class mathematician
  : public virtual person
{
  protected:
    mathematician(const string& proved) : proved(proved) {}
  ...
};

class math_student
  : public student, public mathematician
{
  public:
    math_student(const string& name, const string& passed, const string&
      proved) : person(name), student(passed), mathematician(proved) {}
    virtual void all_info() const override {
        student::all_info();
        mathematician::my_infos();
    }
};
```

Now, `math_student` initializes `person` explicitly to set the `name` there. The two intermediate classes `student` and `mathematician` are refactored to distinguish between inclusive and exclusive member treatment:

- The inclusive handling incorporates the methods from `person`: the two-argument constructor and `all_info`. These methods are `public` and (primarily) intended for `student` and `mathematician` objects.

- The exclusive handling deals only with members of the class itself: the one-argument constructor and my_infos. These methods are protected and thus available in sub-classes only.

The example shows that all three access modifiers are needed:

- private: for data members that will only be accessed within the class;
- protected: for methods needed by sub-classes that will not be used for their own objects; and
- public: for methods intended for objects of the class.

After laying the foundations of the OOP techniques, we will apply them now in a scientific context.

6.4   Dynamic Selection by Sub-typing

⇒ c++11/solver_selection_example.cpp

The dynamic solver selection can be realized with a switch like this:

```cpp
#include <iostream>
#include <cstdlib>

class matrix {};
class vector {};

void cg(const matrix& A, const vector& b, vector& x);
void bicg(const matrix& A, const vector& b, vector& x);

int main (int argc, char* argv[])
{
    matrix A;
    vector b, x;

    int solver_choice= argc >= 2 ? std::atoi(argv[1]) : 0;
    switch (solver_choice) {
        case 0: cg(A, b, x); break;
        case 1: bicg(A, b, x); break;
        ...
    }
}
```

This works but it is not scalable with respect to source code complexity. When we call the solver with other vectors and matrices somewhere else, we must copy the whole switch-case-block for each argument combination. This can be avoided by encapsulating the block into a function and calling this function with different arguments.

The situation becomes much more elaborate when multiple arguments are selected dynamically. For a linear solver, we want to choose the left and right preconditioners (diagonal, ILU, IC, etc.). Then we need nested switch as shown in Section A.8. So we can dynamically select our function objects without OOP, but we have to accept the combinatorial explosion over the parameter space: solvers, left and right preconditioners. If we add a new solver or preconditioner, we will need to expand this monstrous selection block in multiple places.

An elegant solution for our solvers and preconditioners is to use abstract classes as interfaces and derived classes with the specific solvers:

```
struct solver
{
    virtual void operator()( ... )= 0;
    virtual ~solver() {}
};

// potentially templatize
struct cg_solver : solver
{
    virtual void operator()( ... ) override { cg(A, b, x); }
};

struct bicg_solver : solver
{
    virtual void operator()( ... ) override { bicg(A, b, x); }
};
```

In our application, we can define a (smart) pointer of the interface type solver and assign it to the desired solver:

`C++11`

```
unique_ptr<solver> my_solver;
switch (solver_choice) {
  case 0: my_solver= unique_ptr<cg_solver>(new cg_solver);
          break;
  case 1: my_solver= unique_ptr<bicg_solver>(new bicg_solver);
          break;
  ...
}
```

This technique is thoroughly discussed in the design patterns book [14] as the *Factory* pattern. The factory can also be implemented with raw pointers in C++03.

The construction of the unique_ptr is somewhat cumbersome. C++14 introduces the convenience function make_unique that makes this situation really more convenient:

`C++14`

```
unique_ptr<solver> my_solver;
switch (solver_choice) {
  case 0: my_solver= make_unique<cg_solver>(); break;
  case 1: my_solver= make_unique<bicg_solver>(); break;
}
```

It is a good exercise to implement your own make_unique as suggested in Exercise 3.11.13.

Once our polymorphic pointer is initialized, it is straightforward to call our dynamically selected solver:

```
(*my_solver)(A, b, x);
```

The parentheses here mean that we dereference a function pointer and call the referenced function. Without the parentheses, we would (unsuccessfully) try to call the function pointer as a function and dereference its result.

The full power of the factory approach becomes evident when multiple functions are dynamically selected. Then we can avoid the combinatorial explosion shown before. The polymorphic function pointers allow us to decouple the respective selections and to decompose the task into a sequence of factories and a single call with the pointers:

```cpp
struct pc
{
    virtual void operator()( ... )= 0;
    virtual ~pc() {}
};

struct solver { ... };

// Solver factory
// Left Preconditioner factory
// Right Preconditioner factory

(*my_solver)(A, b, x, *left, *right);
```

Now, we have linear code complexity in the factories and a single statement for the function call opposed to the cubic code complexity in the huge selection block.

In our example, we implemented a common super-class. We can also deal with solver classes and functions without a common base class by using `std::function`. This allows us to realize more general factories. Nonetheless, it is based on the same techniques: `virtual` functions and pointers to polymorphic classes. A backward-compatible alternative in C++03 is `boost::function`.

C++ forbids **virtual** template functions (they would render the compiler implementation very complicated: potentially infinite vtables). However, class templates can contain **virtual** functions. This enables generic programming with **virtual** functions by type parameterization of the entire class instead of parameterizing single methods.

| C++11 |

6.5 Conversion

Conversion is a topic not only related to OOP, but we could not discuss it comprehensively without having introduced base and derived classes before. Vice versa, looking at castings between related classes solidifies the understanding of inheritance.

C++ is a strongly typed language. The type of each object (variable or constant) is defined at compile time and cannot be changed during execution.[5] We can think of an object as

- Bits in memory, and

- A type that gives those bits a meaning.

---

5. In contrast, Python variables have no fixed type and are actually merely names referring to some object. In an assignment, the variable just refers to another object and adopts the new object's type.

For several casts, the compiler just looks differently on the bits in memory: either with another interpretation of the bits or with other access rights (e.g., const versus non-const). Other casts actually create new objects.

In C++, there are four different cast operators:

- static_cast

- dynamic_cast

- const_cast

- reinterpret_cast

C as its linguistic root knows only one casting operator: (*type*) *expr*. This single operator is difficult to understand because it can trigger a cascade of transformations to create an object of the target type: for instance, converting a const pointer to int into a non-const pointer to char.

In contrast, the C++ casts only change one aspect of the type at a time. Another disadvantage of C-style casts is that they are hard to find in code (see also [45, Chapter 95]), whereas the C++ casts are easy to discover: just search for _cast. C++ still allows this old-style casting but all C++ experts agree on discouraging its use.

C Casts
Do not use C-style casts.

In this section, we will show the different cast operators and discuss the pros and cons of different casts in different contexts.

6.5.1 Casting between Base and Derived Classes

C++ offers a static and a dynamic cast between classes of a hierarchy.

6.5.1.1 Casting Up

⇒ c++03/up_down_cast_example.cpp

Casting up, i.e., from a derived to a base class, is always possible when there are no ambiguities. It can even be performed implicitly like we did in the function spy_on:

```
void spy_on(const person& p);

spy_on(tom);                    // Upcast student -> person
```

spy_on accepts all sub-classes of person without the need for explicit conversion. Thus, we can pass student tom as an argument. To discuss conversions between classes in a diamond-shaped hierarchy, we introduce some single-letter class names for brevity:

```
struct A
{
    virtual void f(){}
    virtual ~A(){}
    int ma;
};
struct B : A { float mb; int fb() { return 3; } };
struct C : A {};
struct D : B, C {};
```

We add the following unary functions:

```
void f(A a)  { /* ... */ } // Not polymorphic -> slicing!
void g(A& a) { /* ... */ }
void h(A* a) { /* ... */ }
```

An object of type B can be passed to all three functions:

```
B b;
f(b);    // Slices!
g(b);
h(&b);
```

In all three cases, the object b is implicitly converted to an object of type A. However, function f is not polymorphic because it slices object b as discussed in Section 6.1.3. Up-casting only fails when the base class is ambiguous. In the current example, we cannot up-cast from D to A:

```
D d;
A ad(d); // Error: ambiguous
```

because the compiler does not know whether the base class A from B or from C is meant. We can clarify this situation with an explicit intermediate up-cast:

```
A ad(B(d));
```

Or we can share A between B and C with virtual bases:

```
struct B : virtual A { ... };
struct C : virtual A {};
```

Now, the members of A exist only once in D. This is usually the best solution for multiple inheritance in most cases because we save memory and do not risk inconsistent replication of A.

6.5.1.2 Casting Down

Down-casting is the conversion of a pointer/reference to a sub-type pointer/reference. When the actually referred-to object is not of that sub-type, the behavior is undefined. Thus, this cast should be used with utter care and only when absolutely necessary.

Recall that we passed an object of type B to a reference and a pointer of type A& respectively A*:

```
void g(A& a) { ... }
void h(A* a) { ... }

B b;
g(b);
h(&b);
```

Within g and h we cannot access members of B (i.e., mb and fb()) despite the fact that the referred object b is of type B. Being sure that the respective function parameter a refers to an object of type B, we can down-cast a to B& or B* respectively and then access mb and fb().

Before we introduce a down-cast in our program, we should ask ourselves the following questions:

- How do we assure that the argument passed to the function is really an object of the derived class? For instance, with extra arguments or with run-time tests?

- What can we do if the object cannot be down-casted?

- Should we write a function for the derived class instead?

- Why do we not overload the function for the base and the derived type? This is definitively a much cleaner design and always feasible.

- Last but not least, can we redesign our classes such that our task can be accomplished with the late binding of virtual functions?

If after answering all these questions we honestly still believe we need a down-cast, we must then decide which down-cast we apply. There are two forms:

- static_cast, which is fast and unsafe; and

- dynamic_cast, which is safe at some extra cost and only available for polymorphic types.

As the name suggests, static_cast only checks compile-time information. This means in the context of down-casting whether the target type is derived from the source type. We can, for instance, cast a, the function argument of g, to type B& and are then able to call a method of class B:

```
void g(A& a)
{
    B& bref= static_cast<B&>(a);
    std::cout << "fb returns " << bref.fb() << "\n";
}
```

The compiler verifies that B is a sub-class of A and accepts our implementation. When the argument a refers to an object that is not of type B (or a sub-type thereof), the program behavior is undefined—the most likely result being a crash.

In our diamond-shaped example, we can also down-cast pointers from B to D. To this end, we declare pointers of type B* that are allowed to refer to objects of sub-class D:

```
B *bbp= new B, *bdp= new D;
```

The compiler accepts a down-cast to D* for both pointers:

```
dbp= static_cast<D*>(bbp); // erroneous downcast performed
ddp= static_cast<D*>(bdp); // correct downcast (but not checked)
```

Since no run-time checks are performed, it is our responsibility as programmers to only refer to objects of the right type. bbp points to an object of type B, and when we dereference the pointer, we risk data corruption and program crashes. In this small example, a smart compiler might detect the erroneous down-cast by static analysis and emit a warning. In general, it is not always possible to back-trace the actual type referenced by a pointer, especially as it can be selected at run time:

```
B *bxp= (argc > 1) ? new B : new D;
```

In Section 6.6, we will see an interesting application of a static down-cast that is safe since type information is provided as a template argument.

dynamic_cast performs a run-time test whether the actually casted object has the target type or a sub-type thereof. It can only be applied on polymorphic types (classes that define or inherit one or more **virtual** functions, §6.1):

```
D* dbp= dynamic_cast<D*>(bbp); // Error: cannot downcast  to D
D* ddp= dynamic_cast<D*>(bdp); // Okay: bdp points to a D object
```

When the cast cannot be performed, a null pointer is returned so that the programmer can eventually react to the failed down-cast. Incorrect down-casts of references throw exceptions of type std::bad_cast and can be handled in a **try-catch**-block. These checks are realized with *Run-Time Type Information* (RTTI) and take a little extra time.

Advanced background information: dynamic_cast is implemented under the hood as a virtual function. Therefore, it is only available when the user has made a class polymorphic by defining at least one virtual function. Otherwise, all classes would incur the cost of a vtable. Polymorphic functions have these anyway, so the cost of the dynamic_cast is one extra pointer in the vtable.

6.5.1.3 Cross-Casting

An interesting feature of dynamic_cast is casting across from B to C when the referenced object's type is a derived class of both types:

```
C* cdp= dynamic_cast<C*>(bdp); // Okay: B -> C with D object
```

Likewise, we could cross-cast from student to mathematician.

Static cross-casting from B to C:

```
cdp= static_cast<C*>(bdp);       // Error: neither sub- nor super-class
```

Table 6–1: Static versus Dynamic Cast

	static_cast	dynamic_cast
Which classes	all	polymorphic
Cross-casting	no	yes
Run-time check	no	yes
Overhead	none	RTI check

is not allowed because C is neither a base nor a derived class of B. It can be casted indirectly via D:

```
cdp= static_cast<C*>(static_cast<D*>(bdp)); // B -> D -> C
```

Here again it is the programmer's responsibility to determine whether the addressed object can really be casted this way.

6.5.1.4 Comparing Static and Dynamic Cast

Dynamic casting is safer but slower then static casting due the run-time check of the referenced object's type. Static casting allows for casting up and down with the programmer being responsible that the referenced objects are handled correctly.

Table 6-1 summarizes the differences between the two forms of casting:

6.5.2 const-Cast

const_cast adds or removes the attributes const and/or volatile. The keyword volatile informs the compiler that a variable can be modified from somewhere else. For instance, certain memory entries are set by hardware, and we must be aware of this when we write drivers for this hardware. Those memory entries cannot be cached or held in registers and must be read each time from main memory. In scientific and high-level engineering software, externally modified variables are less frequent and we therefore refrain from discussing volatile further in this book.

Both const and volatile can be added implicitly. Removing the volatile attribute of an object that is really volatile leads to undefined behavior since inconsistent values may exist in caches and registers. Conversely, the volatile attribute can only be removed from volatile-qualified pointers and references when they refer to a non-volatile object.

Removing the const attribute invalidates all corresponding const qualifiers on the entire call stack and thus increases the debugging effort tremendously when data is accidentally overwritten. Sadly enough, it is sometimes necessary to do so when dealing with old-style libraries which are often lacking appropriate const qualifiers.

6.5.3 Reinterpretation Cast

This is the most aggressive form of casting and is not used in this book. It takes an object's memory location and interprets its bits as if the object had another type. This allows us, for instance, to change a single bit in a floating-point number by casting it to a bit chain. reinterpret_cast is more important for programming hardware drivers than for advanced flux solvers. Needless to say, it is one of the most efficient ways to undermine the portability of our applications. If you really have to use it, incorporate it in platform-dependent conditional compilation and test your code excessively.

6.5.4   Function-Style Conversion

Constructors can be used to convert values: if a type T has a constructor for arguments of type U, we can create an object of type T from an object of type U:

```
U u;
T t(u);
```

or better:

```
U u;
T t{u};     // C++11
```

Therefore, it makes sense to use the constructor notation for converting values. Let's reuse our example with different matrix types. Assume we have a function for dense matrices and want to apply it to a compressed matrix:

```
struct dense_matrix
{    ... };

struct compressed_matrix
{    ... };

void f(const dense_matrix&) {}

int main ()
{
    compressed_matrix A;
    f(dense_matrix(A));
}
```

Here we take the compressed_matrix A and create a dense_matrix out of it. This requires either

- A constructor in dense_matrix that accepts a compressed_matrix; or

- A conversion operator in compressed_matrix to dense_matrix.

These methods look like this:

```
struct compressed_matrix; // forward decl. needed in constructor

struct dense_matrix
{
    dense_matrix() = default;
    dense_matrix(const compressed_matrix& A) { ... }
};

struct compressed_matrix
{
    operator dense_matrix() { dense_matrix A; ... return A; }
};
```

When both exist, the constructor is preferred. With this class implementation, we can also call f with implicit conversion:

```
int main ()
{
    compressed_matrix A;
    f(A);
}
```

In this case, the conversion operator is prioritized over the constructor. Note that the implicit conversion does not work with an `explicit` constructor or conversion operator. `explicit` conversion operators were introduced in C++11.

The danger of this notation is that it behaves like a C cast with an intrinsic target type, i.e.:

```
long(x);    // corresponds to
(long)x;
```

This allows us to write evil code like

```
double d= 3.0;
double const* const dp= &d;

long l= long(dp);    // OUCH!!! All bets are off!
```

Here we converted a const pointer to const double into a **long**! Although we seemingly asked to create a new value, a const_cast and a reinterpret_cast were performed. Needless to say, the value of l is rather meaningless and so are all values depending on it.

Note that the following initialization:

```
long l(dp);    // Error: cannot initialize long with pointer
```

does not compile. Neither does the braced initialization:

```
long l{dp};    // Same Error (C++11)
```

This leads us to another notation:

```
l= long{dp};   // Error: failed initialization (C++11)
```

With curly braces, we always initialize a new value and even impede narrowing. static_cast allows for narrowing but refuses as well a conversion from a pointer to a number:

```
l= static_cast<long>(dp); // Error: pointer -> long
```

For those reasons, Bjarne Stroustrup advises the use of T{u} Tu for well-behaved construction and named casts like static_cast for other conversions.

6.5.5 Implicit Conversions

The rules of implicit conversion are not trivial. The good news is that we get along most of the time with knowing the most important rules and can usually be agnostic to their priorities. A complete list, for instance, can be found in the "C++ Reference" [7]. Table 6–2 gives an overview of the most important conversions.

Table 6–2: Implicit Conversion

From	To
T	Super-type of T
T	const T
T	volatile T
T[N]	T*
T	U, accordingly §6.5.4
Function	Function pointer
nullptr_t	T*
Integrals	Larger integrals
Numeric type	Another numeric type

Numeric types can be converted in different ways. First, integral types can be promoted, i.e., expanded with 0s or sign bits.[6] In addition, every intrinsic numeric type can be converted to every other numeric type when needed for matching function argument types. For the new initialization techniques in C++11, only conversion steps are allowed that do not lose accuracy (i.e., no narrowing). Without the narrowing rules, even conversion between floating-point and `bool` is allowed with the intermediate conversion to `int`. All conversions between user types that can be expressed in function style (§6.5.4) are also performed implicitly when the enabling constructor or conversion operator is not declared `explicit`. Needless to say, the usage of implicit conversions should not be overdone. Which conversion should be expressed explicitly and where we can rely on the implicit rules is an important design decision for which no general rule exists.

6.6   CRTP

This section describes the *Curiously Recurring Template Pattern* (CRTP). It combines template programming very efficiently with inheritance. The term is sometimes confused with the *Barton-Nackman Trick* that is based on CRTP and was introduced by John Barton and Lee Nackman [4].

6.6.1   A Simple Example

⇒ c++03/crtp_simple_example.cpp

We will explain this new technique with a simple example. Assume we have a class named `point` containing an equality operator:

```
class point
{
  public:
    point(int x, int y) : x(x), y(y) {}
```

---

6. Promotion is not a conversion in the purest sense of language laws.

```
      bool operator==(const point& that) const
      { return x == that.x && y == that.y; }
   private:
      int x, y;
};
```

We can program the inequality by using common sense or by applying de Morgan's law:

```
bool operator!=(const point& that) const
{ return x != that.x || y != that.y; }
```

Or we can simplify our life and just negate the result of the equality:

```
bool operator!=(const point& that) const
{ return !(*this == that); }
```

Our compilers are so sophisticated, they can certainly handle de Morgan's law perfectly after inlining. Negating the equality operator this way is a correct implementation of the inequality operator of every type (with an equality operator). We could copy-and-paste this code snippet and just replace the type of the argument each time.

Alternatively, we can write a class like this:

```
template <typename T>
struct inequality
{
    bool operator!=(const T& that) const
    { return !(static_cast<const T&>(*this) == that); }
};
```

and derive from it:

```
class point : public inequality<point> { ... };
```

This class definition establishes a mutual dependency:

- point is derived from inequality, and

- inequality is parameterized with point.

These classes can be compiled despite their mutual dependency because member functions of template classes (like inequality) are not compiled until they are called. We can check that operator!= works:

```
point p1(3, 4), p2(3, 5);
cout << "p1 != p2 is " << boolalpha << (p1 != p2) << '\n';
```

But what really happens when we call p1 != p2?

1. The compiler searches for operator!= in class point → without success.

2. The compiler looks for operator!= in the base class inequality<point> → with success.

3. The this pointer refers to the object of type inequality<point> being part of a point object.

4. Both types are completely known and we can statically down-cast the `this` pointer to `point*`.

5. Since we know that the `this` pointer of `inequality<point>` is an up-casted `this` pointer to `point` it is safe to down-cast it to its original type.

6. The equality operator of `point` is called and instantiated (if not done before).

Every class `U` with an equality operator can be derived from `inequality<U>` in the same manner. A collection of such CRTP templates for operator defaults is provided by Boost.Operators from Jeremy Siek and David Abrahams.

6.6.2 A Reusable Access Operator

⇒ c++11/matrix_crtp_example.cpp

The CRTP idiom allows us to tackle a problem mentioned earlier (§2.6.4): accessing multi-dimensional data structures with the bracket operator with a reusable implementation. At the time we did not know the necessary language features, especially templates and inheritance. Now we do and will apply this knowledge to realize two bracket operator calls by one of a binary call operator, i.e., evaluate `A[i][j]` as `A(i, j)`.

Say we have a matrix type going by the elegant name `some_matrix` whose `operator()` accesses a_{ij}. For consistency with the vector notation, we prefer bracket operators. Those accept only one argument, and we therefore need a proxy that represents the access to a matrix row. This proxy provides in turn a bracket operator for accessing a column in the corresponding row, i.e., yields an element of the matrix:

```
class some_matrix; // Forward declaration

class simple_bracket_proxy
{
  public:
    simple_bracket_proxy(matrix& A, size_t r) : A(A), r(r) {}

    double& operator[](size_t c){ return A(r, c); }     // Error
  private:
    matrix&    A;
    size_t     r;
};

class some_matrix
{
    // ...
    double& operator()(size_t r, size_t c) { ... }

    simple_bracket_proxy operator[](size_t r)
    {
    return simple_bracket_proxy(*this, r);
    }
};
```

The idea is that A[i] returns a proxy p referring to A and containing i. Calling A[i][j] corresponds to p[j] which in turn should call A(i, j). Unfortunately, this code does not compile. When we call some_matrix::operator() in simple_bracket_proxy::operator[], the type some_matrix is only declared but not fully defined. Switching the two class definitions would only reverse the dependency and lead to more uncompilable code. The problem in this proxy implementation is that we need two complete types that depend on each other.

This is an interesting aspect of templates: they allow us to break mutual dependencies thanks to their postponed code generation. Adding template parameters to the proxy removes the dependency:

```
template <typename Matrix, typename Result>
class bracket_proxy
{
  public:
    bracket_proxy(Matrix& A, size_t r) : A(A), r(r) {}

    Result& operator[](size_t c){ return A(r, c); }
  private:
    Matrix& A;
    size_t     r;
};

class some_matrix
{
    // ...
    bracket_proxy<some_matrix, double> operator[](size_t r)
    {
        return bracket_proxy<some_matrix, double>(*this, r);
    }
};
```

Finally, we can write A[i][j] and have it performed internally in terms of the two-argument operator(). Now we can write many matrix classes with entirely different implementations of operator(), and all of them can deploy bracket_proxy in exactly the same manner.

Once we have implemented several matrix classes, we realize that the operator[] looks quite the same in all matrix classes: just returning a proxy with the matrix reference and the row argument. We can add another CRTP class for implementing this bracket operator just once:

```
template <typename Matrix, typename Result>
class bracket_proxy { ... };

template <typename Matrix, typename Result>
class crtp_matrix
{
    using const_proxy= bracket_proxy<const Matrix, const Result>;
  public:
    bracket_proxy<Matrix, Result> operator[](size_t r)
    {
```

C++11

```
                return {static_cast<Matrix&>(*this), r};
        }

        const_proxy operator[](size_t r) const
        {
                return {static_cast<const Matrix&>(*this), r};
        }
};

class matrix
  : public crtp_matrix<matrix, double>
{
  // ...
};
```

Note that the C++11 features are just used for brevity; we can implement this code as well in C++03 with little more verbosity. This CRTP matrix class can provide the bracket operator for every matrix class with a two-argument application operator. In a full-fledged linear-algebra package, however, we need to pay attention to which matrices are mutable and whether references or values are returned. These distinctions can be safely handled with meta-programming techniques from Chapter 5.

Although the proxy approach creates an extra object, our benchmarks have shown that the usage of the bracket operator is as fast as that of the application operator. Apparently, sophisticated reference forwarding in modern compilers can eliminate the actual creation of proxies.

6.7   Exercises

6.7.1   Non-redundant Diamond Shape

Implement the diamond shape from Section 6.3.2 such that the name is only printed once. Distinguish in derived classes between all_info() and my_infos() and call the two functions appropriately.

6.7.2   Inheritance Vector Class

Revise the vector example from Chapter 2. Introduce the base class vector_expression for size and operator(). Make vector inherit from this base class. Then make a class ones that is a vector of all ones and also inherits from vector_expression.

6.7.3   Clone Function

Write a CRTP class for a member function named clone() that copies the current object—like the Java function clone (http://en.wikipedia.org/wiki/Clone_%28Java_method%29). Consider that the return type of the function must be the one of the cloned object.

Chapter 7

Scientific Projects

In the preceding chapters, we focused primarily on language features of C++ and how we can best apply them to relatively small study examples. This last chapter should give you some ideas for how to build up larger projects. The first section (§7.1) from the author's friend Mario Mulansky deals with the topic of interoperability between libraries. It will give you a look behind the curtain at odeint: a generic library that seamlessly inter-operates with several other libraries in a very tight fashion. Then we will provide some background on how executables are built from many program sources and library archives (§7.2.1) and how tools can support this process (§7.2.2). Finally, we discuss how program sources are appropriately distributed over multiple files (§7.2.3).

7.1 Implementation of ODE Solvers

Written by Mario Mulansky

In this section we will go through the major steps for designing a numerical library. The focus here is not to provide the most complete numerical functionality, but rather to arrive at a robust design that ensures maximal generality. As an example, we will consider the numerical algorithms for finding the solution of *Ordinary Differential Equations* (ODEs). In the spirit of Chapter 3, our aim is to make the implementation as versatile as possible by using generic programming. We start by briefly introducing the mathematical background of the algorithms followed by a simple, straightforward implementation. From this, we will be able to identify individual parts of the implementation and one by one make them exchangeable to arrive at a fully generic library. We are convinced that after studying this detailed example of a generic library design, the reader will be able to apply this technique to other numerical algorithms as well.

7.1.1 Ordinary Differential Equations

Ordinary differential equations are a fundamental mathematical tool to model physical, biological, chemical, or social processes and are one of the most important concepts in science and engineering. Except for a few simple cases, the solution of an ODE cannot be found with analytical methods, and we have to rely on numerical algorithms to obtain at least an approximate solution. In this chapter, we will develop a generic implementation of the Runge-Kutta-4 algorithm, a general-purpose ODE solver widely used due to its simplicity and robustness.

Generally, an ordinary differential equation is an equation containing a function $x(t)$ of an independent variable t and its derivatives x', x'', ...:

$$F(x, x', x'', \ldots, x^{(n)}) = 0. \tag{7.1}$$

This is the most general form, including implicit ODEs. However, here we will only consider *explicit* ODEs, which are of the form $x^{(n)} = f(x, x', x'', \ldots, x^{(n-1)})$ and are much simpler to address numerically. The highest derivative n that appears in the ODE is called the *order* of the ODE. But any ODE of order n can be easily transformed into an n-dimensional ODE of the first order [23]. Therefore, it is sufficient to consider only first-order differential equations where $n = 1$. The numerical routines presented later will all deal with initial value problems (IVPs): ODEs with a value for x at a starting point $x(t = t_0) = x_0$. Thus, the mathematical formulation of the problem that will be numerically addressed throughout the following pages is

$$\frac{d}{dt}\vec{x}(t) = \vec{f}(\vec{x}(t), t), \qquad \vec{x}(t = t_0) = \vec{x}_0. \tag{7.2}$$

Here, we use the vector notation $\vec{x}$ to indicate that the variable $\vec{x}$ might be a more-dimensional vector. Typically, the ODE is defined for real-valued variables, i.e., $\vec{x} \in \mathbb{R}^N$, but it is also possible to consider complex-valued ODEs where $\vec{x} \in \mathbb{C}^N$. The function $\vec{f}(\vec{x}, t)$ is called the right-hand side (RHS) of the ODE. The most simple physical example for an ODE is probably the *Harmonic Oscillator*, i.e., a point mass connected to a spring. Newton's equation of motion for such a system is

$$\frac{d^2}{dt^2}q(t) = -\omega_0^2 q(t), \tag{7.3}$$

where $q(t)$ denotes the position of the mass and ω_0 is the oscillation frequency. The latter is a function of the mass m and the stiffness of the spring k: $\omega_0 = \sqrt{k/m}$. This can be brought into form (7.2) by introducing $p = dq/dt$, using $\vec{x} = (q, p)^T$ and defining some initial conditions, e.g., $q(0) = q_0$, $p(0) = 0$. Using the shorthand notation $\dot{\vec{x}} := d\vec{x}/dt$ and omitting explicit time dependencies, we get

$$\dot{\vec{x}} = \vec{f}(\vec{x}) = \begin{pmatrix} p \\ -\omega_0^2 q \end{pmatrix}, \qquad \vec{x}(0) = \begin{pmatrix} q_0 \\ 0 \end{pmatrix}. \tag{7.4}$$

Note that $\vec{f}$ in Eq. (7.4) does not depend on the variable t, which makes Eq. (7.4) an *Autonomous* ODE. Also note that in this example the independent variable t denotes the time and $\vec{x}$ a point in phase spaces, hence the solution $\vec{x}(t)$ is the *Trajectory* of the harmonic oscillator. This is a typical situation in physical ODEs and the reason for our choice of variables t and $\vec{x}$.[1]

For the harmonic oscillator in Eq. (7.4), we can find an analytic solution of the IVP: $q(t) = q_0 \cos \omega_0 t$ and $p(t) = -q_0 \omega_0 \sin(\omega_0 t)$. More complicated, non-linear ODEs are often impossible to solve analytically, and we have to employ numerical methods to find

---

1. In mathematics, the independent variable is often called x and the solution is $y(x)$.

an approximate solution. One specific family of examples is systems exhibiting *Chaotic Dynamics* [34], where the trajectories cannot be described in terms of analytical functions. One of the first models where this has been explored is the so-called Lorenz system, a three-dimensional ODE given by the following equations for $\vec{x} = (x_1, x_2, x_3)^T \in \mathbb{R}^3$:

$$
\begin{aligned}
\dot{x}_1 &= \sigma(x_2 - x_1) \\
\dot{x}_2 &= Rx_1 - x_2 - x_1 x_3 \\
\dot{x}_3 &= x_1 x_2 - b x_3,
\end{aligned}
\tag{7.5}
$$

where σ, R, $b \in \mathbb{R}$ are parameters of the system. Figure 7–1 depicts a trajectory of this system for the typical choice of parameters $\sigma = 10$, $R = 28$, and $b = 10/3$. For these parameter values the Lorenz system exhibits a so-called *Chaotic Attractor*, which can be recognized in Figure 7–1.

Although such a solution is impossible to find analytically, there are mathematical proofs regarding its *existence* and *uniqueness* under some conditions on the RHS $\vec{f}$, e.g., the Picard-Lindelöf theorem, which requires $\vec{f}$ to be Lipschitz-continuous [48]. Provided that this condition is fulfilled and a unique solution exists—as is the case for almost all practical problems—we can apply an algorithmic routine to find a numerical approximation of this solution.

7.1.2 Runge-Kutta Algorithms

The most common general-purpose schemes for solving initial value problems of ordinary differential equations are the so-called *Runge-Kutta* (RK) methods [23]. We will focus on the *explicit* RK schemes as those are easier to implement and well suited for GPUs. They are a family of iterative one-step methods that rely on a temporal discretization to compute an approximate solution of the IVP. Temporal discretization means that the approximate solution is evaluated at time points t_n. So we use $\vec{x}_n$ for the numerical approximation of the solution $x(t_n)$ at time t_n. In the simplest but most frequently used case of an equidistant discretization with a constant step size Δt, one writes for the numerical solution:

$$
\vec{x}_n \approx \vec{x}(t_n), \quad \text{with} \quad t_n = t_0 + n \cdot \Delta t.
\tag{7.6}
$$

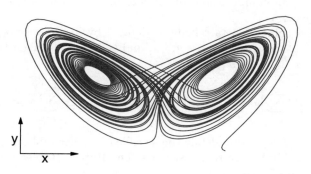

Figure 7–1: Chaotic trajectory in the Lorenz system with parameters $\sigma = 10$, $R = 28$, and $b = 10/3$

The approximate points $\vec{x}_n$ are obtained sequentially using a numerical algorithm that can be written in its most general form as

$$\vec{x}_{n+1} = \vec{F}_{\Delta t}(\vec{x}_n). \tag{7.7}$$

The mapping $\vec{F}_{\Delta t}$ here represents the numerical algorithm, i.e., the Runge-Kutta scheme, that performs one iteration from $\vec{x}_n$ to $\vec{x}_{n+1}$ with the time step Δt. The numerical scheme is said to have the order m if the solution it generates is exact up to some error of order $m + 1$:

$$\vec{x}_1 = \vec{x}(t_1) + O(\Delta t^{m+1}), \tag{7.8}$$

where $\vec{x}(t_1)$ is the exact solution of the ODE at t_1 starting from the initial condition $\vec{x}(t_0) = \vec{x}_0$. Hence, m denotes the order of accuracy of a *single step* of the scheme.

The most basic numerical algorithm to compute such a discrete trajectory x_1, x_2, ... is the *Euler Scheme*, where $F_{\Delta t}(\vec{x}_n) := \vec{x}_n + \Delta t \cdot \vec{f}(\vec{x}_n, t_n)$, which means the next approximation is obtained from the current one by

$$\vec{x}_{n+1} = \vec{x}_n + \Delta t \cdot \vec{f}(\vec{x}_n, t_n). \tag{7.9}$$

This scheme has no practical relevance because it only offers accuracy of order $m = 1$. A higher order can be reached by introducing intermediate points and thus dividing one step into several stages. For example, the famous *RK4* scheme, sometimes called the Runge-Kutta method, has $s = 4$ stages and also order $m = 4$. It is defined as follows:

$$\vec{x}_{n+1} = \vec{x}_n + \frac{1}{6}\Delta t(\vec{k}_1 + 2\vec{k}_2 + 2\vec{k}_3 + \vec{k}_4), \quad \text{with}$$

$$\vec{k}_1 = \vec{f}(\vec{x}_n, t_n),$$

$$\vec{k}_2 = \vec{f}\left(\vec{x}_n + \frac{\Delta t}{2}\vec{k}_1, t_n + \frac{\Delta t}{2}\right),$$

$$\vec{k}_3 = \vec{f}\left(\vec{x}_n + \frac{\Delta t}{2}\vec{k}_2, t_n + \frac{\Delta t}{2}\right), \tag{7.10}$$

$$\vec{k}_4 = \vec{f}\left(\vec{x}_n + \Delta t\,\vec{k}_3, t_n + \Delta t\right).$$

Note how the subsequent computations of the intermediate results $\vec{k}_i$ depend on the result of the previous stage $\vec{k}_{j<i}$.

More generally, a Runge-Kutta scheme is defined by its number of stages s and a set of parameters $c_1 \ldots c_s$, $a_{21}, a_{31}, a_{32}, \ldots, a_{ss-1}$, and $b_1 \ldots b_s$. The algorithm to calculate the next approximation x_{n+1} is then given by

$$x_{n+1} = x_n + \Delta t \sum_{i=1}^{s} b_i k_i, \qquad \text{where} \qquad k_i = f(x_n + \Delta t \sum_{j=1}^{i-1} a_{ij}k_j, \Delta t\, c_i). \tag{7.11}$$

The parameter sets $a_{i,j}$, b_i, and c_i define the so-called Butcher tableau (see Figure 7–2) and fully describe the specific Runge-Kutta scheme. The Butcher tableau for the RK4 scheme above is given in Figure 7–2(b).

(a) Generic Butcher Tableau with s stages

c_1				
c_2	$a_{2,1}$			
c_3	$a_{3,1}$	$a_{3,2}$		
$\vdots$	$\vdots$		$\ddots$	
c_s	$a_{s,1}$	$a_{s,2}$	$\cdots$	$c_{s,s-1}$
	b_1	b_2	$\cdots$	b_{s-1} b_s

(b) Coefficients for the Runge-Kutta-4 method

0				
0.5	0.5			
0.5	0	0.5		
1.0	0	0	1.0	
	1/6	1/3	1/3	1/6

Figure 7–2: Butcher tableaus

7.1.3 Generic Implementation

Implementing the Runge-Kutta scheme introduced above in C++ in a straightforward manner does not create any difficulty. For example, we can use std::vector<double> to represent the state $\vec{x}$ and the derivatives $\vec{k}_n$ and use a template parameter to allow some generality for the RHS function $\vec{f}(\vec{x}, t)$. The code in Listing 7–1 shows a quick and easy implementation of the Euler scheme introduced above. For simplicity, we restrict our examples to the Euler scheme to keep the code snippets brief, but the following points hold for similar implementations of more complicated Runge-Kutta schemes as well.

Listing 7–1: Basic implementation of the Euler scheme

```
typedef std::vector<double> state_type;

template<class System>
void euler_step(System system, state_type &x,
                const double t, const double dt)
{
    state_type k(x.size());
    system(x, k, t);
    for(int i=0; i<x.size(), ++i)
        x[i] += dt*k[i];
}
```

Defining the RHS system as a template parameter already gives us some nice generality: the euler_step function takes function pointers, as well as functors and C++ lambda objects, as system parameters. The only requirement is that the system object is callable with the parameter structure system(x, dxdt, t) and that it computes the derivative in dxdt.

Although this implementation works perfectly fine in many cases, it has several serious problems as soon as you come across some non-standard situations. Such situations might be

- Different state types, i.e., a fixed-size array (std::array) that might give better performance;

- ODEs for complex numbers;

- Non-standard containers, i.e., for ODEs on complex networks;
- Necessity of higher precision than `double`;
- Parallelization, e.g., via OpenMP or MPI; and
- Usage of GPGPU devices.

In the following, we will generalize the implementation in Listing 7–1 in such a way that we can deal with the situations mentioned above. Therefore, we will first identify the computational requirements of the Runge-Kutta schemes and then address each of these requirements individually. The result will be a highly modularized implementation of those algorithms that will allow us to exchange specific parts of the computation so that we can provide solutions to the before-mentioned problems.

7.1.3.1   Computational Requirements

To obtain a generic implementation of the Euler scheme (Listing 7–1), we need to separate the algorithm from the implementation details. For that, we first have to identify the computational requirements that are involved in the Euler scheme. From inspecting Eq. (7.9) or (7.10) together with the basic Euler implementation in Listing 7–1, we can identify several required parts for the computation.

First, the mathematical entities have to be represented in the code, namely, the state variable $\vec{x}(t)$ of the ODE as well as the independent variable t and the constants of the Runge-Kutta scheme a, b, c. In Listing 7–1, we use `std::vector<double>` and `double` respectively, but in a generic implementation this will become a template parameter. Second, memory allocation has to be performed to store the intermediate results $\vec{k}$. Furthermore, an iteration over the possibly high-dimensional state variable is required, and finally scalar computation involving the elements of the state variable x_i, the independent variable t, Δt, as well as the numerical constants a, b, c has to be performed. To summarize, the Runge-Kutta schemes introduced before require the following computational components:

1. Representation of mathematical entities,

2. Memory management,

3. Iteration, and

4. Elementary computation.

Having identified those requirements, we can now design a generic implementation where each requirement is addressed by a modularized piece of code that will be exchangeable.

7.1.3.2   Modularized Algorithm

In our modularized design, we will introduce separate code structures for the four requirements identified before. We start with the types used to represent the mathematical objects: the state $\vec{x}$, the independent variable (time) t, and the parameters of the algorithms a, b, c (Figure 7–2(a)). The standard way to generalize algorithms for arbitrary types is to introduce template parameters. We also follow this approach and hence define three template parameters: `state_type`, `time_type`, and `value_type`. Listing 7–2 shows the class definition of

Listing 7–2: Runge-Kutta class with templated types

```
template<
    class state_type,
    class value_type = double,
    class time_type = value_type
    >
class runge_kutta4 {
    // ...
};
typedef runge_kutta4< std::vector<double> > rk_stepper;
```

the Runge-Kutta-4 scheme with those template arguments. Note how we use double as the default arguments for value_type and time_type so in most cases only the state_type needs to be specified by the user.

Next, we address the memory allocation. In Listing 7–1 this is done in terms of the std::vector constructor which expects the vector size as a parameter. With generic state_types, this is not acceptable anymore, as the user might provide other types such as std::array that are not constructed with the same signature. Therefore, we introduce a templated helper function resize that will take care of the memory allocations. This templated helper function can be specialized by the user for any given state_type. Listing 7–3 shows the implementation for std::vector and std::array as well as its usage in the runge_kutta4 implementation. Note how the resize function allocates memory for the state out based on the state in. This is the most general way to implement such memory allocation; it also works for sparse matrix types where the required size is not so trivial. The resizing approach in Listing 7–3 provides the same functionality as the non-generic version in Listing 7–1 as again the runge_kutta4 class is responsible for its own memory management. It immediately works with any vector type that provides resize and size functions. For other types, the user can provide resize overloads and in that way tell the runge_kutta4 class how to allocate memory.

Next are the function calls to compute the RHS equation $\vec{f}(\vec{x}, t)$. This is already implemented in a generic way in Listing 7–1 by means of templates, and we will keep this solution.

Finally, we have to find abstractions for the numerical computations. As noted above, this involves iteration over the elements of $\vec{x}$ and the basic computations (summation, multiplication) on those elements. We address both parts separately by introducing two code structures: Algebra and Operation. While Algebra will handle the iterations, Operation will be in charge of the computations.

We start with Algebra. For the RK4 algorithm, we need two functions that iterate over three and six instances of state_type respectively. Keeping in mind that the state_type typically is a std::vector or std::array, it is reasonable to provide an algebra that can deal with C++ containers. To ensure as much generality as possible for our basic algebra, we will use the std::begin and std::end functions introduced with C++11 as part of the standard library.

Listing 7–3: Memory allocation

```cpp
template<class state_type>
void resize(const state_type &in, state_type &out) {
  // standard implementation works for containers
  using std::size;
  out.resize(size(in));
}

// specialization for std::array
template<class T, std::size_t N>
void resize(const std::array<T, N> &, std::array<T,N>& ) {
  /* arrays don't need resizing */
}

template< ... >
class runge_kutta4 {
  // ...
  template<class Sys>
  void do_step(Sys sys, state_type &x,
               time_type t, time_type dt)
  {
    adjust_size(x);
    // ...
  }

  void adjust_size(const state_type &x) {
    resize(x, x_tmp);
    resize(x, k1);
    resize(x, k2);
    resize(x, k3);
    resize(x, k4);
  }
};
```

Advice

The correct way to use free functions such as std::begin in a generic library is by locally lifting them into the current namespace with using std::begin and then accessing them without a namespace qualifier, i.e., begin(x), as is done in Listing 7–4. This way, the compiler can also utilize begin functions defined in the same namespace as the type of x via argument-dependent name lookup (ADL) if necessary.

Listing 7–4 shows such a container_algebra. The iterations are performed within for_each functions that are part of the struct called container_algebra. Those functions expect a number of container objects as well as an operation object and then simply perform an iteration over all containers and execute the given operation element-wise. The Operation performed for each element is a simple multiplication and addition and will be described next.

Listing 7–4: Container algebra

```cpp
struct container_algebra
{
    template<class S1, class S2, class S3, class Op>
    void for_each3(S1 &s1, S2 &s2, S3 &s3, Op op) const
    {
        using std::begin;
        using std::end;

        auto first1 = begin(s1);
        auto last1 = end(s1);
        auto first2 = begin(s2);
        auto first3 = begin(s3);
        for( ; first1 != last1 ; )
            op(*first1++, *first2++, *first3++);
    }
};
```

The final pieces are the fundamental operations that will consist of functor objects again gathered in a struct. Listing 7–5 shows the implementation of those operation functors. For simplicity, we again present only the scale_sum2 functor that can be used in for_each3 (Listing 7–4). However, the extension to scale_sum5 to work with for_each6 is rather straightforward. As seen in Listing 7–5, the functors consist of a number of parameters alpha1, alpha2,.. and a function call operator that computes the required product-sum.

Listing 7–5: Operations

```cpp
struct default_operations {
    template<class F1=double, class F2=F1>
    struct scale_sum2 {
        typedef void result_type;

        const F1 alpha1;
        const F2 alpha2;

        scale_sum2(F1 a1, F2 a2)
            : alpha1(a1), alpha2(a2) { }

        template<class T0, class T1, class T2>
        void operator()(T0 &t0, const T1 &t1, const T2 &t2) const
        {
            t0 = alpha1 * t1 + alpha2 * t2;
        }
    };
};
```

Having collected all the modularized ingredients, we can implement the Runge-Kutta-4 algorithm based on the parts described above. Listing 7–6 shows this implementation. Note how all the parts introduced above are supplied as template parameters and are therefore configurable.

Listing 7–6: Generic Runge-Kutta-4

```
template<class state_type, class value_type = double,
         class time_type = value_type,
         class algebra = container_algebra,
         class operations = default_operations>
class runge_kutta4 {
public:
    template<typename System>
    void do_step(System &system, state_type &x,
                         time_type t, time_type dt)
    {
        adjust_size( x );
        const value_type one = 1;
        const time_type dt2 = dt/2, dt3 = dt/3, dt6 = dt/6;

        typedef typename operations::template scale_sum2<
                  value_type, time_type> scale_sum2;

        typedef typename operations::template scale_sum5<
                  value_type, time_type, time_type,
                  time_type, time_type> scale_sum5;

        system(x, k1, t);
        m_algebra.for_each3(x_tmp, x, k1, scale_sum2(one, dt2));

        system(x_tmp, k2, t + dt2);
        m_algebra.for_each3(x_tmp, x, k2, scale_sum2(one, dt2));

        system(x_tmp, k3, t + dt2);
        m_algebra.for_each3(x_tmp, x, k3, scale_sum2(one, dt));

        system(x_tmp, k4, t + dt);
        m_algebra.for_each6(x, x, k1, k2, k3, k4,
                            scale_sum5(one, dt6, dt3,
                                       dt3, dt6));
    }
private:
    state_type x_tmp, k1, k2, k3, k4;
    algebra m_algebra;

    void adjust_size(const state_type &x) {
        resize(x, x_tmp);
        resize(x, k1); resize(x, k2);
        resize(x, k3); resize(x, k4);
    }
};
```

The following code snippet shows how this Runge-Kutta-4 stepper can be instantiated:

```
typedef runge_kutta4< vector<double>, double, double ,
                      container_algebra,
                      default_operations> rk4_type;
// equivalent shorthand definition using the default parameters:
// typedef runge_kutta4< vector<double> > rk4_type;

rk_stype rk4;
```

7.1.3.3 A Simple Example

In the end, we present a small example of how to use the generic Runge-Kutta-4 implementation above to integrate a trajectory of the famous Lorenz system. Therefore, we only have to define the state type, implement the RHS equation of the Lorenz system, and then use the `runge_kutta4` class from above with the standard `container_algebra` and `default_operations`. Listing 7–7 shows an example implementation requiring only 30 lines of C++ code.

7.1.4 Outlook

We have arrived at a generic implementation of the Runge-Kutta-4 scheme. From here, we can continue in numerous directions. Obviously, more Runge-Kutta schemes can be added, potentially including step-size control and/or dense output facility. Although such methods might be more difficult to implement and will require more functionality from the back ends (algebra and operations), they conceptually fit into the generic framework outlined above. Also, it is possible to expand to other explicit algorithms such as multi-step methods or predictor-corrector schemes, as essentially all explicit schemes only rely on RHS evaluations and vector operations as presented here. Implicit schemes, however, require higher-order algebraic routines like solving linear systems and therefore would need a different class of algebra than the one introduced here.

Furthermore, we can provide other back ends besides `container_algebra`. One example could be to introduce parallelism with `omp_algebra` or `mpi_algebra`. Also, GPU computing could be addressed, e.g., by `opencl_algebra` and the corresponding data structures. Another use case would be to rely on some linear-algebra package that provides `vector` or `matrix` types which already implement the required operations. There, no iteration is required and a dummy algebra should be used that simply forwards the desired computation to the `default_operations` without iterating.

As you can see, the generic implementation offers ample ways to adjust the algorithm to non-standard situations, like different data structures or GPU computing. The strength of this approach is that the actual algorithm does not need to be changed. The generality allows us to replace certain parts of the implementation to adapt to different circumstances, but the implementation of the algorithm remains.

An expansive realization of generic ODE algorithms following the approach described here is found in the Boost.odeint library.[2] It includes numerous numerical algorithms and several back ends, e.g., for parallelism and GPU computing. It is actively maintained and

---

2. http://www.odeint.com

Listing 7–7: Trajectory in the Lorenz system

```
typedef std::vector<double> state_type;
typedef runge_kutta4< state_type > rk4_type;

struct lorenz {
    const double sigma, R, b;
    lorenz(const double sigma, const double R, const double b)
        : sigma(sigma), R(R), b(b) { }

    void operator()(const state_type &x,state_type &dxdt,
                    double t)
    {
        dxdt[0] = sigma * ( x[1] - x[0] );
        dxdt[1] = R * x[0] - x[1] - x[0] * x[2];
        dxdt[2] = -b * x[2] + x[0] * x[1];
    }
};


int main() {
    const int steps = 5000;
    const double dt = 0.01;

    rk4_type stepper;
    lorenz system(10.0, 28.0, 8.0/3.0);
    state_type x(3, 1.0);
    x[0] = 10.0;  // some initial condition
    for( size_t n=0 ; n<steps ; ++n ) {
        stepper.do_step(system, x, n*dt, dt);
        std::cout << n*dt << ' ';
        std::cout << x[0] << ' ' << x[1] << ' ' << x[2]
                  << std::endl;
    }
}
```

widely used and tested. Whenever possible, it is strongly recommended to use this library instead of reimplementing these algorithms. Otherwise, the ideas and code presented above could serve as a good starting point to implement new, more problem-specific routines in a generic way.

7.2   Creating Projects

How we design our programs is not really critical as long as they are short. For larger software projects, of say over 100,000 lines of code, it is vital that the sources are well structured.

First of all, the program sources must be distributed in a well-defined manner over files. How large or small single files should be varies from project to project and is out of this book's scope. Here, we only demonstrate basic principles.

7.2.1   Build Process

The build process from source files to executables contains four steps. Nonetheless, many programs with few files can be built with a single compiler call. Thus, the term "compilation" is used ambiguously for the actual compilation step (§7.2.1.2) and the entire build process when performed by a single command.

Figure 7–3 depicts the four steps: preprocessing, compilation, assembly, and linkage. The following sections will discuss these steps individually.

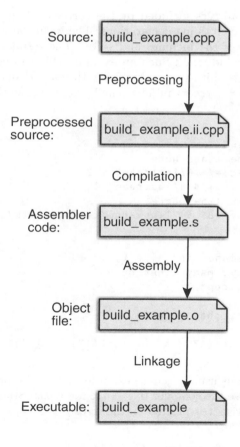

Figure 7–3: Simple build

7.2.1.1   Preprocessing

⇒ c++03/build_example.cpp

The (direct) input of the preprocessing is a source file containing implementations of functions and classes. For a C++ project, this is a file with one of the following typical extensions: .cpp, .cxx, .C, .cc, or .c++,[3] for instance, build_example.cpp:

```
#include <iostream>
#include <cmath>

int main (int argc, char* argv[])
{
    std::cout << "sqrt(17) is " << sqrt(17) << '\n';
}
```

⇒ c++03/build_example.ii.cpp

The indirect inputs are all files included by the corresponding #include directive. These includes are header files containing declarations. The inclusion is a recursive process that expands to the includes of the includes and so on. The result is a single file containing all direct and indirect include files. Such an expanded file can consist of several hundred thousand lines when large third-party libraries with massive dependencies like Boost are included. Only including <iostream> inflates small programs like the preceding toy example to about 20,000 lines:

```
# 1 "build_example.cpp"
# 1 "<command-line>"
// ... skipped some lines here
# 1 "/usr/include/c++/4.8/iostream" 1 3
# 36 "/usr/include/c++/4.8/iostream" 3
// ... skipped some lines here
# 184 "/usr/include/x86_64-linux-gnu/c++/4.8/bits/c++config.h" 3
namespace std
{
  typedef long unsigned int size_t;
// ... skipped many, many lines here
# 3 "build_example.cpp" 2

int main (int argc, char* argv[])
{
    std::cout << "sqrt(17) is " << sqrt(17) << '\n';
}
```

Preprocessed C++ programs usually get the extension .ii (.i for preprocessed C). To execute the preprocessing only, use the compiler flag -E (/E for Visual Studio). The output should be specified with -o; otherwise it is printed on the screen.

---

3. File name extensions are just conventions and do not matter to the compiler. We could use .bambi as an extension for our programs and they would still compile. The same applies to all other extensions in the remainder of this build discussion.

In addition to the inclusion, macros are expanded and conditional code selected. The whole preprocessing step is pure text substitution, mostly independent (ignorant) of the programming language. As a consequence, it is very flexible but also extremely error-prone as we discussed in Section 1.9.2.1. The set of files that are merged during the preprocessing is called a *Translation Unit*.

7.2.1.2 Compilation

⇒ c++03/build_example.s

The (actual) compilation translates the preprocessed sources into assembler code of the target platform.[4] This is a symbolic representation of the platform's machine language, e.g.:

```
        .file   "build_example.cpp"
        .local  _ZStL8__ioinit
        .comm   _ZStL8__ioinit,1,1
        .section        .rodata
.LC0:
        .string "sqrt(17) is "
        .text
        .globl  main
        .type   main, @function
main:
.LFB1055:
        .cfi_startproc
        pushq   %rbp
        .cfi_def_cfa_offset 16
        .cfi_offset 6, -16
        movq    %rsp, %rbp
        .cfi_def_cfa_register 6
        subq    $32, %rsp
        movl    %edi, -4(%rbp)
        movq    %rsi, -16(%rbp)
        movl    $.LC0, %esi
        movl    $_ZSt4cout, %edi
        call    _ZStlsISt11char_traitsIcEERSt13basic_ostreamIcT_ES5_PKc
        movq    %rax, %rdx
; just a bit more code
```

Surprisingly, the assembler code is much shorter (92 lines) than the preprocessed C++ for this example because it only contains the operations that are really performed. Typical extensions for assembler programs are .s and .asm.

The compilation is the most sophisticated part of the build process where all the language rules of C++ apply. The compilation itself consists of multiple phases: front end, middle end, and back end, which in turn can consist of multiple passes.

In addition to the code generation, the names of the C++ program are decorated with type and namespace (§3.2.1) information. This decoration is called *Name Mangling*.

---

4. A C++ compiler is not obliged by the standard to generate assembler code but all common compilers do so.

7.2.1.3   Assembly

The assembly is a simple one-to-one transformation from the assembler into the machine language where the commands are replaced by hexadecimal code and labels by true (relative) addresses. The resulting files are called *Object Code* and their extension is usually .o and on Windows .obj. The entities in the object files (code snippets and variables) are called *Symbols*.

Object files can be bundled to archives (extensions .a, .so, .lib, .dll, and the like). This process is entirely transparent to the C++ programmer and there is nothing that we can do wrong such that we get errors in this part of the build process.

7.2.1.4   Linking

In the last step, the object files and archives are *Linked* together. The two main tasks of the linker are

- Matching the symbols of different object files, and

- Mapping addresses relative to each object file onto the application's address space.

In principle, the linker has no notion of types and matches the symbols only by name. Since, however, the names are decorated with type information, a certain degree of type safety is still provided during linkage. The name mangling allows for linking function calls with the right implementation when the function is overloaded.

Archives—also called link libraries—are linked in two fashions:

- **Statically:** The archive is entirely contained in the executable. This linkage is applied to .a libraries on Unix systems and .lib libraries on Windows.

- **Dynamically:** The linker only checks the presence of all symbols and keeps some sort of reference to the archive. This is used for .so (Unix) and .dll (Windows) libraries.

The impact is obvious: executables that are linked against dynamic libraries are much smaller but depend on the presence of the libraries on the machine where the binary is executed. When a dynamic library is not found on Unix/Linux, we can add its directory to the search path in the environment LD_LIBRARY_PATH. On Windows, it requires a little more work.

7.2.1.5   The Complete Build

Figure 7–4 illustrates how the application for a flux simulator might be generated. First we preprocess the main application in fluxer.cpp which includes standard libraries like <iostream> and domain-specific libraries for meshing and solving. The expanded source is then compiled to the object file fluxer.o. Finally, the application's object file is linked with standard libraries like libstdc++.so and the domain libraries whose headers we included before. Those libraries can be linked statically like libsolver.a or dynamically like libmesher.so. Frequently used libraries like those from the system are often available in both forms.

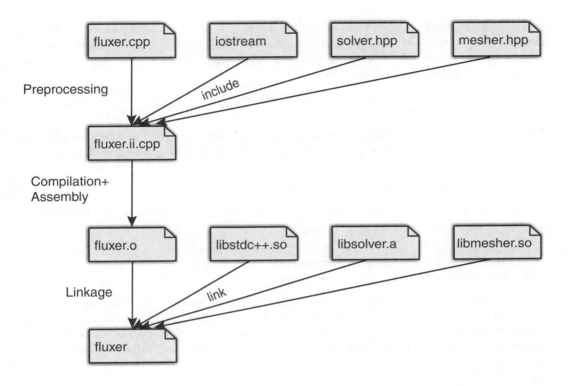

Figure 7–4: Complex build

7.2.2 Build Tools

When we build our applications and libraries from program sources and already-compiled libraries, we can either type in lots of commands over and over or use suitable tools. In this section, we present two of the latter: make and CMake. As a case study we consider a scenario like in Figure 7–4: a fluxer application that is linked with a mesher and a solver library which in turn are built from the appropriate source and header files.

7.2.2.1 make

⇒ buildtools/makefile

We do not know what you have heard about make, but it is not as bad as its reputation.[5] Actually it works pretty well for small projects. The basic idea is that we express dependencies

---

5. Rumor has it that its author showed it to his colleagues before leaving on vacation. When he came back, already regretting the design, it was being used all over the company and it was too late to retract it.

between targets and their sources, and when a target is older than its sources or missing, that target is generated with the given commands. These dependencies are written to a makefile and automatically resolved by make. In our example, we have to compile fluxer.cpp to the corresponding object file fluxer.o:

```
fluxer.o: fluxer.cpp mesher.hpp solver.hpp
    g++ fluxer.cpp -c -o fluxer.o
```

The line(s) with the command(s) must start with a tabulator. As the rules for all object files are similar enough, we write a generic rule instead for all that originate from C++ sources:

```
.cpp.o:
    ${CXX} ${CXXFLAGS} $^ -c -o $@
```

The variable ${CXX} is preset to the default C++ compiler and ${CXXFLAGS} to its default flags. We can change these variables:

```
CXX= g++-5
CXXFLAGS= -O3 -DNDEBUG        # Release
# CXXFLAGS= -O0 -g            # Debug
```

Here we changed the compiler or applied aggressive optimization (for release mode). As a comment, we also demonstrated the debug mode with no optimization and symbol tables within object files needed by debugging tools. We used automatic variables: $@ for the rule's target and $^ for its sources. Next we have to build our mesher and solver libraries:

```
libmesher.a: mesher.o # more mesher sources
    ar cr $@ $^

libsolver.a: solver.o # more solver sources
    ar cr $@ $^
```

For simplicity we build both with static linkage (deviating from Figure 7–4). Finally, we link the application and the libraries together:

```
fluxer: fluxer.o libmesher.a libsolver.a
    ${CXX} ${CXXFLAGS} $^ -o $@
```

If we used the default linker instead of the C++ compiler here, we would need to add C++ standard libraries and possibly some flags specific to C++ linkage. Now we can build our project with one single command:

```
make fluxer
```

This triggers the following commands:

```
g++   fluxer.cpp -c -o fluxer.o
g++   mesher.cpp -c -o mesher.o
ar cr libmesher.a mesher.o
g++   solver.cpp -c -o solver.o
ar cr libsolver.a solver.o
g++   fluxer.o libmesher.a libsolver.a -o fluxer
```

If we change mesher.cpp, the next build process only generates targets depending on it:

```
g++  mesher.cpp -c -o mesher.o
ar cr libmesher.a mesher.o
g++  fluxer.o libmesher.a libsolver.a -o fluxer
```

By convention, the first target not starting with a dot is considered the default target:

```
all: fluxer
```

so we can just write make.

7.2.2.2 CMake

⇒ buildtools/CMakeLists.txt

CMake is a tool of higher abstraction than make as we will demonstrate in this section. Our build project is specified here in a file named CMakeLists.txt. It typically starts with declaring which tool version is needed and naming a project:

```
cmake_minimum_required (VERSION 2.6)
project (Fluxer)
```

Generating a new library is easily done by just declaring its sources:

```
add_library(solver solver.cpp)
```

Which commands are used and how they are parameterized is decided by CMake unless we insist on more detailed specification. A library with dynamic linkage can be generated as easily:

```
add_library(mesher SHARED mesher.cpp)
```

Our final goal is the creation of the fluxer application that is linked against these two libraries:

```
add_executable(fluxer fluxer.cpp)
target_link_libraries(fluxer solver mesher)
```

It is good practice to build CMake projects in separate directories so that we can toss all generated files at once. One typically creates a sub-directory named build and runs all commands there:

```
cd build
cmake ..
```

Now CMake searches for compilers and other tools, including their flags:

```
-- The C compiler identification is GNU 4.9.2
-- The CXX compiler identification is GNU 4.9.2
-- Check for working C compiler: /usr/bin/cc
-- Check for working C compiler: /usr/bin/cc -- works
-- Detecting C compiler ABI info
-- Detecting C compiler ABI info - done
-- Check for working CXX compiler: /usr/bin/c++
```

```
-- Check for working CXX compiler: /usr/bin/c++ -- works
-- Detecting CXX compiler ABI info
-- Detecting CXX compiler ABI info - done
-- Configuring done
-- Generating done
-- Build files have been written to: ... /buildtools/build
```

Finally it builds a makefile that we call now:

```
make
```

Running:

```
Scanning dependencies of target solver
[ 33%] Building CXX object CMakeFiles/solver.dir/solver.cpp.o
Linking CXX static library libsolver.a
[ 33%] Built target solver
Scanning dependencies of target mesher
[ 66%] Building CXX object CMakeFiles/mesher.dir/mesher.cpp.o
Linking CXX shared library libmesher.so
[ 66%] Built target mesher
Scanning dependencies of target fluxer
[100%] Building CXX object CMakeFiles/fluxer.dir/fluxer.cpp.o
Linking CXX executable fluxer
[100%] Built target fluxer
```

The generated makefiles reflect the dependencies, and when we change some sources the next make will only rebuild what is affected by the changes. In contrast to our simplistic makefile from Section 7.2.2.1, modified header files are considered here. If we changed, for instance, solver.hpp, libsolver.a and fluxer would be freshly built.

The biggest benefit we kept for the end: CMake's portability. From the same CMakeLists.txt file from which we generated makefiles, we can create a Visual Studio project by just using another generator. The author enjoyed this feature a lot: till today he never created a Visual Studio project himself but generated them all with CMake. Nor did he migrate these projects to newer Visual Studio versions. Instead he just created new projects with new versions of the generators. Likewise one can generate Eclipse and XCode projects. KDevelop can build its projects from CMake files and even update them. In short, it is a really powerful build tool and at the time of writing probably the best choice for many projects.

7.2.3   Separate Compilation

Having seen how we can build an executable from multiple sources, we will now discuss how those sources should be designed for avoiding conflicts.

7.2.3.1   Headers and Source Files

Each unit of source code is typically split into

- A header file with declarations (e.g., .hpp), and

- A source file (e.g., .cpp).

The source file contains the realization of all algorithms from which the executable will be generated.[6] The header file contains declarations of the functions and classes that are implemented in the other file. Some functions may be used only internally and thus omitted in the header file. For instance, the math functions of our friend Herbert will be split into

```
// File: herberts/math_functions.hpp
#ifndef HERBERTS_MATH_FUNCTIONS_INCLUDE
#define HERBERTS_MATH_FUNCTIONS_INCLUDE

typedef double hreal; // Herbert's real numbers

hreal sine(hreal);
hreal cosine(hreal);
...
#endif

// File: herberts/math_functions.cpp
#include <herberts/math_functions.hpp>

hreal divide_by_square(hreal x, hreal y) { ... }

hreal sine(hreal) { ... }
hreal cosine(hreal) { ... }
...
```

We leave it to the reader's fantasy why Herbert introduced his own real number type.

To use Herbert's magnificent functions, we need two things:

- The declarations by

    - Including the header file herberts/math_functions.hpp or

    - Declaring all desired functions ourselves.

- The compiled code by

    - Linking against math_functions.o (.obj under Windows) or

    - Linking against a library containing math_functions.o.

The declarations tell the compiler that the code for the functions with the given signatures exists somewhere and that they can be called in the current compilation unit.

The linkage step then brings together the function calls with their actual code. The simplest way to link the compiled functions to some application is passing the object file or the archive as an argument to the C++ compiler. Alternatively, we could use a standard linker, but then we would need a handful of C++-specific extra flags.

7.2.3.2 Linkage Problems

During the linkage, the C++ entities like functions and variables are represented by symbols. C++ uses *Name Mangling*: decorating the symbol names with type and namespace (§3.2.1) information.

---

6. The terminology is not mathematically sharp: inline and template functions are defined in headers.

There are three things that can go wrong during the linkage:

1. Symbols (functions or variables) are not found;

2. Symbols are found twice; or

3. There is no `main` function (or multiple).

Not finding a symbol can have different causes:

- The symbols for the declaration and the implementation do not match.

- The corresponding object file or archive is not linked.

- The archives are linked in the wrong order.

A missing symbol is in most cases just a typo. As the symbol names contain type information due to name mangling, it can also be a type mismatch. Another possibility is that the source code is compiled with incompatible compilers where the names are mangled differently.

To avoid problems during linkage or execution, it must be verified that all sources are compiled with compatible compilers; i.e., names are equally mangled and function arguments placed in the same order on the stack. This does not only apply to our own object files and those of third-party libraries but also to the C++ standard library which is always linked in. In Linux, one should use the default compiler which is guaranteed to work with all precompiled software packages. If an older or newer compiler version is not available as a package, it is often an indicator of compatibility issues. It can still be used, but this is perceivably more work (manual installation, careful configuration of our own build processes, . . .).

When the linker complains about redefinition of symbols, it is possible that the same name is declared and used in multiple implementations. More often it is caused by defining variables and functions in header files. This works as long as such a header is only included in one translation unit. When headers with (certain) definitions are included more than once, the linkage fails.

For illustration purposes, we come back to our friend Herbert's infamous math functions. Next to many magnificent math functions, the header contains the following critical definitions:

```
// File: herberts/math_functions.hpp
..
double square(double x) { return x*x; }
double pi= 3.14159265358979323846264338327950288419716939;
```

After including this header into multiple translation units, the linker will complain:

```
g++-4.8 -o multiref_example multiref1.cpp multiref2.cpp
/tmp/cc65d1qC.o:(.data+0x0): multiple definition of 'pi'
/tmp/cc1slHbY.o:(.data+0x0): first defined here
/tmp/cc65d1qC.o: In function 'square(double)':
multiref2.cpp:(.text+0x0): multiple definition of 'square(double)'
/tmp/cc1slHbY.o:multiref1.cpp:(.text+0x63): first defined here
collect2: error: ld returned 1 exit status
```

Let us first deal with the function and then with the variable.

The first aid against redefinition is static:

```
static double square(double x) { return x*x; }
```

It declares the function local to the translation unit. The C++ standard calls this *Internal Linkage* (as opposed to external linkage evidently). The drawback is code replication: when the header is included n times, the function's code appears n times in the executable.

An inline declaration:

```
inline double square(double x) { return x*x; }
```

has a similar effect. Whether or not the function is actually inlined, an inline function always has internal linkage.[7] Conversely, functions without an inline specifier have external linkage and cause linker errors even when the programmer chooses to inline them.

Alternatively, we can avoid the redefinition by defining the function in only one translation unit:

```
// File: herberts/math_functions.hpp
double square(double x);
```

```
// File: herberts/math_functions.cpp
double square(double x) { return x*x; }
```

This is the preferable approach for large functions.

Function Definition

Short functions should be inline and defined in headers. Large functions should be declared in headers and defined in source files.

For data, we can use similar techniques. A static variable:

```
static double pi= 3.14159265358979323846264338327950288419716939;
```

is replicated in all translation units. This solves our linker problem but probably causes others as the following not-so-smart example illustrates:

```
// File: multiref.hpp
static double pi= 17.4;
```

```
// File: multiref1.cpp
int main (int argc, char* argv[])
{
    fix_pi();
    std::cout << "pi = " << pi << std::endl;
}
```

```
// File: multiref1.cpp
void fix_pi() { pi= 3.14159265358979323846264338327950288419716939; }
```

---

7. Advanced: In contrast to static functions, the code is not necessarily replicated. Instead it can be represented by a weak symbol that causes no linker error in redefinitions.

It is better to define it once in a source file and declare it in the header using the attribute extern:

```
// File: herberts/math_functions.hpp
extern double pi;
```

```
// File: herberts/math_functions.cpp
double pi= 3.14159265358979323846264338327950288419716939;
```

Finally, we will do the most reasonable: declaring π as a constant. Constants also have internal linkage[8] (unless previously declared extern) and can be safely defined in header files:

```
// File: herberts/math_functions.hpp
const double pi= 3.14159265358979323846264338327950288419716939;
```

Headers should not contain ordinary functions and variables.

7.2.3.3 Linking to C Code

Many scientific libraries are written in C, e.g., PETSc. To use them in C++ software, we have two options:

- Compile the C code with a C++ compiler or
- Link the compiled code.

C++ started as a superset of C. C99 introduced some features that are not part of C++ and even in old C there exist some academic examples that are not legal C++ code. However, in practice most C programs can be compiled with a C++ compiler.

For incompatible C sources or software that is only available in compiled form, it is possible to link the C binaries to C++ applications. However, C has no name mangling like C++. As a consequence, function declarations are mapped to different symbols by C and C++ compilers.

Say our friend Herbert developed in C the best algorithm for cubic roots, ever. Hoping for a Fields medal, he refuses to provide us the sources. As a great scientist he takes the liberty of stubbornness and feels that compiling his secret C functions with a C++ compiler would desecrate them. However, in his infinite generosity, he offers us the compiled code. To link it, we need to declare the functions with C naming (without mangling):

```
extern "C" double cubic_root(double);
extern "C" double fifth_root(double);
...
```

To save some typing, we can use the block notation:

```
extern "C" {
    double cubic_root(double);
    double fifth_root(double);
    ...
}
```

---

8. Advanced: They may be stored only once as weak symbols in the executable.

Later he became even more generous and offered us his precious header file. With that we can declare the entire set of functions as C code with a so-called *Linkage Block*:

```
extern "C" {
  #include <herberts/good_ole_math_functions.h>
}
```

In this style, `<math.h>` is included in `<cmath>`.

7.3   Some Final Words

I hope you have enjoyed reading this book and are eager to apply many of the freshly learned techniques in your own projects. It was not my intention to cover all facets of C++; I tried my best to demonstrate that this powerful language can be used in many different ways and provide both expressiveness and performance. Over time you will find your own personal way of making the best use of C++. "Best use" was a fundamental criterion for me: I did not want to enumerate uncountable features and all subtleties vaguely related to the language but rather to show which features or techniques would best help you reach your goals.

In my own programming, I have spent a lot of time squeezing out as much performance as possible and have conveyed some of that knowledge in this book. Admittedly, such tuning is not always fun, and writing C++ programs without ultimate performance requirements is much easier. And even without playing the nastiest tricks, C++ programs are still in most cases clearly faster than those written in other languages.

Thus, before focusing on performance, pay attention to productivity. The most precious resource in computing is not the processor time or the memory but your development time. And no matter how focused you are, it always takes longer than you think. A good rule of thumb is to make an initial guess, multiply it by two, and then use the next-larger time unit. The additional time is okay if it leads to a program or computing result that really makes a difference. You have my wholehearted wishes for that.

Appendix A

Clumsy Stuff

This appendix is dedicated to details that cannot be ignored but would slow down the pace we aim for in this book. The early chapters on basics and classes should not hold back the reader from the intriguing advanced topics—at least not longer than necessary. If you would like to learn more details and do not find the sections in this appendix clumsy, the author would not blame you; to the contrary: it would be a pleasure to him. In some sense, this appendix is like the deleted scenes of a movie: they did not make it to the final work but are still valuable to part of the audience.

A.1 More Good and Bad Scientific Software

The goal of this appendix is to give you an idea of what we consider good scientific software and what we do not. Thus, if you do not understand what exactly happens in these programs before reading this book, do not worry. Like the example programs in the Preface, the implementations only provide a first impression of different programming styles in C++ and their pros and cons. The details are not important here, only the general perception and behavior.

As the foundation of our discussion, we consider an iterative method to solve a system of linear equations $Ax = b$ where A is a (sparse) symmetric positive-definite (SPD) matrix, x and b are vectors, and x is searched. The method is called *Conjugate Gradients* (CG) and was introduced by Magnus R. Hestenes and Eduard Stiefel [24]. The mathematical details do not matter here, but rather the different styles of implementation. The algorithm can be written in the following form:

Algorithm A–1: Conjugate gradient algorithm

Input: SPD matrix A, vector b, and left preconditioner L, termination criterion ε
Output: Vector x such that $Ax \approx b$

1 $r = b - Ax$
2 **while** $|r| \geqslant \varepsilon$ **do**
3 $\quad z = L^{-1}r$
4 $\quad \rho = \langle r, z \rangle$
5 $\quad$ **if** *First iteration* **then**
6 $\quad\quad p = z$
7 $\quad$ **else**
8 $\quad\quad p = z + \frac{\rho}{\rho'}p$
9 $\quad q = Ap$
10 $\quad \alpha = \rho / \langle p, q \rangle$
11 $\quad x = x + \alpha p$
12 $\quad r = r - \alpha q$
13 $\quad \rho' = \rho$

Programmers transform this mathematical notation into a form that a compiler understands by using operations from the language. For those who came here from Chapter 1, we want to introduce our anti-hero Herbert who is an ingenious mathematician and considers programming a necessary evil for demonstrating how magnificently his algorithms work. Implementing other mathematicians' algorithms is even more annoying to him. His hastily typed version of CG—which you should only skim over—looks like this:

Listing A–1: Low-abstraction implementation of CG

```cpp
#include <iostream>
#include <cmath>

void diag_prec(int size, double *x, double* y)
{
    y[0] = x[0];

    for (int i= 1; i < size; i++)
        y[i] = 0.5 * x[i];
}

double one_norm(int size, double *vp)
{
    double sum= 0;
    for (int i= 0; i < size; i++)
         sum+= fabs(vp[i]);
    return sum;
}

double dot(int size, double *vp, double *wp)
{
    double sum= 0;
    for (int i= 0; i < size; i++)
```

```
                sum+= vp[i] * wp[i];
        return sum;
}

int cg(int size, double *x, double *b,
        void (*prec)(int, double*, double*), double eps)
{
        int i, j, iter= 0;
        double rho, rho_1, alpha;
        double *p= new double[size];
        double *q= new double[size];
        double *r= new double[size];
        double *z= new double[size];

        // r= A*x;
        r[0] = 2.0 * x[0] - x[1] ;
        for (int i= 1; i < size-1; i++)
                r[i] = 2.0 * x[i] - x[i-1] - x[i+1];
        r[size-1] = 2.0 * x[size-1] - x[size-2];

        // r= b-A*x;
        for (i= 0; i < size; i++)
                r[i]= b[i] - r[i];

        while (one_norm(size, r) >= eps) {
                prec(size, r, z);
                rho= dot(size, r, z);
                if (!iter) {
                        for (i= 0; i < size; i++)
                                p[i]= z[i];
                } else {
                        for (i= 0; i < size; i++)
                                p[i]= z[i] + rho / rho_1 * p[i];
                }

                // q= A * p;
                q[0] = 2.0 * p[0] - p[1] ;
                for (int i= 1; i < size-1; i++)
                        q[i] = 2.0 * p[i] - p[i-1] - p[i+1];
                q[size-1] = 2.0 * p[size-1] - p[size-2];

                alpha= rho / dot(size, p, q);
                // x+= alpa * p; r-= alpha * q;
                for (i= 0; i < size; i++) {
                        x[i]+= alpha * p[i];
                        r[i]-= alpha * q[i];
                }
                iter++;
}
```

```
        delete [] q; delete [] p; delete [] r; delete [] z;

        return iter;
    }

void ic_0(int size, double* out, double* in) { /* .. */ }

int main (int argc, char* argv[])
{
    int size=100;

    // set nnz and size

    double *x=    new double[size];
    double *b=    new double[size];

    for (int i=0; i<size; i++)
        b[i] = 1.0 ;

    for (int i=0; i<size; i++)
        x[i] = 0.0 ;

    // set A and b

    cg(size, x, b, diag_prec, 1e-9);

    return 0 ;
}
```

Let us discuss it in a general fashion. The good thing about this code is that it is self-contained—a virtue shared with much other bad code. However, this is about the only advantage. The problem with this implementation is its low abstraction level. This creates three major disadvantages:

- Bad readability,
- No flexibility, and
- High proneness to errors.

The bad readability manifests itself in the fact that almost every operation is implemented in one or multiple loops. For instance, would we have found the matrix vector multiplication $q = Ap$ without the comments? Probably. We would easily catch where the variables representing q, A, and p are used, but to see that this is a matrix vector product takes a closer look and a good understanding of how the matrix is stored.

This leads us to the second problem: the implementation commits to many technical details and only works in precisely this context. Algorithm A-1 only requires that matrix A is symmetric positive-definite, but it does not demand a certain storage scheme, even less a specific matrix. Herbert implemented the algorithm for a matrix that represents a discretized

1D Poisson equation. Programming at such a low abstraction level requires modifications every time we have other data or other formats.

The matrix and its format are not the only details the code commits to. What if we want to compute in lower (float) or higher (long double) precision? Or solve a complex linear system? For every such new CG application, we need a new implementation. Needless to say, running on parallel computers or exploring GPGPU (General-Purpose Graphic Processing Units) acceleration needs reimplementations as well. Much worse, every combination of the above needs a new implementation.

Some readers might think: "It is only one function of 20 or 30 lines. Rewriting this little function, how much work can this be? And we do not introduce new matrix formats or computer architectures every month." Certainly true, but in some sense it is putting the cart before the horse. Because of such inflexible and detail-obsessed programming style, many scientific applications grew into the hundred thousands and millions of lines of code. Once an application or library reaches such a monstrous size, it is arduous to modify features of the software and it is only rarely done. The road to success is starting software from a higher level of abstraction from the beginning, even when it is more work initially.

The last major disadvantage is how prone the code is to errors. All arguments are given as pointers, and the size of the underlying arrays is given as an extra argument. We as programmers of function cg can only hope that the caller did everything right because we have no way to verify it. If the user does not allocate enough memory (or does not allocate it at all), the execution will crash at some more or less random position or, even worse, will generate some nonsensical results because data and even the machine code of our program can be randomly overwritten. Good programmers avoid such fragile interfaces because the slightest mistake can have catastrophic consequences, and the program errors are extremely difficult to locate. Unfortunately, even recently released and widely used software is written in this manner, either for backward compatibility to C and Fortran or because it is written in one of these two languages. Or the developers are just resistant to any progress in software development. In fact, the implementation above is C and not C++. If this is how you like software, you probably will not like this book.

So much about software we do not like. In Listing A–2, we show a version that comes much closer to our ideal.

Listing A–2: High-abstraction implementation of CG

```
template < typename Matrix, typename Vector,
          typename Preconditioner >
int conjugate_gradient(const Matrix& A, Vector& x, const Vector& b,
                       const Preconditioner& L, const double& eps)
{
    typedef typename Collection<Vector>::value_type Scalar;
    Scalar rho= 0, rho_1= 0, alpha= 0;
    Vector p(resource(x)), q(resource(x)), r(resource(x)),
                                           z(resource(x));

    r= b - A * x;
    int iter = 0 ;
```

```
        while (one_norm(size, r) >= eps) {
            prec( r, z );
            rho = dot(r, z);

            if (iter.first())
                p = z;
            else
                p = z + (rho / rho_1) * p;
            q= A * p;
            alpha = rho / dot(p, q);

            x += alpha * p;
            r -= alpha * q;
            rho_1 = rho;
            ++iter;
        }
        return iter;
    }

int main (int argc, char* argv[])
{
    // initiate A, x, and b
    conjugate_gradient(A, x, b, diag_prec, 1.e-5);
    return 0 ;
}
```

The first thing you might realize is that the CG implementation is readable without comments. As a rule of thumb, if other people's comments look like your program sources, then you are a really good programmer. If you compare the mathematical notation in Algorithm A-1 with Listing A–2 you will realize that—except for the type and variable declarations at the beginning—they are identical. Some readers might think that it looks more like MATLAB or Mathematica than C++. Yes, C++ can look like this if one puts enough effort into good software.

Evidently, it is also much easier to write algorithms at this abstraction level than expressing them with low-level operations.

The Purpose of Scientific Software

Scientists do research. Engineers create new technology.

Excellent scientific and engineering software is expressed only in mathematical and domain-specific operations without any technical detail exposed.

At this abstraction level, scientists can focus on models and algorithms, thus being much more productive and advancing scientific discovery.

Nobody knows how many scientists are wasting how much time every year dwelling on small technical details of bad software like Listing A–1. Of course, the technical details have to be realized in some place but not in a scientific application. This is the worst possible location. Use a two-level approach: write your applications in terms of expressive mathematical operations, and if they do not exist, implement them separately. These mathematical operations must be carefully implemented for absolute correctness and optimal performance. What is optimal depends on how much time you can afford for tuning and on how much benefit the extra performance gives you. Investing time in your fundamental operations pays off when they are *reused* very often.

Advice
Use the right abstractions!
    If they do not exist, implement them.

Speaking of abstractions, the CG implementation in Listing A–2 does not commit to any technical detail. In no place is the function restricted to a numerical type like `double`. It works as well for `float`, GNU's multiprecision, complex, interval arithmetic, quaternions, ...

The matrix A can be stored in any internal format, as long as A can be multiplied with a vector. In fact, it does not even need to be a matrix but can be any linear operator. For instance, an object that performs a Fast Fourier Transformation (FFT) on a vector can be used as A when the FFT is expressed by a product of A with the vector. Similarly, the vectors do not need to be represented by finite-dimensional arrays but can be elements of any vector space that is somehow computer-representable as long as all operations in the algorithm can be performed.

We are also open to other computer architectures. If the matrix and the vectors are distributed over the nodes of a parallel supercomputer and corresponding parallel operations are available, the function runs in parallel without changing any single line. (GP)GPU acceleration can also be realized without changing the algorithm's implementation. In general, any existing or new platform for which we can implement matrix and vector types and their corresponding operations is supported by our *Generic* conjugate gradient function.

As a consequence, sophisticated scientific applications of several thousand lines on top of such abstractions can be ported to new platforms without code modification.

A.2 Basics in Detail

This section accumulates the outsourced details from Chapter 1.

A.2.1 More about Qualifying Literals

Here we want to expand the examples for literal qualifications from Section 1.2.2 a bit.

Availability: The standard library provides a (template) type for complex numbers where the type for the real and imaginary parts can be parameterized by the user:

```
std::complex<float> z(1.3, 2.4), z2;
```

These complex numbers of course provide the common operations like addition and multiplication. For unknown reasons, these operations are only provided between the type itself and the underlying real type. Thus, when we write:

```
z2= 2 * z;     // Error: no int * complex<float>
z2= 2.0 * z;   // Error: no double * complex<float>
```

we will get an error message that the multiplication is not available. More specifically, the compiler will tell us that there is no operator*() for int and std::complex<float> respectively for double and std::complex<float>.[1] To get the simple expression above compiled, we must make sure that our value 2 has the type float:

```
z2= 2.0f * z;
```

Ambiguity: At some point in this book, we introduced function overloading: a function with different implementations for different argument types (§1.5.4). The compiler selects that function overload which fits best. Sometimes the best fit is not clear, for instance, if function f accepts an unsigned or a pointer and we call:

```
f(0);
```

The literal 0 is considered an int and can be implicitly converted into unsigned or any pointer type. None of the conversions is prioritized. As before, we can address the issue by a literal of the desired type:

```
f(0u);
```

Accuracy: The accuracy issue comes up when we work with long double. On the author's computer, the format can handle at least 19 digits. Let us define 1/3 with 20 digits and print out 19 of them:

```
long double third= 0.3333333333333333333;
cout.precision(19);
cout << "One third is " << third << ".\n";
```

The result is

```
One third is 0.3333333333333333148.
```

The program behavior is more satisfying if we append an l to the number:

```
long double third= 0.3333333333333333333l;
```

yielding the printout that we hoped for:

```
One third is 0.3333333333333333333.
```

---

1. Since the multiplication is implemented as a template function, the compiler does not convert the int and double to float.

A.2.2   `static` Variables

In contrast to the scoped variables from Section 1.2.4 which die at the end of the scope, `static` variables live till the end of the program. Thus, declaring a local variable as `static` has an effect only when the contained block is executed more than once: in a loop or a function. Within a function, we could implement a counter for how often the function was called:

```
void self_observing_function()
{
    static int counter= 0;          // only executed once
    ++counter;
    cout << "I was called " << counter << " times.\n";
    ...
}
```

To reuse the `static` data, the initialization is only performed once. The major motivation for `static` variables is to reuse helper data like lookup tables or caches in the next function call. However, if the management of the helper data reaches a certain complexity, a class-based solution (Chapter 2) probably leads to a cleaner design.

The effect of the keyword `static` depends on the context but the common denominator is:

- Persistence: data of `static` variables remains in memory for the rest of the program execution.

- File scope: `static` variables and functions are only visible in the compilation of the actual file and do not collide when multiple compiled programs are linked together. This is illustrated in Section 7.2.3.2.

Thus, the impact on global variables is to limit their visibility as they already live until the program ends. Conversely, the effect on local variables is the lifetime extension since their visibility is already limited. There is also a class-related meaning of `static` which is discussed in Chapter 2.

A.2.3   More about `if`

The condition of an `if` must be a `bool` expression (or something convertible to `bool`). Thus, the following is allowed:

```
int i= ...
if (i)                      // bad style
    do_something();
```

This relies on the implicit conversion from `int` to `bool`. In other words, we test whether `i` is different from 0. It is clearer to say this instead:

```
if (i != 0)                 // better
    do_something();
```

An `if`-statement can contain other `if`-statements:

```
if (weight > 100.0) {
    if (weight > 200.0) {
```

```
            cout ≪ "This is extremely heavy.\n";
        } else {
            cout ≪ "This is quite heavy.\n";
        }
    } else {
        if (weight < 50.0) {
            cout ≪ "A child can carry this.\n";
        } else {
            cout ≪ "I can carry this.\n";
        }
    }
}
```

In the above example, the parentheses could be omitted without changing the behavior but it is clearer to have them. The example is more readable when we reorganize the nesting:

```
if (weight < 50.0) {
    cout ≪ "A child can carry this.\n";
} else if (weight <= 100.0) {
    cout ≪ "I can carry this.\n";
} else if (weight <= 200.0) {
    cout ≪ "This is quite heavy.\n";
} else {
    cout ≪ "This is extremely heavy.\n";
}
```

The parentheses can be omitted here as well, and it requires less effort to figure out what is going on.

At the end of our discussion on if-then-else, we want to do something sophisticated. Let us take the then-branch of the second-last example without braces:

```
if (weight > 100.0)
    if (weight > 200.0)
        cout ≪ "This is extremely heavy.\n";
    else
        cout ≪ "This is quite heavy.\n";
```

It looks like the last line is executed when weight is between 100 and 200 assuming the first if has no else-branch. But we could also assume the second if comes without an else-branch and the last line is executed when weight is less than or equal to 100. Fortunately, the C++ standard specifies that an else-branch always belongs to the innermost possible if. So, we can count on our first interpretation. In case the else-branch belongs to the first if we need braces:

```
if (weight > 100.0) {
    if (weight > 200.0)
        cout ≪ "This is extremely heavy.\n";
} else
    cout ≪ "This is not so heavy.\n";
```

Maybe these examples will convince you that it is more productive to set more braces and save the time guessing what the branches belong to.

A.2.4 Duff's Device

The continued execution in `switch` cases allows us also to implement short loops without the termination test after each iteration. Say we have vectors with dimension $\leqslant 5$. Then we could implement a vector addition without a loop:

```
assert(size(v) <= 5);
int i= 0;
switch (size(v)) {
  case 5: v[i]= w[i] + x[i]; ++i;      // keep going
  case 4: v[i]= w[i] + x[i]; ++i;      // keep going
  case 3: v[i]= w[i] + x[i]; ++i;      // keep going
  case 2: v[i]= w[i] + x[i]; ++i;      // keep going
  case 1: v[i]= w[i] + x[i];           // keep going
  case 0: ;
}
```

This technique is called Duff's device. It is usually not used stand-alone as above (but as a cleanup of unrolled loops). Such techniques should not be used in the main development of projects but only as final tuning of performance-critical kernels.

A.2.5 More about `main`

Arguments containing spaces must be quoted. In the first argument, we can also see when the program is called with path information; e.g.:

```
../c++11/argc_argv_test first "second third" fourth
```

prints out:

```
../c++11/argc_argv_test
first
second third
fourth
```

Some compilers also support a vector of strings as `main` arguments. This is more convenient but not portable.

For calculating with the arguments, they must be converted first:

```
cout ≪ argv[1] ≪ " times " ≪ argv[2] ≪ " is "
     ≪ stof(argv[1]) * stof(argv[2]) ≪ ".\n";
```

which could provide such impressive knowledge to us:

```
argc_argv_test 3.9 2.8
3.9 times 2.8 is 10.92.
```

Unfortunately, the conversion from strings to numbers does not tell us when the complete string is not convertible. As long as the string starts with a number or plus or minus, the reading is stopped if a character is found that cannot belong to a number and the sub-string read up to this point is converted to a number.

In Unix-like systems, the exit code of the last command can be accessed by `$?` in the shell. We can also use the exit code to execute multiple commands in a row under the condition that the preceding succeeded:

```
do_this && do_that && finish_it
```

In contrast to C and C++, the command shell interprets an exit code of 0 as true in the sense of okay. However, the handling of && is similar to that of C and C++: only when the first sub-expression is true do we need to evaluate the second. Likewise, a command is only executed when the preceding one was successful. Dually, || can be used for error handling because the command after an || is only performed when the preceding one failed.

A.2.6   Assertion or Exception?

Without going into detail, exceptions are more expensive than assertions since C++ cleans up the run-time environment when an exception is thrown. Turning off exception handling can accelerate applications perceivably. Assertions, on the other hand, immediately kill the program and do not require the cleanup. In addition, they are usually disabled in release mode anyway.

As we said before, unexpected or inconsistent values that originate from programming errors should be handled with assertions and exceptional states with exceptions. Unfortunately, this distinction is not always obvious when we encounter a problem. Consider our example of a file that cannot be opened. The reason can be either that an incorrect name was typed by a user or found in a configuration file. Then an exception would be best. The wrong file can also be a literal in the sources or the result of an incorrect string concatenation. Such program errors cannot be handled and we prefer the program to terminate with an assertion.

This dilemma is a conflict between avoiding redundancies and immediate sanity checks. At the location where the file name is entered or composed, we do not know whether it is a programming error or erroneous input. Implementing the error handling at these points could require repeating the opening test many times. This causes extra programming effort for repeated check implementation and bears the danger that the tests are not consistent with each other. Thus, it is more productive and less error-prone to test only once and not to know what caused our current trouble. In this case, we shall be prudent and throw an exception so that a cure is possible in some situations at least.

Corrupt data is usually better handled by an exception. Assume the salaries of your company are computed and the data of a newbie is not yet fully set. Raising an assertion would mean that the entire company (including you) would not be paid that month or at least until the problematic data set is fixed. If an exception is thrown during the data evaluation, the application could report the error in some way and continue for the remaining employees.

Speaking of program robustness, functions in universally used libraries should never abort. If the function is used, for instance, to implement an autopilot, we would rather turn off the autopilot than have the entire program terminated. In other words, when we do not know all application domains of a library, we cannot tell the consequences of a program abort.

Sometimes, the cause of a problem is not 100 % certain in theory but sufficiently clear in practice. The access operator of a vector or matrix should check whether the index is in a valid range. In principle, an out-of-range index could originate from user input or a configuration file, but in practically all cases it comes from a program bug. Raising an assertion is appropriate here. To comply with the robustness issue, it might be necessary to allow the user to decide between assertion and exception with compile flags (see §1.9.2.3).

A.2.7 Binary I/O

Conversions from and to strings can be quite expensive. Therefore, it is often more efficient to write data directly in their respective binary representations into files. Nonetheless, before doing so it is advisable to check with tools whether file I/O is really a significant bottleneck of the application.

When we decide to go binary, we should set the flag `std::ios::binary` for impeding implicit conversions like adapting line breaks to Windows, Unix, or Mac OS. It is not true that the flag makes the difference between text and binary files: binary data can be written without the flag and text with it. However, to prevent the before-mentioned surprises it is better to set the flag appropriately.

The binary output is performed with the `ostream`'s member function `write` and input with `istream::read`. The functions take a `char` address and a size as arguments. Thus, all other types have to be casted to pointers of `char`:

```cpp
int main (int argc, char* argv[])
{
    std::ofstream outfile;
    with_io_exceptions(outfile);
    outfile.open("fb.txt", ios::binary);

    double o1= 5.2, o2= 6.2;
    outfile.write(reinterpret_cast<const char *>(&o1), sizeof(o1));
    outfile.write(reinterpret_cast<const char *>(&o2), sizeof(o2));
    outfile.close();

    std::ifstream infile;
    with_io_exceptions(infile);
    infile.open("fb.txt", ios::binary);

    double  i1, i2;
    infile.read(reinterpret_cast<char *>(&i1), sizeof(i1));
    infile.read(reinterpret_cast<char *>(&i2), sizeof(i2));
    std::cout << "i1 = " << i1 << ", i2 = " << i2 << "\n";
}
```

An advantage of binary I/O is that we do not need to worry about how the stream is parsed. On the other hand, non-matching types in the read and write commands result in completely unusable data. In particular, we must be utterly careful when the files are not read on the same platform as they were created: a `long` variable can contain 32 bits on one machine and 64 bits on another. For this purpose, library `<cstdint>` provides what sizes are identical on each platform. The type `int32_t`, for instance, is a 32-bit `signed` `int` on every platform. `uint32_t` is the corresponding `unsigned`.

The binary I/O works in the same manner for classes when they are self-contained, that is, when all data is stored within the object as opposed to external data referred to by pointers or references. Writing structures containing memory addresses—like trees or graphs—to files requires special representations since the addresses are obviously invalid in a new program run. In Section A.6.4, we will show a convenience function that allows us to write or read many objects in a single call.

A.2.8   C-Style I/O

The old-style I/O from C is also available in C++:

```
#include <cstdio>

int main ()
{
    double x= 3.6;
    printf("The square of %f is %f\n", x, x*x);
}
```

The command `printf` stands not so surprisingly for print-formatted. Its corresponding input is `scanf`. File I/O is realized with `fprintf` and `fscanf`.

The advantage of these functions is that the formatting is quite compact; printing the first number in 6 characters with 2 decimal places and the second number in 14 characters with 9 decimal places is expressed by the following format string:

```
printf("The square of %6.2f is %14.9f\n", x, x*x);
```

The problem with the format strings is that they are not *Type-Safe*. If the argument does not match its format, strange things can happen, e.g.:

```
int i= 7;
printf("i is %s\n", i);
```

The argument is an `int` and will be printed as a C string. A C string is passed by a pointer to its first character. Thus, the 7 is interpreted as an address and in most cases the program crashes. More recent compilers check the format string if it is provided as a literal in the `printf` call. But the string can be set before:

```
int i= 7;
char s[]= "i is %s\n";
printf(s, i);
```

or be the result of string operations. In this case, the compiler will not warn us.

Another disadvantage is that it cannot be extended for user types. C-style I/O can be convenient in log-based debugging, but streams are much less prone to errors and should be preferred in high-quality production software.

C++11 ## A.2.9   **Garbarge Collection**

Garbage Collection (GC) is understood as the automatic release of unused memory. Several languages (e.g., Java) from time to time discharge memory that is not referred to in the program any longer. Memory handling in C++ is designed more explicitly: the programmer controls in one way or another when memory is released. Nonetheless, there is interest among C++ programmers in GC either to make software more reliable—especially when old leaky components are contained which nobody is willing or able to fix—or when interoperability to other languages with managed memory handling is desired. An example of the latter is *Managed C++* in .NET.

Given that interest, the standard (starting with C++11) defines an interface for garbage collectors. However, garbage collection is not a mandatory feature, and so far we do not know a compiler that supports it. In turn, applications relying on GC do not run with common compilers. Garbage collection should only be the last resort. Memory management should be primarily encapsulated in classes and tight to their creation and destruction, i.e., RAII (§2.4.2.1). If this is not feasible, one should consider `unique_ptr` (§1.8.3.1) and `shared_ptr` (§1.8.3.2) which automatically release memory that is not referred to. Actually, the reference counting by a `shared_ptr` is already a simple form of GC (although probably not everybody will agree with this definition). Only when all those techniques are non-viable due to some form of tricky cyclic dependencies, and portability is not an issue, should one resort to garbage collection.

A.2.10   Trouble with Macros

For instance, a function with the signature

```
double compute_something(double fnm1, double scr1*}, double scr2)
```

compiles on most compilers but yields a bizarre error message on Visual Studio. The reason is that `scr1` is a macro defining a hexadecimal number which is substituted for our second argument name. Obviously, this is not legal C++ code any longer, but the error will contain our original source before the substitution took place. Thus, we cannot see anything suspicious. The only way to resolve such problems is to run the preprocessor and check the expanded sources, e.g.:

```
g++ my_code.cpp -E -o my_code.ii.cpp
```

This might take some effort since the expanded version contains the sources of all directly and indirectly included files. Eventually, we will find what happened with the source code line rejected by the compiler:

```
double compute_something(double fnm1, double 0x0490, double scr2)
```

We can fix this simply by changing the argument name, once we know that it is used as a macro somewhere.

Constants used in computations should not be defined by macros:

```
#define pi 3.141592653589793238462643383279502884l // Do Not!!!
```

but as true constants:

```
const long double pi= 3.141592653589793238462643383279502884L;
```

Otherwise, we create exactly the kind of trouble that `scr1` caused in our preceding example. In C++11, we can also use `constexpr` to ascertain that the value is available during compilation, and C++14 also offers template constants.

Function-like macros offer yet a different spectrum of funny traps. The main problem is that macro arguments only behave like function arguments in simple use cases. For instance, when we write a macro `max_square`:

```
#define max_square(x, y) x*x >= y*y ? x*x : y*y
```

the implementation of the expression looks straightforward and we probably will not expect any trouble. But we will get into some when we use it with a sum or difference:

```
int max_result= max_square(a+b, a-b);
```

Then it will be evaluated as

```
int max_result= a+b*a+b >= a-b*a-b ? a+b*a+b : a-b*a-b;
```

yielding evidently wrong results. This problem can be fixed with some parentheses:

```
#define max_square(x, y) ((x)*(x) >= (y)*(y) ? (x)*(x) : (y)*(y))
```

To protect against high-priority operators, we also surrounded the entire expression with a pair of parentheses. Thus, macro expressions need parentheses around each argument and around the entire expression. Note that this is a necessary, not a sufficient, condition for correctness.

Another serious problem is the replication of arguments in expressions. If we call `max_square` as in

```
int max_result= max_square(++a, ++b);
```

the variables a and b are incremented four times.

Macros are a quite simple language feature, but implementing and using them is more complicated and dangerous than it seems at first glance. The hazard is that they interact with the entire program. Therefore, new software should not contain macros at all. Unfortunately, existing software already contains many of them and we have to deal with them.

Regrettably, there is no general cure for trouble with macros. Here are some tips that work in most cases:

- Avoid names of popular macros. Most prominently, `assert` is a macro in the standard library and giving that name to a function is asking for trouble.

- Un-define the macro with `#undef`.

- Include macro-heavy libraries after all others. Then the macros still pollute your application but not the other included header files.

- Impressively, some libraries offer protection against their own macros: one can define a macro that disables or renames macros' dangerously short names.[2]

A.3　Real-World Example: Matrix Inversion

> *"The difference between theory and practice is larger in practice than in theory."*
>
> —Tilmar König

To round up the basic features, we apply them to demonstrating how we can easily create new functionality. We want to give you an impression of how our ideas can evolve naturally into reliable and efficient C++ programs. Particular attention is paid to clarity and reusability. Our programs should be well-structured inside and intuitive to use from outside.

---

2. We have seen a library that defined a single underscore as a macro which created a lot of problems.

 To simplify the realization of our study case, we use (the open-source part of) the author's library *Matrix Template Library 4*—see `http://www.mtl4.org`. It already contains a lot of linear-algebra functionality that we need here.[3] We hope that future C++ standards will provide such functionality out of the box. Maybe some of the book's readers will contribute to it.

As a software development approach, we will use a principle from *Extreme Programming*: writing tests first and implementing the functionality afterward—known as *Test-Driven Development* (TDD). This has two significant advantages:

- It protects us as programmers (to some extent) from *Featurism*—the obsession to add more and more features instead of finishing one thing after another. If we write down what we want to achieve, we work more directly toward this goal and usually accomplish it much earlier. When writing the function call, we already specify the interface of the function that we plan to implement. When we set up expected values for the tests, we say something about the semantics of our function. Thus, *tests are compilable documentation*. The tests might not tell everything about the functions and classes we are going to implement, but what it says does it very precisely. Documentation in text can be much more detailed and comprehensible but also much vaguer than tests (and procrastinated eternally).

- If we start writing tests after we finally finish the implementation—say, on a late Friday afternoon—*we do not want to see it fail.* We will write the test with nice data (whatever this means for the program in question) and minimize the risk of failure. Or we might decide to go home and swear that we will test it on Monday.

For those reasons, we will be more honest if we write our tests first. Of course, we can modify our tests later if we realize that something does not work out as we imagined or we evolved the interface design out of the experience we gained so far. Or maybe we just want to test more. It goes without saying that verifying partial implementations requires commenting out parts of our test—temporarily.

Before we start implementing our inverse function and its tests, we have to choose an algorithm. We can choose among different direct solvers: determinants of sub-matrices, block algorithms, Gauß-Jordan, or LU decomposition with or without pivoting. Let's say we prefer LU factorization with column pivoting so that we have

$$LU = PA,$$

with a unit lower triangular matrix L, an upper triangular matrix U, and a permutation matrix P. Thus it is

$$A = P^{-1}LU$$

and

$$A^{-1} = U^{-1}L^{-1}P. \tag{A.1}$$

We use the LU factorization from MTL4, implement the inversion of the lower and upper triangular matrices, and compose it appropriately.

---

3. It actually already contains the inversion function `inv` we are going for, but let us pretend it does not.

⇒ c++11/inverse.cpp

Now, we start with our test by defining an invertible matrix and printing it out:

```
int main(int argc, char* argv[])
{
    const unsigned size= 3;
    using Matrix= mtl::dense2D<double>;   // type from MTL4
    Matrix    A(size, size);
    A=   4, 1, 2,
         1, 5, 3,
         2, 6, 9;

    cout << "A is:\n" << A;
```

For later abstraction, we define the type Matrix and the constant size. Using C++11, we could set up the matrix with uniform initialization:

```
Matrix    A= {{4, 1, 2}, {1, 5, 3}, {2, 6, 9}};
```

However, for our implementation we get along with C++03.

The LU factorization in MTL4 is performed in place. So as not to alter our original matrix, we copy it into a new one.

```
Matrix LU(A);
```

We also define a vector for the permutation computed in the factorization:

```
mtl::dense_vector<unsigned> Pv(size);
```

These are the two arguments for the LU factorization:

```
lu(LU, Pv);
```

For our purpose, it is more convenient to represent the permutation as a matrix:

```
Matrix P(permutation(Pv));
cout << "Permutation vector is " << Pv << "\nPermutation matrix is\n" << P;
```

This allows us to express the row permutation by a matrix product:[4]

```
cout << "Permuted A is \n" << Matrix(P * A);
```

We now define an identity matrix of appropriate size and extract L and U from our in-place factorization:

```
Matrix I(matrix::identity(size, size)), L(I + strict_lower(LU)),
       U(upper(LU));
```

Note that the unit diagonal of L is not stored and needs to be added for the test. It could also be treated implicitly, but we refrain from it for the sake of simplicity. We have now

---

4. You might wonder why a matrix is created from the product $P * A$ although the product is already a matrix. Well, it is not, technically. For efficiency reasons, it is an expression template (see Section 5.3) that evaluates the product in certain expressions. Output is not one of those expressions—at least not in the public version.

finished the preliminaries and come to our first test. Once we have computed the inverse of U, named UI, their product must be the identity matrix (approximately). Likewise for the inverse of L:

```
constexpr double eps= 0.1;

Matrix UI(inverse_upper(U));
cout ≪ "inverse(U) [permuted] is:\n" ≪ UI ≪ "UI * U
                                is:\n" ≪ Matrix(UI * U);
assert(one_norm(Matrix(UI * U - I)) < eps);
```

Testing results of non-trivial numeric calculation for equality is quite certain to fail. Therefore, we used the norm of the matrix difference as the criterion. Likewise, the inversion of L (with a different function) is tested.

```
Matrix LI(inverse_lower(L));
cout ≪ "inverse(L) [permuted] is:\n" ≪ LI ≪ "LI * L
                                is:\n" ≪ Matrix(LI * L);
assert(one_norm(Matrix(LI * L - I)) < eps);
```

This enables us to calculate the inverse of A itself and test its correctness:

```
Matrix AI(UI * LI * P);
cout ≪ "inverse(A) [UI * LI * P] is \n" ≪ AI ≪ "A * AI
                              is \n" ≪ Matrix(AI * A);
assert(one_norm(Matrix(AI * A - I)) < eps);
```

We also check our inverse function with the same criterion:

```
Matrix A_inverse(inverse(A));
cout ≪ "inverse(A) is \n" ≪ A_inverse ≪ "A * AI
                    is \n" ≪ Matrix(A_inverse * A);
assert(one_norm(Matrix(A_inverse * A - I)) < eps);
```

After establishing tests for all components of our calculation, we start with their implementations.

The first function that we program is the inversion of an upper triangular matrix. This function takes a dense matrix as an argument and returns a dense matrix as well:

```
Matrix inverse_upper(const Matrix& A) {

}
```

Since we do not need another copy of the input matrix, we pass it as a reference. The argument should not be changed so we can pass it as const. The constancy has several advantages:

- We improve the reliability of our program. Arguments passed as const are guaranteed not to change; if we accidentally modify them, the compiler will tell us and abort the compilation. There is a way to remove the constancy, but this should only be used as a last resort, e.g., for interfacing to obsolete libraries written by others. Everything you write yourself can be realized without eliminating the constancy of arguments.

- Compilers can better optimize when the objects are guaranteed not to be altered.

- In case of references, the function can be called with expressions. Non-const references are required to store the expression into a variable and pass the variable to the function.

Another comment: people might tell you that it is too expensive to return containers as results and it is more efficient to use references. This is true—in principle. For the moment, we accept this extra cost and pay more attention to clarity and convenience. Later in this book, we will introduce techniques for how to minimize the cost of returning containers from functions.

So much for the function signature; let us now turn our attention to the function body. The first thing we do is verify that our argument is valid. Obviously the matrix must be square:

```
const unsigned n= num_rows(A);
if (num_cols(A) != n)
    throw "Matrix must be square";
```

The number of rows is needed several times in this function and is therefore stored in a variable, well, constant. Another prerequisite is that the matrix has no zero entries in the diagonal. We leave this test to the triangular solver.

Speaking of which, we can get our inverse triangular matrix with a triangular solver of a linear system, which we find in MTL4; more precisely, the k-th vector of U^{-1} is the solution of

$$Ux = e_k$$

where e_k is the k-th unit vector. First we define a temporary variable for the result:

```
Matrix Inv(n, n);
```

Then we iterate over the columns of Inv:

```
for (unsigned k= 0; k < n; ++k) {

}
```

In each iteration we need the k-th unit vector:

```
dense_vector<double> e_k(n);
for (unsigned i= 0; i < n; ++i)
    if (i == k)
        e_k[i]= 1.0;
    else
        e_k[i]= 0.0;
```

The triangular solver returns a column vector. We could assign the entries of this vector directly to entries of the target matrix:

```
for (unsigned i= 0; i < n; ++i)
    Inv[i][k]= upper_trisolve(A, e_k)[i];
```

This is nice and short but we would compute upper_trisolve n *times!* Although we said that performance is not our primary goal at this point, the increase of overall complexity from order 3 to 4 is too wasteful of resources. Many programmers make the mistake of optimizing too early, but this does not mean that we should accept (without serious reasons) an implementation with a higher order of complexity. To avoid the superfluous recomputations, we store the triangle solver result and copy the entries from there.

```
dense_vector<double> res_k(n);
res_k= upper_trisolve(A, e_k);

for (unsigned i= 0; i < n; ++i)
    Inv[i][k]= res_k[i];
```

Finally, we return the temporary matrix. The function in its complete form looks as follows:

```
Matrix inverse_upper(Matrix const& A)
{
    const unsigned n= num_rows(A);
    assert(num_cols(A) == n); // Matrix must be square

    Matrix Inv(n, n);

    for (unsigned k= 0; k < n; ++k) {
        dense_vector<double> e_k(n);
        for (unsigned i= 0; i < n; ++i)
            if (i == k)
                e_k[i]= 1.0;
            else
                e_k[i]= 0.0;

    dense_vector<double> res_k(n);
    res_k= upper_trisolve(A, e_k);

    for (unsigned i= 0; i < n; ++i)
        Inv[i][k]= res_k[i];
    }
    return Inv;
}
```

Now that the function is complete, we first run our test. Evidently, we have to comment out part of the test because we have only implemented one function so far. Nonetheless, it is good to know early whether this first function behaves as expected. It does, and we could be happy with it now and turn our attention to the next task; there are still many. But we will not.

Well, at least we can be glad to have a function running correctly. Nevertheless, it is still worth spending some time to improve it. Such improvements are called *Refactoring*. Experience has shown that it takes much less time to refactor immediately after implementation than later when bugs are discovered or the software is ported to other platforms. Obviously, it is much easier to simplify and structure our software immediately when we still know what is going on than after some weeks/months/years.

The first thing we might dislike is that something so simple as the initialization of a unit vector takes five lines. This is rather verbose:

```
for (unsigned i= 0; i < n; ++i)
    if (i == k)
        e_k[i]= 1.0;
    else
        e_k[i]= 0.0;
```

We can write this more compactly with the conditional operator:

```
for (unsigned i= 0; i < n; ++i)
    e_k[i]= i == k ? 1.0 : 0.0;
```

The conditional operator ?: usually takes some time to get used to but it results in a more concise representation.

Although we have not changed anything semantically in the program and it seems obvious that the result will still be the same, it cannot hurt to run our test again. You will see that often you are sure that your program modifications could never change the behavior—but still they do. The sooner we find an unexpected behavior, the less work it is to fix it. With the test(s) that we have already written, it only takes a few seconds and makes us feel more confident.

If we would like to be really cool, we could explore some insider knowhow. The expression i == k returns a boolean, and we know that bool can be converted implicitly into int and subsequently to double. In this conversion, false turns into 0 and true into 1 according to the standard. These are precisely the values that we want as double:

```
e_k[i]= static_cast<double>(i == k);
```

In fact, the conversion from int to double is performed implicitly and can be omitted as well:

```
e_k[i]= i == k;
```

As cute as this looks, it is some stretch to assign a logical value to a floating-point number. It is well defined by the implicit conversion chain bool → int → double, but it will confuse potential readers and you might end up explaining to them what is happening on a mailing list or adding a comment to the program. In both cases you end up writing more text for the explication than you saved in the program.

Another thought that might occur to us is that it is probably not the last time that we need a unit vector. So, why not write a function for it?

```
dense_vector<double> unit_vector(unsigned k, unsigned n)
{
    dense_vector<double> e_k(n, 0.0);
    e_k[k]= 1;
    return e_k;
}
```

Since the function returns the unit vector, we can just take it as an argument for the triangular solver:

```
res_k= upper_trisolve(A, unit_vector(k, n));
```

For a dense matrix, MTL4 allows us to access a matrix column as a column vector (instead of a sub-matrix). Then, we can assign the result vector directly without a loop:

```
Inv[irange(0, n)][k]= res_k;
```

As a short explanation, the bracket operator is implemented in such a manner that integer indices for rows and columns return the matrix entry while ranges for rows and columns return a sub-matrix. Likewise, a range of rows and a single column gives us a column of the corresponding matrix—or part of this column. Conversely, a row vector can be extracted from a matrix with an integer as a row index and a range for the columns.

This is an interesting example of how to deal with the limitations as well as the possibilities of C++. Other languages have ranges as part of their intrinsic notation; e.g., Python has a symbol : for expressing ranges of indices. C++ does not provide such a symbol, but we can introduce a new type—like MTL4's `irange`—and define the behavior of `operator[]` for this type. This leads to an extremely powerful mechanism!

Extending Operator Functionality

Since we cannot introduce new operators into C++, we define new types and give operators the desired behavior when applied to those types. This technique allows us to provide a very broad functionality with a limited number of operators.

The operator semantics on user types must be intuitive and must be consistent with the operator priority (see an example in §1.3.10).

Back to our algorithm. We store the result of the solver in a vector and then we assign it to a matrix column. In fact, we can assign the triangular solver's result directly:

```
Inv[irange(0, n)][k]= upper_trisolve(A, unit_vector(k, n));
```

The range of all indices is predefined as `iall`:

```
Inv[iall][k]= upper_trisolve(A, unit_vector(k, n));
```

Next, we explore some mathematical background. The inverse of an upper triangular matrix is also upper triangular. Thus, we only need to compute the upper part of the result and set the remainder to 0—or the whole matrix to zero before computing the upper part. Of course, we need smaller unit vectors now and only sub-matrices of A. This can be nicely expressed with ranges:

```
Inv= 0;
for (unsigned k= 0; k < n; ++k)
    Inv[irange(0, k+1)][k]=
        upper_trisolve(A[irange(0, k+1)][irange(0, k+1)],
                       unit_vector(k, k+1));
```

Admittedly, the `irange` makes the expression hard to read. Although it looks like a function, `irange` is a type, and we just created objects on the fly and passed them to the `operator[]`. As we use the same range three times, it is shorter to create a variable (or a constant) for it:

```
for (unsigned k= 0; k < n; ++k) {
    const irange r(0, k+1);
    Inv[r][k]= upper_trisolve(A[r][r], unit_vector(k, k+1));
}
```

This not only makes the second line shorter, it is also easier to see that this is the same range every time.

Another observation: after shortening the unit vectors, they all have the 1 in the last entry. Thus, we only need the size of the vector and the position of the 1 is implied:

```
dense_vector<double> last_unit_vector(unsigned n)
{
    dense_vector<double> v(n, 0.0);
    v[n-1]= 1;
    return v;
}
```

We choose a different name to reflect the different meaning. Nonetheless, we wonder if we really want such a function. What is the probability that we will need this again? Charles H. Moore, the creator of the programming language Forth, once said that "the purpose of functions is not to hash a program into tiny pieces but to create highly reusable entities." All this said, we prefer the more general function that is much more likely to be useful later.

After all these modifications, we are now satisfied with the implementation and go to the next function. We still might change something at a later point in time, but having it made clearer and better structured will make the later modification much easier for us (or somebody else). The more experience we gain, the fewer steps we will need to achieve the implementation that makes us happy. And it goes without saying that we tested the inverse_upper repeatedly while modifying it.

Now that we know how to invert triangular matrices, we can do the same for the lower triangular. Alternatively we can just transpose the input and output:

```
Matrix inverse_lower(Matrix const& A)
{
    Matrix T(trans(A));
    return Matrix(trans(inverse_upper(T)));
}
```

Ideally, this implementation would look like this:

```
Matrix inverse_lower(Matrix const& A)
{
    return trans(inverse_upper(trans(T)));
}
```

The explicit creation of the two Matrix objects is a technical artifact.[5] With future C++ standards or later versions of MTL4, we will certainly not need this artifact any longer.

Somebody may argue that the transpositions and copies are more expensive. In addition, we know that the lower matrix has a unit diagonal and we did not explore this property, e.g., for avoiding the divisions in the triangular solver. We could even ignore or omit the diagonal and treat this implicitly in the algorithms. This is all true. However, we prioritized here the simplicity and clarity of the implementation and the reusability aspect over performance.[6]

We now have everything to put the matrix inversion together. As above, we start with checking the squareness:

---

5. To turn a lazy into an eager evaluation, see §5.3.
6. People who really care about performance do not use matrix inversion in the first place.

```
Matrix inverse(Matrix const& A)
{
    const unsigned n= num_rows(A);
    assert(num_cols(A) == n); // Matrix must be square
```

Then, we perform the LU factorization. For performance reasons this function does not return the result but takes its arguments as mutable references and factorizes in place. Thus, we need a copy of the matrix and a permutation vector of appropriate size:

```
Matrix                      PLU(A);
dense_vector<unsigned>      Pv(n);

lu(PLU, Pv);
```

The upper triangular factor PU of the permuted A is stored in the upper triangle of PLU. The lower triangular factor PL is (partly) stored in the strict lower triangle of PLU. The unit diagonal is omitted and implicitly treated in the algorithm. We therefore need to add the diagonal before inversion (or alternatively handle the unit diagonal implicitly in the inversion).

```
Matrix  PU(upper(PLU)), PL(strict_lower(PLU) + matrix::identity(n, n));
```

The inversion of a square matrix according to Eq. (A.1) can then be performed in one single line:[7]

```
return Matrix(inverse_upper(PU) * inverse_lower(PL) * permutation(Pv));
```

In this section, we have seen that most of the time we have alternatives for how to implement the same behavior—most likely you have had this experience before. Despite our possibly giving the impression that every choice we made is the most appropriate, there is not always THE single best solution, and even while trading off pros and cons of the alternatives, one might not come to a final conclusion and just pick one. We also illustrated that the choices depend on the goals; for instance, the implementation would look different if performance was the primary goal.

This section showed as well that that non-trivial programs are not written in a single sweep by an ingenious mind—exceptions might prove the rule—but are the result of a gradually improving development. Experience will make this journey shorter and more direct, but we will not write the perfect program at the first go.

A.4   Class Details

A.4.1   Pointer to Member

Pointers to Members are class-local pointers that can store the address of a member relative to the class:

```
double complex::* member_selector= &complex::i;
```

---

7. The explicit conversion can probably be omitted in later versions of MTL4.

The variable member_selector has the type double complex::*, a pointer to a double within the class complex. It refers to the member i (which is public in this example).

With the operator .* we can access the member i of any complex object and likewise with ->* that member for a pointer to complex:

```
double complex::* member_selector= &complex::i;

complex c(7.0, 8.0), c2(9.0);
complex *p= &c;

cout << "c's selected member is " << c.*member_selector << '\n';
cout << "p's selected member is " << p->*member_selector << '\n';

member_selector = &complex::r; // focus on another member
p= &c2;                        // point to another complex

cout << "c's selected member is " << c.*member_selector << '\n';
cout << "p's selected member is " << p->*member_selector << '\n';
```

Class-related pointers can also be used to choose a function out of a class's methods during run time.

A.4.2   More Initialization Examples

An initializer list can end with a trailing , to distinguish it from a listing of arguments. In the example above, it did not change the interpretation of the argument list. Here are some more combinations of wrapping and listing:

```
vector_complex v1= {2};
vector_complex v1d= {{2}};

vector_complex v2= {2, 3};
vector_complex v2d= {{2, 3}};
vector_complex v2dc= {{2, 3}, };
vector_complex v2cd= {{2, 3, }};
vector_complex v2w= {{2}, {3}};
vector_complex v2c= {{2, 3, }};
vector_complex v2dw= {{{2}, {3}}};

vector_complex v3= {2, 3, 4};
vector_complex v3d= {{2, 3, 4}};
vector_complex v3dc= {{2, 3}, 4};
```

The resulting vectors are

```
v1 is [(2,0)]
v1d is [(2,0)]

v2 is [(2,0), (3,0)]
v2d is [(2,3)]
v2dc is [(2,3)]
v2cd is [(2,3)]
```

```
v2w is [(2,0), (3,0)]
v2c is [(2,3)]
v2dw is [(2,3)]

v3 is [(2,0), (3,0), (4,0)]
v3d is [(2,0), (3,0), (4,0)]
v3dc is [(2,3), (4,0)]
```

All this said, we have to pay attention that the initialization of nested data is really performed as we intended. It is also worthwhile to reflect on the most comprehensible notation, especially when we share our sources with other people.

Uniform initialization favors constructors for `initializer_list<>`, and many other constructors are hidden in the brace notation. As a consequence, we cannot replace all parentheses with braces in constructors and expect the same behavior:

```
vector_complex v1(7);
vector_complex v2{7};
```

The first vector has seven entries with value 0 and the second vector one entry with value 7.

A.4.3 Accessing Multi-dimensional Arrays

Let us assume that we have a simple class like the following:

```
class matrix
{
  public:
    matrix(int nrows, int ncols)
      : nrows(nrows), ncols(ncols), data( new double[nrows * ncols] ) {}

    matrix(const matrix& that)
      : nrows(that.nrows), ncols(that.ncols),
        data(new double[nrows * ncols])
    {
    for (int i= 0, size= nrows*ncols; i < size; ++i)
        data[i]= that.data[i];
    }

    void operator=(const matrix& that)
    {
        assert(nrows == that.nrows && ncols == that.ncols);
        for (int i= 0, size= nrows*ncols; i < size; ++i)
            data[i]= that.data[i];
    }

    int num_rows() const { return nrows; }
    int num_cols() const { return ncols; }

  private:
    int                 nrows, ncols;
    unique_ptr<double>  data;
};
```

So far, the implementation is done in the same manner as before: variables are private, the constructors establish defined values for all members, the copy constructor and the assignment are consistent, size information is provided by a constant function.

What we are missing is access to the matrix entries.

Be Aware!
The bracket operator accepts only one argument.

That means we cannot define

```
double& operator[](int r, int c) { ... }
```

A.4.3.1   Approach 1: Parentheses

The simplest way to handle multiple indices is replacing the square brackets with parentheses:

```
double& operator()(int r, int c)
{
    return data[r*ncols + c];
}
```

Adding range checking—in a separate function for better reuse—can save us a lot of debug time in the future. We also implement the constant access:

```
private:
  void check(int r, int c) const { assert(0 <= r && r < nrows &&
                                          0 <= c && c <= ncols); }
public:
  double& operator()(int r, int c)
  {
      check(r, c);
      return data[r*ncols + c];
  }
  const double& operator()(int r, int c) const
  {
      check(r, c);
      return data[r*ncols + c];
  }
```

The access of matrix entries is accordingly denoted with parentheses:

```
matrix         A(2, 3), B(3, 2);
// ... setting B
// A= trans(B);
for (int r= 0; r < A.num_rows(); r++)
    for (int c= 0; c < A.num_cols(); c++)
        A(r, c)= B(c, r);
```

This works well, but the parentheses look more like function calls than access to matrix elements. Maybe we can find another way of using brackets if we try harder.

A.4.3.2 Approach 2: Returning Pointers

We mentioned that we cannot pass two arguments in one bracket, but we could pass them in two brackets, e.g.:

```
A[0][1];
```

This is also how two-dimensional built-in arrays are accessed in C++. For our dense `matrix`, we can return the pointer to the first entry in row `r` and when the second bracket with the column argument is applied on this pointer C++ will perform the address calculation:

```
double* operator[](int r) { return data + r*ncols; }
const double* operator[](int r) const { return data + r*ncols; }
```

This method has several disadvantages. First, it only works for dense matrices that are stored row-wise. Second, there is no possibility of verifying the range of the column index.

A.4.3.3 Approach 3: Returning Proxies

Instead of returning a pointer, we can build a specific type that keeps a reference to the matrix and the row index and that provides an `operator[]` for accessing matrix entries. Such helpers are called *Proxies*. A proxy must be therefore a friend of the matrix class to reach its private data. Alternatively, we can keep the operator with the parentheses and call this one from the proxy. In both cases, we encounter cyclic dependencies.

If we have several matrix types, each of them would need its own proxy. We would also need different proxies for constant and mutable access respectively. In Section 6.6, we showed how to write a proxy that works for all matrix types. The same templated proxy will handle constant and mutable access. Fortunately, it even solves the problem of mutual dependencies. The only minor flaw is that eventual errors cause lengthy compiler messages.

A.4.3.4 Comparing the Approaches

The previous implementations show that C++ allows us to provide different notations for user-defined types, and we can implement them in the manner that seems most appropriate to us. The first approach was replacing square brackets with parentheses to enable multiple arguments. This was the simplest solution, and if one is willing to accept this syntax, one can save oneself the effort of coming up with a fancier notation. The technique of returning a pointer is not complicated either, but it relies too strongly on the internal representation. If we use some internal blocking or some other specialized internal storage scheme, we will need an entirely different technique. For that reason, it always helps to encapsulate the technical details and to provide a sufficiently abstract interface for the user. Then our applications do not depend on technical details. Another drawback is that we cannot test the range of the column index.

A.5 Method Generation

C++ has six methods (four in C++03) with a default behavior:

- Default constructor
- Copy constructor

- Move constructor (C++11 or higher)

- Copy assignment

- Move assignment (C++11 or higher)

- Destructor

The code for these can be generated by the compiler—saving us from boring routine work and thus preventing oversights.

Shortcut: If you want to ignore the technical details (for the moment) and prefer to play by the rules, you can go directly to the design guides in Section A.5.3 with a stopover in Section A.5.1.

Assume that our class declares several member variables like this:

```
class my_class
{
    type1   var1;
    type2   var2;
    // ...
    typen   varn;
};
```

Then the compiler adds the six before-mentioned operations (as far as the member types allow) and our class behaves as if we had written:

```
class my_class
{
  public:
    my_class()
       : var1(),
         var2(),
         // ...
         varn()
    {}

    my_class(const my_class& that)
       : var1(that.var1),
         var2(that.var2),
         //...
         varn(that.varn)
    {}

    my_class(my_class&& that)                          // C++11
       : var1(std::move(that.var1)),
         var2(std::move(that.var2)),
         //...
         varn(std::move(that.varn))
    {}

    my_class& operator=(const my_class& that)
```

```
        {
            var1= that.var1;
            var2= that.var2;
            // ...
            varn= that.varn;
            return *this;
        }

        my_class& operator=(my_class&& that)          // C++11
        {
            var1= std::move(that.var1);
            var2= std::move(that.var2);
            // ...
            varn= std::move(that.varn);
            return *this;
        }

        ~my_class()
        {
            varn.~typen();                             // member destructor
            // ...
            var2.~type2();
            var1.~type1();
        }

    private:
        type1   var1;
        type2   var2;
        // ...
        typen   varn;
};
```

The generation is straightforward. The six operations are respectively called on each member variable. The careful reader will have realized that the constructors and the assignment are performed in the order of variable declaration. The destructors are called in reverse order to correctly handle members that depend on other members constructed earlier.

A.5.1   Controlling the Generation   C++11

C++11 provides two declarators to control which of these special methods are generated: default and delete. The names are self-explanatory: default causes a generation in a default fashion as we have shown before, and delete suppresses the generation of the marked method. Say, for instance, we want to write a class whose objects can only be moved but not copied:

```
class move_only
{
  public:
    move_only() = default;
    move_only(const move_only&) = delete;
    move_only(move_only&&) = default;
    move_only& operator=(const move_only&) = delete;
```

```
      move_only& operator=(move_only&&) = default;
      ~move_only() = default;
      // ...
  };
```

unique_ptr is implemented in this style to prevent two unique_ptr objects from referring to
the same memory.

Remark A.1. *Explicitly declaring that an operation will be generated in the* default *way is
considered a user-declared implementation. Likewise, a declaration to* delete *an operation.
As a consequence, other operations may not be generated and the class may surprise us with
unexpected behavior. The safest way to prevent such surprises is to declare all or none of
these six operations explicitly.*

> **Definition 1–1.** For the sake of distinction, we use the term *Purely User-Declared*
> for operations declared with a default or delete and *User-Implemented* for operations
> with an actual, possibly empty, implementation block. Operations that are either purely
> user-declared or user-implemented are called *User-Declared* as in the standard.

A.5.2   Generation Rules

To understand implicit generation, we have to understand several rules. We will walk through
them step by step.

For illustration purposes, we will use a class called tray:

```
class tray
{
  public:
    tray(unsigned s= 0) : v(s) {}
    std::vector<float>  v;
    std::set<int>       s;
    // ..
};
```

which is modified for each demonstration.

A.5.2.1   Rule 1: Generate What the Members and Bases Allow

We said before that C++ generates all special methods as long as we do not declare any of
them. If one of the generatable methods does not exist in

- One of the member types,

- One of the direct base classes (Section 6.1.1), and

- One of the virtual base classes (Section 6.3.2.2),

it is not generated in the class in question. In other words, the generated methods are the
intersection of those available in their members and base classes.

For instance, if we declare a member of the before-defined `move_only` class in `tray`:

```
class tray
{
  public:
    tray(unsigned s= 0) : v(s) {}
    std::vector<float>  v;
    std::set<int>       s;
    move_only           mo;
};
```

its objects can no longer be copied and copy-assigned. Of course, we are not obliged to rely on the generated copy constructor and assignment; we can write our own.

The rule applies recursively: a method deleted in some type implicitly deletes this method in all classes where it is contained and everywhere those classes are contained and so on. For instance, in the absence of user-defined copy operations, a class `bucket` containing `tray` cannot be copied; neither can a class `barrel` containing `bucket`, or a class `truck` containing `barrel`, and so on.

A.5.2.2   Difficult Member Types

Types not providing all six generatable methods can create problems when they are used as member types. The most prominent examples are:

- References are not default-constructible. Thus, every class with a reference has no default constructor unless the user implements one. This in turn is difficult too because the referred address cannot be set later. The easiest work-around is using a pointer internally and providing a reference externally. Unfortunately, the default constructor is needed quite often, e.g., for creating containers of the type.

- `unique_ptr` is neither copy-constructible nor copy-assignable. If the class needs one of the copy operations, we have to use another pointer type, e.g., a raw pointer, and live with all its risks, or a `shared_pointer` and accept the performance overhead.

C++11

A.5.2.3   Rule 2: Destructors Are Generated Unless the User Does

This is certainly the simplest rule: either the programmer writes a destructor or the compiler does. Since all types must provide a destructor, Rule 1 is irrelevant here.

A.5.2.4   Rule 3: Default Constructors Are Generated Alone

The default constructor is the shyest operation when it comes to implicit generation. As soon as *any* other constructor is defined, the default constructor is not generated any longer, e.g.:

```
struct no_default1
{
    no_default1(int) {}
};

struct no_default2
```

```
{
    no_default2(const no_default2&) = default;
};
```

Both classes will not contain a default constructor. In combination with Rule 1, this implies, for instance, that the following class cannot be compiled:

```
struct a
{
    a(int i) : i(i) {}    // Error

    no_default1  x;
    int          i;
};
```

The member variable x does not appear in the initialization list and the default constructor of no_default1 is called. Or the call is made unsuccessfully.

    The motivation for omitting an implicit default constructor in the presence of any other user-defined constructor is that the other constructors are assumed to initialize member data explicitly whereas many default constructors—especially for intrinsic types—leave the members uninitialized. To avoid member data accidentally containing random garbage, the default constructor must be defined or explicitly declared as default when other constructors exist.

A.5.2.5   Rule 4: When Copy Operations Are Generated

For the sake of conciseness, we use the C++11 declarators default and delete. The examples behave in the same manner when we write out the default implementations. A copy constructor and a copy assignment operator are

- Not generated implicitly when a user-defined move operation exists;

- Generated implicitly (still) when the respective other is user-defined;

- Generated implicitly (still) when the destructor is user-defined.

In addition, a copy assignment is

- Not generated implicitly when a non-static member is a reference;

- Not generated implicitly when a non-static member is a const.

Any move operation immediately disables both copy operations:

```
class tray
{
  public:
    // tray(const tray&) = delete;    // implied
    tray(tray&&) = default;           // considered user-defined
    // tray& operator=(const tray&) = delete; // implied
    // ...
};
```

The implicit generation of one copy operation in the presence of its counterpart is branded
as deprecated in C++11 and C++14 but willingly provided by compilers (usually without
protest):

```
class tray
{
  public:
    tray(const tray&) = default; // considered user-defined
    // tray& operator=(const tray&) = default; // deprecated
    // ...
};
```

Likewise, when the destructor is user-defined, the generation of copy operations is deprecated
but still supported.

A.5.2.6   Rule 5: How Copy Operations Are Generated

The copy operations take constant references as arguments, under normal conditions. It is
allowed to implement copy operations with mutable references, and we discuss this here for
completeness' sake rather than for practical relevance (and as kind of a warning example). If
any of a class's members requires a mutable reference in a copy operation, the generated
operation also requires a mutable reference:

```
struct mutable_copy
{
    mutable_copy() = default;
    mutable_copy(mutable_copy& ) {}
    mutable_copy(mutable_copy&& ) = default;
    mutable_copy& operator=(const mutable_copy& ) = default;
    mutable_copy& operator=(mutable_copy&& ) = default;
};

class tray
{
  public:
    // tray(tray&) = default;
    // tray(tray&&) = default;
    // tray& operator=(const tray&) = default;
    // tray& operator=(tray&&) = default;
    mutable_copy     m;
    // ...
};
```

The class `mutable_copy` only accepts mutable references in its copy constructor. Therefore,
that of `tray` also requires a mutable reference. In the case that the compiler generates it, it
will be non-const. An explicitly declared copy constructor with a `const` reference:

```
class tray
{
    tray(const tray&) = default;
```

```
    mutable_copy      m;
    // ...
};
```

would be rejected.

In contrast to the constructor, the copy assignments in our example accept a constant reference. Although this is legal C++ code, it is very bad practice: related constructors and assignments should be consistent in their argument types and semantics—everything else leads to unnecessary confusion and sooner or later to bugs. There might be reasons for using mutable references in copy operations (probably to cope with bad design decisions in other places), but we can run into strange effects that distract us from our main tasks. Before using such a feature it is really worth the time to search for a better solution.

C++11 A.5.2.7 Rule 6: When Move Operations Are Generated

A move constructor and a move assignment operator are not generated implicitly when

- A user-defined copy operation exists;

- The other move operation is user-defined;

- The destructor is user-defined.

In addition to the preceding rules, a move assignment is not generated implicitly when

- A non-static member is a reference;

- A non-static member is a const.

Please note that these rules are more rigid than for copy operations: here the operations are always deleted, not just considered deprecated in some cases. As often happens in computer science when things do not match perfectly, the reasons for this are historical. The rules of the copy operations are legacies of C++03 and were kept for backward compatibility. The rules for the move operations are newer and reflect the design guides from the next section.

As an example for the rules above, the definition of the copy constructor deletes both move operations:

```
class tray
{
  public:
    tray(const tray&) = default;
    // tray(tray&&) = delete; // implicit
    // tray& operator=(tray&&) = delete; // implicit
    // ...
};
```

Since the implicit generation is disabled for many reasons, it is advisable to declare the move operation as the default when it is needed.

A.5.3   Pitfalls and Design Guides

In the previous section, we saw the rules of the standard which are a compromise of legacy and the aim for correct class behavior. When we design new classes, we are free not to concede to obsolete dangerous practices. This is expressed by the following rules.

A.5.3.1   Rule of Five

The motivation for this rule is user-managed resources. They are the main reason that users implement copy and move operations and destructors. For instance, when we use classic pointers, the automatically generated copy/move does not copy/move the data and the destructor does not release the memory. So, for correct behavior we have to implement all or none of the following:

- Copy constructor,

- Move constructor,

- Copy assignment,

- Move assignment, and

- Destructor.

The same applies to C-style file handles and other manually managed resources.

When we write an implementation for one of the five operations, we are usually managing resources, and it is very likely that we need to implement the other four as well for correct behavior. In cases where one or more operations have default behavior or will not be used, it is better to declare this explicitly with `default` and `delete` than to rely on the preceding rules. In short:

Rule of Five
Declare all five of the operations above or none of them.

A.5.3.2   Rule of Zero

In the previous section, we illustrated that resource management is the primary reason for user-implemented operations. In C++11, we can replace classic pointers with `unique_ptr` or `shared_ptr` and leave the resource management to these smart pointers. In the same manner, we do not need to close files if we use file streams instead of obsolete file handles. In other words, if we rely on RAII for all our members, the compiler generates the appropriate operations for us.

Rule of Zero
Do not implement any of the five operations above.

Please note that this rule forbids the implementation and not the declaration as `default` or `delete`. There might be cases where the standard library does not provide a class that manages the resource we are interested in. Then we do ourselves a favor when we write a small set of classes that manage the resources as discussed in Section 2.4.2.4 and all high-level classes use those resource managers, and the default behavior of the five operations in the high-level classes is well defined.

A.5.3.3   Explicit versus Implicit Deletion

Please compare the following two variations of an otherwise identical class implementation:

```
class tray
{
  public:
    tray(const tray&) = default;
    // tray(tray&&) = delete;                // implied
    tray& operator=(const tray&) = default;
    // tray& operator=(tray&&) = delete;    // implied
    // ..
};
```

versus

```
class tray
{
  public:
    tray(const tray&) = default;
    tray(tray&&) = delete;
    tray& operator=(const tray&) = default;
    tray& operator=(tray&&) = delete;
    // ..
};
```

In both cases, the copy operations have default behavior while the move operations are deleted. They should therefore behave equally. But they do not in C++11 when an rvalue is passed:

```
tray b(std::move(a));
c= std::move(b);
```

The first variant of `tray` compiles with the snippet above. However, the values are actually not moved but copied. The second variant of `tray` yields a compiler error saying that the move operations are explicitly deleted. The reason for this discrepancy is that the explicitly deleted operations are considered in the overload resolution where they are better matches than the copy operations. In a later compile phase, it will be detected that they cannot be used. Implicitly deleted operations do not exist at all during the overload resolution and the copy operations are the best matches.

Fortunately, this inconsistency disappears in C++14 since explicitly deleted move operations are not considered in the overload resolution either. Thus, copy-only classes will not be possible any longer and every class that cannot be moved will be copied implicitly.

In the meantime, we can help ourselves by defining move operations that call the corresponding copy operations explicitly:

Listing A–3: Implement move by copy explicitly

```cpp
class tray
{
  public:
    tray(const tray&) = default;
    // move constructor actually copies
    tray(tray&& that) : tray(that) {}
    tray& operator=(const tray&) = default;
    // move assignment actually copies
    tray& operator=(tray&& that) { return *this= that; }
    // ...
};
```

The move constructor and assignment receive the rvalue that which in turn is an lvalue within the methods (having a name). Passing this lvalue to a constructor or assignment calls the copy constructor and assignment respectively. Explaining this silent transformation of the rvalue into an lvalue in a comment does not manifest missing C++ expertise. It can also stop somebody else from adding an alleged missing std::move (which can lead to ugly crashes).

A.5.3.4 Rule of Six: Be Explicit

The preceding examples demonstrated that the implicit generation of the fundamental operations:

- Default constructor,

- Copy constructor,

- Move constructor,

- Copy assignment,

- Move assignment, and

- Destructor.

depends on the interplay of several rules. To find out which of these six operations are actually generated, the source code of all members and direct and virtual base classes must be inspected—especially annoying when those classes are from third-party libraries. Sooner or later, we will find out but this time is just wasted.

We therefore suggest for frequently used classes with non-trivial content:

Rule of Six

Regarding the six operations above, implement as little as possible and declare as much as possible. Any operation not implemented should be declared as default or delete.

To delete the move operations explicitly, we can use the declarators and limit ourselves to C++14 or use the short implementation from Listing A–3. In contrast to the other design guides, we include the default constructor here since its implicit generation also depends on members and base classes (Rule 1 in §A.5.2.1).

We could drop the destructor from the list since every destructor that is not implemented will be generated as `default` as every class needs a destructor. However, long class definitions would need to be read entirely to ascertain that no user-implemented destructor exists. Scott Meyers proposed the quite similar *Rule of Five Defaults* saying the five default-generated constructors and assignments should not be omitted in the class definition but declared as `default` [31].

A.6   Template Details

C++11 ### A.6.1   Uniform Initialization

In Section 2.3.4, we introduced uniform initialization. This technique can be used in function templates as well. However, the brace elimination is now dependent on the type parameter. That is, the number of eliminated braces can vary from instantiation to instantiation. This simplifies many implementations but it can lead to surprising or unintended behavior in some situations. This phenomenon can be observed in pretty simple functions.

Malte Skarupke demonstrated in his blog [39] that something so simple as the following `copy` function can fail:

```
template<typename T>
inline T copy(const T& to_copy)
{
    return T{ to_copy };
}
```

The function works with almost every copy-constructible type. Exceptions are containers of `boost::any`, e.g., `std::vector<boost::any>`. `boost::any` is a utility class for storing objects of copy-constructible classes by type erasure. Since `boost::any` can store (almost) anything, it can also store `std::vector<boost::any>`, and the result of the `copy` operation is a vector that contains the original vector as a single element.

A.6.2   Which Function Is Called?

Thinking about all the possibilities in C++ of overloading functions multiple times in multiple namespaces, everybody will ask himself/herself sooner or later: "How can I know which one is finally called?" Well, we can run the program in a debugger. But as scientists, we want to understand what is going on. To this end, we have to consider multiple concepts in C++:

- Namespaces,

- Name hiding,

- Argument-dependent lookup, and

- Overload resolution.

Let us jump into it and start with a challenging example. For conciseness, we choose short names: c1 and c2 for the namespaces containing a class and f1 and f2 containing the calling function:

```
namespace c1 {
    namespace c2 {
        struct cc {};
        void f(const cc& o) {}
    } // namespace c2
    void f(const c2::cc& o) {}
} // namespace c1

void f(const c1::c2::cc& o) {}

namespace f1 {
    void f(const c1::c2::cc& o) {}
    namespace f2 {
        void f(const c1::c2::cc& o) {}
        void g()
        {
            c1::c2::cc o;
            f(o);
        }
    } // namespace f2
} // namespace f1
```

Now the evil question: Which f is called in f1::f2::g? Let us look at each overload first:

- c1::c2::f: is a candidate by ADL;

- c1::f: is no candidate as ADL does not consider outer namespaces;

- f: in the outer namespace of g but hidden by f1::f2::f;

- f1::f: same as f; and

- f1::f2::f: a candidate because it is in the same namespace as f1::f2::g.

At least, we could rule out three of five overloads and have only c1::c2::f and f1::f2::f left. There remains the question which overload is prioritized. The answer is none; the program is ambiguous.

Now we can entertain ourselves with subsets of the five overloads. First, we could drop c1::f; it did not matter anyway. What would happen if we also omitted c1::c2::f? Then the situation would be clear: f1::f2::f would be called. What if we kept c1::c2::f and removed f1::f2::f? The situation would be ambiguous: between c1::c2::f and c1::f which would be visible now?

So far, all overloads have the same argument type. Let us consider the scenario where the global f takes a non-const reference:

```
void f(c1::c2::cc& o) {}

namespace f1 {
    void f(const c1::c2::cc& o) {}
    namespace f2 {
```

```
            void f(const c1::c2::cc& o) {}
            void g()
            {
                c1::c2::cc o;
                f(o);
            }
        } // namespace f2
    } // namespace f1
```

Regarding overload resolution, the global f is the best match. However, it is still hidden by f1::f2::f despite the different signatures. In fact, everything (class, namespace) named f would hide the function f.

Name Hiding

Any item (function, class, typedef) from an outer namespace is invisible whenever the same name is used in an inner namespace—even for something entirely different.

To make the global f visible for g, we can apply a using declaration:

```
void f(c1::c2::cc& o) {}

namespace f1 {
    void f(const c1::c2::cc& o) {}
    namespace f2 {
        void f(const c1::c2::cc& o) {}
        using ::f;
        void g()
        {
            c1::c2::cc o;
            f(o);
        }
    } // namespace f2
} // namespace f1
```

Now, the functions in c1::c2 and the global namespace are both visible for g; and the global f is the better match due to the mutable reference.

Is the following situation unambiguous? And if so, which overloads of f would be selected?

```
namespace c1 {
    namespace c2 {
        struct cc {};
        void f(cc& o) {}                    // #1
    } // namespace c2
} // namespace c1

void f(c1::c2::cc& o) {}

namespace f1 {
    namespace f2 {
        void f(const c1::c2::cc& o) {} // #2
```

```
        void g()
        {
            c1::c2::cc o;
            const c1::c2::cc c(o);
            f(o);
            f(c);
        }
        void f(c1::c2::cc& o) {}          // #3
    } // namespace f2
} // namespace f1
```

For the const object c, only overload #2 is admissible and that one is visible. Fine, case closed. For the mutable object o, we need a closer look. The last overload of f (#3) is defined after g and therefore not visible in g. The global function f is hidden by #2. Thus remain #1 and #2 of which the former is the better match (no implicit conversion to const).

Summarizing, the general strategy for determining which function overload is called consists of three steps:

1. Find all overloads defined before the call

   - In the namespace of the caller;
   - In its parent namespaces;
   - In the namespace of the arguments (ADL);
   - In imported namespaces (using directive); and
   - By imported names (using declaration).

   If this set is empty, the program will not compile.

2. Eliminate the hidden overloads.

3. Select the best match among the available overloads. If this is ambiguous, the program will not compile.

The examples in this sub-section were certainly somewhat tiresome, but as Monk would say: "You will thank me later." The good news is: in your future programmer's life it will rarely be as bad as our made-up examples.

A.6.3 Specializing for Specific Hardware

Speaking of platform-specific assembler hacks, maybe we are eager to contribute code that explores SSE units by performing two computations in parallel. This might look like the following:

```
template <typename Base, typename Exponent>
Base inline power(const Base& x, const Exponent) { ... }

#ifdef SSE_FOR_TRYPTICHON_WQ_OMICRON_LXXXVI_SUPPORTED
std::pair<double> inline power(std::pair<double> x, double y)
{
    asm ("
#       Yo, I'm the greatestest geek under the sun!
```

```
        movapd xmm6, x
        ...
    ")
    return whatever;
}
#endif

#ifdef ... more hacks ...
```

What is there to say about this code snippet? If you do not like to write such a specialization (which technically is an overload), we do not blame you. But if we do so, *we must put such hacks into conditional compilation.* We have to make sure as well that our build system only enables the macro when it is definitely a platform that supports the assembler code. For the case that it does not, we must guarantee that the generic implementation or another overload can deal with pairs of double. Otherwise, we could not call the specialized implementation in portable applications.

Standard C++ allows us to insert assembler code in our program. It looks as if we called a function named asm with a string literal as argument. The content of that string, i.e., the assembler code, is of course platform-dependent.

The usage of assembler in scientific applications should be well thought out. In most cases, the benefit will not justify the effort and the disadvantages. Testing the correctness and even the compatibility can be much more laborious and error-prone. The author had such an experience with a C++ library that worked smoothly on Linux and was practically unusable on Visual Studio due to aggressive tuning in assembler. All this said, when we start tuning performance with assembler snippets, it not only dramatically increases our development and maintenance costs, but we also risk losing the users' confidence in our software when we are in the open-source domain.

C++11 ## A.6.4 Variadic Binary I/O

Section A.2.7 gave an example of binary I/O. It contained repetitive pointer casts and sizeof. Using language features like type deduction and variadic function, we can provide a much more convenient interface:

```cpp
inline void write_data(std::ostream&) {}

template <typename T, typename ...P>
inline void write_data(std::ostream& os, const T& t, const P& ...p)
{
    os.write(reinterpret_cast<const char *>(&t), sizeof t);
    write_data(os, p...);
}

inline void read_data(std::istream&) {}

template <typename T, typename ...P>
inline void read_data(std::istream& is, T& t, P& ...p)
{
    is.read(reinterpret_cast<char *>(&t), sizeof t);
```

```
        read_data(is, p...);
}

int main (int argc, char* argv[])
{
    std::ofstream outfile("fb.txt", ios::binary);
    double o1= 5.2, o2= 6.2;
    write_data(outfile, o1, o2);
    outfile.close();

    std::ifstream infile("fb.txt", ios::binary);
    double  i1, i2;
    read_data(infile, i1, i2);
    std::cout << "i1 = " << i1 << ", i2 = " << i2 << "\n";
}
```

These variadic functions allow us to write or read as many self-contained objects as we want in each function call. The full power of variadic templates is unleashed in combination with meta-programming (Chapter 5).

A.7 Using `std::vector` in C++03

The following program shows how the vector usage from Section 4.1.3.1 can be realized in C++03:

```
#include <iostream>
#include <vector>
#include <algorithm>

int main ()
{
    using namespace std;
    vector<int> v;
    v.push_back(3); v.push_back(4);
    v.push_back(7); v.push_back(9);
    vector<int>::iterator it= find(v.begin(), v.end(), 4);
    cout << "After " << *it << " comes " << *(it+1) << '\n';
    v.insert(it+1, 5);          // insert value 5 at pos. 2
    v.erase(v.begin());         // delete entry at pos. 1
    cout << "Size = " << v.size() << ", capacity = "
         << v.capacity() << '\n';
    // The following block emulates shrink_to_fit() in C++11
    {
        vector<int> tmp(v);
        swap(v, tmp);
    }
    v.push_back(7);
    for (vector<int>::iterator it= v.begin(), end= v.end();
```

```
            it != end; ++it)
            cout ≪ *it ≪ ",";
    cout ≪ '\n';
}
```

In contrast to C++11, we have to spell out all iterator types and to deal with quite cumbersome initialization and shrinking. Only when backward compatibility is really important should we bother with this old-style coding.

A.8   Dynamic Selection in Old Style

The following example demonstrates the verbosity of dynamic selection with nested `switch` statements:

```
int solver_choice= std::atoi(argv[1]), left= std::atoi(argv[2]),
    right= = std::atoi(argv[3]);
switch (solver_choice) {
    case 0:
        switch (left) {
            case 0:
                switch (right) {
                    case 0: cg(A, b, x, diagonal, diagonal); break;
                    case 1: cg(A, b, x, diagonal, ILU); break;
                        ... more right preconditioners
                }
                break;
            case 1:
                switch (right) {
                    case 0: cg(A, b, x, ILU, diagonal); break;
                    case 1: cg(A, b, x, ILU, ILU); break;
                        ...
                }
                break;
            ... more left preconditioners
        }
    case 1:
        ... more solvers
}
```

For each new solver and preconditioner, we have to expand this gigantic block in multiple places.

A.9   Meta-Programming Details

A.9.1   First Meta-Program in History

Meta-Programming was actually discovered by accident. Erwin Unruh wrote in the early 90s a program that printed prime numbers as error messages and thus demonstrated that C++

compilers are able to compute. Because the language has changed since Erwin Unruh wrote the example, here is a version adapted to today's standard C++:

```
1   // Prime number computation by Erwin Unruh
2
3   template <int i> struct D { D(void*); operator int(); };
4
5   template <int p, int i> struct is_prime {
6     enum { prim = (p==2) || (p%i) && is_prime<(i>2?p:0), i-1> :: prim };
7   };
8
9   template <int i> struct Prime_print {
10    Prime_print<i-1> a;
11    enum { prim = is_prime<i, i-1>::prim };
12    void f() { D<i> d = prim ? 1 : 0; a.f();}
13  };
14
15  template<> struct is_prime<0,0> { enum {prim=1}; };
16  template<> struct is_prime<0,1> { enum {prim=1}; };
17
18  template<> struct Prime_print<1> {
19    enum {prim=0};
20    void f() { D<1> d = prim ? 1 : 0; };
21  };
22
23  int main() {
24    Prime_print<18> a;
25    a.f();
26  }
```

When we compile this code with g++ 4.5,[8] we see see the following error message:

```
unruh.cpp: In member function »void Prime_print<i>::f() [with int i = 17]«:
unruh.cpp:12:36:   instantiated from »void Prime_print<i>::f() [with int i = 18]«
unruh.cpp:25:6:    instantiated from here
unruh.cpp:12:33: error: invalid conversion from »int« to »void*«
unruh.cpp:12:33: error:   initializing argument 1 of »D<i>::D(void*) [with int i = 17]«
unruh.cpp: In member function »void Prime_print<i>::f() [with int i = 13]«:
unruh.cpp:12:36:   instantiated from »void Prime_print<i>::f() [with int i = 14]«
unruh.cpp:12:36:   instantiated from »void Prime_print<i>::f() [with int i = 15]«
unruh.cpp:12:36:   instantiated from »void Prime_print<i>::f() [with int i = 16]«
unruh.cpp:12:36:   instantiated from »void Prime_print<i>::f() [with int i = 17]«
unruh.cpp:12:36:   instantiated from »void Prime_print<i>::f() [with int i = 18]«
unruh.cpp:25:6:    instantiated from here
unruh.cpp:12:33: error: invalid conversion from »int« to »void*«
unruh.cpp:12:33: error:   initializing argument 1 of »D<i>::D(void*) [with int i = 13]«
unruh.cpp: In member function »void Prime_print<i>::f() [with int i = 11]«:
unruh.cpp:12:36:   instantiated from »void Prime_print<i>::f() [with int i = 12]«
unruh.cpp:12:36:   instantiated from »void Prime_print<i>::f() [with int i = 13]«
unruh.cpp:12:36:   instantiated from »void Prime_print<i>::f() [with int i = 14]«
unruh.cpp:12:36:   instantiated from »void Prime_print<i>::f() [with int i = 15]«
unruh.cpp:12:36:   instantiated from »void Prime_print<i>::f() [with int i = 16]«
```

---

8. Other compilers give similar analysis but we found that this message is best suited to show the effect.

```
unruh.cpp:12:36:    instantiated from »void Prime_print<i>::f() [with int i = 17]«
unruh.cpp:12:36:    instantiated from »void Prime_print<i>::f() [with int i = 18]«
unruh.cpp:25:6:   instantiated from here
unruh.cpp:12:33: error: invalid conversion from »int« to »void*«
unruh.cpp:12:33: error:   initializing argument 1 of »D<i>::D(void*) [with int i = 11]«
unruh.cpp: In member function »void Prime_print<i>::f() [with int i = 7]«:
unruh.cpp:12:36:    instantiated from »void Prime_print<i>::f() [with int i =  8]«
... message continues
```

When we filter the error message for `initializing`,[9] we see clearly how well our compiler computes:

```
unruh.cpp:12:33: error:    initializing argument 1 of »D<i>::D(void*) [with int i = 17]«
unruh.cpp:12:33: error:    initializing argument 1 of »D<i>::D(void*) [with int i = 13]«
unruh.cpp:12:33: error:    initializing argument 1 of »D<i>::D(void*) [with int i = 11]«
unruh.cpp:12:33: error:    initializing argument 1 of »D<i>::D(void*) [with int i =  7]«
unruh.cpp:12:33: error:    initializing argument 1 of »D<i>::D(void*) [with int i =  5]«
unruh.cpp:12:33: error:    initializing argument 1 of »D<i>::D(void*) [with int i =  3]«
unruh.cpp:12:33: error:    initializing argument 1 of »D<i>::D(void*) [with int i =  2]«
```

After people realized the computational power of the C++ compiler, it was used to realize very powerful performance optimization techniques. In fact, one can perform entire applications during compile time. Krzysztof Czarnecki and Ulrich Eisenecker wrote a Lisp interpreter that evaluated expressions of a sub-set of Lisp during a C++ compilation [9].

On the other hand, excessive usage of meta-programming techniques can end in quite long compilation time. Entire research projects were canceled after spending many millions of dollars of funding because even short applications of fewer than 20 lines took weeks to compile on parallel computers. Another scary example from people whom the author knows personally: they managed to produce an 18MB error message which originated mostly from a single error. Although this is probably a world record, they are not particularly proud of this achievement.

Despite this history, the author has used a fair amount of meta-programming in his scientific projects and still avoided exhaustive compile time. Also, compilers have improved significantly in the last decade and are today much more efficient in handling massive template code.

A.9.2 Meta-Functions

A Fibonacci number can be computed during compilation by recursion:

```
template <long N>
struct fibonacci
{
    static const long value= fibonacci<N-1>::value
                            + fibonacci<N-2>::value;
};

template <>
struct fibonacci<1>
{
    static const long value= 1;
```

---

9. With bash: `make unruh 2>&1 | grep initializing`; with tcsh: `make unruh |& grep initializing`.

```
};

template <>
struct fibonacci<2>
{
    static const long value= 1;
};
```

A class template that defines a member named value which is known at compile time is called a *Meta-Function*. A class member variable is available during compilation if it is declared both static and const. A static member exists only once per class, and when it is also constant, it can also be set at compile time.

Back to our code example. Note that we need the specialization for 1 and 2 to terminate the recursion. The following definition:

```
template <long N>
struct fibonacci
{
    static const long value= N < 3 ? 1 :
        fibonacci<N-1>::value + fibonacci<N-2>::value; // Error
};
```

would end in an infinite compile loop. For $N = 2$, the compiler would evaluate the expression

```
template <2>
struct fibonacci
{
    static const long value= 2 < 3 ? 1 :
        fibonacci<1>::value + fibonacci<0>::value; // error
};
```

This requires the evaluation of fibonacci<0>::value as

```
template <0>
struct fibonacci
{
    static const long value= 0 < 3 ? 1 :
        fibonacci< -1>::value + fibonacci< -2>::value; // error
};
```

which needs fibonacci< -1>::value .... Although the values for $N < 3$ are not used, the compiler will nevertheless generate an infinite number of these terms and die at some point.

We said before that we implemented the computation recursively. In fact, all repetitive calculations must be realized recursively as there is no iteration[10] for meta-functions.

When we write, for instance,

```
std::cout << fibonacci<45>::value << "\n";
```

_____

10. The Meta-Programming Library (MPL) provides compile-time iterators but even those are internally realized recursively.

the value is already calculated during the compilation and the program just prints it. If you do not believe us, you can read the assembler code (e.g., compile with `g++ -S fibonacci.cpp -o fibonacci.asm`).

We mentioned long compilations with meta-programming at the beginning of Chapter 5. The compilation for Fibonacci number 45 took less than a second. Compared to it, a naïve run-time implementation:

```
long fibonacci2(long x)
{
    return x < 3 ? 1 : fibonacci2(x-1) + fibonacci2(x-2);
}
```

took 14s on the same computer. The reason is that the compiler keeps intermediate results while the run-time version recomputes everything. We are, however, convinced that every reader of this book can rewrite `fibonacci2` without the exponential overhead of re-computations.

C++03 A.9.3 Backward-Compatible Static Assertion

When we have to work with an old compiler that does not support `static_assert`, we can use the macro `BOOST_STATIC_ASSERT` from the Boost library collection instead:

```
// #include <boost/static_assert.hpp>

template <typename Matrix>
class transposed_view
{
    BOOST_STATIC_ASSERT((is_matrix<Matrix>::value)); // Must be a matrix
    // ...
};
```

Unfortunately, the error message is not very meaningful, not to say pretty confusing:

```
trans_const.cpp:96: Error: Invalid application of »sizeof«
on incomplete type
    »boost::STATIC_ASSERTION_FAILURE<false>«
```

If you see an error message with STATIC ASSERTION in it, don't think about the message itself—it is meaningless—but look at the source code line that caused this error and hope that the author of the assertion provided more information in a comment. With a recent Boost version and a C++11-compliant compiler, the macro is expanded to `static_assert` and at least the condition is printed as an error message. Note that `BOOST_STATIC_ASSERT` is a macro and doesn't understand C++. This manifests itself in particular when the argument contains one or more commas. Then the preprocessor will interpret this as multiple arguments of the macro and get confused. This confusion can be avoided by enclosing the argument of `BOOST_STATIC_ASSERT` in parentheses as we did in the example (although it was not necessary here).

A.9.4   Anonymous Type Parameters   C++11

Starting with the 2011 standard, the SFINAE technique can be applied to template parameter types. This makes the implementations clearly more readable. Function templates are much better structured when the enabling type treatment doesn't distort the return type or an argument but is expressed as an unused and unnamed type parameter. The last example would be accordingly:

```
template <typename T,
          typename= enable_if_t<is_matrix<T>::value
                          && !is_sparse_matrix<T>::value>>
inline Magnitude_t<T> one_norm(const T& A);

template <typename T,
          typename= enable_if_t<is_sparse_matrix<T>::value>>
inline Magnitude_t<T> one_norm(const T& A);
```

As we are now no longer interested in the type defined by enable_if_t, we can take its default for the unused type parameter.

⇒ c++11/enable_if_class.cpp

At this point, we want to pick up the topic of controlling the availability of member functions by class template parameters. They are not relevant to SFINAE, and so enable_if expressions are errors. Say we want apply a bitwise AND to each entry of a vector, i.e., implement &= with a scalar. This only makes sense when the vector has integer values:

```
template <typename T>
class vector
{
    ...
    template <typename= enable_if_t<std::is_integral<T>::value>>
    vector<T>& operator&=(const T& value); // error
};
```

Unfortunately, this code doesn't compile. The substitution failure must depend on a template parameter of the function and of the class.

According to Jeremiah Wilcock, it only has to *seem* dependent on a template parameter. Thus, our operator&= must depend on some parameter, say U, so that we can apply enable_if on U:

```
template <typename T>
class vector
{
    template <typename U>
    struct is_int : std::is_integral<T> {};

    template <typename U, typename= enable_if_t<is_int<U>::value> >
    vector<T>& operator&=(const U& value);
};
```

The trick is that this condition can depend indirectly on T and does actually only depend on T and not on U. Here the function has a free template parameter and SFINAE can be used:

```
vector<int>    v1(3);
vector<double> v2(3);

v1&= 7;
v2&= 7.0;      // Error: operator disabled
```

Now we managed to enable a method with respect to a template parameter of the class. The error message from clang 3.4 even let us know that the overload is disabled:

```
enable_if_class.cpp:87:7: error: no viable overloaded '&='
    v2&= 7.0; // not enabled
    ~~^  ~~~
enable_if_class.cpp:6:44: note: candidate template ignored:
    disabled by 'enable_if' [with U = double]
using enable_if_t= typename std::enable_if<Cond, T>::type;
```

Okay, our enabling mechanism refers to the class parameter. Unfortunately, only to that. The function's template parameter doesn't matter in our implementation. We could "and" a double scalar with an int vector:

```
v1&= 7.0;
```

This function call is enabled (it doesn't compile, thus). Our original implementation took the value type of the vector (i.e., T) as a function argument, but this did not allow us to use SFINAE. To apply SFINAE and only accept T as an argument, we have to ascertain that T and U are equal:

```
template <typename T>
class vector
{
    template <typename U>
    struct is_int
      : integral_constant<bool, is_integral<T>::value
                             && is_same<U, T>::value> {};
    // ...
}
```

This technique is admittedly not particularly elegant and we should try to find simpler alternatives. Fortunately, most operators can be implemented as free functions and enable_if can be applied much more easily:

```
template <typename T,
          typename= enable_if_t<is_integral<T>::value>>
vector<T>& operator|=(vector<T>& v, int mask);

template <typename T,
          typename= enable_if_t<is_integral<T>::value>>
vector<T>& operator++(vector<T>& v);
```

Such implementations are in any case preferable to the questionable indirection with faked template parameters. The latter is only necessary for operators that must be defined inside the class like assignment or bracket operators and for methods (§2.2.5).

In scientific applications, we have many transformation operations like permutation or factorization. An important design decision is whether such transformations should create new objects or modify existing ones. The creation of new objects is too expensive for large amounts of data. On the other hand, modifications that pass references cannot be nested:

```
matrix_type A= f(...);
permute(A);
lu(A);
normalize(A); ...
```

A more natural notation would be

```
matrix_type A= normalize(lu(permute(f(...))));
```

To avoid excessive copying, we require that the argument is an rvalue:

```
template <typename Matrix>
inline Matrix lu(Matrix&& LU) { ... }
```

However, the &&-notation with a general template is a forward reference and accepts lvalues as well, e.g.:

```
auto B= normalize(lu(permute(A))); // Overwrites A
```

To limit our function to rvalues, we introduce a filter based on substitution failure:

```
template <typename T>
using rref_only= enable_if_t<!std::is_reference<T>::value>;
```

It explores the fact that in a universal reference the type parameter is substituted to a reference when the argument is an lvalue. An LU factorization can now be implemented as follows:

```
template <typename Matrix, typename= rref_only<Matrix> >
inline Matrix lu(Matrix&& LU, double eps= 0)
{
    using std::abs;
    assert(num_rows(LU) != num_cols(LU));

    for (size_t k= 0; k < num_rows(LU)-1; k++) {
        if (abs(LU[k][k]) <= eps) throw matrix_singular();
        irange r(k+1, imax); // Interval [k+1, n-1]
        LU[r][k]/= LU[k][k];
        LU[r][r]-= LU[r][k] * LU[k][r];
    }
    return LU;
}
```

Passing an lvalue:

```
auto B= lu(A);      // Error: no match
```

would be an error since we disabled the function for lvalue arguments. Recent compilers will tell us that about the SFINAE-based disabling while older compilers just claim the miss of an overload (or fail to compile the anonymous type parameter).

Of course, we can declare everything to be an rvalue with `std::move` and shoot ourselves in the foot with such a lie. Instead, we should create an anonymous copy like

```
auto B= normalize(lu(permute(clone(A))));
```

Here, we first create a copy of A and all transformations are performed on this copy. The same copy is finally taken over by the move constructor of B. Altogether, we only created one single copy of A whose transformed data is finally kept in B.

A.9.5 Benchmark Sources of Dynamic Unrolling

⇒ c++11/vector_unroll_example.cpp

The following program was used for benchmarking in Section 5.4.3:

```
#include <iostream>
#include <chrono>
// ...

using namespace std::chrono;

template <typename TP>
double duration_ms(const TP& from, const TP& to, unsigned rep)
{
    return duration_cast<nanoseconds>((to - from) / rep).count() / 1000.;
}

int main()
{
    unsigned s= 1000;
    if (argc > 1) s= atoi(argv[1]); // read (potentially)
                                    // from command line
    vector<float> u(s), v(s), w(s);
    vector<float> u(s), v(s), w(s);

    for (unsigned i= 0; i < s; ++i) {
        v[i]= float(i);
        w[i]= float(2*i + 15);
    }

    // Load to L1 or L2 cache
    for (unsigned j= 0; j < 3; j++)
        for (unsigned i= 0; i < s; ++i)
            u[i]= 3.0f * v[i] + w[i];

    const unsigned rep= 200000;
```

```
    using TP= time_point<steady_clock>;
    TP unr= steady_clock::now();
    for (unsigned j= 0; j < rep; j++)
        for (unsigned i= 0; i < s; ++i)
            u[i]= 3.0f * v[i] + w[i];
    TP unr_end= steady_clock::now();
    std::cout << "Compute time unrolled loop is "
              << duration_ms(unr, unr_end, rep)
              << " μs.\n";
}
```

A.9.6   Benchmark for Matrix Product

The following backward-compatible benchmark function:

```
template <typename Matrix>
void bench(const Matrix& A, const Matrix& B, Matrix& C,
           const unsigned rep)
{
    boost::timer t1;
    for (unsigned j= 0; j < rep; j++)
        mult(A, B, C);
    double t= t1.elapsed() / double(rep);
    unsigned s= A.num_rows();

    std::cout << "Time mult is "
              << 1000000.0 * t << " μs. These are "
              << s * s * (2*s - 1) / t / 1000000.0 << " MFlops.\n";
}
```

is used in Section 5.4.7.

Appendix B

Programming Tools

In this chapter, we introduce some basic programming tools that can help us to achieve our programming goals.

B.1 gcc

One of the most popular C++ compilers is g++, the C++ version of the C compiler gcc. The acronym used to stand for Gnu C Compiler, but the compiler supports several other languages (Fortran, D, Ada, ...) and the name was changed to *Gnu Compiler Collection* while keeping the acronym. This section gives a short introduction to how to use it.

The following command:

```
g++ -o hello hello.cpp
```

compiles the C++ source file hello.cpp into the executable hello. The flag -o can be omitted. Then the executable will be named a.out (for bizarre historical reasons as an abbreviation of "assembler output"). As soon as we have more than one C++ program in a directory, it will be annoying that executables overwrite each other all the time; thus it is better to use the output flag.

The most important compiler options are

- -I *directory*: Add *directory* to include path;

- -O *n*: Optimize with level *n*;

- -g: Generate debug information;

- -p: Generate profiling information;

- -o *filename*: name the output *filename* instead of a.out;

- -c: Compile only, do not link;

- -L *directory*: Directory for the next library;

- -D *macro*: Define *macro*;

- -l *file*: Link with library lib*file*.a or lib*file*.so.

A little more complex example is

```
g++ -o myfluxer myfluxer.cpp -I/opt/include -L/opt/lib -lblas
```

It compiles the file myfluxer.cpp and links it with the BLAS library in directory /opt/lib. Include files are searched in /opt/include in addition to the standard include path.

For generating fast executables, we have to use at least the following flags:

```
-O3 -DNDEBUG
```

-O3 is the highest optimization in g++. -DNDEBUG defines a macro that lets assert disappear in the executable by conditional compilation (#ifndef NDEBUG). Disabling assertion is very important for performance: MTL4, for instance, is almost an order of magnitude slower since each access is then range-checked. Conversely, we should use certain compiler flags for debugging as well:

```
-O0 -g
```

-O0 turns off all optimizations and globally disables inlining so that a debugger can step through the program. The flag -g lets the compiler store all names of functions and variables and labels of source lines in the binaries so that a debugger can associate the machine code with the source. A short tutorial for using g++ is found at http://tinf2.vub.ac.be/~dvermeir/manual/uintro/gpp.html.

B.2 Debugging

For those of you who play Sudoku, let us dare a comparison. Debugging a program is somewhat similar to fixing a mistake in a Sudoku: it is either quick and easy or really annoying, rarely in between. If the error was made quite recently, we can rapidly detect and fix it. When the mistake remains undetected for a while, it leads to false assumptions and causes a cascade of follow-up errors. As a consequence, in the search for the error we find many parts with wrong results and/or contradictions but which are consistent in themselves. The reason is that they are built on false premises. Questioning everything that we have created before with a lot of thought and work is very frustrating. In the case of a Sudoku, it is often best to ditch it altogether and start all over. For software development, this is not always an option.

Defensive programming with elaborate error handling—not only for user mistakes but for our own potential programming errors as well—not only leads to better software but is also quite often an excellent investment of time. Checking for our own programming errors (with assertions) takes a proportional amount of extra work (say, 5–20 %) whereas the debugging effort can grow infinitely when a bug is hidden deep inside a large program.

B.2.1 Text-Based Debugger

There are several debugging tools. In general, graphical ones are more user-friendly, but they are not always available or usable (especially when working on remote machines). In this section, we describe the gdb debugger, which is very useful to trace back run-time errors.

The following small program using GLAS [29] will serve as a case study:

```cpp
#include <glas/glas.hpp>
#include <iostream>

int main()
{
    glas::dense_vector< int > x( 2 );
    x(0)= 1; x(1)= 2;

    for (int i= 0; i < 3; ++i)
        std::cout << x(i) << std::endl;
    return 0 ;
}
```

Running the program in gdb yields the following output:

```
> gdb myprog
1
2
hello: glas/type/continuous_dense_vector.hpp:85:
T& glas::continuous_dense_vector<T>::operator()(ptrdiff_t) [with T = int]:
Assertion 'i<size_' failed.
Aborted
```

The reason why the program fails is that we cannot access x(2) because it is out of range. Here is a printout of a gdb session with this program:

```
(gdb) r
Starting program: hello
1
2
hello: glas/type/continuous_dense_vector.hpp:85:
T& glas::continuous_dense_vector<T>::operator()(ptrdiff_t) [with T = int]:
Assertion 'i<size_' failed.

Program received signal SIGABRT, Aborted.
0xb7ce283b in raise () from /lib/tls/libc.so.6
(gdb) backtrace
#0  0xb7ce283b in raise () from /lib/tls/libc.so.6
#1  0xb7ce3fa2 in abort () from /lib/tls/libc.so.6
#2  0xb7cdc2df in __assert_fail () from /lib/tls/libc.so.6
#3  0x08048c4e in glas::continuous_dense_vector<int>::operator() (
    this=0xbfdafe14, i=2) at continuous_dense_vector.hpp:85
#4  0x08048a82 in main () at hello.cpp:10
(gdb) break 7
Breakpoint 1 at 0x8048a67: file hello.cpp, line 7.
(gdb) rerun
The program being debugged has been started already.
Start it from the beginning? (y or n) y
```

```
Starting program: hello

Breakpoint 1, main () at hello.cpp:7
7          for (int i=0; i<3; ++i) {
(gdb) step
8              std::cout << x(i) << std::endl ;
(gdb) next
1
7          for (int i=0; i<3; ++i) {
(gdb) next
2
7          for (int i=0; i<3; ++i) {
(gdb) next
8              std::cout << x(i) << std::endl ;
(gdb) print i
$2 = 2
(gdb) next
hello: glas/type/continuous_dense_vector.hpp:85:
T& glas::continuous_dense_vector<T>::operator()(ptrdiff_t) [with T = int]:
Assertion 'i<size_' failed.

Program received signal SIGABRT, Aborted.
0xb7cc483b in raise () from /lib/tls/libc.so.6
(gdb) quit
The program is running.  Exit anyway? (y or n) y
```

The command backtrace tells us where we are in the program. From this back-trace, we can see that the program crashed in line 10 of our main function because an assert was raised in glas::continuous_dense_vector<int>::operator() when i was 2.

B.2.2   Debugging with Graphical Interface: DDD

More convenient than debugging on the text level is using a graphical interface like DDD (Data Display Debugger). It has more or less the same functionality as gdb and in fact it runs gdb internally (or another text debugger). However, we can see our sources and variables as illustrated in Figure B–1.

The screen shot originates from a debugging session of vector_unroll_example2.cpp from Section 5.4.5. In addition to the main window, we see a smaller one like that in Figure B–2, usually on the right of the large window (when there is enough space on the screen). This control panel lets us navigate through the debug session in a way that is easier and more convenient than text debugging. We have the following commands:

Run: Start or restart the program.

Interrupt: If our program does not terminate or does not reach the next break point, we can stop it manually.

Step: Go one step forward. If our position is a function call, jump into the function.

```
 File  Edit  View  Program  Commands  Status  Source  Data                                                      Help
(): main

156 {
157     unsigned s= 1000;
158     if (argc > 1) s= atoi(argv[1]);
159     vector<float> u(s), v(s), w(s);
160
161     for (unsigned i= 0; i < s; i++) {
162         v[i]= float(i);
163         w[i]= float(2*i + 15);
164     }
165     const unsigned rep= 1000000;
166
167     boost::timer t;
168     for (unsigned j= 0; j < rep; j++)
169         u= v + v + w;
170
171     std::cout << "Compute time is " << 1000000.0 * t.elapsed() / double(rep) << " mmicros.\n";
172     std::cout << "u is " << u << '\n';
173
174     return 0 ;

Copyright © 1995-1999 Technische Universität Braunschweig, Germany.
Copyright © 1999-2001 Universität Passau, Germany.
Copyright © 2001 Universität des Saarlandes, Germany.
Copyright © 2001-2004 Free Software Foundation, Inc.
Reading symbols from /home/pgottsch/svn/pgottsch/text/books/cpp_for_scientists/examples/vector_unroll_debug2...done.
(gdb)
\ Welcome to DDD 3.3.11 "Rhubarb" (I486-pc-linux-gnu)
```

Figure B-1: Debugger window

Figure B-2: DDD control panel

Next: Go to the next line in our source code. If we are located on a function call, do not jump into it unless there is a break point set inside.

Stepi and Nexti: This are the equivalents on the instruction level. This is only needed for debugging assembler code.

Until: When we position our cursor in our source, the program runs until it reaches this line. If our program flow does not pass this line, the execution will continue until the end of the program is reached or until the next break point or bug. Alternatively, the program might run eternally in an infinite loop.

Finish: Execute the remainder of the current function and stop in the first line outside this function, i.e., the line after the function call.

Cont: Continue our execution till the next event (break point, bug, or end).

Kill: Kill the program.

Up: Show the line of the current function's call; i.e., go up one level in the call stack (if available).

Down: Go back to the called function; i.e., go down one level in the call stack (if available).

Undo: Revert the last action (works rarely or never).

Redo: Repeat the last command (works more often).

Edit: Call an editor with the source file currently shown.

Make: Call `make` to rebuild the executable.

An important new feature in `gdb` version 7 is the ability to implement pretty printers in Python. This allows us to represent our types concisely in graphical debuggers; for instance, a matrix can be visualized as a 2D array instead of a pointer to the first entry or some other obscure internal representation. IDEs also provide debugging functionality, and some (like Visual Studio) allow for defining pretty printers.

With larger and especially parallel software, it is worthwhile to consider a professional debugger like `DDT` and `Totalview`. They allow us to control the execution of a single, some, or all processes, threads, or GPU threads.

B.3   Memory Analysis

⇒ `c++03/vector_test.cpp`

In our experience, the most frequently used tool set for memory problems is the `valgrind` distribution (which is not limited to memory issues). Here we focus on the `memcheck`. We apply it to the `vector` example used, for instance, in Section 2.4.2:

```
valgrind --tool=memcheck vector_test
```

memcheck detects memory-management problems like leaks. It also reports read access of uninitialized memory and partly out-of-bounds access. If we omitted the copy constructor of our vector class (so that the compiler would generate one with aliasing effects), we would see the following output:

```
==17306== Memcheck, a memory error detector
==17306== Copyright (C) 2002-2013, and GNU GPL'd, by Julian Seward et al.
==17306== Using Valgrind-3.10.0.SVN and LibVEX; rerun with -h for copyright info
==17306== Command: vector_test
==17306==
[1,1,2,-3,]
z[3] is -3
w is [1,1,2,-3,]
w is [1,1,2,-3,]
==17306==
==17306== HEAP SUMMARY:
==17306==     in use at exit: 72,832 bytes in 5 blocks
==17306==   total heap usage: 5 allocs, 0 frees, 72,832 bytes allocated
==17306==
==17306== LEAK SUMMARY:
==17306==    definitely lost: 128 bytes in 4 blocks
==17306==    indirectly lost: 0 bytes in 0 blocks
==17306==      possibly lost: 0 bytes in 0 blocks
==17306==    still reachable: 72,704 bytes in 1 blocks
==17306==         suppressed: 0 bytes in 0 blocks
==17306== Rerun with --leak-check=full to see details of leaked memory
==17306==
==17306== For counts of detected and suppressed errors, rerun with: -v
==17306== ERROR SUMMARY: 0 errors from 0 contexts (suppressed: 0 from 0)
```

All these errors can be reported in verbose mode with the corresponding source line and the function stack:

```
valgrind --tool=memcheck -v --leak-check=full \
         --show-leak-kinds=all vector_test
```

Now we see significantly more details which we refrain from printing here for reasons of size. Please try it on your own.

Program runs with memcheck are slower, in extreme cases up to a factor of 10 or 30. Especially software that uses raw pointers (which hopefully will be an exception in the future) should be checked regularly with valgrind. More information is found at **http://valgrind.org**.

Some commercial debuggers (like DDT) already contain memory analysis. Visual Studio offers plug-ins for finding memory leaks.

B.4 gnuplot

A public-domain program for visual output is gnuplot. Assume we have a data file results.dat with the following content:

```
0 1
0.25 0.968713
0.75 0.740851
```

```
1.25  0.401059
1.75  0.0953422
2.25  -0.110732
2.75  -0.215106
3.25  -0.237847
3.75  -0.205626
4.25  -0.145718
4.75  -0.0807886
5.25  -0.0256738
5.75  0.0127226
6.25  0.0335624
6.75  0.0397399
7.25  0.0358296
7.75  0.0265507
8.25  0.0158041
8.75  0.00623965
9.25  -0.000763948
9.75  -0.00486465
```

The first column represents the x-coordinate and the second column contains the corresponding values for u. We can plot these values with the following command in gnuplot:

```
plot "results.dat" with lines
```

The command

```
plot "results.dat"
```

only plots stars, as depicted in Figure B–3. 3D plots can be realized with the command splot.

For more sophisticated visualization, we can use Paraview which is also freely available.

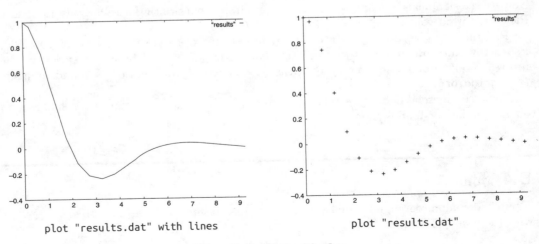

plot "results.dat" with lines   plot "results.dat"

Figure B–3: Plots with plot

B.5   Unix, Linux, and Mac OS

Unix systems like Linux and Mac OS provide a rich set of commands that allow us to realize many tasks with little or no programming. Some of the most important commands are:

- `ps`: List (my) running processes.

- `kill` *id*: Kill the process with id *id*; `kill -9` *id*, force it with signal 9.

- `top`: List all processes and their resource use.

- `mkdir` *dir*: Make a new directory with name *dir*.

- `rmdir` *dir*: Remove an empty directory.

- `pwd`: Print the current working directory.

- `cd` *dir*: Change the working directory to *dir*.

- `ls`: List the files in the current directory (or *dir*).

- `cp` *from to*: Copy the file *from* to the file or directory *to*. If the file *to* exists, it is overwritten, unless we use `cp -i` *from to* which asks for permission.

- `mv` *from to*: Move the file *from* to directory *to* if such a directory exists; otherwise rename the file. If the file *to* exists, it is overwritten. With the flag `-i`, we are asked for our permission to overwrite files.

- `rm` *files*: Remove all the files in the list *files*. `rm *` removes everything—be careful.

- `chmod` *mode files*: Change the access rights for files.

- `grep` *regex*: Find the regular expression *regex* in the terminal input (or a specified file).

- `sort`: Sort the input.

- `uniq`: Filter duplicated lines.

- `yes`: Write y infinitely or *my text* with `yes 'my text'`.

The special charm of Unix commands is that they can be piped; i.e., the output of one program is the input of the next. When we have an installation `install.sh` for which we are certain that we will respond y to all questions, we can write:

```
yes | ./install.sh
```

Or when we want to know all words of length 7 composed of the letters *t, i, o, m, r, k,* and *f*:

```
grep -io '\<[tiomrkf]\{7\}\>' openthesaurus.txt |sort| uniq
```

This is how the author cheats in the game 4 Pics 1 Word—sometimes.

Of course, we are free to implement similar commands in C++. This is even more efficient when we can combine our programs with system commands. To this end, it is advisable to generate simple output for easier piping. For instance, we can write data that can be processed directly from gnuplot.

More information on Unix commands is found for instance at `http://www.physics.wm.edu/unix_intro/outline.html`. Obviously, this section is only an appetizer for their power. Likewise, the entire appendix only scratches the surface of the benefits that we can gain from appropriate tools.

Appendix C
Language Definitions

This appendix is intended as a reference for definitions relevant to this book.

C.1 Value Categories

C++ distinguishes among different categories of values. The most important are lvalue and rvalue.

Definition C–1 (lvalue). An *Lvalue* (so called, historically, because lvalues can appear on the left-hand side of an assignment expression) designates a function or an object.

More pragmatically, an lvalue is an entity from which we can get an address. This does not exclude that they may be constant—although this is somewhat inconsistent with the terminology. The reason for this is that early versions of C had no const attribute so all lvalues were allowed on the left side of an assignment.

The counterpart is:

Definition C–2 (rvalue). An *Rvalue* (so called, historically, because rvalues can appear on the right-hand side of an assignment expression) is an expired value (e.g., an object casted to an rvalue reference), a temporary object or sub-object thereof, or a value that is not associated with an object.

The definitions are adapted from the ISO standard.

C.2 Operator Overview

Table C–1: Operator Summary

Description	Notation	Assoc.
Parenthesized expression	(*expr*)	–
Lambda	[*capture_list*] *lambda_declarator* { *stmt_list* }	–
Scope resolution	*class_name* :: *member*	–
Scope resolution	*namespace_name* :: *member*	–
Global namespace	:: *name*	–
Global namespace	:: *qualified-name*	–

(continues)

Table C–1: Continued

Description	Notation	Assoc.
Member selection	*object* . *member*	⟸
Dereferenced member selection	*pointer* -> *member*	⟸
Subscripting	*expr* [*expr*]	⟸
Subscripting (user-defined)	*object* [*expr*]	⟸
Function call	*expr* (*expr_list*)	⟸
	expr { *expr_list* }	⟸
Value construction	*type* (*expr_list*)	⟸
	expr { *expr_list* }	⟸
Post-increment	*lvalue* ++	–
Post-decrement	*lvalue* --	–
Type identification	typeid (*type*)	–
Run-time type identification	typeid (*expr*)	–
Run-time checked conversion	dynamic_cast < *type* > (*expr*)	–
Compile-time checked conversion	static_cast < *type* > (*expr*)	–
Unchecked conversion	reinterpret_cast < *type* > (*expr*)	–
const conversion	const_cast < *type* > (*expr*)	–
Size of object	sizeof *expr*	–
Size of type	sizeof (*type*)	–
Number of arguments	sizeof... (*argumentpack*)	–
Number of type arguments	sizeof... (*typepack*)	–
Alignment	alignof (*expr*)	–
Alignment of type	alignof (*type*)	–
Pre-increment	++ *lvalue*	–
Pre-decrement	-- *lvalue*	–
Complement	~ *expr*	–
Not	! *expr*	–
Unary minus	- *expr*	–
Unary plus	+ *expr*	–
Address of	& *lvalue*	–
Dereference	* *lvalue*	–
Create (allocate)	new *type*	–
Create (allocate and initialize)	new *type* (*expr_list*)	–
Create (place)	new (*expr_list*) *type*	–
Create (place and initialize)	new (*expr_list*) *type* (*expr_list*)	–
Destroy (deallocate)	delete *pointer*	–
Destroy array	delete [] *pointer*	–
C-style cast	(*type*) *expr*	⟹
Member selection	*object* .* *pointer_to_member*	⟸
Member selection	*pointer* ->* *pointer_to_member*	⟸
Multiply	*expr* * *expr*	⟸
Divide	*expr* / *expr*	⟸
Modulo (remainder)	*expr* % *expr*	⟸
Add (plus)	*expr* + *expr*	⟸
Subtract (minus)	*expr* - *expr*	⟸

(continues)

Table C–1: Continued

Description	Notation	Assoc.
Shift left	*expr* ≪ *expr*	⇐
Shift right	*expr* ≫ *expr*	⇐
Less than	*expr* < *expr*	⇐
Less than or equal	*expr* <= *expr*	⇐
Greater than	*expr* > *expr*	⇐
Greater than or equal	*expr* >= *expr*	⇐
Equal	*expr* == *expr*	⇐
Not equal	*expr* != *expr*	⇐
Bitwise AND	*expr* & *expr*	⇐
Bitwise exclusive OR (XOR)	*expr* ^ *expr*	⇐
Bitwise inclusive OR	*expr* | *expr*	⇐
Logical AND	*expr* && *expr*	⇐
Logical OR	*expr* || *expr*	⇐
Conditional expression	*expr* ? *expr* : *expr*	⇒
Simple assignment	*lvalue* = *expr*	⇒
Multiply and assign	*lvalue* *= *expr*	⇒
Divide and assign	*lvalue* /= *expr*	⇒
Modulo and assign	*lvalue* %= *expr*	⇒
Add and assign	*lvalue* += *expr*	⇒
Subtract and assign	*lvalue* -= *expr*	⇒
Shift left and assign	*lvalue* ≪= *expr*	⇒
Shift right and assign	*lvalue* ≫= *expr*	⇒
Bitwise AND and assign	*lvalue* &= *expr*	⇒
Bitwise inclusive OR and assign	*lvalue* |= *expr*	⇒
Bitwise exclusive OR and assign	*lvalue* ^= *expr*	⇒
Throw an exception	throw *expr*	—
Comma (sequencing)	*expr* , *expr*	⇐

The table is taken from [43, §10.3]; we provided the associativity of the binary and ternary operators. Unary operators of the same priority are evaluated from inside out. In expressions with left-associative operators, the left sub-expression is evaluated first; for instance:

```
a + b + c + d + e          // Corresponds to:
((((a + b) + c) + d) + e
```

Assignments are right-associative; that is:

```
a= b= c= d= e              // Corresponds to:
a= (b= (c= (d= e)))
```

A noteworthy detail is the definition of sizeof. It can be applied directly to expressions like objects but needs parentheses when applied to a type:

```
int i;
sizeof i;                  // Okay: i is an expression
```

```
sizeof(i);              // Okay as well: extra () do not harm
sizeof int;             // Error: parentheses needed for types
sizeof(int);            // Okay
```

If you have doubts about whether parentheses are needed, you can always include extra parentheses.

C.3   Conversion Rules

Integer, floating-point, and bool values can be freely mixed in C++ as each of these types can be converted to any other. Wherever possible, values are converted such that no information is lost. A conversion is *Value-Preserving* when the conversion back to the original type yields the original value. Otherwise the conversion is *Narrowing*. This paragraph is the short version of [43, Intro §10.5].

C.3.1   Promotion

An implicit conversion that preserves the value is referred to as *Promotion*. Short integral or floating-point values can be converted exactly to longer integral or floating-point types respectively. Conversions to int and double are preferred (over longer types) when possible as these are considered to have the "natural" size in arithmetic operations (i.e., being best supported by hardware). The integral promotions are, in detail:

- A char, signed char, unsigned char, short int, or unsigned short int is converted to an int if int can represent all source type values; otherwise, it is converted to unsigned int.

- A char16_t, char32_t, wchar_t, or plain enum is converted to the first of the following types that is able to hold all source type values: int, unsigned int, long, unsigned long, and unsigned long long.

- A bit-field is converted to an int if it can represent all values of the former; otherwise to an unsigned int under the same conditions. Otherwise, no promotion applies.

- A bool is converted to an int: false becomes 0 and true turns into 1.

Promotions are used as part of the usual arithmetic conversions (§C.3.3). Source: [43, §10.5.1].

C.3.2   Other Conversions

C++ performs the following potentially narrowing conversions implicitly:

- Integer and plain enum types can be converted to any integer type. If the target type is shorter, leading bits are cut off.

- Floating-point values can be converted to shorter floating-point types. If the source value lies between two destination values, the result is one of them; otherwise, the behavior is undefined.

- Pointers and references: Any pointer to object types can be converted to void* (evil old-style hacking, though). In contrast, pointers to functions or members cannot be converted to void*. Pointer/references to derived classes can be implicitly converted to pointer/references to (unambiguous) base classes. 0 (or an expression yielding 0) can be converted to any pointer type, resulting in a null pointer. nullptr is preferable. T* can be converted to const T*, likewise T& to const T&.

- bool: Pointers, integral, and floating-point values can be converted to bool: zero values become false, all others true. None of these conversions contributes to understanding programs.

- Integer⇔floating-point: When a floating-point is converted to an integer, the fractional part is discarded (rounding toward 0). If the value is too large to be represented, the behavior is undefined. The conversion from integer to a floating-point type is exact when the former is representable in the target type. Otherwise, the next lower or higher floating-point value is taken (which one is implementation-dependent). In the unlikely case that it is too large for the floating-point type, the behavior is undefined.

Source: [43, §10.5.2] and standard.

C.3.3 Usual Arithmetic Conversions

These conversions are performed on operands of a binary operator to turn them into a common type which is then used as a result type:

1. If either operand is long double, the other is converted to long double;

    - Otherwise, if either operand is double, the other is converted to double;
    - Otherwise, if either operand is float, the other is converted to float;
    - Otherwise, integral promotion from Section C.3.1 is performed on both operands.

2. Otherwise, if either operand is unsigned long long, the other is converted to unsigned long long;

    - Otherwise, if one operand is a long long and the other an unsigned long, then the unsigned long is converted to long long if the latter can represent all values of the former; otherwise, both are converted to unsigned long long.
    - Otherwise, if one operand is a long and the other an unsigned, then the unsigned is converted to long if the latter can represent all values of the former; otherwise, both are converted to unsigned long.
    - Otherwise, if either operand is long, the other is converted to long;
    - Otherwise, if either operand is unsigned, the other is converted to unsigned;
    - Otherwise, both operands are converted to int.

As a consequence, programs with mixed signed and unsigned integers have platform-dependent behavior since the conversion rules depend on the sizes of integer types. Source: [43, §10.5.3].

C.3.4   Narrowing

A *Narrowing Conversion* is an implicit conversion:

- From a floating-point type to an integer type; or

- From `long double` to `double` or `float`, or from `double` to `float`, except where the source is a constant expression and the actual value after conversion is within the range of values that can be represented (even if it cannot be represented exactly); or

- From an integer type or unscoped enumeration type to a floating-point type, except where the source is a constant expression and the actual value after conversion will fit into the target type and will produce the original value when converted back to the original type; or

- From an integer type or unscoped enumeration type to an integer type that cannot represent all the values of the original type, except where the source is a constant expression and the actual value after conversion will fit into the target type and will produce the original value when converted back to the original type.

Source: ISO standard.

Bibliography

[1] D. Abrahams and A. Gurtovoy, *C++ Template Metaprogramming: Concepts, Tools, and Techniques from Boost and Beyond*. Addison-Wesley, 2004.

[2] D. Adams, "Life, the Universe and Everything." *The Hitchhiker's Guide to the Galaxy*, Pan Macmillan, 1980.

[3] M. H. Austern, *Generic Programming and the STL: Using and Extending the C++ Standard Template Library*. Professional Computing Series. Addison-Wesley, 1998.

[4] J. J. Barton and L. R. Nackman, *Scientific and Engineering C++*. Addison-Wesley, 1994.

[5] L. S. Blackford, A. Petitet, R. Pozo, K. Remington, R. C. Whaley, J. Demmel, J. Dongarra, I. Duff, S. Hammarling, G. Henry, et al., "An updated set of basic linear algebra subprograms (blas)," *ACM Transactions on Mathematical Software*, vol. 28, no. 2, pp. 135–151, 2002.

[6] W. E. Brown, "Three <random>-related proposals, v2," Tech. Rep. N3742, ISO/IEC JTC 1, Information Technology, Subcommittee SC 22, Programming Language C++, August 2013.

[7] "C++ reference: Implicit cast." `http://en.cppreference.com/w/cpp/language/implicit_cast`.

[8] K. Czarnecki and U. W. Eisenecker, *Generative Programming: Methods, Tools, and Applications*. ACM Press/Addison-Wesley, 2000.

[9] K. Czarnecki and U. Eisenecker, "Meta-control structures for template metaprogramming." `http://home.t-online.de/home/Ulrich.Eisenecker/meta.htm`.

[10] I. Danaila, F. Hecht, and O. Pironneau, *Simulation Numérique en C++*. Dunod, Paris, 2003.

[11] L. Dionne, "Boost.hana." `http://ldionne.com/hana/index.html`, 2015.

[12] S. Du Toit, "Hourglass interfaces for c++ apis." `http://de.slideshare.net/StefanusDuToit/cpp-con-2014-hourglass-interfaces-for-c-apis`, 2014.

[13] M. A. Ellis and B. Stroustrup, *The Annotated C++ Reference Manual*. Addison-Wesley, 1990.

[14] E. Gamma, R. Helm, R. Johnson, and J. Vlissides, *Design Patterns: Elements of Reusable Object-Oriented Software*. Addison-Wesley, 1994.

[15] B. Ganter and R. Wille, *Formal Concept Analysis: Mathematical Foundations*. Springer Science & Business Media, 2012.

[16] P. Gottschling, "Code reuse in class template specialization," Tech. Rep. N3596, ISO IEC JTC1/SC22/WG21, 2013. `http://www.open-std.org/jtc1/sc22/wg21/docs/papers/2013/n3596.pdf`.

[17] P. Gottschling, *Matrix Template Library 4*. SimuNova, 2014. `mtl4.org`.

[18] P. Gottschling, *Mixed Complex Arithmetic*. SimuNova, 2011. `https://simunova.zih.tu-dresden.de/mtl4/docs/mixed__complex.html`, Part of Matrix Template Library 4.

[19] P. Gottschling and A. Lumsdaine, "Integrating semantics and compilation: Using c++ concepts to develop robust and efficient reusable libraries," in *GPCE '08: Proceedings of the 7th International Conference on Generative Programming and Component Engineering*, pp. 67–76, ACM, 2008.

[20] P. Gottschling, D. S. Wise, and A. Joshi, "Generic support of algorithmic and structural recursion for scientific computing," *The International Journal of Parallel, Emergent and Distributed Systems (IJPEDS)*, vol. 24, no. 6, pp. 479–503, December 2009.

[21] D. Gregor, "ConceptGCC," 2007. `http://www.generic-programming.org/software/ConceptGCC/`.

[22] A. Gurtovoy and D. Abrahams, *The Boost Meta-Programming Library*. Boost, 2014. `www.boost.org/doc/libs/1_56_0/libs/mpl`.

[23] E. Hairer, S. Nørsett, and G. Wanner, *Solving Ordinary Differential Equations I: Nonstiff Problems*. Springer Series in Computational Mathematics, Springer Berlin Heidelberg, 2008.

[24] M. R. Hestenes and E. Stiefel, "Methods of conjugate gradients for solving linear systems," *J. Res. Nat. Bur. Standards*, vol. 49, no. 6, pp. 409–436, December 1952.

[25] R. W. Hockney, *The Science of Computer Benchmarking*, vol. 2. SIAM, 1996.

[26] N. Josuttis, *The C++ Standard Library: A Tutorial and Reference, 2nd Edition*. Addison-Wesley, 2012.

[27] B. Karlsson, *Beyond the C++ Standard Library*. Addison-Wesley, 2005.

[28] KjellKod.cc, "Number crunching: Why you should never, ever, ever use linked-list in your code again." `http://www.codeproject.com/Articles/340797/Number-crunching-Why-you-should-never-ever-EVER-us`, August 2012.

[29] K. Meerbergen, *Generic Linear Algebra Software*. K.U. Leuven, 2014. `http://people.cs.kuleuven.be/~karl.meerbergen/glas/`.

[30] K. Meerbergen, K. Fresl, and T. Knapen, "C++ bindings to external software libraries with examples from BLAS, LAPACK, UMFPACK, and MUMPS," *ACM Transactions on Mathematical Software (TOMS)*, vol. 36, no. 4, p. 22, 2009.

[31] S. Meyers, "A concern about the rule of zero." `http://scottmeyers.blogspot.de/2014/03/a-concern-about-rule-of-zero.html`.

[32] S. Meyers, *Effective Modern C++: 42 Specific Ways to Improve Your Use of C++11 and C++14.* O'Reilly Media, Inc., 2014.

[33] Oracle, "Oracle C++ call interface." `http://www.oracle.com/technetwork/database/features/oci/index-090820.html`.

[34] E. Ott, *Chaos in Dynamical Systems.* Cambridge University Press, 2002.

[35] D. Quinlan, "Rose: Compiler support for object-oriented frameworks," *Parallel Processing Letters*, vol. 10, no. 02–03, pp. 215–226, 2000.

[36] J. Rudl, "Skript zur Vorlesung Finanzmathematik," October 2013.

[37] J. G. Siek, L.-Q. Lee, and A. Lumsdaine, *The Boost Graph Library: User Guide and Reference Manual.* Addison-Wesley, 2001.

[38] J. G. Siek and A. Lumsdaine, *A Language for Generic Programming.* PhD thesis, Indiana University, 2005.

[39] M. Skarupke, "The problems with uniform initialization." `http://probablydance.com/2013/02/02/the-problems-with-uniform-initialization`, February 2013.

[40] A. Stepanov, "Abstraction penalty benchmark, version 1.2 (kai)," 1992. `http://www.open-std.org/jtc1/sc22/wg21/docs/D_3.cpp`.

[41] W. Storm, "An in-depth study of the STL deque container." `http://www.codeproject.com/Articles/5425/An-In-Depth-Study-of-the-STL-Deque-Container`.

[42] B. Stroustrup, *The C++ Programming Language, 3rd Edition.* Addison-Wesley, 1997.

[43] B. Stroustrup, *The C++ Programming Language, 4th Edition.* Addison-Wesley, 2013.

[44] H. Sutter, "Why not specialize function templates?" `http://www.gotw.ca/publications/mill17.htm`, 2009.

[45] H. Sutter and A. Alexandrescu, *C++ Coding Standards.* The C++ In-Depth Series, Addison-Wesley, 2005.

[46] A. Sutton, "C++ extensions for concepts," Tech. Rep. N4377, ISO/IEC JTC 1, Information Technology, Subcommittee SC 22, Programming Language C++, February 2015.

[47] X. Tang and J. Järvi, "Generic flow-sensitive optimizing transformations in C++ with concepts," in *SAC'10: Proceedings of the 2010 ACM Symposium on Applied Computing,* Mar. 2010.

[48] G. Teschl, *Ordinary Differential Equations and Dynamical Systems*, vol. 140. American Mathematical Soc., 2012.

[49] T. Veldhuizen, "C++ templates are Turing complete." `citeseer.ist.psu.edu/581150.html`, 2003.

[50] V. Vernon, *Implementing Domain-Driven Design*. Addison-Wesley, 2013.

[51] R. Whaley, A. Petitet, and J. Dongarra, "Automated empirical optimization of software and the ATLAS project," *Parallel Computing*, vol. 27, no. 1–2, pp. 3–35, Jan. 2001.

[52] B. Wicht, "C++ benchmark – std::vector vs std::list vs std::deque." `http://baptiste-wicht.com/posts/2012/12/cpp-benchmark-vector-list-deque.html`, 2012.

[53] A. Williams, *C++ Concurrency in Action*. Manning, 2012.

[54] P. Wilmott, *Paul Wilmott Introduces Quantitative Finance*. Wiley, 2007.

Index

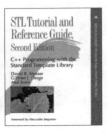

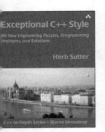

REGISTER YOUR PRODUCT at informit.com/register

Access Additional Benefits and SAVE 35% on Your Next Purchase

- Download available product updates.

- Access bonus material when applicable.

- Receive exclusive offers on new editions and related products.
  (Just check the box to hear from us when setting up your account.)

- Get a coupon for 35% for your next purchase, valid for 30 days. Your code will
  be available in your InformIT cart. (You will also find it in the Manage Codes
  section of your account page.)

Registration benefits vary by product. Benefits will be listed on your account page
under Registered Products.

InformIT.com—The Trusted Technology Learning Source

InformIT is the online home of information technology brands at Pearson, the world's foremost
education company. At InformIT.com you can

- Shop our books, eBooks, software, and video training.
- Take advantage of our special offers and promotions (informit.com/promotions).
- Sign up for special offers and content newsletters (informit.com/newsletters).
- Read free articles and blogs by information technology experts.
- Access thousands of free chapters and video lessons.

Connect with InformIT–Visit informit.com/community

Learn about InformIT community events and programs.

informIT.com
the trusted technology learning source

Addison-Wesley · Cisco Press · IBM Press · Microsoft Press · Pearson IT Certification · Prentice Hall · Que · Sams · VMware Press

ALWAYS LEARNING   PEARS